D0917478

Shepherds after my
own heart

Titles in this series:

NEW STUDIES IN BIBLICAL THEOLOGY 20

Series editor: D. A. Carson

Shepherds after my own heart

PASTORAL TRADITIONS AND LEADERSHIP IN THE BIBLE

Timothy S. Laniak

APOLLOS

INTERVARSITY PRESS
DOWNERS GROVE, ILLINOIS 6051

InterVarsity Press, USA
P.O. Box 1400, Downers Grove, IL 60515-1426, USA
World Wide Web: www.ivpress.com
Email: email@ivpress.com

APOLLOS (an imprint of Inter-Varsity Press, England)
Norton Street, Nottingham NG7 3HR, England
Website: www.ivpbooks.com
Email: ivp@ivpbooks.com

InterVarsity Press ®, USA, is the book-publishing division of InterVarsity Christian Fellowship/USA ®, a student movement active on campus at hundreds of universities, colleges and schools of nursing in the United States of America, and a member movement of the International Fellowship of Evangelical Students. For information about local and regional activities, write Public Relations Dept., InterVarsity Christian Fellowship/USA, 6400 Schroeder Rd., P.O. Box 7895, Madison, WI 53707-7895, or visit the IVCF website at <www.intervarsity.org>.

Inter-Varsity Press, England, is closely linked with the Universities and Colleges Christian Fellowship, a student movement connecting Christian Unions throughout Great Britain, and a member movement of the International Fellowship of Evangelical Students. Website: www.uccf.org.uk.

All Scripture quotations, unless otherwise indicated, are taken from the Holy Bible, New International Version®. NIV®. Copyright © 1973, 1978, 1984 by International Bible Society. Used by permission of Zondervan Publishing House. Distributed in the U.K. by permission of Hodder and Stoughton Ltd. All rights reserved. "NIV" is a registered trademark of International Bible Society. UK trademark number 1448790.

USA ISBN 978-0-8308-2621-6
UK ISBN 978-1-84474-127-4

Set in Monotype Times New Roman
Typeset in Great Britain by CRB Associates, Reepham, Norfolk
Printed in the United States of America ∞

Library of Congress Cataloging-in-Publication Data

A catalog record for this book is available from the Library of Congress.

British Library Cataloguing in Publication Data

A catalogue record for this book is available from the British Library.

P	19	18	17	16	15	14	13	12	11	10	9	8
Y	22	21	20	19	18	17	16	15	14	13		

Affectionately dedicated to Wayne Goodwin,
a mentor and friend who has inspired countless 'shepherds'
to reflect theologically on the nature of ministry.

Contents

Series preface

New Studies in Biblical Theology is a series of monographs that address key issues in the discipline of biblical theology. Contributions to the series focus on one or more of three areas: 1. the nature and status of biblical theology, including its relations with other disciplines (e.g. historical theology, exegesis, systematic theology, historical criticism, narrative theology); 2. the articulation and exposition of the structure of thought of a particular biblical writer or corpus; and 3. the delineation of a biblical theme across all or part of the biblical corpora.

Above all, these monographs are creative attempts to help thinking Christians understand their Bibles better. The series aims simultaneously to instruct and to edify, to interact with the current literature, and to point the way ahead. In God's universe, mind and heart should not be divorced: in this series we will try not to separate what God has joined together. While the notes interact with the best of scholarly literature, the text is uncluttered with untransliterated Greek and Hebrew, and tries to avoid too much technical jargon. The volumes are written within the framework of confessional evangelicalism, but there is always an attempt at thoughtful engagement with the sweep of the relevant literature.

Some books give insight at multiple levels. This is one of them. Entirely in line with the goals of NSBT, Dr Laniak develops a biblical theology of 'shepherd' imagery throughout the Bible. This entails careful listening to a large number of remarkably disparate texts, with the aim of understanding how shepherd imagery functions in each book and corpus of the Bible. Then it demands a careful attempt to delineate how such imagery develops over time. Even the slightest acquaintance with the Bible calls to mind numerous passages (e.g. the beloved Psalm 23) and themes: in the Old Testament, God is the shepherd, the king is the shepherd, religious leaders are shepherds. Carefully adjusted, shepherd imagery is used to describe both good and bad shepherds – see, for instance, Ezekiel 34. All of us remember that John's Gospel portrays Jesus as 'the good shepherd' – and inevitably that raises questions about the nature of the imagery that feeds into this assertion. But pastors are shepherds: that is what 'pastor' means. What bearing does the Bible's extensive choice of such imagery have on how we think of church life?

So at one level, this biblical theology develops one line of 'messianic' development, and pushes for a nuanced but holistic reading of shepherd imagery as it develops across the canon of Scripture. But there are enriching and humbling practical entailments: so extensive is this imagery in the domain of Christian leadership that it contributes a great deal to what Christians ought to understand about leadership itself, and how they will practise it. That is no small matter: it is part of faithfulness to Jesus Christ, who alone is the chief shepherd, not only commanding his undershepherds, but demonstrating in his own life and death and resurrection what Christian leaders are privileged, and morally obligated, to become.

D. A. Carson
Trinity Evangelical Divinity School

Author's preface

It is with profound gratitude that I recall the individuals and organizations who contributed to this project. Through their generous sabbatical policy the trustees of Gordon-Conwell Theological Seminary relieved me of teaching responsibilities for a full academic year. The presidential round-tables of Gordon-Conwell's Center for the Development of Evangelical Leadership provided the early inspiration for this work. My thanks go also to the trustees of the American Schools of Oriental Research who granted me the 2003–04 Annual Professorship at the Albright Institute for Archaeological Research in Jerusalem.

The Albright environment was rich in resources, both material and human. Albright fellows Benjamin Saidel and Eveline van der Steen were especially helpful in my journey into the world of pastoralism. Generous with his time and contacts, AIAR director Sy Gitin helped me make the most of my precious research time. Thanks to Shalom Paul for the opportunity to research at the Hebrew University as a visiting professor. A word of appreciation goes to Joan Westenholz who took time out of her busy work at the Bible Lands Museum to discuss shepherd imagery in the ancient world. The nearby Ecole Biblique – known to its users as the best biblical studies library in the world – was an archaeological adventure of its own. My most illuminating experiences came, however, during field work among the Bedouin in Jordan, Israel and Sinai. My life has been immeasurably enriched by the stories of these remarkable people, stories made accessible by translator and friend Sate Massadeh.

Returning to Gordon-Conwell, I enjoyed immensely helpful interaction with faculty, students and ministry colleagues for the following year. I treasure the thoughtful feedback I received from GCTS faculty members Wayne Goodwin, Sid Bradley, Bob Cooley, Gary Pratico, Bill Murray, Steve Klipowicz, Bob Mayer, Jim White, Rod Cooper, Rick Lints and Sean McDonough. Among the many other thoughtful leaders who gave important suggestions, I must thank John Shuler,

Bob Thompson, Tamara Park, Steve Withrow, Russ Rosser, Dean Faulkner, Misty Mowrey and George Davis. For close reading and careful criticism, I am especially indebted to Dave Baer, a scholar and leader (and my personal 'editor for life'), and Bob Hubbard, a biblical theologian who has modelled for so many of us scholarship in the service of the church.

My research assistant Nicole Minford deserves praise for moving the manuscript through its various iterations to a more uniform state. (Who would have thought the NIV-UK had so many differences?) For managing the ever-expanding bibliography on this project I am eternally grateful for the diligent and patient support of GCTS librarians Bob Mayer and Freemon Barton. (I promise to stick to my book quota from now on!)

While these readers, supporters and countless others helped me decide what to include in the manuscript, one person was most helpful in *removing* material. Jamie Henderson accepted the challenge to reduce the book by 10% when my own efforts to cut led only to polishing. NSBT series editor Don Carson and Philip Duce at IVP were most gracious and patient as they moved me to the required word limit. I appreciate their work in keeping biblical theology alive for the church in this series.

A final recognition is reserved for my wife, Maureen, a shepherdess to many who might otherwise lose their way, including our 'kids', Aaron, Jesse and Adrienne.

Timothy S. Laniak

Foreword

Looking back over fifty years of ministry, I celebrate the high points through rejoicing and the low points as times of special formation and instruction. Alfred Sloan, Peter Drucker, Robert Greenleaf and Warren Bennis were the role models for understanding leadership theory and practice. The very nature of ministry was forged through corporate and business influence; an influence that was limited in its awareness of themes inherent in biblical texts that demonstrate what it means to lead in the Kingdom of God. Persons called to ministry in the twenty-first century now have in Professor Tim Laniak's *Shepherds After My Own Heart* a scholarly study of the biblical metaphor that most often conceptualizes leadership.

Dr. Laniak served as the biblical theologian on the program staff of The Center for the Development of Evangelical Leadership, Gordon-Conwell Theological Seminary. In this role he directed seminary presidents in their consideration of the truths resident in Jeremiah 3:15. Calling, character, competency and community became the watchwords for the development of an understanding of leadership that was rooted in an identity – shepherd leadership. Roundtable participants have now responded to Professor Laniak's exegetical study.

Ian Chapman, Chancellor of Northern Baptist Theological Seminary, says, 'I appreciated the way your exegetical work brought new insights and deeper understandings to the pastoral role. The concept of a shepherd may have little meaning to some in an urban culture but the clarity of your work overcomes that limitation. I found myself wishing that your book had been written years ago; it would have been of great help to me personally and professionally.'

Jackson W. Carroll, Williams Professor Emeritus of Religion and Society, Duke University Divinity School and one of the President's Roundtable Presenters, states regarding the exegesis of the texts that draw on shepherd themes, 'Laniak paints a picture of the pastor's shepherd leadership, reflecting God's and Jesus' shepherding, as a set of tasks that include, among others, oversight, protection, provision, care and guidance of the flock entrusted to the shepherd. Those pastors who make the effort to read this study with care will be richly rewarded.'

Byron Klaus, President of The Assemblies of God Theological Seminary, comments, 'Dr. Laniak provides a significant resource for all who will dare believe that biblical texts on leadership are more than curious commentary on ancient leadership case studies, but serve as foundation and authoritative sources to guide the DNA of leadership for the church in the twenty-first century.'

The church expects effective ministry and pastoral leadership. The work of the ministry is finding more and more people having to exercise leadership within the life of the congregation. This book provides the biblical foundations for understanding God's gift to the church – 'I will give you shepherds after my own heart, who will lead you with knowledge and understanding.' Indeed, Laniak's study of shepherd imagery is his gift to all who are called to lead.

Robert E. Cooley, President Emeritus
Gordon-Conwell Theological Seminary

Abbreviations

AB	Anchor Bible
AOS	American Oriental Series
ATANT	Abhandlungen zur Theologie des Alten und Neuen Testaments
ASOR	American Schools of Oriental Research
b.	Babylonian Talmud
BA	*Biblical Archaeologist*
BAR	*Biblical Archaeological Review*
BASOR	*Bulletin of the American Schools of Oriental Research*
BAGD	W. Bauer, W. F. Arndt, F. W. Gingrich and F. W. Danker, *A Greek–English Lexicon of the New Testament and Other Early Christian Literature*, 2nd edn, Chicago, IL: Chicago University Press, 1979
BDB	F. Brown, *The New Brown–Driver–Briggs–Gesenius Hebrew and English Lexicon*, Peabody, MA: Hendrickson, 1979
BECNT	Baker Exegetical Commentary on the New Testament
BETL	Bibliotheca ephemeridum theologicarum lovaniensium
BR	*Biblical Research*
BTB	*Biblical Theology Bulletin*
CAD	J. Gelb (ed.), *The Assyrian Dictionary of the Oriental Institute of the University of Chicago*, Chicago: Oriental Institute, 1956–
CBQ	*Catholic Biblical Quarterly*
CBQMS	Catholic Biblical Quarterly Monograph Series
ConBOT	Coniectanea biblical, Old Testament
CD	Damascus Code (Qumran document)
CurTM	*Currents in Theology and Mission*
DSS	Dead Sea Scrolls

Dtr	Deuteronomic Literature (Joshua, Judges, Samuel, Kings)
ETCSL	*Electronic Text Corpus of Sumerian Literature* (http://www-etcsl.orient.ox.ac.uk)
HDR	History of David's Rise (to Kingship)
HSM	Harvard Semitic Monograph
HSS	Harvard Semitic Studies
ICC	International Critical Commentary
IDB	*Interpreter's Dictionary of the Bible*
IEJ	*Israel Exploration Journal*
JAAR	*Journal of the American Academy of Religion*
JBL	*Journal of Biblical Literature*
JCS	*Journal of Cuneiform Studies*
JETS	*Journal of the Evangelical Theological Society*
JJS	*Journal of Jewish Studies*
JNES	*Journal of Near Eastern Studies*
JNSL	*Journal of Northwest Semitic Languages*
JSNT	*Journal for the Study of the New Testament*
JSNTS	*Journal for the Study of the New Testament Supplement*
JSOT	*Journal for the Study of the Old Testament*
JSOTS	*Journal for the Study of the Old Testament Supplement*
JSS	*Journal of Semitic Studies*
JTS	*Journal of Theological Studies*
KJV	King James Version
LCL	Loeb Classical Library
LXX	The Septuagint (Greek version of the Old Testament)
m.	Mishnah
MT	Masoretic Text
NA[26]	E. Nestle and E. Nestle E., *Novum Testamentum Graece*, 26 ed., Stuttgart: Deutsche Bibelstiftung, 1981
NAC	New American Commentary
NASB	New American Standard Bible
NIBC	New International Bible Commentary
NICNT	New International Commentary on the New Testament
NICOT	New International Commentary on the Old Testament
NIGTC	New International Greek Testament Commentary

NovT	*Novum Testamentum*
NRSV	New Revised Standard Version
NTS	*New Testament Studies*
NTTS	New Testament Tools and Studies
OB	Old Babylonian
OIP	Oriental Institute Publications
OTL	Old Testament Library
QM	War Rule (of Qumran)
QS	Community Rule (of Qumran)
SBLDS	Society of Biblical Literature Dissertation Series
SBLMS	Society of Biblical Literature Monograph Series
SBT	Studies in Biblical Theology
Str-B	H. L. Strack and P. Billerbeck, *Kommentar zum Neuen Testament aus Talmud und Midrasch*, 6 vols., München: C. H. Beck'sche Verlagsbuchhandlung, 1922–28
SWJT	*Southwestern Journal of Theology*
TDOT	R. L. Harris, G. L. Archer & B. K. Waltke, *Theological Wordbook of the Old Testament*, 2 vols., Chicago: Moody, 1980
TOTC	Tyndale Old Testament Commentary
UF	*Ugarit-Forschungen*
VAS	Vorder asiatische Schriftdenkmäler
VT	*Vetus Testamentum*
WBC	Word Biblical Commentary
WUNT	Wissenschaftliche Untersuchungen zum Neuen Testament
ZAR	*Zeitschrift für altorientalische und biblische Rechtsgeschichte*
ZAW	*Zeitschrift für die alttestamentliche Wissenschaft*
ZNW	*Zeitschrift für die neutestamentliche Wissenschaft*

Introduction

At a time when books on leadership are being published at a dizzying pace, one wonders if the Bible has anything to say about it. While the Bible does say a lot about the topic, there has been no survey like the one you are about to read. One of the primary metaphors by which biblical authors conceptualized leadership is shepherding. This is quite consistent throughout Old and New Testaments. Yet no exegetical resource orients the culturally removed contemporary 'pastor' to this wealth of material. It is my hope that the following journey through Scripture will prompt rich reflection on the nature of the pastor's identity as God's undershepherd.[1]

Translating the term 'shepherd' is problematic, though not for lack of English vocabulary. We use the term 'pastor' – an anglicized form of the Latin/French word for shepherd – but it has no appreciable metaphorical significance. For most modern readers in the industrialized, urbanized West there is little first-hand familiarity with the cultural realities that inform the *meaning* of the metaphor. The familiarity we may think we have comes from idyllic scenes that have made their way into our imaginations through museum paintings or simple Sunday school stories.

Shepherding has a figurative meaning in certain contemporary religious settings where it has been 'applied' in reductionist ways. Some groups have used it to emphasize strict accountability. Many denominations use the language of 'pastoral care' exclusively to refer to ministry among the sick and needy. Such associations have their relative merits, but they are not anchored in or controlled by the cultural realities and texts of the biblical world. In contrast to such restricted and distorted images, the Bible promotes robust, comprehensive shepherd leadership, characterized as much by the judicious use of authority as by sympathetic expressions of compassion.

---

[1] Though the shepherd metaphor is a standard point of departure in the field of 'pastoral theology' (e.g. Oden 1983 and Tidball 1997), it is not typically accompanied by rigorous exegesis of the texts that reflect pastoral traditions.

The apostle Paul assumed shepherds were among the Lord's gifts to the church: 'It was he who gave some to be apostles, some to be prophets, some to be evangelists, and some to be pastors [shepherds] and teachers' (Eph. 4:11).[2] The pastoral role was central to the ongoing life of local churches in the Christian movement, just as it is today. Still, the biblical background of this pastoral language, especially in the Old Testament, has been largely unexplored.

The title of this book comes from Jeremiah, one of several prophets who frequently applied the shepherd designation to Israel's leaders. Through Jeremiah God promises, 'I will give you *shepherds after my own heart*, who will lead you with knowledge and understanding' (Jer. 3:15). On the eve of the destruction of ancient Israel, the prophet was painfully aware that God's chosen people had been misled by self-serving shepherd leaders. They were abused and abandoned not just by their kings, but also by their prophets and priests. The promise in this verse summarizes much of what will surface throughout our investigation. It illustrates what we will call a 'divine preference for human agency'. The God of Scripture chooses regularly to engage humans in the tasks of leadership. Appointment by God implies calling, stewardship and accountability.

This short promise also speaks of a capacity to care for God's flock with self-sacrificing diligence and compassion. It is not just 'heart', however, but *'after my own* heart' that matters. A good shepherd is one who sees what the Owner sees and does what the Owner does. He is a follower *before* he is a leader. He is a leader *because* he is a follower. The shepherds whom God judges in the Bible are those who forget that the people in their care are not their own.

Finally, the promised shepherds are those who will lead 'with knowledge and understanding'. A shepherd needs God's heart, but also a sharp, godly mind. The challenges of leadership require deep reservoirs of discernment and wisdom. This kind of 'knowledge and understanding' comes, in part, from an awareness of the mission and destiny of this flock. Shepherd leaders are anchored theologically in the historic journey of God's people in their various wildernesses.

Shepherd leaders in the Old Testament are understood as a part of the wilderness drama of God's people. Jeremiah, like Isaiah and Ezekiel, finds in the ancient Sinai desert a symbolic setting for the

---

[2] All biblical quotations are taken from the NIV-UK unless otherwise noted.

divine Shepherd's work of provision, protection and guidance. To the exiled community those prophetic voices predict a second exodus in their exilic wilderness, a new covenant and a renewed community. These prophetic anticipations form the background for the ministry of the 'good shepherd' in the Gospels. How Jesus is represented in the Gospels and what he expected of his disciples emerge poignantly from this background. The disciples were sent as shepherds to feed his sheep. They were also sent out as sheep among wolves. They were called to lead God's people as pilgrim tent-dwellers, living on the margins of settled society, to their eternal home. If we are to understand the scope of these related traditions, we need first to engage the discipline of biblical theology.

An exercise in biblical theology

The discipline of biblical theology represents an effort to describe the major themes and concerns of biblical authors at a level beyond a single text. In a sense, it is exegetical theology. We are giving the ancient authors 'voice' about the topics of greatest concern to them, to hear them, in so far as it is possible, as they were heard in their world, and within the context of their literary creations.

It might help to think of this book as a sequence of conversations. Imagine sitting with Ezekiel and trying to understand why he used the image of shepherd to describe good and bad leadership. In the course of the conversation we come to appreciate his historical setting and the people to whom he wrote. Naturally we take into consideration the overall structure of his book and where, how and why the particular issue of leadership comes to its surface.

The presence of other 'voices' complicates the conversation. Ezekiel reflects upon the ancient wilderness traditions of Moses and the royal traditions of David, but also upon the more recent prophetic indictments of Jeremiah. Listening to Ezekiel means listening through him (or with him) to these other voices. Ezekiel will in turn be quoted by later biblical writers who utilize his contributions to shepherd leadership for their own literary and theological purposes. Biblical theology places a premium on the discernible tone and texture of each of these individual voices. We discover a choral masterpiece, with common themes that are sung throughout at different times, in disparate ways, by numerous participants. The trained ear will recognize the theme whenever it appears, but will also discern the individuality and contribution of each voice.

Biblical theology engages an interest both in the individual emphases of various authors in their own settings, and in the common themes or traditions [3] that course through the Scriptures. In our case, we are tracing the development of a tradition – an evolving canonical conversation – about the topic of shepherd leadership. Any theme in the Bible will naturally interact with others. The challenge in a study like this is to contain the investigation. In one source, for example, shepherd imagery is embedded in royal traditions. In another it is attached to second exodus traditions. In the Gospels it may play a role in presenting Jesus as a new Moses, a new David, or both. It is important to ask why each author used the shepherd image and how it was related to these traditions, but we will constantly negotiate how much space to give to the answers. While this may create some frustration, to treat our topic as though it were unrelated to these others would do injustice to the developing conversation.

Imagine the great themes of the Bible as rivers, many of which begin in the lofty heights of the Pentateuch. A particular river sometimes comes into full view as rushing rapids. At other times it moves in secret through subterranean passages. Wherever the water flows there is movement and sound, but at the more remote depths it requires keener powers of observation and better tools to locate it. The evidence of a given river at regular intervals 'above ground' makes the discovery of the intervening segments below more likely. The thesis of this present work is that a discernible pastoral 'stream of tradition' flows through Scripture. This tradition provides a broader context for understanding the nature of leaders in the covenant community, and for understanding the nature of that community as the flock of the divine Shepherd.

Most of the Bible's pastoral imagery is embedded in two traditions. These might be thought of as the springs or fountainheads of the watercourses we will trace. The first is the exodus/wilderness complex. Looking back on this time in Israel's history, inspired writers saw YHWH [4] revealing himself as protector, provider and guide, the ultimate Shepherd of his flock. In this setting Moses functioned as God's undershepherd. When Israel subsequently requests a king,

---

[3] 'Tradition' is a better term than 'theme' for this kind of inquiry because it appreciates, alongside the literary interest, a sense of history. We are investigating a way of reflecting about leadership and community life that took place at key moments in the history of salvation. The pastoral theology that evolves is the dynamic product of both the history and the reflection.

[4] YHWH (pronounced 'Yahweh') is a transliteration of the consonants used in the divine name.

another major tradition emerges that is associated with the shepherd king David and his dynasty. Many messianic promises are situated in this latter stream. These two traditions provide prototypes for the leaders who follow.[5] Moses and David are prototypical leaders. More importantly, YHWH reveals himself as the true Shepherd Ruler of Israel.

After investigating these two springs, we will follow the river where it leads.[6] Four prophets in the Old Testament make sustained use of pastoral imagery: Isaiah, Jeremiah, Ezekiel and Zechariah. Each in his own way recalls the exodus and/or wilderness. Each reflects on the Davidic covenant, emphasizing pastoral motifs in the process. In turn, each propels the river forward, adding new energy and dimensions to the images, creating expectation for a second exodus and a unique shepherd king.

The next section traces the river through the four Gospels, again a mix of ancient deposits with new emphases and revelations. Each in their own way, the Gospels depict a shepherd who has come to lead God's flock in the promised new kingdom. Mark focuses on the shepherd of the second exodus. Matthew reveals the compassionate Davidic shepherd. Luke presents the seeking and saving shepherd. John describes the self-sacrificing shepherd.

The final two chapters consider the reflections of Peter in his first epistle and of John in the book of Revelation. Although one might have assumed that this 'pastoral theology' would lead us to the 'pastoral epistles',[7] it takes us, instead, to these eschatological letters that emphasize the marginalization of the community. In these two books Christians are understood still to be in exile. Here leaders are challenged to follow the divine Shepherd who became their sacrificial lamb. In Revelation it becomes clear that following the Shepherd Lamb entails dying for him.

This investigation is balanced in some intentional ways. It gives proportionate weight to both Testaments as it searches for continuity among these themes. What is foundational is valued, as well as what is cumulative. Our approach also balances interest in both cultural

[5] The notion of prototypes is discussed in the first introductory chapter. This bears certain similarities to the theological category of typology.

[6] The Bible has much more to say about Moses and the wilderness or David and the Messiah than we will discuss. Our interest will rest upon those passages where shepherd imagery is significant.

[7] Although Paul is quite 'pastoral' in his ministry, engages second exodus theology at times (W. D. Davies 1997) and refers to church leaders as shepherds occasionally, pastoral imagery is not a central, organizing rubric in the Pauline corpus.

background and literary context. Research on shepherd passages has often been focused exclusively on pastoral realities *or* on textual traditions (including extrabiblical parallels). Good biblical theology, like good exegesis, respects context – Old and New, cultural and literary – when attempting to discern meaning.

The convergence of interests in both the natural and textual worlds is necessary especially when the topic is a metaphor. Figures of speech typically generate their force and meaning through culturally informed associations. For this reason I provide an introductory chapter on the work of shepherds before investigating any texts. Yet metaphors are figures of *speech*, and they must be analysed as strategic rhetorical devices. Consequently, a separate introductory chapter surveys the use of pastoral language for shepherd rulers in extrabiblical texts. This provides background for understanding how such imagery was used in official documents throughout the ancient world.

Critical paths for reading

This book will likely appeal to two different kinds of readers. Consequently two 'critical paths' should be considered. The *New Studies in Biblical Theology* series will obviously engage those interested in biblical theology as an academic discipline. For these readers everything is included. There are three introductory chapters for conceptual, cultural and extrabiblical backgrounds, two foundational chapters on biblical 'prototypes' and ten chapters devoted to the contributions of different biblical authors. Interaction with biblical terminology is in the original languages when appropriate and, with secondary sources, noted throughout. All of the chapters have an ample supply of cross references and footnotes so that the 'academic' reader can follow comments to their sources for further research.

A second kind of reader is the thoughtful pastor who wants to consider biblical perspectives on leadership. For many, pastoral ministry involves an almost constant identity crisis. The following survey provides some historical and theological anchors that should be helpful. Several pastors read through the manuscript and made important suggestions to enhance its usefulness. They also recommend a strategy for their peers. First of all, decide what level of interest you have regarding the introductory chapters. This background is appropriate for the ensuing discussion, but you may not have sufficient interest in it, at least not at the beginning. Perhaps these chapters can be skimmed for the purpose of getting started with the biblical passages as soon as possible. When you do move into these passages you will still find dense prose with italicized original language words, and footnotes with references to collateral research. Throughout the book you may need to skim at times with an eye towards the main points. Consider especially the introductions and concluding summary statements in each chapter, and hang on till the end. Those who have 'stuck with it' say that it is worth the effort of getting acquainted with these various biblical sources. One described its cumulative effect as being like a tide. Each wave will move you a little, and by the end you will find yourself surprisingly far up the shore.

In light of the current interest in leadership, and in the face of our culture's tendency to package concepts in tidy boxes, one might expect this to be a contribution to a new model called 'shepherd leadership'. Principles will surface in this study, and these will be highlighted in the 'Concluding observations and reflections'. However, pastors who have read this work have described a different benefit, a more subtle but profound change in their sense of *identity*. This might be the product of a fresh connection to the historic plan of God with his people. It might be a sense of awe at being called to serve behind the Great Shepherd. For some it is a renewed regard for their vocation as a robust and significant calling. The shepherd image is about perspective as much as praxis. These are the kinds of effects (and affects) a metaphor should have. Rather than providing twelve 'steps' to shepherd leadership, here are twelve successive invitations to reconsider leadership from within the prism of pastoral imagery. The mounting force of the metaphor should make some lasting impressions.

I
Background

Chapter One

Metaphors for the moment

Metaphors: ornamental or fundamental?

Definitions

Reflection on the value of metaphor has a long history. While Plato was suspicious of anything beyond plain speech,[1] Aristotle appreciated the unique value of metaphor: 'Ordinary words convey only what we know already; it is from metaphor that we can best get hold of something fresh' (*Rhetoric* 1410b). Therefore he considered the making of metaphors a worthwhile pursuit: 'But the greatest thing by far is to be a master of metaphor. That alone cannot be learned; it is the token of genius. For the right use of metaphor means a perception of the similarity in dissimilar things' (*Poetics* 1459a).

What was the basis for debate among the Greeks was an established tradition in the Near East. Figurative language is evident in a wide variety of genres and appears to be as natural in human communication as literal speech. The Bible is a rich repository of figures of speech that contribute to its communicative efficacy (cf. Bullinger 1968).[2]

In order to understand the nature and uses of metaphor, we need to appreciate the nature of figurative language in general. A trope or figure of speech is a term that is used in a non-literal way. Examples include simile, metaphor, synecdoche, metonymy, anomaly, irony and paradox. Each of these calls on a higher order of cognition for comprehension. Similar to these elements of speech are images and symbols that are typically non-literary in form. Ryken et al. (1998: xiii) define a verbal image as 'any object or action that we picture in

---

[1] In more recent times John Locke (1894: bk 3, 10.34) agreed that figurative speech serves 'for nothing else but to insinuate wrong ideas, move the passions, and thereby mislead the judgment...' This view represents a bias towards rational, literal and objective scientific thought.

[2] For recent interdisciplinary investigations of specific biblical metaphors, see Brettler (1989), Nielsen (1989), Camp & Fontaine (1993), Stienstra (1993) and G. A. Long (1994). On figurative language in the Bible generally, see Caird (1980), Macky (1990) and Ryken et al. (1998).

words'. It is usually rich in overtones and generous with connotations, deployed in order to elicit an experiential reflection. A symbol is closely related. It is 'an image that stands for something else in addition to its literal meaning' (ibid. xiv). Metaphors and similes are frequent symbols in the Bible.

Our primary interest is in those figures of speech that are used to make comparisons.[3] Metaphors are implicitly comparative (e.g. God is my rock, light or shepherd), whereas similes are explicit (e.g. the kingdom of heaven is like . . .). Synecdoche is the use of a part to represent the whole ('Zion' stands for the Holy Land) or the whole to represent the part ('Zion' stands for the temple in Jerusalem). Metonymy is the use of a related object to refer to something. The shepherd's staff, for example, is a metonym for royal office or authority.

Resemblance is central to any definition of metaphor (cf. Ricoeur 1974: 53–55), though it exists in a creative tension with dissimilarity: 'To see the like is to see the same in spite of, and through, the different. This tension between sameness and difference characterizes the logical structure of likeness' (Ricoeur 1979: 146). Readers or listeners are teased by this tension into considering the points of similarity.

Caird (1980: 145–149) notes that the points of comparison can be quite diverse. To say that someone's reputation (lit.) 'stinks' (Gen. 34:30) is to import sensation from one setting into another. To say 'their hearts turned to water' (Josh. 7:5) is to compare effect from one domain to another. That is, their courage dissipated. Comparing a type of activity is more common. Thus, it is common in ancient texts to read of people being '(shep)herded' by rulers and military commanders.[4]

Metaphors are not simply equations with transferable attributes. They create a potential exchange between two domains or environments in which the inner logic or relations between various elements are compared. To compare a king to a shepherd is to download a collection of contextual associations regarding shepherds in relation to their sheep. The metaphor may then highlight resemblance in more than one way. For example, there may be a feeling of protection along with a delineation of shepherding functions.

[3] The native OT terminology for comparison is *māšāl* (from the root meaning 'to be comparable to'), translated 'proverb' or 'parable'.

[4] In metaphor theory three components are distinguished: the subject (or 'tenor'), the object (or 'vehicle') and the similarities being highlighted. In the language of semiotics these elements are referred to as the referent, the sign and the signification(s).

I. A. Richards (1936) was the first to describe the interactive relationship between these two linguistic contexts. A metaphor leads us to reconsider the two distinct domains from the perspective of the shared elements in focus. What happens when these two worlds are placed side by side is a resonating of what M. Black (1962: 40) calls 'systems of associated commonplaces'. These are tantalizing potential extensions, implications or 'entailments' that contribute to a metaphor's multivalence. R. H. Brown (1977: 88) describes an 'electric field of potential elaborations' which helps a metaphor deliver its meaning 'in the interplay of juxtaposed associations'.

While not all metaphors have such extensive surplus meaning, obvious organic associations naturally 'travel' together in familiar configurations. Certainly this is the case with shepherd language in the biblical texts we are about to survey. The metaphor drags a collection of inter-related associations from the source domain into the target domain as *prospects* for comparison. The hearer/reader understands that the selected features of a subject have been recontextualized. Such recontextualizing generates new ways of seeing familiar things.

Appreciating metaphors and their 'associated commonplaces' (as with all figurative language) requires a certain level of cultural competence. Just like jokes, metaphors are often meaningful only to the culturally initiated. Knowing what is (not) implied or inferred is a challenge. For this reason we begin with an effort to understand pastoral realities in the ancient world (ch. 2). The next chapter summarizes the standardized metaphorical associations in extrabiblical literature (ch. 3). Awareness of conventional entailments prepares us to appreciate the likely correspondences biblical authors had in mind. Together these introductory chapters provide a measure of cultural competence in preparation for our investigation of the Bible's shepherd passages.

The importance of social context and culture in the interpretation of metaphor has been emphasized by a number of theorists (e.g. Quinn 1987, 1991). Language has both semantic (linguistic) and pragmatic (social) dimensions. Metaphors work in a given context because of 'socially binding connotations' (Dittmer 1977: 570) that form a tacit consensus about a legitimate range of meanings. The irony (as in all figurative language) is that the bending of the normal rules of literal speech is only successfully accomplished when readers/listeners are aware of the rules and in expectance of general compliance with them. Metaphors create a bridge between two

33

specific phenomenal worlds, one that can only be crossed by two parties (speaker/listener) who are similarly socialized. In this sense, metaphors are made for the moment.

Ezekiel provides an interesting test case for a reader's cultural competence. In real life, the primary purpose in raising flocks is to gain income. Herding is an economic choice, a livelihood. Any shepherd, ancient or modern, would be surprised if he were criticized for raising animals only for their fibre, milk and meat. Yet this is Ezekiel's critique of the 'shepherds of Israel' in Ezekiel 34. The criticism only makes sense if the leaders of Israel are *under*shepherds. In that case they have no right to the products. The parable goes right to the heart of the matter: the rulers behaved like owners rather than hired servants.

The way we think

To this point we have acknowledged the unique place figures of speech have in language. But metaphor is now recognized as fundamental to thought as well.[5] Our earliest efforts at conceptualization require analogical thinking. The mental categories we construct for the world we sense are built by seeking and seeing order, similarity and pattern. To move from the familiar to the unfamiliar we must categorize on the basis of comparison. Analogical thinking is therefore natural and necessary.

Rosch (1978) has shown that this cognitive process is a search for 'family resemblance'[6] among objects, judging them (unconsciously) in terms of prototypes. Prototypes are exemplars for phenomenological categories, ideal members that possess the primary attributes by which we define a class. While leaving room for ambiguity, our cognition categorizes new objects in terms of learned prototypes.[7] The ensuing discussion about shepherd rulers begins with an investigation of two prototypical shepherd rulers in biblical literature, Moses and David. To use theological language, these figures 'typologically' anticipate the role of Christ as the ultimate shepherd.

---

[5] The most accessible introduction to this view is Lakoff & Johnson (1980). While their philosophical presuppositions are radically constructivist (assuming that 'reality' is socially and cognitively constructed rather than objectively 'out there'), their insights regarding the way people conceive of the world are useful.

[6] Using a phrase made popular by Wittgenstein.

[7] Stereotyping is a similar, natural mechanism for interpreting what would otherwise be a bewildering variety of individuals.

Because of this natural, conceptualizing movement from the known to the unknown, a majority of metaphors make use of concrete or physical realities to describe less tangible realities. The physical world is 'mapped' onto our symbolic and spiritual world. We use elements of and effects from physical phenomena to understand and describe transcendent realities. Theology is, therefore, metaphor-dependent and metaphor-rich (McFague 1982; Soskice 1985). We need metaphors if we are to understand God. Anthropomorphism is an indispensable means by which biblical writers convey their thoughts about God (Caird 1980: 172–182). The metaphorical phrase 'God is my shepherd' is thus, in the words of Ortony (1975), 'necessary and not just nice'. Or, to quote Frederick Ferré, anthropomorphisms are 'necessarily not avoidable' (1987: 188). Thus, the vocation of shepherding itself became a vital medium of revelation.

If metaphors are fundamental to human thought, then we might compare their place in our thinking to scientific models (M. Black 1962). These are comprehensive viewpoints, frames of reference through which we view reality. This may seem like a grand claim for metaphor, but a case can be made at least for central 'root' metaphors functioning this way (see below). Social scientists have chosen different terms for such integrating perspectives: paradigms (Kuhn 1970; Gregory 1983); schemas (Fiedler 1982); frames (Goffman 1974; Bolman & Deal 1997); prisms (Grant & Oswick 1996: 147–165); images (Morgan 1986); symbols (Geertz 1971); epistemes (Iggers 1975:6); implicit theories (Brief & Downey 1983); representations (Sternberg & Frensch 1991); cognitive maps (Weick & Bougon 1986); mental models (Senge 1990); cultural models (Caws 1974); cultural systems (Geertz 1966); and world hypotheses (Pepper 1942).[8] Of course, these terms are neither completely synonymous nor do they all possess the same scope. But each term represents a concession that *knowledge is perspectival.*

This awareness has broken down the rigid boundaries often assumed to exist between the left and right brain, between objective, scientific, abstract thought and subjective, imaginative, concrete thought. No doubt there are varied ways of thinking. But the barrier between them is unexpectedly permeable. Polanyi (1964) exposed the whole scientific enterprise as one propelled more by insight

---

[8] Other terms that have currency include matrices, filters, world-views, constructs, dominant or implicit ontologies, and root metaphors.

('personal knowledge') than by incremental discovery. Kuhn (1970) summarized the history of science as a movement from one paradigm to another, each one simultaneously resisting and inviting bits of new information.

One value of these insights for our study is the awareness that human thought tends towards an economy of explanatory images. We cultivate mental categories that preserve as much information as possible with as little effort as possible (Rosch 1978). This tendency requires mental frameworks that are suitably matched to the world around us. These frameworks are metaphorical in nature.

Metaphorical thought provides coherence to our thinking about the world, but in so doing it also creates limits. While a picture may be 'worth a thousand words', it is only one picture. Might a thousand other pictures be possible? If metaphor provides a 'filter' through which we perceive the world (M. Black 1962: 39–40), then other filters are not only possible but desirable. This is not to suggest an unfettered relativist epistemology. Rather this is recognition that there are numerous (not limitless) valid perspectives on reality. The four Gospel accounts present filters or frames through which we appreciate the nature(s) of Jesus: as New Moses, New David or New Israel. These are complementary metaphorical re-presentations. Similarly, biblical writers talk of God as rock, father, king, judge, hen and shepherd. By highlighting certain attributes with associated affects, a particular image inevitably veils others. We simply cannot conceive of all attributes at once. Thus, the serviceability of a metaphor is its liability.

The likelihood of multiple metaphors prompts a look at 'mixed metaphors'. It appears that biblical writers did not hesitate to combine their images. For example, Matthew's account of Jesus sending out the disciples to minister represents their mission as being sent 'like sheep among wolves' (Matt. 10:16). This disturbing image is partly qualified by the use of two other similes: 'Therefore be as shrewd as snakes and as innocent as doves.' Although the disciples were to take nothing for their own defence, they were to be shrewd. The imaginative combination of sheep, snakes and doves kept innocence from being cheapened to naiveté and shrewdness from being reduced to self-protection. Our study will climax with the sustained, ironic mixed metaphor in Revelation of the Lion-Lamb. The ease with which canonical writers merged their metaphors may be a clue that they appreciated both the constructive and constrictive nature of figurative thought.

Metaphors at work

Classifications

Metaphors may be novel, living and active, or they may be dead, frozen clichés. Others are in between these poles, but likely moving towards lifelessness. Something about metaphors tends to cool off or atrophy with use. Once a figure becomes extensively used it is often mistaken for literal speech. Who, when hearing of the foot of a mountain or head of a pin, pictures the rest of the mountain or pin like a body? The meanings of base or top have, over time, entered the dictionary as denotations.

When we encounter shepherd language in the Near East it is frequently fossilized in titles and epithets. Translators will often supply the word 'rule' in place of verbs for shepherding and 'ruler' for the noun. Perhaps, after time, that is all these terms meant. The 'electric field of potential elaborations' has been turned off. The metaphor is apparently dead. However, in a remarkable number of instances and genres, shepherd language is explicitly elaborated. The metaphor is thawed and revivified for reuse. A king not only calls himself a shepherd but he represents himself as the source of green pastures and safe fold. God is pictured leading his sheep by still waters and along sure paths.

Because of this remarkably persistent reuse of the shepherd construct in the ancient world, it should not be classified as dead, but 'retired' (to use yet another metaphor!). Metaphors can come out of 'retirement', brought back into service at any time by any user, as long as there are hearers who understand the contextual elements. We must pay attention to each context to examine the extent to which various elements are (re)animated. We will find that biblical writers – even more than other Ancient Near Eastern sources – re-employed the pastoral metaphor with intentionality. Time after time, text after text, the shepherd is called back to serve as a frame of reference for evaluating leadership. The durability of the metaphor is all the more striking when one takes into account the fact that in the New Testament period the social status of literal shepherds had been seriously diminished.

Another important distinction can be made between descriptive, conventional metaphors and those that are constructive.[9] Conventional metaphors are typically constitutive of a reigning paradigm.

---

[9] Compare the concepts in this section to Kuhn's distinction between 'normal' and 'revolutionary' science.

There is an 'optimum overlap' of elements, with similarities outweighing the differences (Oswick et al. 2002: 297–298). For example, the earth has been viewed as a mechanism since the rise of modern science. This is not a startling image. It reinforces the standard way of viewing it. Shepherd ruler language was much the same in the ancient world. The gods were viewed as having a certain shepherd-like responsibility for humans, and human rulers were accountable for a similar kind of responsibility with respect to their subjects. This kind of metaphor supports widely held perspectives, and grounds them in natural phenomena.

Constructive metaphors, by contrast, have a ring of novelty and/or irony. They are generative of new ways of thinking that may be disruptive to the standard world view. Jesus used constructive images often in his parables, subverting the frames and models of his listeners. To say that the kingdom of heaven was like leaven was to use a substance typically associated with evil and equate it with something good. To say the kingdom of heaven was like a wedding feast was a conventional metaphor. But then to say that the first list of guests had refused and now everyone was invited – 'good and bad' (Matt. 22:10) – this was scandalous. For Jesus to say 'I am the good shepherd' (John 10:11, 14) was to take a conventional metaphor for God and associate it with himself. This provocative new way of imaging reality came with another disturbing entailment: the religious leaders were the hirelings and thieves!

Another important distinction should be made between 'root' metaphors (Pepper 1942) and isolated, simple metaphors. 'Root' metaphors are so named because they are often implicit in the use of a 'tree' of related figures, lying under the 'soil' of explicit speech. The metaphor of mind-as-computer is a widely accepted though typically unstated analogue. It is implied in an expression like, 'I need more time to *process* that.' Similarly, biblical references to people led to pleasant places, provided with water and given rest indicate a pastoral metaphor underneath the surface. More obviously, any figurative reference to a person or group as sheep automatically triggers the image of a shepherd and potentially images the whole pastoralist system.

Most theorists define root metaphors not only as those that are implicit in discourse, but also as those that are comprehensive in scope. These metaphors tend to explain the use of related metaphors and provide primary organizing rubrics in a culture. They are *integrating* metaphors that have the greatest carrying capacity for meaning. In this sense, root metaphors are similar to and indicative of a world view. We will discover that pastoral imagery contributes to canonical thought in this fundamental way.

Functions of metaphor

Metaphors invite both comprehension and apprehension of perspectives (R. H. Brown 1977: 115–125). Comprehension emphasizes the cognitive aspects of meaning-making through metaphor. This has been a major emphasis in metaphor theory since I. A. Richards. Soskice (1985: 31ff.) calls this the 'incremental' view of metaphor, whereby meaning is achieved by building a comparison.

Apprehension emphasizes the existential aspects of interpretation. Metaphors, like non-literary icons, 'invite, incite, and induce' (M. Black 1979: 29) their readers to *experience* a reality, not just hear about it. Lakoff and Johnson (1980: 71) call this global understanding an 'experiential *gestalt*'. We are familiar with this effect in the context of Gospel parables. They were only understood fully by 'those who had ears to hear and eyes to see'. The images which Jesus painted with his words were not simply sources of information; they were invitations to accept or reject a novel perspective. They forced a choice.

With this existential dimension in mind we should be careful to appreciate the affective and artistic elements of metaphors. Though Classical sources disparaged metaphors as passion-stirring devices, such affects should not be excluded from a fuller analysis of metaphor's utility. It is precisely in the *combining* of cognitive content with affective associations that metaphor gains its power. A simple metaphor, like a small key, can open a whole world and immerse a willing participant in all of its sensory stimulation.

While many metaphors are much more modest in their aims, they all have a capacity to communicate in ways that are unique to figurative language. They are compact, felicitous and engaging. They prompt reflection, feeling, evaluation and action. The meaning of a metaphor, like the meaning of a joke, can be unpacked and, to a certain extent, explained. But the full impact of the image on one's imagination requires an image. Metaphors are irreducible moments of multi-modal communication.

Political symbols, social roles and community narratives

Political language has always been conducive to metaphors. As Seth Thompson (1996) wryly observes, 'Politics without metaphors is like a fish without water.' From a cynical point of view, this is because politics is about manipulating popular impressions and assessments. People need to be coerced into viewing their governments as benevolent or at least benign. They need to be persuaded to give of their resources to an invisible entity that is constantly defining itself to its members by powerful rhetoric.

Governments, of course, do have tangible elements like buildings, programmes and regulations. These constitute what Walter Bagehot calls government's 'efficient' part (Dittmer 1977: 559). But Bagehot also refers to its 'theatrical' part: the symbols, traditions, myths and ideals that form a *sense* of country. Subsequent analysis of political symbolism has uncovered its powerful influence over the way people conceive of their own government as well as those of others.[10] This is an important angle of inquiry, because many of the texts we are investigating are 'official' texts that represent a theo-political perspective.

Contemporary study of political symbolism is indebted to symbolic interactionism, a social psychological perspective rooted in dramatic categories. People in the public sphere are interpreted as 'actors' who 'perform' within the boundaries of prescribed 'roles'. This perspective highlights certain elements of political drama. It locates actors in a narrative that tends to take on mythic proportions. Leaders take role sets that match archetypal patterns played out in 'type scenes'. In a sense, then, roles are metaphors by which people interpret a host of associated implications.

In the case of shepherd language, the metaphor explicitly imports a known role from another domain of human experience. The role expectations of a shepherd in real life are precisely the extensions of the metaphor that characterize a ruler. He must 'play his part' just as a shepherd plays his.

A valuable insight of role theory is that people play different roles simultaneously. Each person must configure a 'role set'. Shepherd is a felicitous metaphor for human leadership because both occupations have a comparable variety of diverse tasks that are constantly negotiated. As we will see in the next chapter, shepherds had to combine broad competencies in animal husbandry with capacities for scouting, defence and negotiation. The use of the shepherd metaphor for leaders affirms the coherence and inner logic of these diverse tasks and competencies. 'Performance' is judged by the expectations

---

[10] See Lasswell (1979–80) and M. Edelman (1971) in general, Kemp (1989) for Egypt, and Larsen (1979) for Mesopotamia.

associated with that role set. A good shepherd is one who does what is required by each circumstance, in each context.

What is most intriguing about the dramatic perspective is that it highlights the human tendency to construct roles within the context of a community's narratives or myths.[11] There is a 'storied nature' to human conduct (Sarbin 1986). Meaning is derived not only through comprehensive root metaphors but also through the stories those metaphors imply. What we will find in the biblical passages discussed below is more than a root metaphor of God or king as shepherd. We will find a persistent, fully developed narrative of the divine Shepherd who, with his undershepherds, looks after the needs of his vulnerable flock as they wander along the margins of settled society. The metaphor triggers a host of associations that root the role of leaders in the great history of salvation.

---

[11] The term 'myth' is used here not in contrast to historical fact, but rather for the foundational, integrating narrative of a community.

Chapter Two

Shepherds in the ancient world

Metaphors assume cultural competence. To understand pastoral imagery, modern Bible readers need an immersion in the sights and sounds (and smells!) of ancient shepherd life. What follows is a brief survey of the social and economic history of shepherding in the ancient world. Our primary interest is the setting of Old Testament realities and images,[1] particularly the pastoral background of the patriarchs and ancient Israelites. This setting will guide our understanding of the earliest references to shepherds in the Bible. It will become apparent that pastoralism was a widely visible and significant sector of all Near Eastern societies from the very beginning of human civilization. Sheep and goats were central to sacrificial cults, their products were necessary for daily sustenance and clothing, and ownership of large flocks marked wealth and status. Our summary of the cultural context of pastoralism encourages a systemic explanation of the challenges and routines of shepherd life. This brief introduction will orient the modern reader to the inner logic and 'associated commonplaces' of pastoral life by exploring it *on its own terms.*

Pastoral realities in the Ancient Near East

Now Abel kept flocks, and Cain worked the soil. (Gen. 4:2)

The patriarchal period

Long before the dawn of urban civilization, people raised small livestock and cattle as a primary form of subsistence. By the seventh millennium BC goats and sheep were domesticated in Mesopotamia

---

[1] Although this survey will extend occasionally into the Roman period, appropriate background for NT passages is provided below.

(Davis 1987: 127), and 'pastoralism'[2] has remained central to economies in the Fertile Crescent up until the modern era. Ancient Mesopotamian states managed flocks numbering in the tens and even hundreds of thousands (Postgate 1986: 198 n. 13; Snell 1997: 38; cf. Job 1:3; 42:12). Herds of similar size were raised in Egypt's Delta region and along the marginal areas to its east (Brewer 2002: 444). Such large flocks – raised for both common and cultic purposes – required a massive administrative system involving many different levels of 'shepherding'.[3]

The social and economic significance of pastoralism in the Ancient Near East is increasingly apparent in second millennium texts. The presence of North-west Semitic Amorites, a people with pastoralist origins, dominated the Levant in the Middle Bronze Age (2300–1550 BC). Their presence was felt even in Egypt during the reign of the Hyksos, Asiatic 'shepherd kings'.[4]

The patriarchal stories of the Bible are set in the context of these Middle Bronze Age dynamics in the Fertile Crescent. Abraham was a wealthy, semi-nomadic pastoralist who moved with all of his family and belongings from Ur (Mesopotamia), to Haran (Syria), to Canaan, to Egypt, and back to Canaan again. God promised him a permanent home in Canaan, but not until 'the sin of the Amorites [had] reached its full measure' (Gen. 15:16). Abraham's descendants, Isaac, Jacob and the twelve sons of Jacob, were all pastoralists in the land of Canaan. They were temporary sojourners in possession only

[2] Terminology in our survey will follow general usage in social anthropology. *Pastoralism* (or pastoral nomadism) describes the work of people-groups (i.e. pastoralists) whose primary source of subsistence and/or production comes from flocks/herds of sheep, goats, cattle, camels, pigs or donkeys (Galaty 1990). *Transhumance* is a similar term that reflects a group's seasonal movement along with their flocks and herds. Transhumants follow a certain pattern in relation to a fixed regional home. The movement may be 'vertical', to different altitudes, or 'horizontal', from one region to another, in search of pasture. The stories of Jacob illustrate the horizontal transhumance typical in the Levant. *Animal husbandry* is a general term used for the complete business of raising domesticated animals. *Shepherding* is reserved simply for the tending of sheep (and goats). We will use the term *pastoral* for any element in the world of shepherds.

[3] The practice of subcontracting shepherds involved three different levels of herders in Uruk (Van Driel 1993: 224–225), the *rab buli* (administrative head), the *naqidu* (chief contractor) and the *re'u* (actual shepherds). Similar terms (*na-gada, nig-shu, i-dab, u-tul*) are found in the documents of Ur (Van de Mieroop 1993: 168–169; cf. similar rankings in Ugaritic [Segert 1987; del Olmo Lete 1993: 192] and Hittite texts [Beckman 1988: 38–40]). The words *naqidu/na-gada* are equivalent to Hebrew *nāgîd* (usually translated 'prince'), and *re'u* is equivalent to Hebrew *rō'eh* (shepherd). This background is relevant to the discussion of 2 Sam. 5:2 below.

[4] Cf. Redford 1992: 106–107. The designation 'shepherd king' comes from Josephus in *Contra Apion* 1, 74, 91.

of a promise of permanence. In this milieu God was understood quite naturally as 'my shepherd' (Gen. 48:15).

Joseph, the beloved son of Jacob, was sold as a slave to Ishmaelite caravaneers[5] by his brothers, who were tending the family flocks (Gen. 37). To their eventual surprise, Joseph became an Egyptian vizier and saved Egypt and his family during an extensive famine.[6] He resettled his family in the Delta region, the geographical setting of the Hyksos' original incursion and the region where Egypt's own pastoralists seasonally herded their flocks. Joseph's advice to his brothers reveals the contempt that Egyptians felt for vocational herders:

> When Pharaoh calls you in and asks, 'What is your occupation?' you should answer, 'Your servants have tended livestock from our boyhood on, just as our fathers did.' Then you will be allowed to settle in the region of Goshen, for *all shepherds are detestable to the Egyptians.* (Gen. 46:33–34)

When Joseph's brothers were introduced to Pharaoh, they identified themselves in terms of the transient nature of their trade: 'Your servants are shepherds . . . just as our fathers were . . . We have come to *live here awhile*, because the famine is severe in Canaan' (Gen. 47:3, 4). Pharaoh was pleased to give them the land of Goshen and offered to put those 'with special [herding] ability' in charge of his own livestock (v. 6). Jacob also emphasized the transitory, pastoral identity of his family: 'The years of my *pilgrimage* are a hundred and thirty. My years have been few and difficult, and they do not equal the years of the *pilgrimage* of my fathers' (v. 9).

The verb *gûr* (to sojourn), used in both of these self-introductions, is central to the identity of the patriarchs, both historically and theologically (cf. Heb. 11:8ff.). While the longing to settle in Canaan was strong (Gen. 47:30; 49:29–32; 50:25), the confession of the Israelites during the festival of Firstfruits was to be a perpetual reminder of their ephemeral heritage: 'my father was a *wandering* Aramean and he went down to Egypt and *sojourned* there . . .' (Deut.

---

[5] The descendants of Ishmael merged with the descendants of Esau (i.e. Edomites) and eventually were associated with the Midianites and the Arabs of the East in biblical genealogies (Gen. 16:12; 28:9; 37:25ff.; Judg. 7; 8:24). These are the ancient Bedouin tribes, known for camel herding and desert trade.

[6] Evidence for the widespread ownership of flocks and cattle among the Egyptians surfaces when they trade in 'their horses, their sheep and goats, their cattle and donkeys' for food in Gen. 47:16–17.

26:5 NASB; cf. Ps. 105:12, 23). In a sense the nomadic 'DNA' of the community was ritually formalized each year by each member.[7] After they settled in Canaan it would be especially important to remember that 'you are but aliens [gērîm] and sojourners [tôšābîm] with me' (Lev. 25:23, author's trans.).

The exodus, conquest and settlement periods

Pastoralism was a central feature of Near East economies for the rest of the second millennium BC. A variety of Hittite sources reveal the significance of herd animals in legal, ritual and military contexts in Anatolia during this period (Beckman 1988). Texts from Ugarit (del Olmo Lete 1993) suggest the same kind of importance for the products, uses and administrative aspects of animal husbandry in northern Canaan (c. 1500–1350 BC). In the fifteenth century Egyptian king Thutmose III boasts of carrying off 20,500 sheep along with 2,000 each of horses, cows and goats in his defeat of the Canaanite city Megiddo (Pritchard 1969: 237). Ramses II, another New Kingdom pharaoh, gloats over terms of peace that included '...cattle, goats, and sheep *by the tens of thousands*...' (ibid.: 257).

The community that left Egypt in the exodus at this time took 'flocks and herds, *a very large number of livestock*' (Exod. 12:38 NASB). Leaving the security of the Nile civilization, they moved into the Sinai wilderness where they became nomadic pastoralists for a generation.

During the Late Bronze Age (c. 1550–1200 BC) Canaan was made up of independent city states that were often harassed by vagrant groups such as the *shasu* and *'apiru*.[8] There is archaeological evidence that these tribal pastoralists were an ongoing threat throughout the region, and that by 1200 BC such groups were in control of new settlements throughout the hill country (Hopkins 1993).[9] The conquest narratives in Numbers, Deuteronomy and Joshua record the arrival of the tribes of Israel in this Late Bronze period (Merrill 1987: 102–121). We will give ample attention below to the pastoral elements in these accounts.

---

[7] This emphasis will be important for the writers of Hebrews and 1 Peter, discussed below.

[8] Though these designations from the Amarna texts are more social than ethnic (Redford 1992: 195, 271), it is possible that *'apiru* is an early reference to the Hebrews (Na'aman 1986: 278).

[9] The tension between 'the desert and the sown' is perennial in the Near East. Once the Israelites were themselves in agrarian settlements, they were subject to desert raiders (Judg. 6:3–6).

The period of the Israelite kingdoms and beyond

As in former time periods, pastoralism was widespread and vital to the economies and societies of the Levant throughout the first millennium BC. During the Neo-Assyrian Empire (1156–626 BC) the smaller kingdoms of Palestine were viewed as desirable vassals along the major trade routes and as sources of small and large cattle. Israel's fat-tail sheep are shown as booty on an eighth-century BC monument from Tiglath-Pileser III (Evenari et al. 1971: 310).[10] In Sennacherib's famous Bull Inscription he describes plundering Hezekiah of large and small cattle 'beyond counting' (701 BC; Pritchard 1969: 288). Similar boasts were made by his successor Essarhadon (ibid. 290–291). There are also in these sources frequent references to the sometimes threatening pastoral nomadic Arab tribes (Eph'al 1984). The Old Testament provides the names of literally hundreds of tribal groups, many of them clearly pastoral nomads.[11]

Pastoralism continued to flourish in Mesopotamia during the Neo-Babylonian Empire (625–539 BC). Flocks for both palace and temple were raised in large quantities (Van Driel 1993)[12] and pastoral products represented a significant portion of that empire's economy. Large-scale pastoral activity throughout the Levant and outside the great urban centres of the Fertile Crescent persisted into the Persian, Hellenistic and Roman periods.[13] Because of the importance of the pastoral economy virtually everyone was at least indirectly acquainted with shepherds' work. Consequently the application of the shepherd's world to that of leaders and communities found a receptive, culturally competent audience.

Pastoral realities in the regions of Israel

The hill country and the wilderness

While it is true that the ancient Israelites left the wilderness and became settled farmers, it is important to appreciate the prevalence of

[10] Tiglath Pileser III also listed the purple wool garments that came from the textile industry in Syria-Palestine (Pritchard 1969: 282–283).

[11] Biblical references to pastoral tribes include Isa. 13:20; 60:7; Jer. 49:29, 32; Ezek. 27:21; 1 Chr. 5:21. 'Tent-dwellers' are mentioned in Isa. 42:11; Jer. 49:29, 31; Ps. 120:5.

[12] King Ashurnasirpal describes a royal banquet for 47,074 persons at which was served (among other foods) '… 1,000 fattened head of cattle, 1,000 calves, 10,000 stable sheep, 15,000 lambs – for my lady Ishtar (alone), 200 head of cattle (and) 1,000 *sihhu*-sheep – 1,000 spring lambs…' (Pritchard 1969: 124; cf. Esth. 1:1–5).

[13] For detail on the Hellenistic and Roman periods specifically, see Isaac (1990) and Safrai (1994).

shepherds and their flocks virtually everywhere in the Promised Land throughout Israel's history. They did not leave pastoralism behind; they simply developed a dimorphic [14] economy like most Near Eastern states. The coastal plains and fertile valleys were more suited to international commerce and agriculture, to be sure, but even there we find consistent biblical and archaeological evidence of flocks and cattle.[15] It was always [16] considered critical to maintain a balanced mixed economy of both farming and herding.[17]

At the centre of the land of promise is the hill country, the mountainous area of Judah and Samaria, averaging just over 700 metres (2,400 ft) in altitude. These are the 'mountains and valleys' that 'drink rain from heaven' (Deut. 11:11), rain that fills underground springs and pools that often survive through the dry season. This land was lauded as a source of 'grain, new wine and oil' (Deut. 7:13 et al.), the characteristic products of hill-country agriculture.

Israel's hilly countryside is known frequently as a land of 'milk and honey' (Deut. 6:3; 11:9 et al.). Such a description is more the dream of pastoralists than farmers. It refers to the milk of the flocks and the produce of uncultivated fields.[18] Moses warns the assembly not to forget the Lord after the land has produced and 'your herds and flocks grow large' (Deut. 8:13). While the primary places for herding were in the more arid areas to be discussed below, we should not assume that the hill country was used exclusively for agriculture.[19] The patriarchal stories mention Abraham and Lot in the hill country near Bethel, Laban's flocks in Syria, Jacob's flocks in Dothan, and Judah's sheep shearing in Timnah. Archaeological evidence points to

[14] A term introduced by Rowton (1974) for the complementary nature of pastoral-agricultural societies. A more nuanced term is 'polymorphous' (Lemche 1985).

[15] Cf. Hesse & Wapnish (2002). The Sharon plains and the Shephelah were used by Judah's kings for herds (1 Chr. 27:29; 2 Chr. 26:10). The prediction (Isa. 65:10) that the forests of Sharon and Galilee would become pasture lands is a description of the undesirable changes in these regions that result from increased population and deforestation through neglect (Bimson & Kane 1985: 17).

[16] An understanding of pastoralism in the ancient world is aided by ethno-archaeology, the controlled study of the past by comparison with modern societies. The description of perennial dynamics in this chapter leads, at times, to a mix of tenses (past and present).

[17] Herding traditionally balanced flocks and cattle at a 2/3 to 1/3 ratio (Sade 1988).

[18] Assuming this is wild honey (Hareuveni 1980: 11–15). Date honey, on the other hand, would suggest that agriculture is also envisioned (cf. Num. 16:13; 13:27).

[19] A mixed economy (cf. Jer. 51:23–25; 31:10–11, 23) has traditionally been the safest economic strategy in the face of natural, social and political threats. The Israelites increased the agricultural use of the hill country, a perennial indication of prosperity. As a result of the Assyrian invasion later in their history, the land returned to a state *only* useful for pastoralism (Isa. 7:21–23, 25; cf. Jer. 37:12–13).

the persistence of animal husbandry throughout the hill country, especially in Judah (Hesse & Wapnish 2002). Biblical writers attest to the presence of shepherds, flocks and tents in the villages and towns of all of Israel's settled areas.[20] Judah even became an exporter of 'lambs, rams and goats' to Arabia (Ezek. 27:21).

Having appreciated the prevalence of flocks throughout all the regions of ancient Israel, it is still appropriate to give our fullest attention to the areas most often associated with shepherd culture. To the east and south of the mountains of Judah lie semi-arid areas which receive less rainfall than required to secure grain production. This is the 'steppe' or wilderness which forms the bridge between the fertile areas and the truly desert regions.

Semi-arid areas are the traditional home to large flocks, fed naturally by wild shrubs and grasses that grow on the slopes and valleys. Yet hillsides that appear to be carpets of green each winter often hide exhausted soils that hold little water. Realistically, these marginal areas were devoted to pastoralism not because they were ideal, but because they were ill-suited for much else, and regions with more rain were developed for agriculture.[21] The semi-arid environments provide the backdrop for David's early life as shepherd of his family's flock (1 Sam. 16) and, later, as protector of Nabal's sizeable herds (1 Sam. 25:2).

The arid areas in the Sinai, the southernmost Negev,[22] and the wilderness areas around the Dead Sea constitute a more drastic ecological region. Though in good years there is enough moisture to produce pastures for intermittent grazing, precipitation here averages 80–150 mm (3–6 in.). Only the hardiest plants and animals (and people) can survive in this environment. Such is the setting for the wilderness sojourn during which divine intervention alone kept the community of Israel alive.

The biblical term 'wilderness' (*midbār*) is used for different geographic regions, a semantic ambiguity that suggests cultural realities are as much in mind. *Midbār* may refer to the desert (i.e. place of thirst, fatigue and death; Ps. 63:1–2), but it can also simply mean pasturelands (Talmon 1966: 40–44).[23] Pastoral work typically takes

---

[20] E.g., Josh. 6:21; Judg. 6:19; 13:15; 1 Sam. 22:19; 1 Kgs 8:56; 12:16; Hos. 9:6; Jer. 6:3; 30:18; 49:29; Zech. 12:7; Mal. 2:12.

[21] A recent study in the Negev documents drought (less than 50 mm/2 in. rainfall) at an average of seven in twenty-four years (Bruins 1986: 196–198).

[22] 'Negev' comes from a root meaning 'to be dry' (BDB §5870).

[23] This awareness explains how the feeding of the 5,000 could take place while they were in the desert, yet sitting on green grass (Mark 6:35, 39).

place in the arid and semi-arid areas of the Negev, but flocks may also graze in the more fertile areas mentioned above. *Midbār* can be used in both contexts (cf. Gen. 37:22; Josh. 8:15; Jer. 12:10–11; Hareuveni 1991: 26–35). One's appreciation for the wilderness as a *symbolic environment* is necessary for understanding most of the biblical traditions we will survey below.

Another biblical term, *nāweh*, resembles *midbār*; it can refer to a place of flocks (2 Sam. 7:8) and shepherds (Jer. 33:12) or to enclosures where sheep are kept in safety (Zeph. 2:6).[24] *Nāweh* is often used in passages with figurative significance (e.g. Ps. 23:2). The most noteworthy symbolism is found in references to Canaan (Exod. 15:13; Ps. 79:7; Jer. 10:25) and, more particularly, Jerusalem (2 Sam. 15:25). Passages picturing the greenery of blessing (Joel 2:22) and the desolation of curse (Jer. 23:10) use the two words together (e.g. 'the pastures in the desert are withered'). The ultimate pastureland of Israel is recognized by their enemies in the sobering words of Jeremiah:

> Whoever found them devoured them;
>   their enemies said, 'We are not guilty,
> for they sinned against the LORD, *their true pasture*,
>   the LORD, the hope of their fathers.'
>
> (Jer. 50:7)

Sheep and goats

> Be sure you know the condition of your flocks,
>   give careful attention to your herds . . .
> When . . . the grass from the hills is gathered in,
> the lambs will provide you with clothing,
>   and the goats with the price of a field.
> You will have plenty of goats' milk
>   to feed you and your family
>   and to nourish your servant girls.
> (Prov. 27:23–27)

Biblical references to shepherding presuppose an understanding not only of the environment but also of the animals themselves. The

---

[24] Other Hebrew terms for pasture include three nouns from the shepherding verb *rā'āh* (*mir'eh*, *mar'ît*, and *rĕ'î*) and *rebeṣ*, a place where sheep can lie down (i.e. in safety; cf. Jer. 50:7; Isa. 65:10). *Gādēr* is used for an enclosed area, i.e. for flocks.

frequency of terms for sheep and goats [25] illustrates the general importance of and familiarity with them in the biblical periods. One evidence of God's covenant blessing was the multiplication of flocks (Deut. 7:13; 28:4). An evidence of curse was their loss (Deut. 28:18, 31, 51). Prophetic depictions of the messianic era envisage flocks once again pasturing securely on the hills of Israel (Jer. 33:12ff.; Zeph. 2:6).

Historically, the primary breed of sheep in this region is the Awassi 'fat tail'.[26] The nickname is descriptive of its unusually large tail which stores energy for the autumn season when nutrition is often negligible.[27] This breed is hardy in regions where the summer heat is intense and water is often minimal. The ability to tolerate dehydration [28] is accompanied by the ability to replenish rapidly the 7–9 litres of water that may be lost over several days (Evenari et al. 1971: 311). To this day Awassi are highly regarded as strong milk producers and good sources of wool and tasty mutton. They are cherished for their docile temperaments, compliant even during shearing and slaughter (Isa. 53:7).

The black-haired 'Sinai' goat has been indigenous to the region for centuries.[29] These goats are well suited to wilderness settings, living off brush and roots, navigating precipitous trails and sustaining themselves in high humidity with little water. Goats have traditionally been valued more as domestic rather than commercial producers, providing, in addition to milk, fibre for tents and blankets. While they reproduce more quickly (within the first year) and yield more milk than sheep, goat products are valued less in the markets and the animals' life expectancy is shorter. The word for goat is used fifty-six times in the Pentateuch (of seventy-four total in the Old Testament), evidence of how common and important they were in the patriarchal and wilderness settings, and in the rituals and architecture of the tabernacle.

Sheep and goats have been herded together through the ages because of their natural, complementary features. Sheep characteristically

[25] There are over 600 biblical references to sheep (typically Heb. $\bar{s}\bar{o}'n$; Gk *probaton*) and goats (typically Heb. *'ēz*; Gk *eriphos*). These animals are *caprids* or small *ruminants*, i.e. herbivores that chew their cud. Large ruminants include cattle.

[26] Though colour variation was more prevalent in biblical times (cf. Gen. 30), the image of the common white Awassi is captured in Song 4:2 (= 6:6): 'Your teeth are like a flock of sheep just shorn, coming up from the washing.'

[27] The tails, weighing up to 10 kg (22 lb) in males and 5 kg (12 lb) in females (Evenari et al. 1971: 311), were prescribed as food for Israel's priests (Exod. 29:22; Lev. 3:9 et al.).

[28] By perspiration and panting, and by the protection of a thick coat.

[29] The sight of a flock of black goats on chalky wilderness hills inspired the poet to write, 'Your hair is like a flock of goats descending from Mount Gilead' (Song 4:1; 6:5).

follow each other closely and 'flock' together, huddling for protection from heat or cold. Goats are smarter, more independent, and often serve as leaders for small groups of sheep (Jer. 50:8). Sheep are discriminating eaters, cropping select grasses evenly above the ground, while goats are indiscriminate 'browsers'. For intensive [30] feeding the goats are often separated to allow the more docile sheep to get their fill.[31] When the flocks are in the wilderness areas at night, the goats may need separate shelter because their thinner coats provide less protection (Jeremias 1963: 206). Sheep, also penned at night, are able to provide warmth for each other during the winter months.

The size of a flock fluctuates considerably and is a function of a number of variables including the purpose of the flock (Cribb 1991: 34–37). Subsistence may be achieved by the work of a family whose flock numbers twenty-five to sixty (Johnson 1969: 10), and surplus is possible with flocks over sixty. These flocks and larger ones that number 200–500 are typically pastured in the wilderness areas except during the summer, when they feed on the stubble of the harvested grain fields. While a competent shepherd can handle as many as 500 sheep and goats alone in open pasturelands, the comprehensive work of animal husbandry over the course of a year (including the making of milk and fibre products) requires a number of able workers.

A typical ratio of one male to ten females characterizes a flock designed to provide milk, wool and meat (Gen. 32:14). Both sheep and goats give birth on the range.[32] The males are culled for market or sacrifice. Shepherds since antiquity could hope for an 80% birthing rate for their flocks in a good year (Postgate & Payne 1975: 5), with birth losses offset by occasional twinning. Jacob reports that he had such success there was an annual increase of 100% to Laban's flock (Gen. 31:38). Figuratively, the health and multiplication of a community was a sign of good leadership (Jer. 23:3).

Products of the flock

The products of a mixed flock are numerous and highly valued. For this reason, sheep and goats were regularly used as barter, gifts, tribute and plunder (cf. 2 Kgs 8:4; 2 Chr. 14:12–15; 17:11; Isa. 60:7;

---

[30] 'Intensive' feeding refers to bringing food (usually grain) to the animals either as a supplemental or as the exclusive source of nutrition. 'Extensive' feeding takes place on the open range.
[31] This may be the background for the image of the great judgment as a separating of sheep and goats in Matt. 25.
[32] To protect the newborn, a shepherd must 'gather the lambs in his arms' (Isa. 40:11) and bring them back to the fold until they are strong enough to return to the fields.

Ezek. 27:21). Milking, which lasts as long as five months when the pastures are full, provides fat (for candles, soap, etc.), curd/butter, yoghurt and a variety of cheeses that supply fat and protein essential in an otherwise lean diet. The Awassi, by traditional methods, produce about 100 litres of milk annually (Evenari et al. 1971: 311). Wool was valued in Israel as it was throughout the ancient world (Lev. 13:47; 2 Kgs 3:4; Job 31:20; Ezek. 34:3; Prov. 31:13). Goat hair was useful for sacks, rope and tents,[33] and it provided the raw material for the tabernacle (Exod. 25:4; 26:7; 35:6).

Another traditional use of flocks was for natural fertilizer in the ploughed fields. This simple datum is one of the important links in the symbiotic relationship between agricultural and pastoral economies. Once the grain fields are harvested the flocks move in for their summer nourishment. This is necessary for the shepherd who loses his spring pastures with the termination of the spring rains. But it is also in the farmer's best interest to open his fields during the 'off season'.[34]

Goats and sheep were especially valuable after they were slaughtered. Both animals were among the most common sacrifices in the ancient world (B. J. Collins 2002) and were raised in large numbers for such use (cf. 1 Kgs 8:63).[35] In Israelite ritual, the firstborn of the flock was to be designated the possession of YHWH (Exod. 13:12; Deut. 15:19) and a tithe of the flock was assigned to him (Lev. 27:32). Flawless sheep and goats were used for burnt, peace, sin and guilt offerings (Lev. 1:10; 3:6; 5:6, 15). The pilgrimage festival of Passover required of each family a year-old sheep or goat, also without blemish (Exod. 12:5ff.). Rams were specifically designated for most of the flock offerings. They were offered for Nazirite vows (Num. 6:14, 17, 19), at the new-moon festival (Num. 28:11–14), Passover (Num. 28:19–20), Pentecost (Lev. 23:18), for peace offerings (Lev. 9:4ff.) and on the Day of Atonement (Lev. 16:3, 5). A lamb submitting silently to slaughter is a poignant image of the Servant in Isaiah (Isa. 53:7).

The animals were used as meat apart from ritual settings. However, it is likely that only the nobility could afford meat on a regular basis (Borowski 1998). Solomon's table featured one hundred sheep and goats daily (1 Kgs 4:23). Lambs (typically the freshly weaned males, two to five months old) have been the most desirable traditionally,

---

[33] The apostle Paul was a tent-maker from Tarsus, a city famous in the Mediterranean world for its goat-hair tents.

[34] As well as making good fertilizer, herd dung was also useful as fuel and medicine.

[35] Of the 114 references to *kebeś* (lamb) in the OT, 111 indicate a sacrificial context.

but females and males no longer useful for reproduction were regularly culled and sold for meat as well. Jacob's deception of Esau featured a quickly prepared meal of goat, disguised as hunted game (Gen. 27:9ff.).

Animal skins were useful containers for wine and water and served as butter churns. Skins became clothing (Gen. 3:1), rugs and other kinds of coverings (Exod. 26:14). The skins of sheep were utilized as inflatable rafts as early as the Neo-Assyrians in the ninth century BC (Borowski 1998: 64–65). Sheepskin parchment is first depicted on a Neo-Assyrian relief (c. 800 BC; Ryder 1993: 12). A variety of tools and instruments for both ritual and profane use were made from the sinew, bones and horns.[36]

A shepherd's duties

> He makes me lie down in green pastures,
> he leads me beside quiet waters,
>> he restores my soul.
> He guides me in paths of righteousness
>> for his name's sake.
> Even though I walk
>> through the valley of the shadow of death,
> I will fear no evil,
>> for you are with me;
> your rod and your staff,
>> they comfort me.
>
> (Ps. 23:2–4)

We have begun to anticipate a shepherd's challenges by exploring the biological make-up of the animals and the particular environmental and socio-economic contexts in which they were raised. The condition and growth of a flock depends greatly on the care, attentiveness and skill of the shepherd. The primary verbs for shepherding (Heb. *rā'āh*; Gk *poimainō*) can mean feeding, leading (i.e. to pasture) and general tending (oversight). Some shepherds were owners or managers of enormous herds, with hired 'undershepherds' who were responsible to them for smaller sub-flocks (cf. Gen. 29 – 31). Family herds were also common, and the work of animal husbandry was shared by all

---

[36] Several of the artefacts used by the Israelite priests in their rituals came from sheep. Along with the sacrifice itself, there was the ram's horn and, by the second century BC, untanned leather parchment for the sacred text.

members, young and old, male and female (Gen. 24:13ff.; 29:6ff.; 37:2; Exod. 2:16; 1 Sam. 16:11; 17:15).

One of the most pressing challenges for shepherds is to provide food and water for animals in environments that frequently withold these essential elements for life and production. In the hot, arid summer, sheep must drink water daily or they risk dehydration and death. A shepherd needs to keep within a 32-kilometre (20-mile) grazing radius of an adequate water source in cold weather and within 15–20 kilometres (10–12 miles) in the summer (Evenari 1971: 311; cf. Matthews 1978: 70, n. 26). Water is available from a number of different sources, and these sources are perennially protected and contested. Natural springs are the simplest and most envied sources of 'permanently' available water, though they can be contaminated (Exod. 15:22–27; Jas 3:11–12) or dry up. Wells provide access to the water table and, once dug, can be maintained for generations. The story of Isaac at Beer-sheba in Genesis 26 illustrates the importance of such wells in the Negev and the contentiousness surrounding them.[37] Shepherds require the winter rains to bring green life to the hillsides and to turn the dry valleys into streams. This water settles into temporary pools of 'quiet waters' (Ps. 23:2; 2 Kgs 3; cf. Hareuveni 1991: 55–66) which sometimes last for months. Pastoralists are known for leading rainwater into man-made cisterns,[38] which they keep covered for use throughout the year.

A shepherd must make sure that the flocks (especially sheep) have access to a variety of vegetation, and also be careful not to graze too soon or overgraze an area.[39] A balanced diet may require moving several times in the course of a given day. Sheep are typically *led* from in front, though they are occasionally *driven* from behind[40] according to the shepherd's plan. The good shepherd must 'lead with compassion' (*nhl*; cf. Gen. 33:14; Ps. 23:3; Isa. 40:11; 49:10), knowing that the pregnant and nursing ewes need more rest and extra nutrition in

---

[37] For other stories of shepherds and (conflicts over) springs/wells, see Gen. 16, 21, 24, 26, 29; Exod. 2.

[38] Some of these crude cisterns have been known to hold enough water from a desert flood for two years (Evenari 1971: 161).

[39] Sensitivity to an area's 'carrying capacity' is reflected in the Abraham and Lot story of Gen. 13:5–7 (cf. Bruins 1986: 56–57) and in a Hittite legend: 'Who [are you], who continually graze on [ou]r meadow? [I]f you [continue to eat?] the fresh greenery, you will destroy our meadow!' (Beckman 1988: 40).

[40] Flocks typically follow a shepherd but are 'driven' from behind when the animals might be distracted by agricultural fields (in which they are not allowed to feed). Amos was called from (lit.) 'behind the sheep' (Amos 7:15; cf. Gen. 31:18; 32:17, 19 [H 18, 20]; 2 Sam. 7:8), but compare references to 'leading' them in Pss. 23:2; 77:20 [H 21]; 80:1.

the winter and spring, as do the lambs and kids. Shepherds have to watch their animals carefully; the right balance of eating, drinking and resting is essential.

Rest is not only a function of being well provided for. It is a state of security that comes from the shepherd's protective presence.[41] The image of a gathered flock lying down in green pastures was commonly used to picture satisfaction and safety (Isa. 32:18). There are many threats in the environment that require the herder's vigilance. The weather itself can be an enemy. Cold nights with frost, driving rain or hail, or summer days with the hot east *hamsin* winds can wreak havoc on a herd. Because the climate is so variable in the marginal areas, shepherds have to predict not only the weather, but also the amount of water and pasture needed in anticipation of each move they make. Neglecting the mothers and young, or driving the flocks too hard can bring on fatalities (Gen. 33:13). Protection is provided most fully each night as the shepherd leads his flock into some kind of pen.[42] These 'folds' are places where the sheep can be counted, moving under the hand of the shepherd into safety (cf. Num. 32:16; Judg. 5:16; Jer. 33:12–13; Ezek. 20:37).[43]

There are many menacing threats in the wilderness. Shepherds had to be vigilant regarding diseases that easily ravage a flock. The threat of epidemics could be as great as that of drought. Wild animals often take the young, especially at night. Wolves, bears, leopards and lions are named in Scripture as natural enemies of a flock.[44] David's courage with Goliath came from his experience with such predators (1 Sam. 17:34–36). Shepherds have had to face human threats as well (Job 1:14–15). Shrewd thieves that break in and steal (John 10:1, 10) can remove a whole flock.[45] Finally, the desert itself can be a haunting, confusing and frightening environment (Jer. 50:6;

---

[41] Keller (1970: 35ff.) identifies four factors that inhibit sheep from lying down (i.e. with a sense of security): fear (especially of threats in the environment); tension from strife among the flock; aggravation by pests (e.g. parasites and flies); and hunger.

[42] Separate stone pens (Borowski 1998: 41–42), caves (cf. 1 Sam. 24:3), or simple extensions of the tent dwelling were used to protect the flocks at night, and to provide safety and special provisions for the sick and young during the day. For references to literal folds/pens, see Num. 32:16; 1 Sam. 24:3; 2 Chr. 32:28; Ps. 78:70; John 10:1; and as imagery, Zeph. 2:6.

[43] In settled areas, folds were stone enclosures or, in some regions, they were under a typical Israelite two- or four-room house (Netzer 1992: 196–198). This may explain to a certain extent Jephthah's rash vow in Judg. 11 (expecting perhaps an animal to come out first) and also the kind of setting for Jesus' birth in Luke 2, discussed below.

[44] Amos 3:12; Isa. 11:6; Jer. 5:6; 50:17; John 10:12; cf. Gen. 31:39; Sir. 13:17.

[45] I interviewed one shepherd who had his flock stolen three times!

Hareuveni 1991: 95ff.). Shepherd and sheep can only be safe on 'right paths'.[46]

To face these various challenges a shepherd carried two simple but versatile implements. His staff (*maṭṭeh*) was useful for support, picking off branches, snagging a trapped animal with the crook, or redirecting misbehaving members of the herd. The staff became a symbol for the protective presence of the shepherd (Ps. 23:4). *Maṭṭeh* is commonly used for tribe, perhaps suggesting the tribal head who leads by (or leans on) his staff. The staff became a symbol of the tribe (cf. Num. 17:2–10 [H 17–25]) and of authority and rule (as sceptre) in general (Ps. 110:2; Jer. 48:17). Supernatural power was located in the staffs of Moses (Exod. 4:2, 4, 17 et al.; 17:9, 11–12), Aaron (Exod. 7:9–10, 12, 19; Num. 17:8 [H 23]) and Elisha (2 Kgs 4:29, 31).

The shorter club or rod (*šēbeṭ*) was a crude weapon, also made from a tree branch. Used to beat cumin (Isa. 28:27) and as a weapon in battle (2 Sam. 23:21), the rod was a traditional shepherd's standby for defence [47] and the implement used for counting a flock (Lev. 27:32; Ezek. 20:37). The security of the flock was often tied to the protective capacity of a shepherd (Ps. 23:4). The rod was the symbol for discipline in the family (Prov. 13:24 et al.; cf. 1 Cor. 4:21) and among the nations (2 Sam. 7:14; Ps. 2:9; Isa. 10:15). The *šēbeṭ* (i.e. as sceptre) became the symbol of military might and authority for ancient kings (Gen. 49:10; Mic. 7:14), and a euphemism for a country's political autonomy (Amos 1:5; Zech. 10:11; cf. Gen. 49:1; Ps. 45:7).

Another term for either of the shepherd's instruments was *maqqēl*, translated either 'rod' or 'staff'. The object lesson in Zechariah 11 involves the breaking of two such staffs, the one representing 'pleasantness' and the other 'union'. These two rods may represent the two functions of the shepherd (ruler): protector from external threats (with the *šēbeṭ*) and peacekeeper among the flocks (with the *maṭṭeh*; cf. Power 1928: 437).[48]

The wide range of activities involved in shepherding is determined by the daily and seasonal needs of the animals. Consequently, attentive and careful shepherds become endeared to their flocks.

---

[46] The verb *nḥh* is often used to emphasize proper shepherd-like guidance to an appointed destination (Exod. 13:21; Ps. 78:53, 72) or, figuratively, on paths of righteousness (Pss. 5:8 [H 9]; 23:3).

[47] David kills Goliath with a slingshot, another useful weapon mastered by traditional shepherds. In that context David assured Saul that he had successfully 'struck ... and ... killed' a bear and a lion (1 Sam. 17:34–36).

[48] Note, however, that while both rod and staff bring comfort in Ps. 23:4, both are symbols of oppression in Isa. 9:4 (H 3); 10:24.

Responsible shepherds know every member of their flocks in terms of their birth circumstances, history of health, eating habits and other idiosyncrasies. It is not uncommon to name each goat and sheep and to call them by name (John 10:3ff.). One of the most striking characteristics of the shepherd-flock relationship is that control over the flock is exercised simply by the sound of the shepherd's voice or whistle (John 10:3; cf. Judg. 5:16; Zech. 10:8). Only a special bond between animal and human can explain this responsiveness.

All of these elements – the movement, the isolation, the variety, the adjustments, the demands – contributed to a knowledge base and 'skill set' that distinguished shepherds as remarkably and broadly capable persons. They were known for independence, resourcefulness, adaptability, courage and vigilance. Their profession cultivated a capacity for attentiveness, self-sacrifice and compassion. Jacob was not exaggerating when he claimed, 'The heat consumed me in the daytime and the cold at night, and sleep fled from my eyes' (Gen. 31:40). This occupation put shepherds in a constant state of negotiation with an unpredictable physical and social environment. For these and other reasons, the shepherd naturally became an icon of leadership.

On some high moor, across which at night hyenas howl, when you meet him, sleepless, far-sighted, weather-beaten, armed, leaning on his staff, and looking out over his scattered sheep, every one on his heart, you understand why the shepherd of Judea sprang to the front in his people's history; why they gave his name to their king, and made him the symbol of Providence; why Christ took him as the type of self-sacrifice. (G. A. Smith 1966: 210)

Chapter Three

Shepherd rulers in the ancient world

Having surveyed the natural world of shepherds, we are now in a position to appreciate the ways in which ancient societies used pastoral imagery to reflect notions of peoplehood and leadership. It is important to consider these extrabiblical textual traditions as background for the images used by later (or contemporaneous) biblical writers. Pastoral images conveyed notions of rulership – both divine and human – in a wide variety of historical periods, geographical regions and literary contexts in the Ancient Near East. Shepherd language was used in stock titles and epithets to define a king's role as just ruler, benevolent provider and/or powerful defender. Ancient sources describe a country's citizenry (or army) as a flock and their experience of plenty as green pastures. Mesopotamian and Egyptian sources will serve as background for Old Testament usage here. A brief survey of Classical sources will provide orientation for the New Testament section below.

Mesopotamian deities

> The god is a shepherd of men, seeking (good) pastures for mankind.[1]

The tradition of shepherd rulers is evident as far back as written history. The myths of the Sumerians identified numerous deities as shepherds in epithets and titles.[2] Indeed, most of the major gods bear the epithet 'shepherd' (van der Toorn 1995: 1460). Typically the designation is descriptive of the gods' role as rulers of humanity, usually with an emphasis on their benevolent concern for humanity.

The ancient deity Dumuzi was associated with the fertility of the pasturelands and the flocks. In a poem he is considered both shepherd and farmer:

---

[1] *CAD*, vol. 7, p. 95.
[2] Cf. Hallo (1957: 129–130) for definitions and examples of both.

> Grant him the staff that guides the land aright, the staff
> and the lead rope...
> May he exercise the shepherdship over their black-headed [3]
> inhabitants,
> He, like a farmer, may establish cultivated fields,
> May he like a faithful shepherd multiply the sheepfolds,
> May there be flax under him, may there be barley under
> him.

(Sefati 1998: 305)

The worship of this pastoral deity extends from the third to the first millennium BC. This is the Dumuzi known later in Assyro-Babylonian times as Tammuz, the shepherd king who was ritually lamented each summer when the fields were barren (Ezek. 8:14).

Another god in the Mesopotamian pantheon described as a shepherd was Enlil, sometimes pictured with a horned cap. In a hymn to Enlil as ruler he is called the 'august leader-goat' (Jacobsen 1987: 102). Elsewhere he is told, 'the shepherd-crook of the gods is under your care' (Pritchard 1969: 576). In a hymn of intercession he is petitioned, 'Like a just shepherd appoint the affairs of the universe. With produce make the surface of the land heavy!' (Lutz 1919: 55–56). He was frequently extolled as provider: 'Enlil, the reliable shepherd of (herds) multiplying one like the other, the herdsman and leader of all in which is breadth of life' (Jacobsen 1987: 107). He was known for his skill and wisdom: 'Enlil you are the reliable shepherd, you know how to herd them, they are having sweet, pleasant times under the speckled stars' (ibid. 110). For over a millennium Enlil was worshipped as a source of fertility and order, as both farmer and shepherd (Jacobsen 1987: 105), the 'Shepherd who decrees the fates' (e.g. Kramer 1972: 47, 44).[4]

The sun, as the primary source of life and fecundity, was a likely object of veneration in pastoral terms. In an Akkadian hymn to the sun god from the end of the second millennium, Shamash is honoured for his constant care and direction:

---

[3] I.e., human.

[4] In the famous 'Lamention over the Destruction of Ur', ritual mourning is shaped by the image of the shepherd god Enlil and his fold: 'He has abandoned his stable, his sheepfold (became) haunted ... Enlil has abandoned the shrine of Nippur, his sheepfold (became) haunted' (Hallo 1997: 535). The refrain 'has abandoned ... his sheepfold' occurs throughout the Lament which concludes, as it began, with Enlil's haunting absence: 'gone is the trustworthy shepherd' (Kramer 1940: 47).

You care for all the peoples of the land . . .
Whatever has breath you shepherd without exception . . .
Every day you pass over the broad earth . . .
Above, you direct all the affairs of men,
Shepherd of that beneath, keeper of that above,
You, Shamash, direct, you are the light of everything.
(Lambert 1960: 126–129)

The hymn ends with an important association between the sun and governance over 'the affairs of men'. This will be a significant connection in our exploration of the role of shepherd kings.

The cosmologies of the ancient Mesopotamians included other deities that were referred to as shepherds. A simple list (see Appendix A)[5] reveals the variety of applications for the image and documents its widespread use in descriptions, titles and epithets from different genres. References to divine shepherds/shepherdesses continue in Mesopotamia into the first century BC (Westenholz 2004: 175). It is fascinating to find the ancient Mesopotamians assuming that these great deities were also their personal shepherd gods. 'Shamash is *my* shepherd' and 'Marduk has provided *me* with pasture' are striking examples.[6]

Depictions of Marduk bring out another dimension of the shepherd's role, that of protection. Militancy is clear in *Enuma Elish*, the Babylonian creation myth that extols Marduk's cosmogonic victory: 'His lordship shall be supreme, he shall have no rival. He shall be the shepherd of the black-headed folk, his creatures' (Hallo 1997: 402). The construction of a new world characterized by peace and order requires concern, wisdom and strength, the characteristic qualities of a shepherd god.

Along with written shepherd titles for the gods, there were suggestive iconographic elements drawn from pastoral life. The shepherd's rod and/or staff, and the sceptre derived from them (Vancil 1975: 31–32), became symbols of royal authority in ancient reliefs.[7] In one myth Enki presents to Inanna 'the exalted scepter,

---

[5] To put these in perspective, there are over 3,000 deities mentioned in texts from ancient Mesopotamia.

[6] These examples are provided by Block (1988: 57), who notes (ibid. fn. 91) that the shepherd title is often used for heads of pantheons, those gods who rule over the 'flock' of lesser gods. See other examples in Westenholz (2004: 175, 185).

[7] For just a few of the many examples, see Du Mesnil du Buisson (1973: 116, fig. 34; 121, fig. 40). Compare also the evidence from Hatti noted in Beckman (1988: 42–43).

staffs,[8] the exalted shrine, shepherdship, kingship' (Kramer 1972: 66).[9] In both picture and word, shepherdship and kingship were equated.

This brief survey supports the following observations. First, shepherd language is used for a variety of gods and goddesses in diverse literary contexts throughout Mesopotamian history. Second, the title of shepherd is found in contexts with explicit references to benevolent rule/leadership (with power, wisdom/justice and mercy; and as those who 'decree the destinies'), generous provision (fertility, healing) and/or able protection (military strength). Shepherd deities were responsible for the promotion and maintenance of both physical life and social order. All hope was gone if a patron god abandoned his or her city. According to the Lamentation over Ur, without a trustworthy shepherd a city's fate is sealed.

Mesopotamian kings

The great gods called me, so I became the beneficent shepherd whose scepter is righteous. (Hammurabi)[10]

The myths of Mesopotamian deities reflected the dynamic realities of emerging city states and their rulers on earth. Human rulers were represented in royal inscriptions as historical recipients of shepherdship from the gods. They in turn ruled over their human 'flock'. In royal hymnody kings emphasized their divine parentage (Kramer 1974: 163–166). They represented themselves as accountable to the divine council for establishing and maintaining the *mes*, cosmic rules that brought harmony among humans. In a summary of Mesopotamian royal titles, W. Hallo (1957: 133) notes that royal self-justification inevitably included, first, an affirmation of divine calling, and second, a description of the nature of that calling as 'shepherding' the country/people of the deity.[11] These twin ideas of calling and accountability as shepherds assumed that the gods were invested in

[8] Biblical evidence for staff and sceptre as separate symbols of leadership is found in Num. 21:18.

[9] Another pictographic symbol associated with shepherd or ram rulers was the horned helmet, the 'distinctive head-gear of divinity' (Van Buren 1945: 104), attested from the earliest times through the Persian Period for both ruling gods and kings. For description and examples see Black & Green (1992: 102 and relevant illustrations).

[10] Pritchard (1969: 177).

[11] Hallo (1957: 147) considers the shepherd epithet the 'one by which the king was most closely linked to his subjects'. He also notes that it is one of the few that often precedes a king's name, thus implying that it was used in personal address.

the affairs of this world. Kings sought to 'prove' that they were good shepherds (i.e. had been faithful to their trust) through their various inscriptions.

Early in the history of Sumer an equation between human shepherdship and rulership took shape. In an epic poem about ancient Uruk, King Enmerker prays to Inanna for the city of Aratta to submit to him. Enmerker – the 'wild goat of the high mountains with noble horns' (Jacobsen 1987: 292) [12] – is promised military conquest by the goddess: '[the people of Aratta will] kneel down for you (to sleep) like highland sheep' (ibid. 286). The king of Aratta at one point describes his people as 'scattered ewes' (ibid. 308). After several tests, the messenger to Erech conveys the image that Enmerker will be their new ruler: 'From in his city may the men walk like sheep, and may he follow after them like their shepherd' (ibid. 310).

Names compounded with 'shepherd' are widely attested [13] during the Ur III period (2100–2000 BC), an era known for a renaissance of Sumerian themes. The first of these kings was Gudea, who used such epithets as 'shepherd', 'shepherd of the first class of Ningirsu', 'faithful shepherd', 'shepherd of his country' (cf. Appendix B). Gudea's shepherdship was the source of pastoral fecundity: 'Let the cattle pens be built on your behalf, let the sheepfolds be renewed on your account, May the people lie down in grassy pastures under your reign, (enjoying) abundance, and let the eyes of all the countries be directed toward Sumer' (ibid. 100).

Shepherd language was continued by other third-millennium kings,[14] and it is found in some early iconography as well. The 'kid-carrier' image is ever present in Mesopotamian records (Muller 1944; Westenholz 2004: 178–182). A goat or sheep was shown either under the arm or against the chest of an official on a variety of media.

Other shepherding accoutrements associated with rulers include the staff, crook, lead rope and/or mace. In a detailed analysis of these symbols of power, Wiggermann (1985–86: 15) states, 'It is abundantly clear that the symbolic staff of rulership, given to the king to

---

[12] In other lines Enmerker is called the beloved provider, thus representing the full range of shepherding roles for his people.

[13] See Goodenough (1929: 173ff.) for a survey. Westenholz (2004: 167) notes many examples of shepherd names for kings in the Sargonic period. Once the Sumerian revival was underway titles were used retroactively for Old Akkadian kings. For example, Naram Sin, in the 'Curse of Agade', is the shepherd king responsible for 'all the lands . . . lying down in grassy pastures, their people experienced happiness' (ibid.).

[14] See Appendix B.

shepherd the people, derives from the staff of the shepherd, with which he guides his flock.'[15] A hymn to Rim-Sin of Larsa assumes the connection: 'You make the shepherd of the land hold in his hands the august staff until distant days' (Charpin 1986: 345). Ishme-Dagan of Isin considered the 'staff which makes the loyal men walk with one step' a gift of the gods (Gadd 1948: 38). Warad-Sin from Larsa (c. 1834 BC) prays for 'a staff to subdue the people' (Thureau-Dangin 1907: 205). This is 'the mighty man, the warrior for Ur, king of Larsa, king of Sumer and Akkad, the shepherd of righteousness who brings to pass the laws' (ibid. 215). The staff is a ubiquitous Near Eastern symbol for rule.

By the beginning of the second millennium BC Akkadian and Amorite kings were using conventional shepherd language to describe themselves. Samples from the kings of Isin will illustrate. A sustained pastoral metaphor is found in relation to Ur-Ninurta, 'the shepherd who offers everything for Nippur, herdsman of Ur' (Frayne 1990: 66). In a hymn dedicated to him it is written:

> Under his rule may the people rest in grassy pastures with him as their herdsman. May Ur-Ninurta make the numerous people follow the just path ... As for sheep, may he search for food (for them) to eat, may he let them have water to drink! ... (Ur-Ninurta) the faithful shepherd who is attentive to you. May you be available to make the black-headed, numerous as sheep, follow your path.[16]

The royal ideology contained in these lines maintains the traditional emphasis on fertility and peace,[17] with a clear interest in presenting the king as a tireless shepherd who is faithful and attentive. Notice

[15] See also Frankfort (1939: 164, 178), van Buren (1945: 142–144) and Pritchard (1969: 114).

[16] Ur-Ninurta D 33f., A 20, 26, and C 20–23, *ETCSL*. Compare words spoken to Iddin-Dagan: 'Enlil has commanded you to keep firm the cosmic bond in Sumer, to keep the people on the track, to let Sumer and Akkad relax under your broad protection, to let the people eat noble food and drink fresh water. Iddin-Dagan, you are the shepherd in his heart, the one whom Enlil has spoken to truly' (Iddin-Dagan B 5–13, *ETCSL*; cf. Beyerlin 1978: 107).

[17] For an intriguing example of shepherd imagery emphasizing well-being and prosperity embedded in an Akkadian prophecy of a coming saviour, see Pritchard (1969: 604). See also the personal lament of King Naram-Sin in the OB Cuthean Legend: 'I am a king who has not protected his land and a shepherd who has not safeguarded his people' (Westenholz 1997: 273). King David similarly forgot his pastoral responsibilities (1 Chr. 21:17).

again the picture of a shepherd guiding his people as sheep along true paths (cf. Ps. 23:3).[18]

These same elements are present in the law code of Hammurabi, the eighteenth-century BC Amorite king of Babylon. His famous law code is introduced by a lengthy, ideologically charged prologue. In it there is obvious interest in anchoring his own reputation in the rich Sumerian heritage of shepherd rulers.[19] He saw himself as one who would:

> cause justice to prevail in the land, to destroy the wicked and the evil, that the strong might not oppress the weak, to rise the sun over the black-headed and to light up the land. *Hammurabi, the shepherd, called by Enlil, am I*; the one who makes affluence and plenty abound ... (Pritchard 1969: 164)

Just rule, military protection, abundant provision: these are the shepherd ruler's traditional responsibilities.

Hammurabi's Code [20] continued the tradition of equating shepherdship with rule in general and justice in particular. He also continued the tradition of linking the epithet of shepherd with the historical announcement at the beginning of one's reign of a *mesharum*-act, that is, some specific, limited dispensation for the good of the people, such as exemption from tax or debt.[21]

Hammurabi's 282 laws were meant to illustrate his passion for justice. These laws were the basis for vindicating himself before the gods who had appointed him to rule. In his epilogue he presents himself to these gods as 'perfect', that is as 'one not careless or neglectful of the black-headed whom Enlil had presented to me, whose shepherding Marduk had committed to me'. He takes credit for providing peace and justice, and for promoting general welfare. Like a good shepherd he could say, 'I made the peoples rest in friendly habitations; I did not let them have anyone to terrorize them. I sought out peaceful regions for them ...' Furthermore,

---

[18] Lipit-Ishtar, another king from Isin, was similarly lauded as 'the wise shepherd, who leads the people, to let them relax in the sweet shade' (Westenholz 2004: 169).

[19] Hammurabi stood in a line of royal law codifiers who saw themselves as good shepherds (Ur-Nammu, Lipit-Ishtar).

[20] It is generally assumed that Hammurabi's 'Code' was more an apology for his own reign of justice than an actual set of laws by which judges made decisions.

[21] Evidence for a similar practice in Egypt is clear at the ascension of Ramses IV (Pritchard 1969: 378–379). See Lemche (1976) for possible connections with the sabbatical and jubilee institutions in Israel.

> The great gods called me, so I became the beneficent shepherd whose scepter is righteous . . . they prospered under my protection; I always governed them in peace; I sheltered them in my wisdom. In order that the strong might not oppress the weak, that justice might be dealt the orphan (and) the widow. (Pritchard 1969: 177–178)[22]

These kings of the Middle Assyrian period (late second millennium BC) continued the emphases of Mesopotamian royal traditions. However, along with the peaceful images of faithful shepherds and green pastures, a militant element increasingly surfaces. In a battle account Shalmaneser I (thirteenth century BC) calls himself 'astonishing great dragon, shepherd of all the settlements', the one whom Assur 'faithfully chose . . . gave me the scepter, weapon and staff to (rule) properly' (Grayson 1987: 182–183). His successor Tukulti-Ninurta presents himself in historical inscriptions as 'attentive shepherd', the one who 'shepherds the four quarters at the heels of the god Shamash, the shepherd who has charge over them, [and the herdsman] who properly administers them' (ibid. 233, 237). Once given 'the scepter for my office of shepherd' by Assur, the king announced that '[I] set my foot upon the neck of the lands (and) shepherded the extensive black-headed people like animals' (ibid. 234).

Tiglath-Pileser I (c. 1100 BC) exonerates himself before the gods as an 'attentive' and 'faithful' shepherd (Grayson 1991: 13). Of his victory he says, 'Their warriors I laid low in battle like sheep' and 'I butchered their troops like sheep' (ibid. 16, 19). Another Assyrian, Assur-nasir-pal I (eleventh century BC), similarly exults that he is:

> Without rival among the princes of the four quarters, the wonderful shepherd, who fears not opposition, the mighty flood who has no conqueror, the king who has brought into subjection those that were not submissive to him, the mighty hero who treads on the neck of his foe, who tramples all enemies under foot, who shatters the might of the haughty. (Luckenbill 1926: 139; cf. 173)[23]

The themes of first-millennium Neo-Assyrian kings (contemporaneous with the Israelite monarchies) continue those of their predecessors: divine calling, source of protection, provision/fertility

---

[22] In giving laws to Israel YHWH was demonstrating his royal wisdom (Deut. 4:5–8).

[23] He also calls himself 'The wonderful shepherd, who fears not the battle' and again mentions the motifs of mighty flood, bringing others to subjection, trampling their necks, etc. (Luckenbill 1926: 169).

and guidance. Shamshi-Adad V (ninth century BC) emphasized the cultic element in a victory stele inscription; he was the 'unrivalled king of the universe, shepherd of the shrines' (Grayson 1996: 182). Sargon II (eighth century BC) also represented himself in piety: 'shepherd of Assyria ... who carefully observes the law of Shamash ... who waits reverently upon the word of the great gods...' (Luckenbill 1926: 80).[24] King Adad-Nirari III (c. 800 BC) emphasized prosperity: '[The gods] made his shepherd's rule good as the plant of life to the people of Assur' (Engnell 1967: 29). Sennacherib (c. 700 BC) combines the various roles of the shepherd ruler: 'the great king, the mighty king, king of Assyria, king without a rival; prayerful shepherd (ruler), worshipper of the great gods; guardian of the right, lover of justice, who lends support, who comes to the aid of the needy, who turns (his thoughts) to pious deeds' (Luckenbill 1926: 48).

The military emphasis is clearer when Sennacherib (like Assurnasirpal) refers to his pastoral insignia as 'the just staff that extends the realm, the *merciless crook for the destruction of enemies*' (OIP 2 85:5).[25] Sennacherib was among the foreign 'shepherds' who plundered Judah, destroying everything but Jerusalem in 701 BC.

Particularly important background for the pre-exilic and exilic prophets is found in the literatures of the Neo-Babylonian kings who followed the Assyrians.[26] Nebuchadnezzar (625–561 BC) uses shepherd language to emphasize his faithfulness, wisdom and devotion to the cult: 'I Nebuchadnezzar, the righteous king, faithful shepherd who leads the peoples, director of the regions belonging to Bel, Samas, and Marduk, the contented, seeker after wisdom, regardful of life, exalted one who wearies not, caretaker of Esagila and Ezida, son of Nabopolassar king of Babylon am I' (Langdon 1905: 83).[27]

Another noteworthy inscription comes from a *kudduru* (boundary stone) regarding Babylonian King Merodach-baladan II: 'Let him be the shepherd who collects the dispersed (flock); and entrusts to him the just staff (and) the crook which maintains the welfare of the people' (VAS 1 37 I, 32–36). The staff and crook are familiar symbols

---

[24] Sargon II (eighth century BC) makes a claim about his own ascent to the throne on the back of criticism of the previous ruler, an unfit shepherd (Hallo 2000: 295).

[25] It is not surprising to find shepherd language so resilient among the Mesopotamian kings. The Assyrian rulers, like the Amorites, were intent on tracing their lineage back to the golden Sumerian age (Westenholz 2000).

[26] For examples in Neo-Babylonian building inscriptions, see Langdon (1905: 61, 71 [twice], 79, 83 [twice], 93, 101, 103, 111, 145, 147, 153 [twice], 155, 169).

[27] For another pertinent Neo-Babylonian example from King Neriglissar, see Goodenough (1929: 176).

66

of justice and well-being, as we have seen (cf. Ps. 23:4). The notion of gathering a scattered flock is somewhat unique, but will be a significant, recurring motif in biblical passages from this period (e.g. Jer. 23:1–4; Ezek. 34:5ff.; cf. John 11:52).

The official literature of ancient Mesopotamia reveals that the image of shepherd rulers was used widely and consistently with a number of essential elements. Gods[28] depicted as shepherds were typically caring providers whose wisdom ('light') and beneficence was necessary for life. Kings chose to equate the shepherd title with their own calling and their faithfulness to their charge given by the divine council. It is common to find shepherd titles/epithets used to represent the king as the source of justice (order in the community), prosperity and peace (subjugation of enemies), and as the pious supporter of the cult. The phrase 'sheep without a shepherd' was a useful description of people without a (good) king (Lambert 1960: 229).

Egyptian deities

Well directed are men, the cattle of the god. (King Kheti)[29]

The earliest evidence of Egyptian civilization suggests the remarkably sudden emergence of a highly developed society in the late fourth millennium BC. Written language, urban infrastructure, social stratification and a ruling dynasty with widespread control all seem to have emerged without precedent or evolution and then continued through centuries of relative stability. The earliest records also reveal a dynamic and diverse collection of gods who were represented with a variety of images. The first deity to be represented in human form was the predynastic Khnum, a man with a ram's head.[30] Among the gods depicted as shepherds are two of the most popular 'great' deities, Amun-Re (the creator and sun god) and Osiris (god of fertility/ resurrection and ruler of the dead).[31]

---

[28] Although the evidence is limited, gods in the Canaanite pantheon were represented occasionally as shepherds (J. Gray 1952; Korpel 1990: 448–449; Driver 1956: 67). For Hittite texts, see Pritchard (1969: 210, 398).

[29] This line comes from some self-flattering advice from King Kheti to Merikare (Beyerlin 1978: 46; cf. Williams 1964).

[30] Other gods were depicted with ram's horns, the most significant of which was Amun.

[31] Osiris was regularly shown with a shepherd's crook and flail. In some contexts he was called 'the sacred ram' (Hornung 1982: 90, 94). Osiris was unique in his accessibility to commoners throughout Egypt's history (Knapp 1988: 107).

The sun was revered for its life-giving and life-sustaining powers and was, consequently, worshipped as the shepherd of the cosmos. The sun god Amun-Re became the chief deity in Egypt by the New Kingdom and his ram cult was symbolized by the rows of ram statues which, to this day, line the causeway from Karnak to Luxor. In the Middle Kingdom (2040–1630 BC), Amun-Re is referred to implicitly as the herder of his people: 'the good god, the beloved, who gives life to all that is warm and to all good cattle (people)' (Pritchard 1969: 365). He brings beneficence to his own but judgment to his enemies: 'Good shepherd who appears in the white crown, Lord of the rays, who makes brilliance, to whom the gods offer hymns, who extends his arms to the one whom he loves, whereas his enemy is consumed by a flame: it is his eye which brings the enemy down' (Beyerlin 1978: 13).

Elsewhere in this creation hymn, Amun-Re is extolled as the creator, judge of the weak, hearer of the captive, life-giver, sustainer and guardian of all life. In words that resemble those in the biblical psalter, Amun-Re is praised for his ceaseless concern over his flock: '... who spends the night wakeful when all the world sleeps, and seeks what is useful for the flock ... Jubilation for you, because you weary yourself with us, honour to you because you created us' (ibid. 15; cf. Ps. 121).

The image of the sun god as a courageous shepherd who leads, feeds and protects his herd is present in New Kingdom (1551–1087 BC) hymns as well. One hymn describes the god as the 'valiant herdsman, driving his cattle, their refuge and the maker of their living' (Pritchard 1969: 368). Another says to him, 'You are mighty as a herdsman, tending them for all eternity ... You are good at all times. All the world lives from your countenance...' (Beyerlin 1978: 26). While this hymn emphasizes protection and provision throughout, the most endearing language is used at the close: 'Your ears are open to hear them, and you fulfil their wishes, You our Ptah, who loves his likeness, you shepherd, who loves his flock' (ibid. 27).

The image of a god concerned for the affairs of his people led to hymns (frequent in the Ramesside period) with explicit personal focus: 'Amun, shepherd, early in the morning you care for your flock and drive the hungry to pasture. The shepherd drives the cattle to the grass; Amun, you drive me, the hungry one, to food, for Amun is indeed a shepherd, a shepherd who is not idle' (Beyerlin 1978: 40). Thus the notion of a caring, personal divine shepherd was familiar in both Mesopotamia and Egypt [32] even before the Israelites experienced YHWH's comprehensive care in the deserts of Sinai.

Pharaoh as shepherd

He is the herdsman of all; there is no evil in his heart. His herds are few, but he spends the day herding them. (Ipuwer) [33]

As we move our focus to the pastoral imagery used of human kings in Egypt, we are immediately struck by the ambiguity of the identity of their kings: the pharaoh was portrayed as both human and – to some extent – divine. Alive, the king was incarnate Horus, 'the Great God, the Lord of Heaven' (Frankfort 1939: 37). In his death he was Osiris. In titulary he is regularly referred to as good, mighty or perfect god. This perspective matches the iconography [34] of pharaohs who were usually depicted as god-sized among men and of equal status with other deities.

As a god-man,[35] Pharaoh was mediator between the two realms. He was the chief priest of the divine realm, mediating divine blessing through his ritual performances. But he was more. Pharaoh was a terrestrial king, a political leader of both Upper and Lower Egypt. Rather than being subject to law (as in Mesopotamia), pharaohs saw themselves as the source of law. In his own person he was the embodiment of the self-contained state and the source of its cosmic law and order, known as *ma'at*.[36] The king was 'for ever and ever, setting order (*ma'at*) in place of disorder' (Baines 1995: 11). In the words of Knapp, 'The eternal rightness of ma'at bespoke an ordered stability that in turn confirmed and consolidated the continuing rule of pharaoh. Suffused with the benefits of ma'at, the divine office of pharaoh served as a basic unifying element for the Egyptian state' (Knapp 1988: 103).

The shepherd's crook became one of the symbols of comprehensive kingship; its hieroglyphic value was 'rule'. Royal coronation

---

[32] Shepherd titles for deities (and kings) were much more widespread in Mesopotamia than in Egypt.

[33] J. Wilson (1951: 159).

[34] Engraved symbols were an important means of imposing Egypt's official world view onto the perceptions of the public – and the gods (Hornung 1982).

[35] For nuanced discussion of Egyptian views of the king, see O'Connor & Silverman (1995).

[36] *Ma'at* was also an Egyptian goddess who personified the principles of order and truth.

ceremonies (*Sed* festivals) included the presentation to the king of the crook and flail, the characteristic emblems of Osiris. Other insignia of rulers included the mace and sceptre, which are also likely to be traced to pastoral prototypes.[37]

Before surveying explicit shepherd titles, it is revealing to consider provocative pastoral images in critiques of royal indifference to social injustice. The excerpts that follow are all the more remarkable when we consider the totalitarian governments they criticized.[38] Criticism came in a variety of forms and its preservation suggests that the prophetic voices in Egypt – like those we find in Scripture – were given some hearing.

The 'Admonitions of Ipuwer', probably from early in the Middle Kingdom period (2040–1640 BC), provide a description of an ideal ruler. This is actually a negative evaluation of the current Pharaoh's policies written by an unknown (to us) critic: 'See now, the land is deprived of kingship by a few people who ignore custom ... See all the ranks, they are not in their place, *like a herd that roams without a herdsman*. See, cattle stray with none to bring them back, everyone fetches for himself and brands with his name...' (Lichtheim 1973: 156, 158). Scattered herds reflect the absence of social order and economic prosperity. For Ipuwer this chaos was evidence of a sleeping shepherd.

Ipuwer's assumption was that the king was accountable for the condition of his 'herd'. J. Wilson (1951: 133) understands this new perspective to represent a major modification in the understanding of kingship during the Middle Kingdom: 'The concept of the good shepherd rather than the distant and lordly owner of the flocks shifted the idea of kingship from possession as a right to responsibility as a duty.'[39]

An interesting dimension to Ipuwer's critique is a 'messianic' prediction of a model future king. In a better world '... one would say: "He is the herdsman of all; there is no evil in his heart. His herds

---

[37] Cf. Mercer 1952 I: 67; IV: 58–60; Hayes 1953: 28, 192–194; 285.

[38] Other texts critical of kings are noted in Baines (1995: 19ff.) and analysed throughout Posener (1960).

[39] The theme of injustice is evident in other genres as well. The 'Dispute over Suicide' is a purported discussion between a man and his soul, perhaps written during the First Intermediate Period (2134–2040 BC) or soon after (ibid. 163–169). Suicide appeared the only reasonable alternative to the pressure of the chaos around him. The Middle Kingdom 'Tale of the Eloquent Peasant' (ibid. 169–184) is another narrative expression of critique. In it a poor man's right to impartial justice is illustrated. These are examples of royal propaganda in which kings characterized/promoted their rule as just and compassionate.

are few, but he spends the day herding them"' (ibid. 159). Ipuwer's words carry the same combination of criticism and idealized hope that is heard from later prophets in Israel.

The Middle Kingdom (2040–1640 BC) was a period during which kings were at pains to represent themselves as just kings. J. Wilson (1951: 133) concludes that these rulers 'responded by taking formal throne names which expressed their desire and obligation to render *ma'at* to men and gods. This was another formulation of the concept of the good shepherd.' Sesostris I declared that Re had 'made me the herdsman of this land, for he knew that I would maintain it in order for him' (Beyerlin 1978: 28).

The Second Intermediate Period brought the stability of the Middle Kingdom to an end. The New Kingdom (1551–1087 BC) began when the kings of the eighteenth dynasty established and reinforced their legitimacy, in part by appealing to the traditional image of the shepherd ruler. For example, Amenhotep III, amid claims of deity, presents himself as 'the good shepherd, vigilant for all people, whom the maker therof has placed under his authority, lord of plenty' (Breasted 1906–7: 2, 365–366). Seti I exalts himself as 'the good shepherd who keeps his army alive, a father and mother to everyone' (Kitchen 1993: 56). It was during the New Kingdom period that Israel's sojourn with their divine Shepherd in the wilderness took place.

Following the successful rout of the Libyan invasion, Merneptah [40] represents himself as shepherd protector and parent: 'I am the Ruler who shepherds you; I spend (all) day in searching out [. . . caring for] you (just) as a father sustains his children. Are you foolish like the birds, not knowing the goodness of what he does?' (Kitchen 2003: 4).

An encomium (literary tribute) to the twentieth-dynasty king Ramesses V (ruler during the Israelite Settlement period) represents the militant dimension of the image: 'Thou herdsman of To-meri (Egypt) . . . thou stripling son of Buto, good god, lord of power (?), great of strength over every land to slay Kharu (Syria), and to crush Kush (Ethiopia)' (Gardiner 1931: 41).

The evidence for shepherd names and imagery among Egyptian kings is not nearly as widespread as it is in the Mesopotamian contexts. However, the themes associated with it are similar. At least by the mid-second millennium BC kings represented themselves as accountable to the gods for their rule. They were expected to provide

---

[40] This is the first Pharaoh to mention the people 'Israel' in Palestine.

for and protect their people, as a good shepherd would. Herding imagery was especially useful for criticizing royalty when there was evidence of neglect.

Greek gods and kings

... he must also be a lover of men, for it would be strange for a shepherd to be a hater of sheep and ill disposed toward his own flock. (Archytas)[41]

While Mesopotamian and Egyptian precedents have the most direct bearing on Old Testament texts, similar shepherd traditions from Classical Greece emerged, evolved and joined those influences that exercised themselves upon the New Testament writers. A brief overview will suffice.

As in earlier civilizations, Greek writers saw themselves in a universe overseen by shepherd deities. The image of Hermes *kriophoros* is the most well known example of a kid/ram-carrying shepherd god. Along with Hermes, other shepherd gods include Apollo, Pan and Dionysus.[42]

In this period the notion of a shepherd ruler was much more developed with respect to human leaders, especially military commanders. Homer's *Iliad* and *Odyssey* (c. 800 BC) repeatedly refer to individual heroes of the past with the phrase *poimēn laon*, 'shepherd of the people'.[43] Agamemnon, holder of the ancestral sceptre (*Iliad* 2.243, 254), is one of the most celebrated military shepherds (*Iliad* 10.3; 11.187; 19.25). Atreus, Achilles, Machaeon, Mentor and Nestor were also pastoral commanders.[44] Non-Greek military leaders were considered shepherds as well.[45]

Xenophon (*Memorabilia* 2.1–4; c. 400 BC) relays the explanation that Socrates gave when asked why Homer called Agamemnon 'shepherd of the people'. He said:

[41] Cited in Goodenough (1928: 61).
[42] See (respectively) the 'Hymn to Hermes' 496–498; the 'Hymn to Apollo' 47; *Anthologia Graeca* 6:96; and *Anthologia Graeca* 9:524.
[43] Like the noun, the verb *poimainō* had a range of metaphorical connotations including rule, protection and nurture (BAGD 6021).
[44] See, respectively, *Iliad* 2.105; *Iliad* 16.2; *Iliad* 11.506, 597, 650; *Odyssey* 24.456; *Iliad* 2.78–83; 10.73; 23.411; *Odyssey* 3.469; 14.109. Homer's tradition was carried on by Hesiod, who refers to Jason (*Theogony* 1000) and Amphitryon (*Shield of Heracles* 39–41) as (military) shepherds.
[45] The Trojan leader Hector is so designated in the *Iliad* (10.406; 22.277).

Isn't it because a shepherd must see to it that his sheep are safe and have food, and that the object for which they are raised is obtained; while a general too must see to it that his soldiers are safe and have supplies, and that the goal for which they are in the army will be attained? . . . A king is chosen not to take good care of himself, but so that the men who chose him may prosper. It is not easy to find anything finer than this goal or anything more disgraceful than its opposite.

Xenophon concludes, 'Socrates reduced leadership to the ability to bring prosperity to one's followers.'

The metaphor is apparent in other genres. All three major tragic poets of the Classical period engage the image of shepherd rulers. Aeschylus frequently pictures Greek commanders and rulers in pastoral terms.[46] He also depicts Persian king Xerxes as a shepherd (*Persians* 73–79).[47] Sophocles (*Ajax* 360) and Euripides[48] show fondness for the image as well.

Plato (c. 400 BC) gave one of the most thoughtful presentations on leadership in the Classical world. In his *Republic* (1.342–346) he summarized the ideal view of rule in a dialogue between Thrasymachus and Socrates. Thrasymachus assumed 'sheep' were meant to be exploited by their 'shepherds'. Socrates argued that the essence of a shepherd's art is selfless concern for his flock; otherwise he is no shepherd at all. Worse, careless shepherds are like the wolves from which they are expected to protect their sheep (3.415–416; cf. 4.440). This is precisely the argument Ezekiel makes in his indictment on the false shepherd leaders of Israel (ch. 34).

Plato believed that in mythic/primeval time the gods ruled directly over flocks of humans as shepherds. Human rule was meant to be an extension of that beneficent rule in the age of human history. Originally the gods shepherded the people without political constitutions (*Statesman* 271), motivated simply by their love.

Archytas described this ideal ruler as a benevolent shepherd. He must:

> . . . not only be understanding and powerful in ruling well, but he must also be a lover of men, for it would be strange for a shepherd

---

[46] Cf. *Suppliants* 348, 642, 767; *Agamemnon* 657, 669, 795; *Eumenides* 78–79, 197, 249.

[47] Like Isaiah, Xenophon speaks of Cyrus as a shepherd (*Cyropaedia* 8, 2.14). There he is emphasizing his generosity and benevolence.

[48] *Alcestis* 579; *Hippolytus* 153; *Phoenissae* 1140; *Suppliants* 674.

to be a hater of sheep and ill disposed toward his own flock. And he must be lawful as well, for so he will have understanding of rulership. For by his knowledge he will be able to judge correctly; by his power to punish; by his excellence, to benefit; and by the laws, to do all these with reference to reason ... he would do nothing in his own interest, but only for the sake of his subjects, just as law exists not for its own sake but only for those subject to it. (Goodenough 1928: 61)

Whereas the Near Eastern sources treat law codes as embodying the divine will, these Greek philosophers posit a view of leadership that is above law. If motivated properly by love and led by understanding, a good shepherd follows his inclinations for the good of all.

Goodenough (ibid.) states that the Pythagorean view was the official political ideology of the Hellenistic era, the cultural backdrop of the New Testament writings. Ecphantus summarized this perspective in *Stobaeus*,[49] emphasizing the intimacy implied:

He who rules in accordance with virtue is called, and is, the king, for he has the same love and communion with his subjects as God has with the universe. And there must exist complete good will, first on the part of the king toward his subjects, and second on their part toward the king, such as is felt by a father toward his son, a shepherd toward his sheep, and a law toward those who use it.

Greek literature has, thus, provided in its shepherd metaphors the most militant and the most tender images of leadership. As we draw closer to the period of the New Testament the latter was apparently the more dominant view at large.[50]

At this point we must draw to a close our survey of extrabiblical materials. To be sure, there are more connections to be made. These will be noted alongside texts which they illuminate, as appropriate.

---

[49] Cited in Goodenough (1928).
[50] Virgil, also from this period, wrote *bucolic* poetry which idealized the life and work of shepherds.

II
Biblical prototypes

Our survey of extrabiblical texts has provided an introduction to the conventional associations of shepherd imagery for ruling deities and humans. Not surprisingly, biblical authors make use of these familiar traditional meanings. However, the persistence of the metaphor in a broad variety of biblical texts from different periods suggests that the image of a shepherd ruler had special significance. This persistence is due, in part, to Israel's foundational story, which took place in a real wilderness. God's chosen leader Moses was trained for his role as a shepherd of flocks in the deserts of Sinai. In that same setting Israel's journey to nationhood began. The ideal of a shepherd ruler is further reinforced when Israel's ideal king, David, is similarly called from tending flocks to become the shepherd of God's people. These two figures are leadership prototypes, serving as models for leaders who follow them. But they are themselves extensions of the divine Shepherd who leads the covenant community by their hands.

Chapter Four

YHWH, Moses and the 'flock' of God in the wilderness

Our journey through the Bible begins with the earliest traditions regarding Israel's origins in the wilderness, traditions [1] that occasionally employ pastoral imagery for YHWH and his chosen leaders. It is important to investigate this context of shepherd language because the 'associated commonplaces' of a metaphor are often engaged *implicitly*. Pastoral imagery encompasses shepherds and their flocks as well as the realities of the wilderness, the challenging environment equated with them. Were we to restrict our attention to Pentateuchal texts that use the term 'shepherd' metaphorically, we would be limited to few references (Gen. 48:15; 49:24; Num. 27:17). But with the help of inspired poets and prophets of a later period, we recognize the latent shepherd imagery present throughout the wilderness narratives. In so doing, we will begin to understand the paradigmatic value of the desert period for later readers, and leaders. [2]

The literary setting of the wilderness stories

While it is important to read the wilderness stories in terms of their geographical and cultural setting, we must also pay close attention to their literary contexts. A 'canonical' reading appreciates the narrative movement that frames the entire Torah. Its teleologically driven plot centres on the promises made to Abraham in Genesis 12:1–3 for a name, a nation, a land and a blessing for the world (Kaiser 1978). The Pentateuch presents a story of this promise and its persistent efficacy in the lives of Abraham's descendants.

---

[1] 'Traditions' involve written materials (of various genres) comprised of historically grounded complexes of concepts, themes and motifs. Though discerning traditions involves a measure of subjectivity, our interest will be in the highly visible complexes that are indisputably present in the Pentateuch.

[2] While biblical theology has a preference for diachronic development, there is a place for reading former texts in light of later ones.

In this 'exemplar history' (Tunyogi 1962: 388) foundational events and persons appear and become paradigmatic in the rest of Scripture. Moses is the archetypal prophet whose leadership becomes a pattern that influences the representations of later figures in canonical history. The exodus is the prototypical expression of liberation, the basis for other liberations from other slaveries (such as sin in the NT). The wilderness is a category of liminal time and place in which God could be present in extraordinary ways (Cohn 1981).

In many ways the book of Genesis provides keys to understanding the narratives of Exodus, Numbers and Deuteronomy.[3] This first book is truly a prologue to the whole Pentateuch. The theme of creation from Genesis 1 echoes in the new creation of God's people (Nohrnberg 1995: 227–249).[4] Like Moses who follows,[5] Abraham and his sons were tent-dwelling shepherds, sojourners in the land of others, in possession (only) of the promise of a homeland. Moses recalls the promise to the patriarchs in Deuteronomy 9:5 as the only reason for God's faithfulness to Israel.

Most important for our study is the theme[6] of divine presence and guidance in the patriarchal narratives (e.g. Gen. 28:10–22; cf. Terrien 1978: 63–105; Mann 1977: 106–113). This theme, especially in the context of the wilderness, is central to the books of Exodus (Greenberg 1969: 16–17; Durham 1987: xxi–xxiii) and Numbers.[7] A chiasm in Exodus–Numbers (and in the Pentateuch as a whole)[8] emerges when we recognize the Sinai covenant at its centre with the wilderness episodes on either side of it (M. S. Smith 1997: 298–299). Deuteronomy provides Moses' perspective on this foundational

---

[3] See Sailhamer (1992). M. Noth (1972) had anticipated the thematic study of the Pentateuch twenty years earlier, noting the importance of the guidance/wilderness theme in particular.

[4] See, for example, the importance of water in the two accounts (and in the flood). More subtle is the placement of the graphic term *tōhû* (wasteland) in the bookend sections of the Pentateuch, Gen. 1:2 and Deut. 32:10. This word is featured later in Isaiah, where the wilderness has pronounced metaphorical significance as a place of new beginnings/new exodus. Isaiah uses the technical term *br'* for the creation of the world (40:26; 42:5 et al.) and Israel (43:1).

[5] For more Abraham-Moses parallels, see Rendtorff (1997).

[6] I understand 'theme' (with Clines 1978) to be a dominating idea that represents the orientation of the author and gives shape to the content, structure and development of a work.

[7] The Hebrew name for Numbers means 'in the wilderness'.

[8] This structural device provides a better explanation of the 'duplicate' accounts of Exodus and Numbers (e.g. Exod. 16 and Num. 11; Exod. 17:1–17 and Num. 20:1–13) than the source-critical reconstructions typically proposed.

period in Israel's life and lays out a covenantal hermeneutic for interpreting the history that follows.[9]

The leadership of YHWH in the wilderness

> In a desert land he found him,
> in a barren and howling waste.
> He shielded him and cared for him . . .
> The LORD alone led him . . .
> (Deut. 32:10–12)

The presence of God

With this thematic sketch of the Pentateuch in mind, we may now look in more detail at the characterization of YHWH as the leader of Israel in the wilderness traditions. Divine presence is certainly an appropriate place to begin; YHWH's presence,[10] physically manifest in the glory-cloud (*kābôd*) and pillar of fire, was the means by which Israel was *led* (*nḥh*). In Exodus 33 Moses makes a revealing statement to God in a moment when the destiny of the rebellious generation hangs in the balance. In his anger YHWH warns that his continued presence would be lethal for Israel. Moses protests, 'If your Presence does not go with us, do not send us up from here. How will anyone know that you are pleased with me and with your people unless you go with us? What else will distinguish me and your people from all the other people on the face of the earth?' (Exod. 33:15–16)

Israel's identity was inextricably tied to the presence of God, first demonstrated to the patriarchs and then to his chosen people in the wilderness sojourn.[11] The tabernacle was known as the *miškān*, the place of God's 'dwelling'.[12] The ark of the covenant became the visible centre of the community at rest and moved at the head of the tribal

---

[9] It has been common since the work of M. Noth (1981) to call the historical books (or Former Prophets: Joshua–Kings) the 'Deuteronomic' or 'Deuteronomistic' history ('Dtr'). These designations are typically coupled with Noth's assumption that Deuteronomy was composed during the time of Josiah. We are assuming the Mosaic authorship of Deuteronomy, in which case the book's role in shaping the later literature is, to an important extent, a function of its prophetic capacity.

[10] Plastaras (1966: 94–100) makes a plausible case that the name YHWH meant 'The God Who is Present (in Power)' (cf. Coats 1993: 14–17).

[11] Exodus 33 mentions the various manifestations of the God-with-us theme: his face, glory, angel and name (Kelley 1970; Kaiser 1978: 120–121).

[12] See the discussion of Sarna (1991: 158) on the distinctly nomadic connotation of the root *škn* (to dwell).

league when they marched. These spatial locations indicate the theological importance of God's presence among his people.

Protection

> For the LORD your God moves about in your camp to protect you and to deliver your enemies to you. (Deut. 23:14)

The presence of God with Israel had three significant implications that are revealed in the wilderness narratives. The first is the dramatic protection and deliverance provided by YHWH, most obviously in the exodus event itself. Stirred with compassion, YHWH plans to rescue them from oppression (Exod. 3:7–8), to free his 'firstborn son' from slavery (Exod. 4:22–23). As God had protected the ancestral fathers with plagues on their enemies (Gen. 12:17), so he delivers Israel from Egypt by plagues. When the Egyptian army tried to recapture their former slaves, God's fiery cloud moved to the rear of the congregation to create a barrier (Exod. 14:19–20). From that cloud the Divine Warrior threw the Egyptian army into confusion (v. 24).[13] YHWH effectively lured Pharaoh into a trap, sovereignly choosing the time and place to destroy him (Durham 1987: 193). The power of God is emphasized with reference to his 'strong arm' by which Israel was delivered (Exod. 3:19; 6:1; 13:9; 32:11; Deut. 5:15; 6:21; 7:8 et al.).

Other episodes of divine protection from human enemies punctuate the wilderness period. As a ritual Moses was to say whenever the ark set out, 'Rise up, O LORD! May your enemies be scattered; may your foes flee before you' (Num. 10:35). Deliverance from the hands of Amalek is attributed to YHWH's fighting on their behalf (Exod. 17:14, 16), and deliverance *into* the hands of the Amalekites is attributed to YHWH's absence (Num. 14:43). One of the great turning points in the wilderness journey comes when the people fail to believe that God can deliver the Canaanites into their hands. On the basis of God's powerful presence, two of the spies believed that they could take the land:

> The land we passed through and explored is exceedingly good. If the LORD is pleased with us, *he will lead us into that land*, a land

---

[13] Royal and military metaphors are more obvious in these accounts than shepherding ones. However, later inspired recollections of this period resort to a pastoral understanding as well.

flowing with milk and honey, and will give it to us. Only do not rebel against the LORD. And do not be afraid of the people of the land, because we will swallow them up. *Their protection is gone, but the LORD is with us.* Do not be afraid of them. (Num. 14:7–9)

Conflicts become more regular as the Israelites move into Transjordan. In these early conquest accounts the mighty power of God is evident in delivering them from their enemies (Num. 21). Success is explained simply as YHWH 'handing them over' to Israel (Num. 21:34). Balaam is unable to curse Israel because he sees that they are protected by the powerful reality that *'the LORD their God is with them'* (Num. 23:21).

Provision

> Can God spread a table in the desert?
>
> (Ps. 78:19)

> They asked, and he brought them quail
> and satisfied them with the bread of heaven.
> He opened the rock, and water gushed out;
> like a river it flowed in the desert.
>
> (Ps. 105:40–41)

God's presence is consistently equated with divine provision. Of the four wilderness episodes leading up to the Sinai revelation in Exodus, one reveals God as able protector (vs. Amalek) and three reveal him as gracious provider (of water, bread and meat). In Exodus 15, following directly on the heels of the Egyptians' defeat, the Israelites find themselves in Marah ('bitter') without drinkable water. In response to their grumbling, the Lord shows Moses a piece of wood that 'sweetens' the water (Exod. 15:25). Instead of the diseases that befell the Egyptians, they could experience his 'healing' (v. 26).[14]

Healing is one form of divine beneficence that will resurface in the story of the bronze serpent (Num. 21:8–9; cf. 12:13). Although a minor theme in the Pentateuch, it is nevertheless an important manifestation of God's life-giving power (Burden 1994: 48; Coats 1993: 135–150). In Deuteronomy 32:39 (cf. Ps. 107:20) the parallel between life and health is explicit:

---

[14] Literally, 'I am YHWH, your healer' (cf. Num. 21:4–9; Burden 1994: 47–49).

See now that I myself am He!
There is no god besides me.
I put to death and I bring to *life*,
I have wounded and I will *heal*,
and no-one can deliver out of my hand.

An essential element of the portrait of God in the wilderness is that the one with the power of death has the power and the will also to grant life and health.

Another feature of the story of Marah is important in the light of later biblical motifs. Following the miracle of the water sweetening, they came to Elim 'where there were twelve springs and seventy palm trees, and they camped there near the water' (Exod. 15:27). The ample provision of water underscores the bounty YHWH was able and willing to provide. Springs represent perpetual supplies of water. The presence of one for every tribe suggests that they were each well taken care of.[15]

A second water story at Rephidim follows in Exodus 17. At the point of death, the people grumble again. In response to Moses' intercession, the Lord instructs him to use the rod 'with which you struck the Nile' (v. 5) as an instrument not of curse, but now of blessing (Fretheim 1991: 175–176). As instructed, he strikes a rock and water is provided for the community once again. Here again it is clear that the powerful presence of God reflects a preference for good, though it is fully capable of destruction. The shepherd's rod brings both judgment and blessing, both death and life.

The two water stories in Exodus frame the first account of manna and quail in the Torah. Again, the miracle follows the grumbling of the people. They compare the barren wilderness with the bounty they enjoyed ('all ... we wanted') in Egypt (Exod. 16:3). The people doubted YHWH as their feeder, the primary role of the shepherd. The Lord's response was to 'rain down bread from heaven' on them (v. 4). With it the people would be 'filled with bread' (v. 12), but only one day at a time. A jar of manna would be kept in perpetuity as a reminder of this faithful provision (Exod. 16:33). The notion of heavenly bread that satisfies (*śb'*) is present in later reflections on the wilderness period (Neh. 9:15; Ps. 105:40; cf. Ps. 78:25). 'Bread from heaven' is precisely the way Jesus will represent himself in John 6:32.

---

[15] Seventy is the number of Jacob's family that went down to Egypt (Deut. 10:22) and the number of elders serving the wilderness community (Exod. 24:1; Num. 11:16; cf. Luke 10:1 in some manuscripts).

Spiritual sustenance is the ultimate reality to which the feeding miracles refer: 'He humbled you, causing you to hunger and then feeding you with manna, which neither you nor your fathers had known, to teach you that man does not live on bread alone but on *every word that comes from the mouth of the LORD*' (Deut. 8:3; cf. Deut. 32:2; Ezek. 20:11, 13; Wis. 16:26). The most significant 'food' in the wilderness was the Law itself. When Jesus relives Israel's forty-year wilderness experience in his forty-day temptation, he draws support in his hunger from these very words that come from the mouth of God (Matt. 4:4; Luke 4:4).

In the wilderness account the bread is linked to a test regarding a pre-Sinai Sabbath ordinance. They would receive exactly enough bread for each person, each morning. Any extra collected would spoil. On the sixth day there would be a special dispensation: people could gather enough for two days. The extra bread would remain unspoiled through the seventh day when the provision would be absent. As God provided for them every day, he would provide for them more exceptionally on the day of rest. Sabbath observance would become a continual education (and expression of faith) in the more-than-adequate provisions of God. It would also be a day on which they would provide rest for those in their care (Deut. 5:14).

Rest (*nwḥ*) is an important provision in the wilderness narratives (cf. Isa. 63:14). In a moment when God considered destroying the community and rebuilding it with Moses alone, he promises, 'My Presence will go with you, and I will give you rest' (Exod. 33:14; cf. Matt. 11:28). In Numbers 10:33 the ark went before the congregation to 'find them a place to rest [*měnûḥâ*]'.[16] In Deuteronomy 12:9 *měnûḥâ* is equated with the Promised Land itself.

The miracle of bread was accompanied by a miraculous supply of meat. While the manna came with the morning dew, the evening brought quail (Exod. 16:14; cf. Ps. 105:40). In the Numbers account of quail the comparison with the cuisine of Egypt is remembered in exaggerated terms (Num. 11:4). As is more typical in Numbers (compared with Exodus), a stronger view of the people's rebelliousness is emphasized in order to explain the final divine rejection of that generation from the Promised Land. God gives the people meat, but now not just enough to 'satisfy'. He vows to give it to them for a month, 'until it comes out of your nostrils and you loathe it – because you have rejected the LORD, who is among you . . .' (Num 11:20;

---

[16] *Měnûḥâ* comes from the root *nwḥ*. Compare the use of *nwḥ* in Deut. 12:10; 25:19 and in references to the land after the conquest (Josh. 1:13, 15 et al.).

cf. Ps. 78:23–31). Israel had come to doubt the efficacy of God's satisfying presence among them.

The unbelief of the community and their constant murmuring left Moses too burdened to carry the people alone (Num. 11:14). Woven into the story of divine provision of meat is the account of God sharing his Spirit with seventy elders. Moses thus experiences personally the breadth of God's generous presence. Where the Spirit of the Lord is, there is not only the means for physical sustenance and rest, but also relief from the burden of leadership.

A final, significant expression of the provision of God in the wilderness is the Promised Land itself. While the land is, in one sense, outside the Torah, it is the focus of much of its attention and the goal of the narrative. This land, promised to the patriarchs as sure, described by the spies as good, but missed by the rebellious generation, is a pastoralist's dream, 'flowing with milk and honey' (Exod. 3:8, 17 et al.). The Shepherd of Israel was leading his people home to a land that would be fully satisfying: 'a good land – a land with streams and pools of water, with springs flowing in the valleys and hills ... When you have eaten and are satisfied [*śbʿ*], praise the LORD your God for the good land he has given you' (Deut. 8:7–10; cf. 11:15).

Guidance

> In your unfailing love you will lead
> the people you have redeemed.
> In your strength you will guide them
> to your holy dwelling ['pasture'; *nāweh*].
> (Exod. 15:13)

God's guidance in the wilderness begins with his redemption of the people from Egypt and continues throughout their journey to the pastures of the Promised Land. A number of important verbs are used to express the Pentateuchal theme of God's pastoral leading.[17]

The term that implies gentle leading is used in Exodus 15:13, cited above: 'In your strength you will *guide* [*nhl*] them to your holy dwelling.' This verbal root was used in Genesis 33:14 for Jacob's slower pace for his flocks. It is used poetically in Psalm 23:2 for being

---

[17] The most common qualification of the divine name in the Pentateuch is 'the LORD your God, *who brought you out of Egypt*' (e.g. Exod. 20:2). This construction typically uses the Hiphil of the root *yṣʾ*. Compare the Hiphil forms of *ʿlh* (e.g. Lev. 11:45; Isa. 63:11) and *hlk* (Ps. 136:16; Isa. 63:13), which are used together in Amos 2:10.

led by quiet waters, and in Isaiah 40:11 for YHWH *gently leading* the 'nursing ewes' of his 'flock'. Gentleness is also expressed in images of God carrying Israel in his arms (Deut. 1:31; Hos. 11:3; cf. Deut. 32:11; Exod. 19:4). With a different word similar sentiments are expressed in Hosea 11:4:

> I led [*mšk*] them with cords of human kindness,
> with ties of love;
> I lifted the yoke from their neck
> and bent down to feed them.

Nhg – used of Moses driving/herding his flocks in Exodus 3:1 – typically means leading a group of animals (or people) to a specific destination, even against their will (Deut. 4:7).[18] This is the term used (in parallel with *nś'*) in Psalm 78:52: 'But he brought his people out like a flock; he *led* them like sheep through the desert' (cf. Isa. 63:14). Similarly, the exilic psalmist cries out to the God who continues to lead his people: 'Hear us, O Shepherd of Israel, you who *lead* Joseph like a flock . . .' (Ps. 80:1).

A third root, *nḥh*, emphasizes guidance. Personal guidance was the obvious implication of the desert pillars: 'By day the LORD went ahead of them in a pillar of cloud to *guide* them on their way and by night in a pillar of fire to give them light, so that they could travel by day or night' (Exod. 13:21;[19] cf. Pss. 78:14; 105:39; Neh. 9:12, 19).[20] Psalm 77:19–20 (H 20–21) describes God's leadership of the people through his chosen servants after emphasizing the divinely chosen course:[21]

> Your path led through the sea,
>   your way through the mighty waters,
>   though your footprints were not seen.
> You *led* your people like a flock
>   by the hand of Moses and Aaron.

---

[18] This verb is sometimes used in military contexts, i.e. for military leaders taking their armies to war (1 Chr. 20:1). A martial setting is present throughout the wilderness traditions of the Pentateuch (G. I. Davies 1974; Lee 2003).

[19] This verb is used twice in Exod. 13:17–22, a passage Coats (1972) calls the 'exposition for the wilderness theme'. He sees God's leadership as the unifying motif for this theme (p. 292).

[20] In rebellion the people requested another god that would 'go before' them (Exod. 32:23). Below we discuss Jesus' pastoral promise to 'go before' his disciples.

[21] Coats (1972: 290) notes that the noun *derek* functions like the verbal root *nḥh* in pointing to God's guidance (cf. Exod. 13:21; Deut. 1:19, 31; 8:2; Isa. 43:16, 19; 49:11; 51:10; and in the passages in Psalms and Nehemiah noted above).

Nḥh often reflects the capacity by which a capable, visionary leader guides a group towards its destiny:

He *guided* them safely, so they were unafraid;
but the sea engulfed their enemies.[22]
Thus he brought them to the border of his holy land,
to the hill country his right hand had taken.
(Ps. 78:53–54)

The last section of Numbers and the whole of Deuteronomy show Israel poised to enter the land of promise. In the end, Moses could confess, 'The LORD alone *led* him' (Deut. 32:12).

The geographical itineraries in Numbers underscore the intentionality of God's guidance in the wilderness (Childs 1974: 284).[23] The itinerary summary in Numbers 33 reinforces the narrative's message that purposeful progress on the path was only interrupted by the choices of a sinful generation. The important episode with the spies in Numbers 13 – 14 demonstrates not only the tendency to resist the plan of God but also the necessity of moving in accordance with his timing (14:40–45).

But God's guidance of his people extends beyond geographical direction. The leadership of YHWH was expressed through his regular consultations with Moses, especially at the 'Tent of Meeting'. Most importantly, the foundational form of guidance in the Pentateuch is the Torah given on Mount Sinai. This law was to become the basis for God's perpetual guidance, celebrated so often in the Psalms (e.g. Ps. 119:105). In Psalm 23:3 the divine Shepherd *guides* (*nḥh*) his flock on '*paths of righteousness*'.

Ancient shepherd rulers presented themselves as sources of revelation and wisdom. In characterizing himself as a good shepherd, Hammurabi listed laws that would build a stable and equitable society (cf. Deut. 4:6–8). While YHWH shares many of the attributes of Near Eastern shepherd rulers, the strong emphasis on guidance *in the wilderness* is unique (Mann 1977: 236). Guidance in battle and guidance by law were common. But the image of God leading his 'flock' purposefully in a historic journey across a desert towards a

---

[22] Leading *safely* is emphasized similarly in Deut. 8:15: 'He led [*hlk*] you through the vast and dreadful desert, that thirsty and waterless land, with its venomous snakes and scorpions.'

[23] Notice the emphasis on Israel's journey by staged movement (*massaʻ*) in Exod. 17:1 (cf. Exod. 40:36, 38).

permanent pastureland is a novel use of the shepherd metaphor. The passages we have reviewed reveal a God with a travel 'itinerary', the Shepherd who leads Israel on prescribed paths towards a promised destination. But even that destination is not permanent, as we will see. Spiritual leaders in the New Testament are later called to shepherd God's flock in a world that is not their ultimate home.

The leadership of Moses

> You led your people like a flock
> by the hand of Moses and Aaron.
> (Ps. 77:20 [H 21])

A prophet for YHWH

> The LORD used a prophet to bring Israel up from Egypt,
> by a prophet he cared for him.
> (Hos. 12:13 [H 14])

The ways in which YHWH is represented as the Shepherd of Israel correspond to the ways in which Moses is represented as his undershepherd. Moses is the *extension* of God's rule in their lives, the *means* of their provision, the *agent* of their deliverance. This prophet is so central in the Torah that these five books are sometimes considered his biography (Coats 1988; Knierim 1985; Carr 2001). Yet the Torah is, ultimately, a revelation of YHWH. This paradox is at the heart of human leadership, biblically understood.

The personal journey of Moses is one that begins with a misplaced sense of his independent capacity as a leader of his 'own' people (Exod. 2:11). He reacts with indignation over the oppression of a Hebrew slave and then tries to arbitrate between two Hebrews who were fighting. Their response is suggestive for the subsequent narrative: 'Who made you ruler [*śar*] and judge [*šōpēṭ*] over us?' (v. 14). Moses *would* one day be the judge of this people (Exod. 18), but only after he made his own forty-year sojourn in the wilderness that would later become their temporary home. God would call him to be the instrument for delivering '*my* people' (Exod. 3:7, 10). At that point Moses would be more than hesitant to presume such a role (Exod. 3:11).

Moses became an extension of the 'hand of God' leading his people (Ps. 77:20 [H 21]; cf. Exod. 9:3; 13:14). To equip this undershepherd for his mission God endows the staff in his hands with supernatural power. This *maṭṭeh* becomes an important instrument in the upcoming confrontations with Pharaoh and in the wilderness sojourn that follows (cf. Deut. 34:10–12; Hoffmeier 1997: 154–155).[24] It has the power to work the wonders of God, wonders of deliverance and provision. The staff is also a link between Moses' life as a shepherd in Midian and his role as leader of God's 'flock'.

Central to Moses' many roles was the word of God. As a prophet he was YHWH's unique spokesman to the community (Exod. 33:11; cf. Deut. 18:18), an extension of God's guiding, nurturing presence for Israel. Moses was the means by which God led and fed his people in the wilderness.[25] Notice the link between the prophet's role and nurture in Hosea 12:13 [H 14]: 'by a prophet [YHWH] cared for [Israel]'. The verb *šmr* ('cared for') can refer to shepherding (Gen. 30:31; 1 Sam. 17:20) and is used six times in Psalm 121 for God's care in a wilderness setting.

A priest for Israel

> But now, please forgive their sin – but if not, then blot me out of the book you have written. (Exod. 32:32)

Another important dimension of Moses' leadership is his role as mediator/intercessor, often understood in priestly terms (Childs 1974: 356–357; 505–510). The pilgrimage of Moses as a leader moves from an impulsive attempt to mediate for 'his' people, to a state of disbelief that he could ever help them, to a sequence of intercessory experiences through which he becomes more fully identified with them. This journey, it becomes clear, is integral to God's plan for him as their shepherd leader.

Moses' identification with his people is anticipated by the elements of his life that are later mapped onto the experience of the community: his successful escape from Egypt, his forty years of sojourn with his flocks in the wilderness (cf. Exod. 2:22; 18:3), and his encounter with YHWH on Sinai. But existential identification with the people required a fuller mixing of their stories.

Intercession for Moses is first necessitated by the early rejection he experiences from the people he is called to serve (Exod. 5:22–23).

---

[24] The staff of Moses (or staff of God; Exod. 4:20; 17:9) is mentioned almost twenty times in the confrontations with Pharaoh in Exodus. It is also the source of power in the stories of Meribah in Exod. 17:1–7 and Num. 20:1–13.

[25] This is just what Jesus will call his disciples to do in the Gospels.

Time and again Moses, confronted by the people's need, cries out to the Lord on their behalf (e.g. Exod. 15:25; 17:4, 16). Intercession turns to strategic pleading and, eventually, passionate identification as time goes on. Aware of the idolatrous revelry at the foot of Mount Sinai, God expresses his anger to Moses: 'Now leave me alone so that my anger may burn against them and that I may destroy them. Then I will make you into a great nation' (Exod. 32:10; cf. Deut. 9:14; Moberly 1983: 44–109). Moses reacts by questioning how God could have brought his people out of Egypt only to let them die (v. 11). What, he wonders, would that make of YHWH's reputation in Egypt (v. 12; Deut. 9:28; Ezek. 20:9, 14)?[26] Moses' final appeal is to the promises made to the patriarchs (v. 13; cf. Deut. 9:27). In response, YHWH relents.

Although Moses shares the anger of God towards his people in the scene that follows, something has changed. At the very moment in their journey when Moses might have seized his role as God's messenger of judgment to the people, he is captivated by a sense of identity that makes him simultaneously *their* representative before YHWH: 'The next day Moses said to the people, "You have committed a great sin. But now I will go up to the LORD; *perhaps I can make atonement for your sin"'* (Exod. 32:30; cf. Deut. 9:18–21). Moses 'stood in the breach' and saved Israel from God's wrath (Ps. 106:23).

YHWH had thus succeeded in merging the concerns of his own heart (Exod. 3:7, 9, 16; Num. 11:12) with those of his servant. The plight of the people, for better or worse, was now inextricably tied to Moses' own destiny. His prayer for their salvation is remarkable: 'So Moses went back to the LORD and said, "Oh, what a great sin these people have committed! They have made themselves gods of gold. But now, please forgive their sin – but if not, *then blot me out of the book* you have written"' (Exod. 32:31–32; cf. Deut. 9:19–20; Rom. 9:3).

YHWH denies Moses' specific request and recalls him to the task of leadership: 'The LORD replied to Moses, "Whoever has sinned against me I will blot out of my book. Now go, lead [*nḥh*] the people to the place I spoke of, and my angel will go before you"' (vv. 33–34). Having authoritative words to preach to God's people, power to provide for them and a heart to intercede for them, the shepherd of

---

[26] For God to desert his people would mean that he had stopped leading them (Coats 1972: 294). The image of deserted (scattered) sheep is used in critiques of bad shepherd rulers in Jeremiah and Ezekiel.

Israel now needed the will to guide them to their divinely ordained destination.

Moses' previous prayers for 'this people' (Exod. 17:4; 32:31; 33:12) have now become prayer for 'us': 'O Lord, if I have found favour in your eyes ... then let the Lord go with *us*. Although this is a stiff-necked people, forgive *our* wickedness and *our* sin, and take *us* as your inheritance' (Exod. 34:9). The transformation in Moses is set in contrast to (and perhaps prompted by) the seeming change in the divine disposition. YHWH now ironically challenges Moses that 'your people' have become corrupt (Exod. 32:7; cf. Deut. 9:12). While Moses reminds the Lord that the Hebrews are still *his* people (v. 11), his own identification with them is not diminished. He has absorbed their destiny into his own.

Moses spent the last forty years of his life pleading for the lives of God's (and his) people.[27] With a twist of irony, his request to suffer with them is granted in Numbers 20 (cf. Deut. 32:51–52). As a result of dishonouring God, Moses' life ends with the rebellious generation outside the Promised Land. In his final sermons in Deuteronomy the prophet reflects an understanding that their fate had affected his from the beginning of their sojourn: 'Because of you the Lord became angry with me also and said, "You shall not enter it, either" ' (Deut. 1:37; cf. 3:26; 4:21; cf. Ps. 106:32–33). Moses became a type of the vicariously suffering servant[28] that resurfaces in the book of Isaiah (Bentzen 1948: 16–17; Coats 1993: 136; Miller 1993: 309–310) and prefigures the rejected Messiah in the Gospels. To be a shepherd means to lay down one's life for the flock.

Leadership, human and divine

> May the Lord ... appoint a man over this community to go out and come in before them ... so that the Lord's people will not be like sheep without a shepherd. (Num. 27:16–17)

The death of Moses outside the land of promise reinforces the theological perspective of the Pentateuch. Although some have seen these five books as a biography of Moses, he is absent in the beginning and the end. The macro story is larger than this human giant. It encompasses promises made to antecedent heroes like

---

[27] The book of Numbers provides other examples of Moses' intercessory role in 11:2; 12:13; chs. 14 and 16.

[28] He is called the 'servant of YHWH (or Elohim)' five times in the Torah, repeatedly throughout Joshua and Kings, and fourteen times in the Writings.

Abraham, promises that will be fulfilled in the lives of future heroes like Joshua. The central character is the Promise-Maker and Promise-Keeper, YHWH (Beegle 1972: 347–348). Moses shared God's glory, it is true (literally, Exod. 34:29); but he had none of his own. His role was absolutely pivotal in the drama, but he was a *supporting* actor (Blenkinsopp 1992: 135).

A simple summary of Moses' leadership in the wilderness is given in Psalm 77:20 [H 21]: 'You led your people like a flock by the hand of Moses and Aaron.' In this retrospection, it was *God* who led *his* people by the hand of *his* servants. It is somewhat ironic that von Rad's attempt to isolate one source's representation of Moses reduces him to what may be the broadest description of his capacities: 'What then, in J's view, was Moses? He was no worker of miracles, no founder of religion, and no military leader. He was an *inspired shepherd* whom Jahweh used to make his will known to men' (1962: 292, italics added). It would be better to say that Moses was, *as a shepherd*, a prophetic miracle worker, covenant mediator, military leader, priestly intercessor and source of divine direction and provision.[29] He was the human instrument by which God comprehensively shepherded his flock.

When Moses considers the prospect of his own death and the need for a faithful successor he prays, 'May the LORD, the God of the spirits of all mankind, appoint a man over this community to go out and come in before them, one who will lead them out and bring them in,[30] so that the LORD's people will not be like sheep without a shepherd' (Num. 27:16–17).

The shepherd who was to follow Moses needed to have the Spirit of YHWH upon him for this task. On this basis alone could Moses confirm his calling (Num. 27:18). The promise to the new leader was as firm as the one made to Moses: 'No-one will be able to stand up

---

[29] Coats (1988) summarizes Moses' broad set of roles in the Pentateuch as law-giver, prophet, priest, judge, sage, deliverer, covenant mediator, suffering servant and hero. Royal motifs in the story (birth story, beauty, early life as shepherd, supernatural powers, source of law and its interpretation, military leader, succession story) were already noted by Philo (Goodenough 1929: 178–181). In light of our introduction to metaphor and role theory, and in line with typical representations of rulers in Ancient Near Eastern sources, it would seem more appropriate to *expect* a diverse role set for a figure like Moses. His story is a reminder that leadership often transcends institutional roles (cf. Wildavsky 1984).

[30] While the phraseology in this verse has military connotations (cf. Josh. 14:11; 1 Sam. 18:13, 16), its usage together with shepherd language for David in 2 Sam. 5:2 includes the full responsibilities of rule (cf. 1 Kgs 22:17).

against you all the days of your life. As I was with Moses, so I will be with you; I will never leave you nor forsake you' (Josh. 1:5). Leadership continues after Moses' death because the Spirit of God had chosen and would enable his successor. Because human leadership is derivative of divine leadership and dependent on God's own Spirit for its effectiveness, the death or demise of a given leader is not the end of the community's story. Biblically speaking, a human leader is none other than God leading his own people through an anointed servant. As Joshua takes up his place in the front of God's community, the people respond: 'Just as we fully obeyed Moses, so we will obey you. *Only may the LORD your God be with you as he was with Moses*' (Josh. 1:17). They unanimously recognized God's new shepherd.

Formation of the covenant community

> You will be for me a kingdom of priests and a holy nation. (Exod. 19:6)

The wilderness traditions had paradigmatic importance in the life of Israel, for it was during this period that the nation was formed. It was to these foundational moments that later prophets, priests and kings would return in efforts of reform, renewal and reunification.[31] The great challenge was to *remember* the lessons learned in the desert (Deut. 8:2–3). Unfortunately, in pastoral terms, Israel's hearts were prone to 'go astray' (*t'h*; Ps. 95:10).

Regardless of Israel's behaviour, God's commitment to them and to his 'promise-plan' (Kaiser 1978) remained constant. Even if it were necessary to reduce them to one (Exod. 32:10), he would eventually have a community to carry his name. In pastoral terms, this meant 'culling' the flock in order to keep only those that were responsive and productive. Thus 'remnant' theology, common in later exilic literature, was already evident in the first wilderness.[32]

The persistence of God represents ultimate purposes for the covenant beyond the blessing of the Jewish people. The unique relationship God proposed to Israel gave them an identity and a mission *among the nations*. The patriarchal promises that provide the plot for our grand narrative include this important dimension: 'and

---

[31] Note the importance of the feast of Tabernacles in Solomon's temple dedication (1 Kgs 8) and the reform of Nehemiah (Neh. 8), and the feast of Passover in the reforms of Hezekiah (2 Chr. 30) and Josiah (2 Kgs 23).

[32] Precedents for this theology are found at least as early as the story of the flood.

all peoples on earth will be blessed through you' (Gen. 12:3). Just prior to consummating the covenant on Mount Sinai, the Lord described the identity of his people: 'Although the whole earth is mine, you will be for me a kingdom of priests and a holy nation' (Exod. 19:5–6). Israel's holiness and righteousness, emphasized so comprehensively in the laws of Sinai, were meant to reflect God's holiness and righteousness *to the nations* (Deut. 4:6–8).

Being the people of God required Israel to participate in and cooperate with an eschatological agenda that was global in scope. The wilderness journey was a rite of passage designed to transition these pastoral nomads into a nation with historic, missional purpose. Through them the world would have a window on God's wisdom and access to his blessing. The Shepherd of Israel was, through Israel, seeking a remnant from all the nations (cf. Amos 9:12), i.e. 'sheep which are not of this fold' (John 10:16 NASB).

Chapter Five

YHWH, David and the royal traditions

Moses had predicted a day when YHWH's people would have a king. He had in many respects been himself a royal prototype. Shepherd language in the Old Testament, as in the Ancient Near East generally, is attached most often to the institution of kingship (both divine and human). Our focus in this chapter will turn to the rise and reign of Israel's famous shepherd king, David, and to the sometimes creative, sometimes destructive tension between human and divine rule in Israel's experience.

This overview provides the opportunity to consider not only the narratives in the book of Samuel but also some of the Psalms associated with royalty. Though the equation between king and shepherd is infrequent in these passages, the royal tradition is the foundation for the great messianic expectations in the prophets and their fulfilment in the Gospels. Among these later writers there is unreserved use of pastoral language in criticism of poor leadership and in descriptions of the compassionate rule associated with the coming Davidic shepherd Messiah.

Narrative anticipations of David

Kingship in the Pentateuch

> The sceptre will not depart from Judah.
>
> (Gen. 49:10)

There are subtle ways in which David's kingship is foreshadowed in the Pentateuch. Significant royal features are attributed to humans in the creation account.[1] Elements in the stories of Abraham point

---

[1] E.g. in Gen. 1:26–28 (Wildberger 1965: 255–259; Brueggemann 1968; cf. Ps. 8:4–9 [H 5–10]). The Genesis account provides a preview for the primary tension in leadership: humans are *like* God (and serve as his vice-regents), but they are *not* God.

more specifically to the Davidic king: the centrality of Hebron, the conquest of Canaan, the cult of Melchizedek in Jerusalem and the importance of Mount Moriah (Clements 1967). Similarly, Moses anticipates the later king by mention of his law-giving (and adjudicating), military leadership, plans for a sanctuary, symbolic priestly activities and the title 'my servant' (Porter 1963). Perhaps David's experience of delayed promise and 'wilderness wanderings' is foreshadowed by both Moses and the experiences of the community in the Pentateuch.

Explicit anticipations come especially in references to the sceptre of the tribe of Judah in Jacob's blessing (Gen. 49:8–12; Alexander 1995: 32–37). The royal institution in general is predicted by Balaam, who sees a king and kingdom coming out of Jacob (Num. 24:7, 17, 19). Finally, Deuteronomy 17:14–20 provides descriptions of what faithful kings must do, should Israel one day request a king. In this speech Moses provides guidelines to protect Israel against the abuses of typical kings. He clearly sees monarchy as a danger, though inevitable and, in its ideal form, perhaps even desirable (Gerbrandt 1986).

Kingship in Judges

I will not rule over you, nor will my son rule over you. The LORD will rule over you. (Judg. 8:23)

The historical books that follow Deuteronomy are called, in the Hebrew canon, the Former Prophets and, in critical scholarship, the Deuteronomic or Deuteronomistic history ('Dtr').[2] The reason for this latter designation is the continuity of themes and apparent editing of the corpus *in terms of* the book of Deuteronomy. One of the key themes that reaches beyond the final speeches of Moses is kingship and, more specifically, what kind of king Israel should seek.

An early attempt at kingship in the book of Judges provides evidence for Moses' reserve. Gideon is chosen as YHWH's instrument of deliverance from the Midianites. After a victory clearly marked by God's personal intervention, Gideon is asked by the men of Israel to be king, with the prospect of dynasty to follow (8:22). But the 'worthy refuser' (Jobling 1998: 49) sets monarchy against

---

[2] In deference to the traditional designation of this corpus as the Former Prophets and in light of increasing dis-ease with the extent of 'Deuteronomic' editing attributed to a wide variety of biblical books (R. R. Wilson 1999), we will prefer the traditional designation except where the secondary literature is engaged.

theocracy: 'I will not rule over you, nor will my son rule over you. *The LORD will rule over you*' (Judg. 8:23).[3] The royal option (from Deut. 17), though refused by Gideon,[4] is sought by his son Abimelech (lit. 'my father is king'). The bloody story of his short-lived reign offers an important narrative caution against royal rule.

But Judges provides a mixed assessment of the royal institution. While theocracy was preferable to monarchy, the last five chapters of the book reveal a tendency among the people rather towards a third – and less desirable – option: *anarchy*. An ominous refrain punctuates the decline of Israelite life: 'In those days Israel had no king; everyone did as he saw fit' (Judg. 21:25; cf. 17:6; 18:1; 19:1). The implied assessment is that the lack of a king explains the state of chaos. Judges also reflects a distinct preference for the tribe of Judah (the first to take the land in 1:1–2; cf. 20:18) in contrast to Saul's tribe, Benjamin, which was responsible at the end of the book for abusing a Levite's concubine (from Judah). A civil war between the rest of the tribes ensues, during which the Benjaminites are almost completely annihilated (21:17) – with God's help (20:35).

Kingship in 1 Samuel 1 – 15

> It is not you they have rejected, but they have rejected me as their king. (1 Sam. 8:7)

The story continues in 1 Samuel, with the first twelve chapters forming a prologue to the (inevitable?) rise of monarchy (Childs 1979: 271; cf. Eslinger 1994). Kingship is anticipated in the prayer of Hannah, who foresees that 'the LORD will judge the ends of the earth. He will give strength to his king and exalt the horn of his anointed' (1 Sam. 2:10). The major turning point in the prologue begins with the people's request for a king in chapter 8.[5] A complicated interchange between YHWH, Samuel and the people follows, resulting in the new institution, but with qualified divine support for the first king.

---

[3] The tension between divine and human rule in Judges is played out with the root *špt* (to judge). While human agents are called judges throughout the book, the emphasis on YHWH as ultimate Judge is clearly seen in the Jephthah story (11:27; cf. 2:16–18).

[4] The details of the story imply that Gideon did pursue some of the accoutrements of royalty: tribute, a ruling position for his family, a cult centre and many wives (8:24–30; 9:2). Two of these were features of royalty that Moses had prohibited in Deut. 17:17.

[5] The request for a king is highlighted by the names of the two leading figures in the first part of 1 Samuel. Samuel sounds like 'heard of God'; Saul means 'asked (of God)'.

The issues in chapters 8 – 12 provide background for understanding the theology behind the royal institution that emerged in Israel, a theology that bears directly on the concept of shepherd rulers. The request for a king was precipitated by several concerns. The stated reason was the lack of a good successor to the current leader. The elders said to Samuel, 'You are old, and your sons do not walk in your ways; now appoint a king to lead [lit. 'judge'] us, such as all the other nations have' (1 Sam. 8:5). The reference to 'all the other nations' (cf. 8:20) implies a second reason.[6] This may be the most important key to understanding YHWH's response, 'they have rejected *me* as their king' (v. 7).[7] The community was exposing its own belief that security could only be ensured by a human king. The third reason is the Philistine threat, which from an historical perspective was a driving concern of this period.[8] Apparently Israel was no longer willing to accept an occasional judge leading by the power of the heavenly Judge.

The interchange that follows reveals ambivalence on the part of YHWH. He seems alternatively opposed and favourable to the new institution.[9] A coherent reading of the extended narrative (V. P. Long 1989: 236) clarifies that there are three related concerns, each of which prompts a slightly different divine response. First and most strongly, God is opposed to the *intent* – more than the *content* – of the request. The people wanted to be like the other nations. Second, he is opposed to Saul personally, his inappropriate fit signalled almost from the beginning. Third, as is characteristic in the Former Prophets, YHWH is ambivalent about kingship as an institution. The Lord gives the people what they seek, but only after rehearsing the likely abuses (1 Sam. 8:11–18) and providing again the criteria by which the new arrangement could work (10:25; 12:13–15). While the request was sinful, the institution was redeemable (Klein 1983: 79).

---

[6] For the historical influence of 'the other nations' on the monarchy that emerged in Israel, see Herrmann (1985: esp. 127 n. 5 for bibliography) for Egypt, Ishida (1977: 6–25) for Mesopotamia, and Day (1998) for Canaan.

[7] Samuel reminds them that YHWH was the deliverer of Israel and *had been their king all along* (1 Sam. 12:11–12).

[8] This is clear from the archaeological record (Mazar 1990: 300–313). It is also evident in the larger narrative context (1 Sam. 9:16; 16:11, 19; 17:15, 34ff.), though 1 Sam. 12:12 mentions the Ammonites first.

[9] Standard critical explanations have assumed contradictory sources behind the canonical text: anti-monarchic sources in 1 Sam. 8:1–22; 10:17–27; 12:1–25, and pro-monarchic sources in 9:1 – 10:16 and 11:1–15.

The rise and reign of David[10]

The history of David's rise

Your servant has been keeping his father's sheep. (1 Sam. 17:34)

Although God chose Saul and granted blessing over his early reign (1 Sam. 10:6–10; 11:1–15), two incidents signal his demise: the pre-empting of Samuel's role in the sacrifice at Gilgal (1 Sam. 13:8–14) and the ignoring of Samuel's word in regard to the Amalekite ban (1 Sam. 15:13–24). Significantly, both of these actions exhibit contempt for the word of the Lord's prophet and thus manifest presumptuous kingship. Although Saul continues to reign, he has lost the support of Samuel and of God himself. Saul becomes a foil for one better suited to lead the people of YHWH (Roberts 1987: 382–383).

The collection of stories that follows is often referred to as the 'History of David's Rise' (HDR).[11] This narrative begins with the introduction of David into the court of Saul in 1 Samuel 16 and continues through the confirmation of David as king by all Israel in 2 Samuel 5. The themes of the HDR are the divine choice of David (and rejection of Saul), the continuing favour God grants David with the people (and Saul's son), and David's success against the enemies of Israel (and in evading Saul). David's election, initiated by Samuel's secret anointing in 1 Samuel 16 and confirmed by his victory over Goliath in 1 Samuel 17, is rigorously tested by the pursuit of an afflicted king and those loyal to him.

What is most important for our discussion is the significance attached to David's role as a shepherd in the framing of this extended narrative (Brueggemann 1990: 237–238). David is introduced as a literal shepherd twice. In 1 Samuel 16 the prophet is told to find a replacement for Saul from among the sons of Jesse. While reviewing all of Jesse's sons, Samuel receives no divine prompting. He asks if there are any more, to which Jesse replies, 'There is still the youngest ... *but he is tending* [r'h] *the sheep*' (1 Sam. 16:11).

After the secret anointing the shepherd boy becomes, in an important sense, the true king of Israel. The transfer of the divine

---

[10] While the historicity of (Saul and) David is questioned in mainstream scholarship, the biblical accounts fit suitably in the context of late Iron Age 1 realities in Canaan. For a critique of the minimalist approach to this period, see Knoppers (1997).

[11] This terminology for 1 Sam. 16 – 2 Sam. 5 comes from Rost (1926), who also described a distinct 'Succession Narrative' in 2 Sam. 9 – 20 and 1 Kgs 1 – 2.

Spirit [12] from Saul to David signals this dramatic shift in favour of Jesse's son (1 Sam. 16:13–16). Seeking relief from a malevolent spirit that now terrorizes him, Saul is introduced, ironically, to '. . . a son of Jesse of Bethlehem who knows how to play the harp. He is a brave man and a warrior. He speaks well and is a fine-looking man. And the LORD is with him' (1 Sam. 16:18). Although young, David has a reputation already as a musician and a fighter, two ancillary skills of shepherds.

The second introduction to David takes place in the encounter with Goliath that follows. In this account the details of his occupation are once again highlighted. David has been travelling to and fro between flock and palace (1 Sam. 17:15) when his father asks him to bring some supplies to his brothers. Having left his herds with another keeper (v. 20), David finds battle lines drawn up against the Philistines and hears the giant's irreverent challenges to Israel. David's persistent questioning about Goliath's provocation elicits criticism from his brother Eliab: 'Why have you come down here? And *with whom did you leave those few sheep in the desert?*' (v. 28) News of David's questions comes to the king, to whom the shepherd then offers his service. David's lack of experience is obvious to Saul. But the shepherd explains that his confidence is a result of God's help while '*your servant has been keeping his father's sheep*'. He continues, 'When a lion or a bear came and carried off a sheep from the flock, I went after it, struck it and rescued the sheep ... The LORD who delivered me from the paw of the lion and the paw of the bear will deliver me from the hand of this Philistine' (vv. 34–37). Saul portentously blesses him with the words, 'The LORD be with you' (v. 37; cf. 1 Sam. 16:18; 18:12, 14, 28).

David tries on the king's armour which, symbolically, does not 'fit' him. David had learned to fight as a shepherd in the wilderness, and with a shepherd's weapons he would face Goliath: 'Then he took his staff in his hand, chose five smooth stones from the stream, put them in the pouch of his shepherd's bag and, with his sling in his hand, approached the Philistine' (v. 40).

---

[12] God's Spirit, directly evident in the wilderness traditions, is an indispensable element of human leadership, often described as God being 'with' a person and/or symbolized by anointing. This spiritual dynamic is present in succession accounts (e.g. Josh. 1:5, 17; 3:7; 2 Kgs 2:9ff.) and is a regular attribute of effective leadership (Judg. 3:10 et al.; 1 Sam. 10:6ff.; 11:6). The 'sharing' of the Spirit in Numbers 11 provides a symbolic picture of delegated authority.

The unexpected victory over the Philistine(s) is the first narrated testimony of the deliverance of YHWH by the hand of the *shepherd* from Bethlehem. David's continued military success and his meteoric rise to prominence over Saul's other officers (18:5–7) follows. This success becomes the source of Saul's envy which, in turn, puts David on the run until the king's death at the end of 1 Samuel.

At the end of the HDR there are other significant references to David as shepherd, this time as the shepherd leader of God's people. Upon the deaths of Saul and Jonathan, David takes the opportunity to show that in death as in life he respected 'the LORD's anointed' [13] (2 Sam. 1:14–16; cf. 1 Sam. 24:6; 26:9–11). The section 2 Samuel 2:1 – 5:5 is the concluding unit in the story of David's rise to the throne. Its chiastic structure (Fokkelman 1990: 144) moves between the anointing of David by the elders of Judah in 2:1–7 and his anointing by the tribes [14] of Israel in 5:1–5. The wording in chapter 5 is significant:

> All the tribes of Israel came to David at Hebron and said, 'We are your own flesh and blood. In the past, while Saul was king [*melek*] over us, you were the one who led Israel on their military campaigns [lit., 'led them out and brought them in'].' [15] And the LORD said to you, 'You shall shepherd [*r'h*] my people Israel, and you shall become their ruler [*nāgîd*].'
>
> When all the elders of Israel had come to King David at Hebron, the king made a compact with them at Hebron before the LORD, and they anointed David king [*melek*; cf. 2:4, 7] over Israel. (2 Sam. 5:1–3)

Saul had been a transitional figure, in one sense Israel's final judge (cf. Alt 1989: 185–205; Berges 1989). Although he is referred to as a

---

[13] Anointing of kings was not common in the Ancient Near East. In Egypt only ministers of the king were anointed (Redford 1992: 368). Biblical references to anointing likely reflect an emphasis not only on divine choice but on service to the divine King. Consequently, the characteristic phrase 'my servant' is used of David (2 Sam. 3:18; 7:5, 8).

[14] The word *šēbeṭ* may mean either a shepherd's rod or a tribe (with the staff as symbol of authority). McCarter (1984: 130–131, cf. 192) translates it 'staff bearers'.

[15] This phrase typically implies military leadership (1 Sam. 29:6; 2 Sam. 3:25; 2 Kgs 19:27; Ps. 121:8) and often, more specifically, *effective* military leadership (van der Lingen 1992). However, it may also be a *merism* that describes the totality of David's leadership (Fokkelman 1990: 140). The decision to formalize David's role among them as *melek* supports this interpretation.

king (*melek*),[16] his primary role was that of military deliverer.[17] David had demonstrated his exceptional capacities in this area. However, the elders affirm that his calling was to a broader range of responsibilities. As the narrative unfolds, David will become a king in every conventional sense: bringing unity to the tribes, extending the nation's borders, maintaining a standing army, organizing civil institutions and establishing a royal cult centre. Yet David's rule is conditioned by the social covenant (*běrît*) from which it is derived.[18] It is also qualified by the use of *nāgîd* as the preferred term for his leadership.

Nāgîd is used intentionally to emphasize *God's* perspective on Israel's ruler.[19] In 1 Samuel 9:16 (cf. 10:1) YHWH appoints Saul as Israel's first *nāgîd*, the one who would deliver Israel from the Philistines. When Saul begins to fail, Samuel calls his substitute a *nāgîd* (1 Sam. 13:14). Reflecting the prophet's use, Abigail uses the same term in reference to David (1 Sam. 25:30). David describes his replacement of Saul as the *nāgîd* of Israel in his rebuke of Michal (2 Sam. 6:21). The term is cited again by the elders of Israel as a prophetic word to David (2 Sam. 7:8). In the subsequent cases in Samuel–Kings the term is always used by the Lord's prophets.[20]

While some have defined *nāgîd* as crown prince (Mettinger 1976: 151–184; Ishida 1977: 50; Halpern 1981: 1–11), in these books it is clearly a synonym for king. It is better to think of this term as a way of reinforcing the ultimate rule of YHWH (Murray 1998: 281–301). With this term the standard roles of royalty are assumed, *but qualified by implicit reference to the divine Ruler*.[21] The term *nāgîd* creates space for divine kingship (Brueggemann 1990: 238). If Glück (1963) is

---

[16] The root *mlk* is used of Saul previously (1 Sam. 10:24; 11:12, 15; 12:1, 2, 13 et al.). In the following discussion it is important to bear in mind that while the term *melek* may have had grand associations, the actual institution at this time was likely nothing more than a tribal chieftainship (Ishida 1977: 23; cf. Earle 1991). The semantic and sociological overlap between *šōpēṭ*, *nāgîd* and *melek* also suggests an evolution towards full-scale monarchy, rather than a radical, categorical break with previous institutions.

[17] The 'judges' of the book of Judges are primarily military deliverers (Judg. 2:16), but, as Whitelam (1979: 47–69) explains, governance is also assumed.

[18] See the reflections of McCarthy (1982) and Tadmor (1982) on this episode, and Reviv (1989) on the institution of eldership in Israel.

[19] Carlson (1964: 55) similarly interprets *nāgîd* as *ideal* shepherd. Others have emphasized divine designation (Alt 1989: 195 n. 54).

[20] After the David references (1 Sam. 25:30; 2 Sam. 5:2; 6:21; 7:8; cf. 1 Sam. 13:14) see those for Solomon (1 Kgs 1:35), Abijah (2 Chr. 11:22), Jeroboam I (1 Kgs 14:7), Basha (1 Kgs 16:2) and Hezekiah (2 Kgs 20:5).

[21] See especially Murray's (1998: 285–289) comments on Saul as *nāgîd* of YHWH's *naḥălâ* in 1 Sam. 10:1.

correct [22] that *nāgîd* terminology originated with reference to middle-level shepherd contractors, then the parallelism in 2 Samuel 5:2 may be explicit: 'You shall *shepherd* my people Israel, and you shall become their *nāgîd*' (2 Sam. 5:2). Israel received its desired king, but only on the condition that it understand his role as derivative from and dependent upon the rule [23] of YHWH, the flock's true Owner. Kings, beginning with Saul, were to be measured in terms of their responsiveness to the words of that Owner, words mediated regularly through his messengers the prophets.

As king of unified Israel, David makes a strategic decision to turn Jerusalem into a new regal-ritual centre for the nation. But twice he experiences YHWH's resistance to the automatic assumptions of conventional monarchy. First, in Uzzah's death (2 Sam. 6) he learns that meticulous obedience to God's word will determine his success (cf. 1 Chr. 15:13). Second, God's refusal to allow him to build a temple (2 Sam. 7) interrupts the expected sequence of kingdom building in the ancient world (cf. Lundquist 1984).[24] Yet this passage reports a magnificent promise made to David and his lineage. God *will* bless David, *but on God's terms*. The fundamental tension at this pivotal moment in the development of the monarchy is the same one that Samuel articulated when the community had first requested a king. It is summarized suggestively in the title of Murray's (1998) monograph, 'Divine Prerogative and Royal Pretension'.

Chapter 7 is part of an important literary hinge in 2 Samuel [25] and a prologue to the story of David's reign that follows. While the great

---

[22] Although the roots *nqd* and *ngd* should be distinguished (Carlson 1964: 53), both were historically used for high-level herders. Like 'shepherd' (*rō'eh*), *nāgîd* is a general leadership term that can be used in a variety of settings, such as the army (1 Chr. 13:1) or the temple (1 Chr. 9:20). The use of a more flexible term avoids the automatic associations that come with the term 'king'.

[23] Levenson (1985: 70–75) helpfully distinguishes between YHWH's *suzerainty*, his primal and ultimate ownership of Israel (established by the exodus and Sinai covenant and violated by any other treaties), and YHWH's *sovereignty*, his rule which might be mediated by a human king.

[24] Although David's inclinations to create a conventional regal-ritual centre are qualified, the priestly dimension of Israel's monarchy is accepted (Rooke 1998). Like Moses, David and his dynastic heirs were mediators for the people of YHWH.

[25] There is a great deal of discussion about the purpose and placement of chs. 6, 7 and 8 in the literary structure of Samuel. For the importance of ch. 7 either by itself or in relation to ch. 8, see Carlson (1964); McCarthy (1965); Eslinger (1985: 96–99); Petersen (1986: 136); Murray (1998). Mettinger (1976: 41–47) argues that ch. 7 is the conclusion of the HDR, in which case the two references to David as figurative shepherd (in chs. 5 and 7) might effectively echo the two introductory references to David as literal shepherd in 1 Sam. 16 and 17.

promise to David is the focus in this chapter, David's role as shepherd is a significant emphasis. David seeks to build a 'house' (temple) for the Lord, who had given him 'rest from all his enemies around him' (v. 1). Nathan's initial unreflective response is affirmative, because 'the LORD is with you' (v. 3). However, a dream that night brings a different answer from the Lord to 'my servant David' (v. 5). He begins by asking:

> Are you the one to build me a house to dwell in? I have not dwelt in a house from the day I brought the Israelites up out of Egypt to this day. I have been moving from place to place with a tent as my dwelling. Wherever I have moved with all the Israelites, did I ever say to any of their rulers [or 'tribes'; *šibṭê*] whom I commanded to shepherd [*r'h*] my people Israel, 'Why have you not built me a house of cedar?' (2 Sam. 7:5–7)

To 'my servant David' (v. 8) the Lord makes his promise:

> ... I took you from the pasture [*nāweh*] and from following the flock to be ruler [*nāgîd*] over my people Israel. I have been with you wherever you have gone, and I have cut off all your enemies from before you ... And I will provide a place for my people Israel and will plant them so that they can have a home of their own and no longer be disturbed. (2 Sam. 7:8–10)

The prophetic message reinforces the emphasis on divine ownership of the 'flock' of Israel. 'My people' is a leitmotif in chapter 7 (vv. 7, 8, 10, 22, 23, 24). The royal institution in Israel could not unreflectively accumulate the conventional attributes and associations it had in neighbouring Near Eastern societies. By so doing, the initiation of monarchy would constitute rejection of divine rule. As YHWH had first resisted monarchy but then acceded, he now only temporarily opposes the plans for a temple. In both cases the issue of ultimate authority had to be addressed first. *God* would take the initiative in calling Israel's kings. *God* would hold them accountable, blessing and judging them by *God's* word. *God* would build a dynasty for David.[26]

---

[26] The view that a king reigns on behalf of a deity is not uncommon in the ancient world (cf. ch. 3). Unique in the Former Prophets is the emphasis on the *tension* between human and divine rule.

Reference to the wilderness is not only a reminder that God had no need of a temple; it also draws on the rich pastoral symbolism used for divine (and human) leadership. Like a Bedouin, God had moved about in a tent with his 'flock'.[27] His mobile presence with the community (and with David; v. 9) is more fundamental in that relationship than his future residence in a fixed location. God's ruling presence would not be permanently attached to Israel's royal institutions. It had preceded monarchy and it would follow it. Anticipations of a sanctuary had indeed begun in the wilderness (Exod. 15:18), but only within the context of YHWH's eternal kingship (Exod. 15:17).[28] The role of any of Israel's 'shepherds'[29] (1 Sam. 7:7) derives its fundamental orientation from the directing presence of YHWH in the midst of his community.

The end of David's reign

> Instead, he took the ewe lamb that belonged to the poor man. (2 Sam. 12:4)

David's early reign over Israel is marked by divine blessing (2 Sam. 2 – 8), but following the Bathsheba affair it staggers under divine judgment (2 Sam. 12 – 24; cf. Carlson 1964; Keys 1996). David's final years validate the prophetic word that what he had done in secret to Bathsheba and Uriah would be repeated in public by members of his own household (Amnon and Absalom). That word began with a parable Nathan used to illustrate the abuse of power, the perennial problem with monarchy (2 Sam. 12:1–12). With the story of a man whose only sheep was taken by a wealthy neighbour, Nathan taps deep into David's own identity as a shepherd. The prophet succeeds in revealing just how far David had come from being the shepherd of God's people: *rather than protecting them on the battlefield, he was at home sacrificing them for his personal pleasure.* This kind of royal presumption had been anticipated by the words of Moses in Deuteronomy 17:20; his heart had been 'lifted up above his countrymen'

---

[27] Some parallel Mesopotamian sources include the tension between semi-nomadic origins and the emergence of a settled state with permanent temple (Malamat 1980; Laato 1997).

[28] Another link between this passage and 2 Sam. 7 (v. 10) is the notion of 'planting' them (i.e. in Canaan).

[29] This is the first plural use of the term 'shepherds' for leaders. While it may refer to Moses and Aaron (cf. Ps. 77:20 [H 21]), it might also include others who were responsible for the community. This more general sense is present in the prophetic literature (cf. Jer. 3:15; 10:21 et al.).

(NASB).[30] Worse, 'David has usurped the role of Yahweh, by providing, violently, for himself' (Halpern 2001: 36). One of the redeeming features of the census story at the end of David's reign is the king's expressed concern for his people as a flock under his care: 'I am the one who has sinned and done wrong. *These are but sheep.* What have they done?' (2 Sam. 24:17).

The idealization of kingship

> When one rules over men in righteousness,
>   when he rules in the fear of God,
> he is like the light of morning at sunrise
>   on a cloudless morning,
> like the brightness after rain
>   that brings the grass from the earth.
>
> (2 Sam. 23:3–4)

David in the appendix of 2 Samuel

Although the author of 1 and 2 Samuel is brutally realistic about the flaws of King David, the book ends with a summary of his reign as one generally characterized by faithfulness to YHWH. This appendix (chs. 21 – 24) evidences a chiastic structure that balances two narratives, two lists and two songs (McCarter 1984: 18–19). The centre of this chiasm begins with a song of thanksgiving that provides a theological commentary on David's life (ch. 22 = Ps. 18; cf. Satterthwaite 1995: 43–47). Its themes are those of the narrative portions: David's divine election, his personal integrity, God's protective presence, David's success in battle with God's help and David's just rule. Picking up numerous semantic motifs and themes from Hannah's prayer in chapter 2 (Polzin 1993: 30–36; J. W. Watts 1992: 23–29), this psalm contributes to the framing of 1 and 2 Samuel with an emphasis on the ultimate rule of God and the penultimate rule of his king.

David's last words (23:1–7) form the other half of the appendix's centre. Here the king provides an important description of his own reign in the (ideal) categories that we have come to associate with Near Eastern rulers. He represents himself as the military leader who has achieved peace; the wise, righteous and just judge who has taken

---

[30] With this assessment in view, the reader is prepared (prompted?) to anticipate something more stable and closer to the ideal in the future (Satterthwaite 1995). Yet the promised son Solomon will also fail and the royal succession that follows will create a larger gap between the ideal and the real.

up the cause of the oppressed.[31] In pastoral terms, he is protector, provider and guide. Most importantly, he is the divinely appointed king who fears YHWH.

David in Kings and Chronicles

The idealization of David's reign continues in the books of Kings. There, archetypes measure the faithfulness of successive kings. The whole history of the northern kingdom is judged negatively because their rulers followed in the footsteps of Jeroboam, the template for apostate kings. The southern kings are measured by the Davidic standard.[32] Only Hezekiah and Josiah are held up as true Davidides, supporters of Zion as the single place of worship and unifiers of 'all Israel'.[33] In a sense, David lives on in these faithful kings (Provan 1995). The concern at the end of 2 Kings is the future of the Davidic line. With the royal figure in captivity, what can Israel expect of the God who promised David a permanent dynasty? Had their unfaithfulness cancelled the divine plan (cf. Ps. 89:38–39 [H 39–40])? The books of Kings contribute to the development of messianic hope by means of such questions.

While Chronicles shares much in common with Kings, the idealization of David (and Solomon) is more pronounced there. The patrons of Israel's golden age are characterized without reference to their failures.[34] What is especially significant is the equation of the kingdom of the Davidic dynasty and the kingdom of God (1 Chr. 17:13, 14; cf. 1 Chr. 28:5; 29:23; 2 Chr. 9:8; 13:8). While this understanding elevates the Davidic kingship, it is characteristically balanced by an emphasis on the personal reign of God over his people (Japhet 1989: 395–411).[35] In this post-monarchical book, there is

[31] See Whitelam (1979) and Weinfeld (1995) for discussions of the centrality and idealization of royal justice in the Bible in its Ancient Near Eastern context. Weinfeld emphasizes the concrete nature of social justice in the Bible, i.e. something a ruler *does*. On David as ideal judge, see Whitelam, pp. 29–37.

[32] The following kings are compared to David: Solomon (1 Kgs 3:3), Asa (1 Kgs 15:11), Amaziah (2 Kgs 14:3), Ahaz (2 Kgs 16:2), Hezekiah (2 Kgs 18:3) and Josiah (2 Kgs 22:2). Compare also 1 Kgs 9:4; 11:4, 6, 33, 38; 15:3, 5. Notice the emphasis on David's heart in 1 Kgs 11:4; 14:8; 15:3 (cf. 9:4; 2 Kgs 18:3, 6; Ps. 78:72).

[33] The phrase 'all Israel' is used about ninety times in the Former Prophets and about fifty times in Chronicles/Ezra–Nehemiah. God's ideal of a unified people, first realized by David, echoes in the revivals of Hezekiah and Josiah and anticipates the messianic expectations of Ezekiel.

[34] The unique case of the census in 1 Chr. 21 may be a further case of idealizing David, i.e. as Repentant Sinner (Knoppers 1995).

[35] God is ruler not only over his own nation but over all the kingdoms of the world (2 Chr. 20:6; Japhet 1989: 395 n. 1) and their kings (1 Chr. 5:26).

no tension any more between human and divine kingship. The Davidic king is understood simply as God's son, his designated representative on earth (1 Chr. 14:17; 17:13; 22:9–10; 28:6; 32:23; cf. 2 Sam. 7:14).

Psalms of the Davidic covenant[36]

> He also chose David His servant
> And took him from the sheepfolds.
> (Ps. 78:70 NASB)

The perspective of 2 Samuel 23:1–7, echoed in references to David as prototype in Kings and Chronicles, is evident also in the psalms of the Davidic covenant. These psalms (78, 89, 132) exhibit the characteristic emphases of the Samuel narratives: God's promises to David, David's success over the enemies of Israel, his concern for justice and his personal integrity before God. Unlike the royal psalms (discussed below), these psalms are more historically particularized with reference to David.

Psalm 78 summarizes Israel's journey as a people, beginning with their sojourn out of Egypt. It is rich in pastoral detail:

> But he brought his people out like a flock;
> he led them [*nhg*] like sheep through the desert.
> He guided [*nḥh*] them safely, so they were unafraid;
> but the sea engulfed their enemies.
> Thus he brought them to the border of his holy land,
> to the hill country his right hand had taken.
> He drove out nations before them
> and allotted their lands to them as an inheritance
> [*naḥălâ*];
> he settled the tribes of Israel in their homes
> [lit. 'tents'].
> (Ps. 78:52–55)

The psalm concludes by turning its attention to God's favoured royal leader, *thus creating out of Israel's history a seamless pastoral journey from Sinai to Zion*:

---

[36] Cf. Anderson (1983: 237) for the distinction between royal psalms and psalms of the Davidic covenant.

He also chose David His servant
And took him from the sheepfolds;
From the care of the ewes with suckling lambs
He brought him
To shepherd Jacob His people,
And Israel His inheritance.
So he shepherded them according to the integrity
of his heart,
And guided them with his skillful hands.

(Ps. 78:70–72 NASB)

Reference to the care of nursing ewes is meant to illustrate the nurturing role of the shepherd. Responsible oversight and compassionate leadership are in view as the final verse couples David's personal uprightness with understanding (*tĕbûnâ*) and guidance (*nḥh*).

The true Shepherd of Israel

Come, let us bow down in worship,
let us kneel before the LORD our Maker;
for he is our God
and we are the people of his pasture,
the flock under his care.

(Ps. 95:6–7)

Royal and enthronement psalms

You will rule [shepherd] them with an iron sceptre.

(Ps. 2:9)

The issues and themes present in the books of Samuel, Kings and Chronicles are, as we have seen, present as well in some of the psalms. The royal psalms (2, 18, 20, 21, 45, 72, 101, 110, 144:1–11), which contribute significantly to the framing of the psalter,[37] often go beyond the descriptions of any particular ruler[38] and stylize the

[37] The first three 'books' of the psalms are intentionally framed with royal psalms (1 – 41; 42 – 72; 73 – 89; G. H. Wilson 1986; 1993), suggesting that the traditional collection (like the Former Prophets) was oriented around the royal institution generally and the Davidic covenant particularly.

[38] David is only mentioned by name in Ps. 18:20 [H 51]. While almost half of the psalms have a Davidic superscription (preserved in the LXX), these serve primarily to ascribe authorship to David or to correlate a given psalm to an episode in his life, rather than to build a theology of human kingship.

representation of human kingship. Here one finds the closest parallels to the literature of Israel's neighbours. The king is responsible not only for military victory (e.g. 18:37–41 [H 38–42]; 21:8 [H 9]; 110:1, 2), justice (45:6 [H 7]; 72:1–2; 101:3–8)[39] and general prosperity (72:7), but he also has the power to affect the forces of nature (72:3, 16; cf. 89:25 [H 26]) and to reign as sovereign over the nations (110:2). The king's prowess with earthly enemies matches the divine King's control over cosmic and chaotic forces (Flanagan 1988: 206). The symbols of royal rule are the shepherd's rod (*šēbeṭ*; Ps. 2:9) and sceptre (*maṭṭeh*; Ps. 110:2). Royal psalms, echoing Nathan's oracle, call David a son of God (2 Sam. 7:14; cf. Pss. 2:7; 89:26–27) and also depict the king sitting at the right hand of God (Ps. 110:1).[40]

Though these psalms honour the king, it is always in the context of YHWH's ultimate rule. The king's subordination is explicit in references to *YHWH's* king (2:6; 18:51), *YHWH's* anointed (2:2; 20:3; 11:2; 132:13) and *YHWH's* servant (89:51). The royal psalms celebrate the Lord as the primary and ultimate ruler over this world generally and over his chosen people specifically. The direct covenant relationship between YHWH and his people is expressed through the emphatic and continuous use of the phrases '*my* people'[41] and 'the sheep of *his* pasture' (Pss. 74:1; 77:21 [H 20]; 78:52; 79:13; 80:1; 95:7; 100:3). The psalmist can as easily report that '*He* [YHWH] brought his people out like a flock; *he* led them like sheep through the desert' (Ps. 78:52; cf. 80:1) as to confess, 'You led your people like a flock *by the hand of Moses and Aaron*' (Ps. 77:20 [H 21]). Any 'shepherd' leading Israel is a steward of the community purchased by YHWH in the exodus. This is no less true for the one who set the standard for royal conduct in Jerusalem (cf. Ps. 78:70–71).

The royal psalms contribute to the Psalms' emphasis on the kingship of YHWH over Israel and all creation. Commentators rightly claim that the reign of God is the 'root metaphor' for the Psalms (Mays 1994; cf. McCann 1993: 41–50). G. H. Wilson (1985: 215) calls the enthronement of YHWH the 'editorial centre' of the Psalms. While the specific genre of enthronement psalm is typically

---

[39] Justice, equity and social order were standard expressions of shepherd rule in antiquity.

[40] Terms usually reserved for God are sometimes employed (e.g. *hôd* and *hādār* in 45:4 [E 3]).

[41] See Good (1983: 52–55) for the ambiguity of the term *'ām* in reference to people and flocks.

associated with relatively few examples (24, 29, 47, 93 – 99), the theme of God's reign permeates the book.[42]

Psalm 23

The LORD is my shepherd.
(Ps. 23:1)

The direct personal reign of God over his people and his king is affirmed most eloquently in Psalm 23. Here the psalmist expresses trust in the provision, protection and guidance of the divine Shepherd.

> [1] Because the Lord is my shepherd, I lack nothing.
> [2] In green pastures he causes me to lie down.
> To quiet waters he carefully leads me; [3] he restores
>   my vitality.
> He guides me on the right paths for the sake of his
>   honour.
> [4] Though I walk through the valley of deadly [43]
>   darkness, I will fear no calamity.
> For you are with me; your club and staff they
>   comfort me.
> [5] You prepare a table before me in the presence of my
>   enemies.
> You anoint my head with oil; my cup overflows.
> [6] Surely goodness and loving-kindness will pursue me
>   all the days of my life.
> And I will return to stay [44] in the house of YHWH as
>   long as I live.

(Author's translation)

The sentiments conveyed by the simple pastoral imagery of Psalm 23 have captivated believers for generations. It is a psalm of trust attributed to David, Israel's archetypal shepherd ruler. The royal

---

[42] Cf. 5:2 [H 3]; 44:4 [H 5]; 47:2, 6, 7 [H 3, 7, 8]; 48:2 [H 3]; 68:24 [H 25]; 74:12; 84:3 [H 4]; 95:3; 98:6; 145:1; 149:2.

[43] Thomas (1962) defends a superlative force for the root *mwt* in the compound *ṣalmāwet* (cf. Jon. 4:9).

[44] The MT vocalizes the last verb of this psalm as the waw-consecutive perfect of *šwb* ('I will return'), a verb important in v. 3. Most translations amend the vocalization to match the root *yšb* ('I will dwell'; cf. Ps. 27:4). I follow Craigie (1983: 204), who respects the Masoretic pointing but makes sense of the whole line by emphasizing returning *to* dwell.

leader is addressing Israel's divine Shepherd ruler YHWH in personal terms. *Like every Israelite whom he represents, the king is also a dependent subject*, in need of the provision, protection and guidance his divine Shepherd abundantly supplies.

We have noted precedents in Ancient Near Eastern literature for referring to deities as personal shepherds. This was much less attested in those sources than were images of a *community's* divine Shepherd. The same proportions are true in the Hebrew Scriptures.[45] What is remarkable is the way an individual 'sheep' could legitimately conceive of the Lord as *my* shepherd (cf. Ps. 119:176). The intimacy implied from the beginning of the psalm is enhanced by the change in references from 'he' to 'you' beginning in verse 4.

Having surveyed the pastoralist's world (in ch. 2), we are more likely capable of appreciating the natural and cultural elements of the poem. The psalmist celebrates the primary benefits of the good Shepherd's presence: protection, provision and guidance. The journey is complete when he returns to the home of his Master.

The statement in verse 1 that there is no want should be understood in the context of the many threats and needs that exist in the desert environment (cf. vv. 4–5). Bountiful provision includes pastures of fresh vegetation that emerge following the winter rains. There is enough for sheep to lie down, satisfied with excess around them (cf. 2 Sam. 23:4). The good Shepherd knows where to find pastures that are not only lush but safe enough for his flocks to rest in peace. He leads them carefully (*nhl*) to 'still waters', the run-off pools that become calm reservoirs for drinking. Again, it is the skilled shepherd who knows the environment well enough to provide for his animals' needs without compromising their security. This natural bounty is the source of restoration (*šwb*, Polel) for each valued sheep.

The divine Shepherd guides (*nḥh*) his sheep throughout their journey in the right tracks. The wilderness is a confusing environment. Left to themselves, sheep inevitably 'go astray' (Ps. 119:176). The metaphor is obvious: human members of the flock of YHWH need the guidance of their Shepherd to walk in his ways. Righteous (*ṣdq*) ways, i.e. *rules*, are evidence of a good *ruler*, either divine or human (cf. Isa. 11:4–5; Jer. 23:6; 50:7). Ultimately *YHWH's* reputation depends on the standards of the community that bears his name (cf. Exod. 32:12; Deut. 4:6–8).

---

[45] In the Psalms alone see Pss. 74:1–2; 77:20; 78:52f.; 80:1–3; 95:7; 100:3.

The psalmist turns in 23:4–5 to the protection that the good Shepherd affords. Even in the deadly shadows[46] that fall at dusk in the desert's canyons there is safety in his presence. Though easily frightened by nature, this trusting sheep will move through the shadows without fear. The club of the trustworthy Shepherd is ready for any predator. The staff, with which he nudges wandering sheep back in line, is also a source of comfort. Only as a disciplined flock, following the Shepherd's lead together, can they be kept safe. Even surrounded by these hostile enemies they can graze with confidence (v. 5).

The psalm becomes more literal and begins to merge images in the last two verses.[47] The anointed one in verse 5 may be the individual sheep[48] or a human guest who is welcomed by the divine host (cf. Luke 7:46).[49] The cup may be a skin from which the animals drink (Isa. 21:5) or a common cup for guests.[50] Surely by verse 6 it is the human subject who contemplates enjoying God's presence fully in the house of the Lord. While shepherd/sheep imagery may fade towards the end of the psalm, it still provides a comprehensive rubric (root metaphor) for this poetic reflection on God's presence in the life of an individual in his 'flock'. The psalm begins with his presence evident in the journey through the wilderness and appropriately concludes with a return home to enjoy that presence for ever.[51]

While Psalm 23 is celebrated for its timeless appeal,[52] it may provide a retrospective reflection anchored in David's own life. Specifically, his flight from Absalom and his return in 2 Samuel 15 – 19 may be in mind (Lundbom 1986). It is just as likely, however, that the king's personal experience of exodus and return under the care of

---

[46] The term *ṣalmāwet* is used four times in the Psalms, all in shepherding/wilderness contexts (Pss. 44:11–24; 107:10–14).

[47] Most commentators assert that the psalm has changed its metaphor from shepherd to host at v. 5 (with the sheep becoming a guest). Those who insist that shepherd imagery remains intact throughout the psalm often amend *šulḥān* (table) to *šelaḥ* (javelin), assuming dittography of the *nun* from the following word (Power 1928; Koehler 1956). But there is no versional support for this emendation, and it may not be necessary. Biblical images of the divine Shepherd in the wilderness and (new) exodus traditions frequently involve hospitality along with protection and guidance.

[48] Oil was a traditional medicinal treatment for animals and humans in the ancient world.

[49] This may also refer to David's anointing as king (1 Sam. 16:13).

[50] Cup can be a metaphor for fate or destiny (Pss. 11:6; 16:5–6).

[51] At the end of our study we find precisely these themes in 1 Peter.

[52] Mowinckel (1962: 41) suggests, 'Perhaps what gives it priceless value to all ages may be the very fact that it stands there as a pure expression of confidence in God, unhindered by all special historical circumstances ...'

the divine Shepherd are echoes of the *community's* experience in the wilderness traditions. A number of terms in this passage are featured in those traditions (Freedman 1980; Barré & Kselman 1983). Perhaps even more importantly, they are featured again in prophetic passages that predict a *new* exodus from the wilderness of exile.[53]

Being without lack (*ḥsr*; v. 1) was a result of God's watchful presence in the wilderness (Deut. 2:7; Neh. 9:21). Scarcity is the Israelites' experience in exile when they forsake the presence of God (Jer. 44:18). The pastures (*nĕ'ôt*) of verse 2 recall 'your holy pasture' (*nĕwēh qodšĕkā*) to which YHWH led (*nhl*) his people in Exodus 15:13. In exile even the enemies of God's people will recognize that they had forsaken their *nĕwēh ṣedeq* (true pasture; Jer. 50:7; cf. 2 Sam. 15:25). The phrase 'waters of stillness' (v. 2) employs an important term (*mĕnûḥôt*) that represents the ideal for which God had rescued his people in Psalm 95:6–11 (cf. Num. 10:33). The image of sheep lying down (*rbṣ*) under the proper guidance (*nhl*) of their divine Shepherd is taken up in Ezekiel 34:14–16. *Nhl* is a significant root not only in the original exodus account (Exod. 13:21; 15:13), but also in the 'second exodus' traditions of Isaiah (40:11; 49:10), to which we will turn shortly.

The revivification of the sheep imagined in verse 3 employs the root *šwb* (cf. Ruth 4:15; Lam. 1:16), a verb that Jeremiah favours in his calls for repentance and prophecies of coming renewal.[54] Also using the Polel verb form, Jeremiah predicts,

> But I will *bring* Israel *back* to his own pasture
>   and he will graze on Carmel and Bashan;
> his appetite will be satisfied
>   on the hills of Ephraim and Gilead.
>   (Jer. 50:19; cf. Ezek. 39:29; Isa. 49:5–6)

Regathering and restoration are linked together as in the shepherd psalm (T. M. Willis 1987). The Shepherd in Psalm 23:3 guides (*nḥh*)

---

[53] Although there are archaic features of the psalm (Freedman 1980), it is possible that it is exilic as Freedman (ibid. 299) concludes. This view abandons the LXX superscription ('of David') in favour of the Aramaic designation which reads, 'Prophecy concerning the return of the people. A narrative concerning the comforts given the people while they were coming up from Babylon.' If this is the more accurate setting, then the psalm joins the other voices of this period in hopeful trust for divine deliverance with allusions to the original wilderness traditions.

[54] Jer. 2:6 refers to the original desert through which God led his people as a place of *ṣalmāwet* (cf. Ps. 23:4).

his sheep, a form of leadership attributed to God in the wilderness (Exod. 13:21; 15:13; Pss. 77:21 [E 20]; 78:53, 72). Here also the works of God on behalf of Israel were performed for the sake of his 'name' (v. 3; Ps. 106:8).

Righteous (*ṣedeq*) paths recall ancient covenantal standards (Stigers 1980)[55] and anticipate the importance of righteousness in a new wilderness restoration. When the Spirit comes,

> ... the desert becomes a fertile field ...
> Justice will dwell in the desert
>   and righteousness [*ṣĕdāqâ*] live in the fertile field ...
> My people will live in peaceful dwelling-places
>   [*nĕwēh šālôm*],
> in secure homes,
> in undisturbed places [*mĕnûhôt*] of rest.
>   (Isa. 32:15–18; cf. Isa. 51:1–5)

Isaiah will project words of comfort (*nhm*) once again in these desolate areas (Isa. 40:1 et al.; cf. Ps. 23:4). There God will again 'spread his table' (Ps. 78:19).

As the psalm closes in verse 6, it returns to an important motif from the wilderness covenant. Israel had been promised long life (*'orek yāmîm*; Deut. 30:20) if they walked in the paths of righteousness that God had revealed. The psalmist is assured that the eternal dwelling of God is the ultimate destination of his desert journey. Though one cannot be sure that David was the author of Psalm 23, there are important links between its lyrics and the life of the king who personally embodied the story of Israel. Like Moses, who had prefigured him in such dramatic ways, the shepherd ruler of Israel had first learned to trust YHWH as his personal shepherd in the desert. There he was privately prepared to tend the flock of God. Psalm 23 is a reminder that even the king – especially the king – was dependent on the God of Israel for personal nurture and guidance. Israel's kings had to understand that being a member of the flock of God was more fundamental than being an appointed shepherd over that flock.

---

[55] Another word carrying covenantal associations is *hesed* in v. 6 (Glueck 1967; but cf. Sakenfeld 1978). We might also think of good fortune (*ṭôb*; v. 6) as indicative of conventional covenant blessings (contrast *rā'* in v. 4). For covenant language in Ps. 23, see Barré & Kselman (1983).

III
YHWH, the Messiah and promises of a second exodus

The prototypes for later pastoral traditions have now been explored. YHWH led his flock through the wilderness by the hand of Moses. He then chose another shepherd, David, through whom to guide his people in the land of promise. But eventually the monarchy became corrupt and the prospect of returning to a spiritual 'wilderness' became inevitable. We turn now to the prophetic voices who spoke on behalf of the divine King, the true Shepherd of Israel.

Pre-exilic prophets were active in the northern kingdom (Amos, Hosea) prior to Assyria's conquest in 722 BC and in Judah (Micah, Isaiah) prior to Babylon's invasion of Jerusalem in 586 BC. The fall of Jerusalem created a crisis of immense proportions. It called into question the foundations of their society and theology, and brought scrutiny upon the leaders who had failed them. Prophetic oracles probed the causes for this catastrophe within the context of Israel's covenant relationship with YHWH. It was determined that their leaders had failed the Lord through cultic apostasy, social injustice and dependence on political allegiances.

While the sense of impending judgment on Israel/Judah (and their neighbours) casts a dark shadow over this prophetic material, the corpus nevertheless exhibits an ultimate dimension of hope. The anticipation of something better, especially in terms of leadership, is the basis for the messianic traditions. Isaiah's expectations of a coming Davidic king and an era of justice and peace are rooted in the wilderness and royal traditions we have surveyed. These expectations intensified with the trauma of exile. Prophets who ministered in that period (Jeremiah, Ezekiel) gave voice to rich visions of a reconstituted people, a renewed covenant and revitalized leadership. These exilic visions – and those that follow (e.g. Zechariah) – make sustained use of pastoral imagery to explicate the state of the future. The divine Shepherd of Israel will regather Israel from their dispersion and renew his covenant with them in their wilderness.

Chapter Six

Isaiah: the Davidic Messiah and a way in the wilderness

Isaiah's contribution to the wilderness and royal/Messiah traditions cannot be overstated. First among the Latter Prophets, this book addresses most of the key issues and themes found in those that follow. This diverse collection of prophecies attributed to Isaiah ben Amoz derives from his long ministry during the reigns of four of Judah's kings: Uzziah, Jotham, Ahaz and Hezekiah (1:1). Over a period of perhaps sixty years (740–680? BC) Isaiah played a central role in political affairs in Jerusalem. During this period Judah watched the northern kingdom fall to Assyria. King Ahaz gained some time by making Judah a vassal of Assyria. Nevertheless, during Hezekiah's reign the Assyrian military machine rolled into Judah and destroyed almost all of it, except Jerusalem. Hezekiah was 'trapped like a bird in a cage',[1] but the royal city was miraculously spared. Yet in the wake of this miracle, Hezekiah revealed his own vulnerability to political allegiances. His overtures to Babylon at this time (Isa. 39) would eventually turn Judah into a vassal of this next superpower. The myth of Zion's inviolability could continue only a little longer.

While Isaiah had a personal ministry that lasted for decades, his visions and oracles looked ahead to events that transpired over the next two centuries. He predicted that there would be judgment on Judah as there was on Samaria. Controlling these events stood the 'Holy One of Israel', who would hold his 'vineyard' responsible for bearing rotten 'produce' (Isa. 5). The divine Sovereign would use the kings of foreign nations (Assyria, Babylon) to accomplish his purposes among his own people. Many lives would be lost, Isaiah predicts, and of those 'scattered' among the nations, only a remnant would remain. However, these foreign kings would also be punished for their hubris, considering themselves autonomous and god-like in their power. Isaiah's visions look ahead to the day of YHWH's

---

[1] A phrase taken from Sennacherib's famous inscription describing the siege of Jerusalem (Pritchard 1969: 288).

judgment on Babylon. The Lord would use Cyrus, king of Persia, to bring an end to Babylon's might, instructing this chosen 'shepherd' (44:28) to bring Jewish exiles back from captivity. Before Isaiah's prophecies come to a close, the book already has in view details of post-exilic realities in Palestine.

Though debate about (multiple) authorship continues,[2] it is now widely appreciated that the book of Isaiah has been organized quite intentionally. Certain key themes, motifs and rubrics give structure to the book. For example, the contrast between the 'former things' in the past and the 'new things/days' that are coming is an important organizing device (Seitz 1991: 199–202). This rubric is used to inspire hope for a 'second exodus' that will be enjoyed by the remnant (Anderson 1962: 187ff.; cf. Fishbane 1985: 362–368). Another major theme is (the king's) faith in God vs. faith in human power (e.g. Assyria). This theme is dramatically illustrated through prophetic interactions with Ahaz in chapters 7 – 12 and Hezekiah in chapters 36 – 39 (Williamson 1998: 247–248). These interactions highlight the question of *Davidic* leadership in the fate of Israel. If God's judgment is unavoidable, *who then will lead them* in the reconstruction of their world? The question of leadership persists through the final chapters of Isaiah.

'Davidic' rulers and the reign of YHWH

O LORD Almighty, God of Israel, enthroned between the cherubim, you alone are God over all the kingdoms of the earth. (Isa. 37:16)

The book of Isaiah begins with a two-part introduction: chapters 1 – 6 [3] introduce the themes of the whole book (concluded in chs. 65 – 66); chapters 7 – 12 introduce the specific themes of the first portion of the book, chapters 7 – 35.[4] This second introductory section features

[2] The perspective of this chapter is that the eighth-century prophet is the primary author of the book bearing his name, though editing is possible (cf. Oswalt 1986: 17–28; Motyer 1993: 25–30).

[3] Several commentators understand ch. 6 (Isaiah's call) to be a part of the section that follows (e.g. Motyer 1993). It is clearly a hinge between the two introductions (Oswalt 1986: 175), one which places the human rule of Uzziah (who had just died) in the context of the divine rule of YHWH.

[4] There is growing interest in the role of chs. 36 – 39 (Hezekiah's confrontation with Assyria and his indiscretions with Babylon) in the final shaping of Isaiah (cf. Seitz 1991; Beuken 2003). This section is a hinge, bringing to a conclusion concerns surrounding the Assyrian threat (chs. 7 – 35) and anticipating the Babylonian presence that becomes the setting for the messages that follow (chs. 40 – 55).

three messianic prophecies about the house of David that are central to Isaiah's visions of the future. The issue of kingship is recalled as the first half of Isaiah draws to a close (in chs. 28 – 33). Although shepherd language is absent in this portion of the book, its theology of kingship is foundational for the rest of the book and the messianic traditions that this theology promotes.

The first of the three prophecies in chapters 7 – 12 comes to Ahaz while he is under pressure to join the local opposition against the region's major superpower, Assyria. Ahaz's failure to respond in faith is the turning point for 'the house of David', a motif that frames the dialogue (7:2, 13; Motyer 1993: 80–81; cf. v. 17). Juxtaposed to the grand vision of the King of heaven in chapter 6, this passage illustrates an historical contrast with the human kings of history. In this context the prophet mentions a messianic [5] figure whose lineage is shrouded in mystery. The promise of a child named 'God-with-us' ('Immanuel'; v. 14) is enmeshed in a prediction of severe judgment 'on you and on your people and on *the house of your father*' (i.e. David; v. 17).

Isaiah 9:1–7 [H 8:23 – 9:6] [6] provides another prediction of a messianic figure, this time with more detail. Again it is a child who is promised. Again his names are given prominence. These names signify divine qualities: he is the 'Mighty God', the 'Everlasting Father', the 'Prince of Peace' (v. 6). Sitting on the throne of David (v. 7), this ideal ruler will create a reign of peace, established in justice (*mišpāṭ*) and righteousness (*ṣĕdāqâ*) (v. 7).[7] This reign of light that will dawn (v. 2) is initiated by the God who, in words reminiscent of the exodus account, 'shattered the yoke that burdens them, the bar across their shoulders, the rod of their oppressor' (9:4).[8] The birth of the

---

[5] The English term 'Messiah' ('anointed one') is a transliterated form from the Hebrew root *mšḥ*. However, etymology does not explain the theological significance of the term. We will look at those passages which reflect anticipation for a future, ideal king in Israel. That king was expected in the near future and in this sense was realized in the persons of Hezekiah and Josiah. But expectations of someone whose rule would be more far reaching is also evident. This eschatological 'Messiah' and an attendant messianic *era* is envisioned in several passages, as we shall see.

[6] References below will list English versification only.

[7] That these values are important to Isaiah *as leadership values* is evident by their centrality in his critiques of Israel's rulers in the prologue to the book (1:23; 5:7, 16; cf. ch. 3) and beyond (e.g. 10:1–2; chs. 28, 32). Compare also his criticism of the corrupt 'shepherds who lack understanding' in 56:11.

[8] Compare references to 'yoke' (*'ōl*) in Lev. 26:13; 'burden' (*siblôt*) in Exod. 1:11; 2:11; 5:4–5; 6:6–7; 'shoulder' (*šĕkem*) in Ps. 81:7; and 'oppressor' (*nōgēś*) in Exod. 3:7; 5:6, 10–14.

ideal king completes the divine plan by creating a capable human ruler who administers for him. Isaiah 11:1–5 likewise introduces the hope of a coming (Davidic) king (v. 1; cf. v. 10), endowed by the Spirit of the Lord (v. 4).[9] The attributes of his reign resemble those of the ideal king found in royal psalms. He will rule in the 'fear of the LORD' (vv. 2, 3) and in righteousness (*ṣdq*; vv. 4, 5); he will judge (*špṭ*) fairly, especially with regard to the poor (v. 4); he will 'slay the wicked' (v. 4); and he will create a new era of peace where wild and domestic animals will dwell together in harmony (vv. 6–9).

While this oracle shares much with the royal traditions, there are hints of new dimensions. First, the language of the king's reign is more grandiose, with detailed descriptions of an era that is a virtual return to the Garden of Eden (cf. 51:3). Second, the prophet's reticence in using the name 'David' is suggestive. Hope is found (v. 1) in a new shoot (*ḥōṭer*) from the stock (*geza'*) of Jesse, a branch (*nēṣer*)[10] from Jesse's root (*šōreš*). The emphasis on Jesse suggests something more primal than simply another descendant of David. A brand-new start from the *root* is in mind.

These three passages promote a particular kind of hope for Judah. First, they can expect YHWH personally to remain committed to his people, though the shape of his concern may change. He will judge them – especially their leaders – for their unfaithfulness. But eventually a new creation, initiated by God and overseen by divinely selected and inspired leaders,[11] will usher in a bright future. The promise of an ideal king is guaranteed in later oracles: 'See, a king *will* reign in righteousness and rulers *will* rule with justice' (32:1). 'Your eyes *will* see the king in his beauty . . .' (33:17).

But kingship for Isaiah is primarily and ultimately an issue of *YHWH's* reign. What began as a private revelation in 6:5 ('my eyes have seen the King, the LORD Almighty') will become a reality for all the people in 28:5:

---

[9] 'Spirit' (*rûaḥ*) is mentioned four times in this verse, emphasizing the role of God in the rule of the king. Isaiah emphasizes the Spirit more than any other OT writer (cf. Ma 1999). It is important for his understanding of leadership, both human (king and Servant) and divine (in the coming 'second exodus').

[10] Jesus' identity as the predicted *nēṣer* is associated with his home in Nazareth (Matt. 2:23).

[11] A Davidic ruler is only mentioned once elsewhere in the book, again in ambiguous terms, with the promise of a just judge in the (lit.) 'tent of David' (16:5). Another (ominous) reference is the collapse of Eliakim, who holds the 'key to the house of David' (22:20–25).

> In that day the LORD Almighty
> will be a glorious crown,
> a beautiful wreath
> for the remnant of his people.

This section closes conclusively on the same note:

> For the LORD is our judge,
> the LORD is our lawgiver,
> the LORD is our king;
> it is he who will save us.
> (33:22)

This message declares the reign of the expected ideal king to be penultimate. In what becomes increasingly common in the rest of the book, Isaiah describes God's rule over his people and the world as *unmediated*.[12] The human king, occasionally mentioned, has *delegated* authority and thus can never claim to be more than a servant of the Lord (Roberts 1983; Williamson 1998). These are precisely the emphases we found in the Psalms.

This message is reinforced in the second part of the book, beginning with the crisis facing Ahaz's descendant in chapters 36 – 39. Hezekiah exercises the faith[13] that Ahaz had lacked. Facing the threat of 'the great king, the king of Assyria' (36:4, 13), he places his faith in the divine King. His prayer begins, 'O LORD Almighty, God of Israel, enthroned between the cherubim, you alone are God over all the kingdoms of the earth' (37:16). Recognizing the sovereignty of YHWH is what makes Hezekiah a successful monarch. As long as Zion is understood to be the throne *of God*, it will remain safe.

Throughout the rest of the book, the focus of Isaiah's messages continues to be the creating and redeeming power[14] of 'Jacob's King' (41:21). 'I am the LORD, your Holy One, Israel's Creator, your King' (43:15). 'This is what the LORD says – Israel's King and Redeemer, the LORD Almighty: I am the first and I am the last; apart from me there is no God' (44:6). The message to Zion is emphatic: '*Your God reigns!*' (52:7) He is the one who determines the

---

[12] This is especially clear in 59:15–20 and in 63:3–5, where YHWH looks for but finds no-one to help him.

[13] One of the prominent roots in the narrative of chs. 36 – 39 is *bṭḥ* (to trust). For Isaiah, trust in YHWH is a primary indication of a human ruler's understanding that his own role is contingent on the role of the divine King.

[14] Cf. Stuhlmueller (1970).

course of history, even 'anointing' Cyrus (45:1) as his 'shepherd' (44:28).[15] The second half of Isaiah thus reverberates with a vision of the true, exalted King of Israel with which the book began (ch. 6).[16]

A 'second' exodus

> Like a shepherd He will tend His flock,
> In His arm He will gather the lambs
> And carry them in His bosom;
> He will gently lead the nursing ewes.
>
> (Isa. 40:11 NASB)

An important, related theme in Isaiah, especially [17] chapters 40 – 55, is often described as the 'second exodus' (e.g. Anderson 1962). The designation is natural, for Isaiah provides several images of exiles leaving their bondage and returning on a desert highway to the mountain of the Lord. This journey is initiated and supervised by the compassionate Shepherd of Israel (Isa. 40:11). YHWH will not only shepherd his people personally, but he will lead them home by the Persian king, his appointed shepherd (44:28; cf. 63:11). The centrality of this construct prompted Westermann's (1969: 22) accurate observation: 'The place which Deutero-Isaiah gives to the exodus is so conspicuous that all the other events in Israel's history recede into the background.'

The second exodus tradition in Isaiah involves several important related motifs [18] that are introduced in 40:1–11.[19] These motifs recall

[15] The notion of Gentile kings being used to promote the welfare of God's people is common in the latter half of Isaiah (49:7, 23; 60:3, 10, 11, 16; 62:2).

[16] In a detailed comparison of the structure and language of Psalms Book 4 and 'Second Isaiah', Creach (1998) demonstrates that both intentionally place the royal traditions of David within the broader theological context (and confines) of the reign of YHWH.

[17] Earlier references in the book include 4:5–6; 10:24–27; 11:11–16; ch. 12; 19:19–25; 35:5–10 (cf. Fishbane 1979: 126–128).

[18] The discussion that follows agrees with Zimmerli (1960), Anderson (1962, 1976), Fishbane (1979: 121–151) and Hugenberger (1995) that these elements are intentionally reminiscent of the first exodus/wilderness accounts. The reader will also find useful in this regard the works of Stuhlmueller (1970), Holmgren (1973), Patrick (1985) and Merrill (1988). Barstad's (1989) criticism that these motifs have an independent origin should keep the analysis from becoming overblown, but there are enough obvious echoes of the first exodus/wilderness to consider this a true tradition.

[19] Ch. 40, recalling ch. 6 (O'Kane 1996), provides an orientation and overview to many of the themes that follow, especially in chs. 40 – 48 (cf. Seitz 1990).

the original wilderness sojourn during which the Shepherd of Israel
faithfully provided for, protected and guided his people.

> [1] Comfort, comfort my people,
>> says your God.
> [2] Speak tenderly to Jerusalem,
>> and proclaim to her
> that her hard service has been completed,
>> that *her sin has been paid for*,
> that she has received from the LORD's hand
>> double for all her sins.
> [3] A voice of one calling:
> '*In the desert* prepare
>> *the way for the LORD*;
> make straight in *the wilderness*
>> *a highway for our God.*
> [4] *Every valley shall be raised up,*
>> *every mountain and hill made low*;
> *the rough ground shall become level,*
>> *the rugged places a plain.*
> [5] And *the glory of the LORD will be revealed*,
>> and all mankind together will see it.
>>> For the mouth of *the LORD has spoken*' . . .
> [8] The grass withers and the flowers fall,
>> but *the word of our God* stands for ever.
> [9] You who bring good tidings to Zion,
>> go up on a high mountain.
> You who bring *good tidings* to Jerusalem,
>> *lift up your voice with a shout*,
> lift it up, do not be afraid;
>> say to the towns of Judah,
>> 'Here is your God!'
> [10] See, the Sovereign LORD *comes with power*,
>> *and his arm rules* for him.
> See, his reward is with him,
>> and his recompense accompanies him.
> [11] *He tends his flock like a shepherd*:
>> *He gathers the lambs in his arms*
> and *carries them close to his heart*;
>> *he gently leads those that have young.*

(Isa. 40:1–11)

In these words of comfort come the official notice that Israel's slavery is over (v. 2). The call out of cruel bondage in exile is even more dramatic in Isaiah 49:9: 'Say to the captives, "Come out," and to those in darkness, "Be free!"' A comparison with the bondage of Egypt is found early in the book: 'O my people who live in Zion, do not be afraid of the Assyrians, who beat you with a rod [20] and lift up a club against you, as Egypt did' (10:24; cf. 52:4). A similar call to freedom comes in 48:20:

> Leave Babylon,
> flee from the Babylonians!
> Announce this with shouts of joy
> and proclaim it.
> Send it out to the ends of the earth;
> say, 'The LORD has redeemed his servant Jacob.'

The role of God as redeemer (*gô'ēl*) is central to the theology of chapters 40 – 66 (Dijkstra 1999) and integral to the second exodus construct (Holmgren 1973: 71–96). Hope is grounded in YHWH's redemption in 43:1–2:

> But now, this is what the LORD says –
> he who created you, O Jacob,
> he who formed you, O Israel:
> 'Fear not, for I have *redeemed* you;
> I have summoned you by name; you are mine.
> When you pass through the waters,
> I will be with you;
> and when you pass through the rivers,
> they will not sweep over you.'

A second important element is 'the way' of/for the LORD, mentioned in 40:3. Other passages mention the journey along 'roads' through the wilderness (cf. 42:16; 49:9; Ps. 23:3). But the motif of a particular 'way' (*derek*) recalls exodus/wilderness language (Stuhlmueller 1970: 67–73). It was the Lord who 'made a way [*derek*] through the sea, a path [*nĕtîbâ*] through the mighty waters' (43:16). He was the one who 'made a road [*derek*] in the depths of the sea so that the redeemed

---

[20] See J. T. Willis (1990) for discussion of Isaiah's frequent, symbolic use of the word pair 'rod' (*šēbeṭ*) and 'staff' (*maṭṭeh*), especially for Assyrian oppression. Willis reports that the words appear separately in twelve passages and seven times as a pair.

might cross over' (51:10).[21] YHWH will reveal himself again as Israel's true leader.

A third element from the wilderness tradition is the 'glory' (*kĕbôd*) of the Lord which accompanied them (40:5; cf. Exod. 40:34–38; Stuhlmueller 1970: 95–98). In words clearly reminiscent of the first exodus, Isaiah elsewhere promises, 'But you will not leave in *haste*[22] or go in flight; for the LORD will go before you, the God of Israel will be your *rear guard*' (52:12; cf. Exod. 13:21ff.; 14:19–20). While the primary purpose of the original cloud was the revelation of God to his own people, the whole world was also an implied 'audience' (cf. Exod. 14:19ff.; Isa. 66:18; Motyer 1993: 300).

Another important motif in this passage is God's 'word' (*dābār*) which determines the course of history (v. 8). The message of Isaiah 40 – 55 in particular is predicated on the Lord's control over history, that is, his ability to make his word come to pass (e.g. 46:9–10).[23] But God's word as *tôrâ* was also central to the original wilderness journey, and so it is in this part of Isaiah (42:4, 21; 51:4, 7; cf. 2:3).

The word is especially appreciated for its power to create,[24] a featured element in the (creation and) exodus traditions (Stuhlmueller 1970: 169–192; Mann 2000). Theologically, the exodus story gave testimony to a *new creation* (cf. F. M. Cross 1973: 112–144). History – specifically the history of redemption – came to be understood as a continuation of God's creating work (cf. Fretheim 1991: 166–168; Levenson 1988). The prophet anticipates the *re-creation* of God's people (via a purified remnant) and the revivification of Zion as a new Garden of Eden (51:3).[25]

Another second exodus motif prompted Westermann (1969: 12) to call chapters 40 – 66 the 'gospel of joy'. The rejoicing that followed the first exodus (Exod. 15) is echoed in Isaiah 40:9 (cf. 52:8). Commands to exult and rejoice (41:16; 51:11; 52:9; 54:1; 55:1) are

---

[21] The power of God over the sea is, for Isaiah, an important precedent demonstrating God's ability (and intention) to save his people (50:2; 51:10).

[22] The term for 'haste' (*ḥippāzôn*) is only used here and in Exodus passages (Exod. 12:11; Deut. 16:3). For Isaiah 'the way' in the second exodus 'appropriately escalates' (Hugenberger 1995: 124) the elements of the first redemption. The conviction that the new work of God will be better than the first is likely behind the unusual exhortation to 'forget' the former things in 43:18 (cf. 46:9).

[23] Notice the persistence of the first person future (English: 'I will') throughout these chapters.

[24] Isaiah uses *br* for YHWH's new work in 41:20 and 65:17, 18, a verb exclusively used of God in creation contexts (Gen. 1:1 et al.; Isa. 40:26, 28; 42:5 et al.). This term is also used in reference to Israel's origin as a people in Isa. 43:1, 15.

[25] New life is one of the motifs in the shepherd psalm (Ps. 23:3).

directed specifically to local inhabitants (42:11ff.); the ends of the earth (42:10); the sea and desert (42:10ff.); wild beasts of the desert (43:20); heaven and earth; and mountains and trees (44:23; 49:13; 55:12).[26]

Isaiah 40:3–4 illustrates the profound effect of God on the wilderness environment. He is the road-builder who levels the mountains and valleys. In chapter 41 the dramatic transformation of the desert is the result of YHWH's power (and compassion), which produces miraculous fertility[27] and abundant water:

> [17]The poor and needy search for water,
>   but there is none;
>   their tongues are parched with thirst.
> But I the LORD will answer them;
>   I, the God of Israel, will not forsake them.
> [18]I will make rivers flow on barren heights,
>   and springs within the valleys.
> I will turn the desert into pools of water,
>   and the parched ground into springs.
> [19]I will put in the desert
>   the cedar and the acacia, the myrtle and the olive.
> I will set pines in the wasteland,
>   the fir and the cypress together,
> [20]so that people may see and know,
>   may consider and understand,
> that the hand of the LORD has done this,
>   that the Holy One of Israel has created it.
>   (Isa. 41:17–20)

The provision of water is explicitly set against the backdrop of the wilderness traditions in 43:16, 19 (Mann 2000: 144). The one who 'made a way through the sea' is making a new 'way in the desert and streams in the wasteland' (43:19; cf. 48:21). Even the animals know that 'I provide water in the desert . . . give drink to my people, my chosen' (43:20). The one who guides can be expected also to provide.

---

[26] Of all the allusions, this motif is the hardest to defend as necessarily from the first exodus. However, see its prominent place in Ps. 105:43.

[27] The image of a fertile desert is found in 55:12–13, the passage that brings to a close Isa. 40 – 55. Thus, the image of the second exodus is an inclusio framing this important section.

YHWH's role as shepherd becomes explicit in his nurturing activities in 40:11: 'He tends his flock like a shepherd. He gathers the lambs in his arms and carries them close to his heart; he gently leads those that have young.' The comfort and tenderness at the beginning of this passage is, in the concluding line, revealed to characterize YHWH's leadership. As he had done in the first exodus, he will again tend (*r'h*), gather (*qbṣ*), carry (*nś'*) and gently lead (*nhl*) his flock. Such promises are similar to those in 42:16, expressed by other verbs common to the wilderness traditions: 'I will lead [*hlk*, Hiphil] the blind by ways they have not known, along unfamiliar paths I will guide [*drk*, Hiphil] them.'

It is striking that the nurturing role of the divine Shepherd described in 40:11 is preceded by the image of a powerful God whose 'arm rules for him' (v. 10).[28] This is not ironic for those familiar with pastoral realities. The protective shepherd towards outsiders is the providing shepherd towards his own flock. *For Isaiah, the power of God is fundamental to his ability to empower* (vv. 26–31; Mann 2000: 151).[29] The 'arm of the Lord' is an important metaphor for YHWH's strength, especially with respect to human rulers. It was the arm of the Lord that led Israel out of Egypt (Exod. 15:16; cf. Deut. 4:34; 5:15 et al.). The comfort offered the exiles is a result of God's powerful leadership:

> Awake, awake! *Clothe yourself with strength,*
>   *O arm of the* LORD;
> awake, as in days gone by,
>   as in generations of old.
> Was it not you who cut Rahab to pieces,
>   who pierced that monster through?
>   (Isa. 51:9; cf. v. 12)

The second exodus tradition represents a new age of tender compassion coming on the heels of God's judgment of the nations.

[28] Recall here that shepherd language was often used for military leadership in antiquity and in the Bible. Brettler (1998: 118–119) assumes that 'shepherd' is a sub-metaphor of the 'king' metaphor, rather than appreciating it as a general image for rulers, including all the roles associated with kingship (e.g. military).

[29] If, as Carr (1995) suggests, 40:9 is the beginning of a new section, then the themes of God's power and care are joined in this introduction. J. D. W. Watts (1987: 83–89) similarly sees an 'arch' pattern to vv. 10–31, a section he titles 'The Lord Yahweh Comes like a Shepherd'. However, Freedman (1987) defends a view of vv. 1–10 as a chiasm. It is likely that these two verses serve as a (typical) Isaianic bridge that both summarizes and anticipates.

One of the final passages in Isaiah recalls God's leadership by the hands of his human shepherds. Isaiah 63:7 – 64:11 is a communal lament that describes God's history of gracious dealings with his rebellious people in the first wilderness. The purpose of this lament is to invigorate effective intercession, typified by Moses (Clifford 1989), to seek the return of the 'angel of his presence' who had 'carried [nś'] them all the days of old' (63:9; cf. 40:11; Exod. 19:4; Deut. 32:11). In Isaiah 63:11 God is expected once again to remember 'the days of yore – Moses! his people!' (trans. Motyer 1993: 514–515). The lament asks:

Where is He who brought them up out of the sea with the
    shepherds [30] of His flock?
Where is He who put His Holy Spirit in the midst of them,
Who caused His glorious arm to go at the right hand of Moses,
Who divided the waters before them to make for Himself an
    everlasting name,
Who led them through the depths?

(Isa. 63:11–13 NASB)

The lament seeks the return of God's rest- and direction-giving Spirit:

... like cattle that go down to the plain,
    they were given rest [nwḥ] by the Spirit of the LORD.
This is how you guided [nhg] your people
    to make for yourself a glorious name.

(v. 14)

The hope is that now, when Israel had itself become a wilderness (cf. 64:10), God would hear this intercession and remember his ancient promises (63:16).

Servant and servants

Here is my servant, whom I uphold,
    my chosen one in whom I delight;
I will put my Spirit on him
    and he will bring justice to the nations.

(Isa. 42:1)

---

[30] Though some translations use the singular 'shepherd' (assuming only Moses), the MT is plural, indicating either all of Israel's leaders during the wilderness period or, perhaps, the siblings Moses and Aaron (cf. Ps. 77:20 [H 21]).

Second exodus imagery in Isaiah 40 – 55 surrounds references to a distinct but ambiguous figure, the Servant of YHWH. The designation 'Servant' is used most often in these chapters for Jacob/Israel (41:8–9; 43:10; 44:1, 21; 45:4; 49:3). This follows the identification for Israel in Moses' final words specifically in the context of their inevitable exile (Deut. 32:36, 43). However, Isaiah's Servant is also an individual, perhaps with royal qualities (e.g. 49:6–7).[31] Certainly as we have noted, *ṣĕdāqâ* (righteousness), *mišpāṭ* (judgment) and *šālôm* (peace) are characteristics of the reigns of ideal kings. And the notion of king as 'corporate personality' is evident throughout the historical books. But a more comprehensive explanation for the Servant may be as a second Moses, the prototype for both prophets and kings in Israel (Hugenberger 1995).[32] If Hugenberger's explanation is correct, then the evidence for a second Moses and a second exodus is mutually reinforcing.[33]

While granting the plausibility of second Moses typology, the generic (and ambiguous) [34] nature of the Servant should still be appreciated. Kings and prophets were frequently called '(my) servant(s)'. This umbrella term keeps the focus on the accountability that an individual (or group) has before their Lord.[35] Servants do not exist for themselves, but as agents for someone else's purposes. Thus, the role of Isaiah's 'Servant' has more to do with his divinely ordained assignment in the plan of YHWH than with the parameters of his institutional position. In a book laced with criticism for presumptuous rulers, the simple term 'servant' effectively circumscribes the role God has for his human agent(s). Isaiah is clear about the ironies of biblical leadership: to rule is to serve and to suffer, and to lead is to be *both* shepherd and sacrificial lamb.

As this section of Isaiah comes to a close, the notion of an individual 'Servant' is replaced by references to the Lord's

---

[31] Schultz (1995) has recently made a cautious defence for the royal identity of the Servant. This view is supported by the recent studies of Rowe (2002: 63–84), based on literary analysis, and Walton (2003), who proposes a royal enthronement setting for the servant song in 52:13 – 53:12. While this *Sitz im Leben* would explain the unusual references to atoning sacrifice, such an occasion is not described in any of the Bible's historical texts.

[32] See O'Kane's (1996) observations regarding Isaiah himself as a second Moses.

[33] See his discussion on pp. 122–128.

[34] Recall that ambiguity surrounds early references to a 'messianic' figure in Isaiah.

[35] Paul (1968) discusses the interchangeability in cuneiform inscriptions of the terms 'shepherd' and 'servant', both of which emphasize the role of the king as a deputy of the gods.

'servants'.[36] The single mention of this group in 54:17 anticipates its reference ten times in chapters 56 – 66 (56:6; 63:17; 65:8, 9, 13 [3x], 14, 15; 66:14). This democratizing of God's plan is similarly evident when the promise to David is mentioned once in chapter 55, and only as the basis for renewed commitment *to the community*: 'I will make an everlasting covenant with you [pl.], my faithful love promised to David' (55:3; cf. Eissfeldt 1962). Isaiah ends with a grand vision of God's direct reign over his reconstituted community. In the coming age, God's people will take up their original calling as a 'kingdom of priests' (Exod. 19:6): 'And you will be called priests of the LORD, you will be named ministers of our God' (61:6; cf. 4:3). In that new order, members of the nations will join them as priests and Levites for the Lord (66:21). The remarkable presence of foreigners in the final visions of Isaiah (esp. ch. 56; cf. 14:1) anticipates the 'other sheep' of Jesus' ministry in John 10:16. In Isaiah 56:8, 'The Sovereign LORD declares – he who gathers the exiles of Israel: "I will gather *still others* to them besides those already gathered."' But we must first turn to the intervening history the prophet so eloquently foretold.

---

[36] See Beuken (1990), who sees the servants as the main theme of chs. 56 – 66, and Berges (2000), who compares Isaianic 'servants' terminology with usage in Books 4 and 5 of the Psalms.

Chapter Seven

Jeremiah: righteous shepherds

Jeremiah, Moses and the wilderness

They did not ask, 'Where is the LORD,
who brought us up out of Egypt
and led us through the barren wilderness...?
(Jer. 2:6)

As Isaiah had predicted, the kingdom of Judah fell to Babylon in
586 BC. It was the destiny of an unwilling prophet to shepherd the
community through this horrendous ordeal. Jeremiah is known for
his reluctant response to God's call, the irresistible force of God's
word in his life, the rejection he experienced by the people of Judah,
and his transparent 'confessions' through which he voiced honest
criticism of the divine programme. In these ways Jeremiah picks up
the mantle of the ancient prophetic prototype, Moses (cf. Seitz 1989).
Jeremiah returns relentlessly to the Mosaic covenant as the justification for his warnings and as the basis for his faith in its continued
vitality. Like Moses, Jeremiah continues to mediate God's word to
his people as prophet and to intercede for them as priest, even when
forbidden. For both, the burden of leadership was often oppressive.
In one of his many laments, Jeremiah provides a graphic description
of his own experience of rejection, 'like a gentle lamb led to the
slaughter' (11:19). In another he protests, 'I have not run away from
being your shepherd' (17:16).[1] The merging of his own identity
(and fate) with the community's (J. A. Thompson 1980: 88–92) is
remarkably similar to the experience of Moses.

The connection between Moses and Jeremiah runs deeper.[2] At this
crucial hinge in Israel's history Jeremiah realizes that the people are

---

[1] Although some early versions (and later commentators) vocalize the consonants to
read 'trouble' (*mērā'āh*), the MT participle form (*mērō'eh*) employs the metaphor of
shepherd, which is used at least once later for prophets (see below on 50:6).

[2] See Holladay (1989: 35–70) for a full treatment of Jeremiah's interaction with
previous (biblical) traditions. He also provides a useful summary of Jeremiah's
influence on succeeding traditions (ibid. 80–95).

returning, in a theological sense, to the wilderness. His oracles begin purposefully[3] with a reminder of the marital love they had shared in the *midbār*: 'I remember the devotion of your youth, how as a bride you loved me and followed me through the desert, through a land not sown' (Jer. 2:2). As will be typical in Jeremiah's messages, the image is part of a rhetorical snare. Israel forgot the one who had shown her his love in the desert:[4]

> This is what the LORD says:
> 'What fault did your fathers find in me,
>   that they strayed so far from me?
> They followed worthless idols
>   and became worthless themselves.
> They did not ask, "Where is the LORD,
>   who brought us up out of Egypt
> and led us through the barren wilderness,
>   through a land of deserts and rifts,
> a land of drought and darkness,
>   a land where no-one travels and no-one lives?"
> I brought you into a fertile land
>   to eat its fruit and rich produce.
> But you came and defiled my land
>   and made my inheritance detestable.'
>
> (Jer. 2:5–7)

The prophet blames Israel's three types of leaders for this travesty:

> 'The *priests* did not ask,
>   "Where is the LORD?"
> Those who deal with the law did not know me;
>   the leaders [lit. *shepherds*] rebelled against me.
> The *prophets* prophesied by Baal,
>   following worthless idols.

---

[3] Though it is common to see the book of Jeremiah as a mosaic of oracles and editorial additions, there is general agreement that the first twenty chapters reflect messages by the prophet given early in his ministry.

[4] This intimate view of the wilderness period has led some to posit a 'nomadic ideal' in ancient Israel (Budde 1895; Flight 1923). Talmon (1966; cf. Fox 1973) has criticized this view appropriately for retrojecting a monastic ideal into the OT and for ignoring the clear trajectory of the (short) wilderness sojourn towards (long-term) land ownership. However, the desert was the place of birth for the community, a new creation modelled after the Genesis pattern, and a time from which exilic prophets derived hope.

Therefore I bring charges against you again,'
declares the LORD.

(2:8–9)

The means of divine judgment were the 'roaring lions' (foreign kings)[5] that wasted the holy land (v. 15).

The first twenty chapters of Jeremiah are rich in figures of speech, and among the most persistent are these that are grounded in pastoral life. In Jeremiah 3 unfaithful Israel is encouraged to return to her lord, who promises to provide her with 'shepherds after my own heart, who will lead [lit. *shepherd*] you with knowledge and understanding' (v. 15). Here is the first hint that there is a plan to replace – not just remove – the leaders who had failed them. More importantly, the phrase 'after my own heart' provides hope for a promised heir on *David's* throne (cf. 1 Sam. 13:14). These future Davidides will shepherd with knowledge and understanding/prosperity (*śkl*).[6]

The importance of *śkl* as a trait of shepherd rulers[7] is evident further in 10:21 where Jeremiah castigates Judah's kings: 'The shepherds are senseless [*b'r*] and do not enquire [*drš*] of the LORD; so they do not *prosper* [*śkl*] and all their flock is scattered [*pwṣ*]'[8] (cf. 1 Sam. 18:14). By using the root *b'r*, Jeremiah introduces the ironic image of shepherds who have no more sense than the animals for whom they care. Worse, they have the effect of predators, scattering the flock whose protection was their responsibility. As a result of poor leadership, the people of Israel were scattered (i.e. deported) and Jacob's pastureland (*nāweh*; v. 25) was turned into a 'haunt of jackals' (v. 22).

Canaan, once a symbol of agricultural fertility, becomes nothing more than a *midbār* again in chapter 12. The enemies of Judah are 'shepherds [who] will ruin my vineyard and trample down my field; they will turn my pleasant field into a desolate wasteland' (v. 10). This devastation is attributed to lack of good leadership, 'because there is no-one who cares' (v. 11). As northern raiders take captive the

---

[5] Near Eastern royal propaganda regularly depicted kings as devouring lions. While Assyria and Egypt are in mind here, Babylon is the lion elsewhere (4:7; 5:6). Symbolism is used for other pastoral predators and threats: leopards (5:6), serpents (8:17), the desert wind (4:11) and malevolent shepherds (6:3).

[6] Jeremiah frequently uses words with double or ambiguous meanings.

[7] For the attribution of wisdom traits to kings, see McKane (1983; on v. 15 see p. 88).

[8] Scattering is a standard covenant curse (Deut. 4:27; 28:64); divine gathering is a gracious covenant promise (Deut. 30:3).

'LORD's flock' (13:17),[9] the shepherds of Israel are called into account: 'Where is the flock that was entrusted to you, the sheep of which you boasted?' (13:20)

Judgment on Israel's shepherd rulers

> Woe to the shepherds who are destroying and scattering the sheep of my pasture! (Jer. 23:1)

The first twenty chapters of Jeremiah are followed by two appendices, the first of which concerns Judah's royal leaders (21:1 – 23:8).[10] In this section Judah's last kings from Josiah to Jehoiachin are mentioned (explicitly or implicitly),[11] except Zedekiah who was the currently reigning king. This appendix is the 'climax of and response to the collection of oracles about kings' (Klein 1980: 167). Surfacing here is the prophetic tendency to use shepherd language in criticism of royalty (Gottlieb 1967: 199).

Jeremiah's sustained critique reflects the fundamental royal ideal of justice, a value that became severely compromised following Josiah's revival. A summary statement is given to the 'house of David' in 21:12:

> This is what the LORD says:
>
> 'Administer justice every morning;
> rescue from the hand of his oppressor
> the one who has been robbed,
> or my wrath will break out and burn like fire
> because of the evil you have done...'

In 22:1–5 this traditional standard for royal behaviour is elaborated for those who sit on 'David's throne' (mentioned twice in vv. 2, 4). In the centre of the appendix's chiastic structure (Lundbom 1997: 133–136) Jehoiakim especially is criticized for oppression and

---

[9] Pastoral symbolism begins in v. 16 with feet stumbling on 'darkening hills' (i.e. as a flock waits for the morning light) and continues through v. 20 where what meets their eyes are the armies from the north (McKane 1986: 301).

[10] Some commentators begin this section at 21:11, but Lundbom (1997: 45–47) makes a good case for vv. 1–10 matching 23:1–8 as frames for the appendix.

[11] Josiah (implicitly, 22:10); Shallum/Jehoahaz (vv. 11–12); Jehoiakim (vv. 18–19); Jeconiah (vv. 24–30).

violence (22:13–17). He had built his own palace by mistreating workers and shedding innocent blood. This abuse of power was, fundamentally, a failure to understand the character of YHWH; care of the needy is 'what it means to know me' (v. 16; cf. 21:12). Jehoiakim's efforts to 'live like a king' in palaces of cedar [12] would only get him a donkey's burial (v. 19) and no heir on the throne (v. 30). In this grave indictment Jeremiah predicts a wind (i.e. Babylon) that will, literally, 'shepherd away all your shepherds' [13] (v. 22). Captivity will bring the self-exalting cedar-builders to shame and humiliation (v. 22).

Jeremiah does more than condemn this last of several self-centred kings. By predicting that none of his heirs will sit on 'the throne of David' (mentioned again in v. 30), the prophet is calling into question the permanence of the Davidic covenant. If no Davidic heir in this generation will sit on the throne, will there *ever* be one?

The climax to the appendix answers this question. A final woe on Judah's shepherds is followed by an amazing promise of divine intervention, including the installation of a future Davidic king. This passage is worth looking at in detail.

[1]'Woe to the shepherds who are destroying and scattering the sheep of my pasture!' declares the LORD. [2]Therefore this is what the LORD, the God of Israel, says to the shepherds who tend my people: 'Because you have scattered my flock and driven them away and have not bestowed care on them, I will bestow punishment on you for the evil you have done,' declares the LORD. [3]'I myself will gather the remnant of my flock out of all the countries where I have driven them and will bring them back to their pasture, where they will be fruitful and increase in number. [4]I will place [14] shepherds over them who will tend them, and they will no longer be afraid or terrified, nor will any be missing,' declares the LORD.

[5]'The days are coming,' declares the LORD,
'when I will raise up to David a righteous Branch,

---

[12] Dubbink (2001) provides a useful assessment of the emphasis on cedar (used four times in ch. 21), a symbol of royal pretension (cf. 2 Sam. 5, 7). The destruction of the proud cedars provides the backdrop for the blossoming of the sprout of David (Jer. 23:5).

[13] Jeremiah is fond of such verbal redundancy (cf. 23:2, 5).

[14] The Hiphil of *qwm* is used here and in v. 5 ('raise up') for direct divine appointment of leadership.

a King who will reign wisely
and do what is just and right in the land.
[6] In his days Judah will be saved
and Israel will live in safety.
This is the name by which he will be called:
The LORD Our Righteousness.

[7] 'So then, the days are coming,' declares the LORD, 'when people will no longer say, "As surely as the LORD lives, who brought the Israelites up out of Egypt," [8] but they will say, "As surely as the LORD lives, who brought the descendants of Israel up out of the land of the north and out of all the countries where he had banished them." Then they will live in their own land.' (Jer. 23:1–8) [15]

The first four verses follow a chiastic structure (Craigie et al. 1991: 325) that emphasizes the reversal of the flock's fate as a result of YHWH's caring intervention on behalf of *his* flock.[16] He will personally undo the scattering, driving away and lack of care with his own gathering, bringing back and caring for them (Klein 1980).

A Woe to shepherds destroying my flock (v. 1)
  B You yourself[17] scattered, thrust out, didn't 'take care of' my flock (v. 2a)
    C I will 'take care of' you (v. 2b)
  B′ I myself will gather,[18] bring back my flock (v. 3)
A′ I will raise up shepherds who will shepherd the flock (v. 4)

The rulers of Judah had done exactly the opposite of what they were expected to do as shepherds of God's flock. Therefore God holds them personally responsible [19] for the destruction (*'bd*) [20] and scattering

---

[15] While there are discernible sub-sections here (vv. 1–4, 5–6, 7–8), I follow J. A. Thompson (1980: 485–486) and Kuyvenhoven (2003) in seeing the final shape as vv. 1–8.

[16] The personal pronoun is used four times in the first three verses.

[17] The emphasis in the 'B' lines (yourself/myself) is achieved in Hebrew by the use and (first) position of the personal pronoun in each phrase.

[18] Gathering scattered people is a typical refrain in Mesopotamian royal literature, especially present when a king was intent on legitimizing his ascension (Widengren 1984).

[19] It is characteristic of Jeremiah to lay blame for the exile on the leaders, but to insist that there is ultimate divine causality ('the countries where *I* have driven them'; v. 3).

[20] Typically meaning 'to destroy', this verb likely refers in pastoral contexts to losing (i.e. allowing to stray; cf. Ezek. 34:4, 16). However, the verb appropriately captures the prophetic message that passive neglect is tantamount to active killing (cf. Ezek. 34:5).

(*pwṣ*) of his people (v. 1). The principle of *lex talionis*[21] is emphasized by a play in verse 2 on the Hebrew root *pqd* (translated 'bestow care/punishment' in the NIV and 'take care of' in our outline above).[22] As an expression of his ongoing commitment to his flock, the Lord promises to place new shepherds over them, those who will *really* shepherd them (*rō'îm wěrā'ûm*; v. 4; Holladay 1986: 615).[23] The result will be a flock without fear and without loss.[24]

The promise of new shepherds is preceded by hints of a new creation (Craigie et al. 1991: 327; Mulzac 2000: 40). The phrase 'be fruitful and multiply' appears first in the Garden of Eden (Gen. 1:22, 28), then following the flood (Gen. 9:1, 7), and again prior to the creation of the nation of Israel (Exod. 1:7, 10, 12, 20). Fruitfulness (and peace; Jer. 23:6) are covenant blessings (Deut. 6:3 et al.) and symptoms of the age to come (cf. Amos 9:11–15; Hos. 2:21–23; Ezek. 36; Zech. 8:9–13).

The second oracle in this short section is also in chiasm (Craigie et al. 1991: 329):

> **A** God will raise up a legitimate/righteous ruler (v. 5a–c)
>> **B** This king will reign with success/prosperity and righteousness (v. 5d)
>>> **C** He will bring justice and righteousness (v. 5e–f)
>> **B'** Judah/Israel will be delivered and safe (v. 6a–b)
> **A'** God will call him 'YHWH our Righteousness' (v. 6c–d)

Viewing the structure clarifies the emphases: the centre of God's plan is a new king who will reign according to the ideals of justice and righteousness. However, the agent for this plan is God himself, emphasized in the frame (A, A').

Righteousness is an important element throughout the passage. The Davidic ruler would be a *ṣemaḥ ṣaddîq*, a righteous or legitimate shoot who will *really* reign as king (*mālak melek*; v. 5). Jeremiah again toys with the ambiguousness of a Hebrew root (*ṣdq*). His emphasis may be on the formal *legitimacy* of the (Davidic) shoot or on the *character* of his reign in terms of the royal (Davidic)

---

[21] 'An eye for an eye, a tooth for a tooth.'

[22] Turning-of-the-tables judgment is characteristic of Jeremiah (31:28; cf. 29:10) and Dtr literature in general (Deut. 28:63).

[23] Significantly, the future holds a succession of capable rulers and not exclusively the Davidic shepherd mentioned below.

[24] The Niphal of *pqd* is used here with yet another meaning, 'to be missing' (cf. Num. 31:49; 1 Sam. 25:7).

ideal.[25] Verse 5 describes a reign of success/prosperity (*śkl*) as a result of the doing (*'āśâ*) of justice and righteousness (*mišpāṭ uṣĕdāqâ*) in the land. Only in such a realm does the flock of YHWH enjoy safety.

The final use of *ṣdk* comes in the name of the Davidic king, *yhwh ṣidqēnû* ('The LORD our Righteousness'; v. 6). Jeremiah is employing subtle rhetorical strategies again. Zedekiah (*ṣidqiyâ*), whose name means 'My[26] Righteousness is the Lord', is implicated as the one who *should* have been a true son of David. Thus the one unnamed king is perhaps present in the most conspicuous way. The reversal of Israel's fate by the replacement of her leaders is complete when God puts someone on the throne whose name reverses the current king's name (Klein 1980: 170) and gives it true substance. *God's* naming of the promised king is a less-than-subtle reminder that the last rulers of Judah were named by the *Babylonian* king.[27] As puppets of another suzerain, they were unqualified to represent the true King of Israel.

Verses 7–8 provide more evidence that a new covenant is under way. It is not enough for Jeremiah to say that God is going to do something miraculous by bringing Israel back to their land. It is not even enough to say further that this event will be *similar* in scope or purpose to the first exodus and the Sinai covenant. Jeremiah understands this new thing as the reconfiguring and reconstitution of that covenant. The Sinai Torah begins with the identification of YHWH as the one who 'brought you out of Egypt'. That central credal statement is going to be changed. The exilic community will look back to this second exodus as their founding moment: 'As surely as the LORD lives, who brought the descendants of Israel up out of the land of the north and out of all the countries where he had banished them' (v. 8; cf. 16:14–15).

A new covenant with a regathered flock

The people who survive the sword
will find favour in the desert.
(Jer. 31:2)

---

[25] Perhaps Jeremiah wants to maintain ambiguity by suggesting both.

[26] The change in pronoun in the names is important. Righteousness will not only be an attribute of the king but of the whole people. The very purpose for which a shepherd's authority is granted is the care of God's flock (Holladay 1986: 619).

[27] Throne names were given to Shallum (Jehoahaz), Coniah (Jehoiachin) and Mattaniah (Zedekiah).

The merging of promises for a messianic figure and a Messianic Age in chapter 23 anticipate themes more fully developed later in the book. Chapter 33 provides an extended picture of these 'coming days' (v. 14) when a righteous shoot from David will grow and bring justice and righteousness to the earth (v. 15). At that time the city of Jerusalem will wear the name 'The LORD Our Righteousness' (v. 16). YHWH emphasizes the permanence of his promises to David, giving them an immutable character like the seasons (vv. 25–26).

Chapter 33 follows a collection [28] of spectacular promises of Israel's restoration culminating with a new covenant that will exceed the Mosaic covenant in effect (31:33–34). Before this second Sinai YHWH will be a shepherd to them in their wilderness. With covenant language reminiscent of the exodus, the Lord promises Israel's renewal:

> [1] 'At that time,' declares the LORD, '*I will be the God of all the families of Israel, and they shall be My people.*' [2] Thus says the LORD, 'The people who survived the sword *found grace in the wilderness* – Israel, when it went to find its *rest.*' [3] The LORD appeared to him from afar, saying, '*I have loved you with an everlasting love; Therefore I have drawn you with lovingkindness.*' (Jer. 31:1–3 NASB)

Renewal is emphasized with the word 'again' ('*ôd*) in the following verses: '*Again* I will build you and you will be rebuilt, O virgin of Israel! *Again* you will take up your tambourines, and go forth to the dances of the merrymakers. *Again* you will plant vineyards on the hills of Samaria; The planters will plant and will enjoy them' (Jer. 31:4–5 NASB).

Shepherd imagery emerges as explicit connections to exodus traditions increase:

> [8] See, I will *bring them* from the land of the north
> and *gather them* from the ends of the earth.
> Among them will be the blind and the lame,
> expectant mothers and women in labour;
> a great throng will return.
> [9] They will come with weeping;
> they will pray as I bring them back.

---

[28] Chs. 30 – 31 are often called the 'Book of Consolation'. J. A. Thompson (1980: 551ff.) includes chs. 32 – 33.

I will lead them beside streams of water
  on a level path where they will not stumble,
because I am *Israel's father,*
and Ephraim is *my firstborn son.*
[10] Hear the word of the LORD, O nations;
  proclaim it in distant coastlands:
'He who scattered Israel will *gather them*
  and will watch over his flock like a shepherd.'
[11] For the LORD will *ransom* Jacob
  and *redeem* them from the hand of those stronger
    than they.
[12] They will come and *shout for joy on the heights of Zion*;
  they will rejoice in the bounty of the LORD –
the grain, the new wine and the oil,
  the young of the flocks and herds.
They will be like a well-watered garden,
  and they will sorrow no more.

(Jer. 31:8–12)

The Lion of heaven judges the shepherds of Babylon

> Weep and wail, you shepherds;
>   roll in the dust, you leaders of the flock.
> For your time to be slaughtered has come.
>
> (Jer. 25:34)

We now turn our attention to the presence of shepherd language in the sections of the book that give structure to its final shape. The literary hinge of MT Jeremiah is chapter 25 (Kessler 1999). Following the prediction of a seventy-year Babylonian captivity for Judah, the prophet warns of punishment for Nebuchadnezzar, the 'servant of YHWH'.[29] The cup of God's wrath was to be given to all those who participated in punitive measures taken against Israel. The Lion of heaven prepares to pounce on those shepherds who have preyed on the flock of God (cf. 49:19–21).

---

[29] Nebuchadnezzar (25:9; 27:6; 43:10) is among three figures in Jeremiah singled out as a servant of YHWH. Cf. David (33:21, 22, 26) and Jacob (i.e. Israel; 30:10; 46:27, 28). Although Jeremiah is not identified as YHWH's servant, he is one of the prophets who are regularly considered by YHWH as 'my servants' (7:25; 26:5; 29:19; 35:15; 44:4; cf. 25:4).

> [34] Weep and wail, you shepherds;
> roll in the dust, you leaders of the flock.
> For your time to be slaughtered has come;
> you will fall and be shattered like fine pottery.
> [35] The shepherds will have nowhere to flee,
> the leaders of the flock no place to escape.
> [36] Hear the cry of the shepherds,
> the wailing of the leaders of the flock,
> for the LORD is destroying their pasture.
> [37] The peaceful meadows will be laid waste
> because of the fierce anger of the LORD.
> [38] *Like a lion* he will leave his lair,
> and their land will become desolate
> because of the sword of the oppressor
> and because of the LORD's fierce anger.
> (Jer. 25:34–38)

The Lord despises the shepherds and 'majestic ones' (*'addîrîm*; v. 34) [30] of the flocks and will destroy (*šdd*) their pastures (*mar'îtām*; v. 36). Just as punishment for the leaders of Israel followed the law of retribution, so also the judgment of the proud rulers of the nations will mirror their own abusive behaviour.

Babylon is the primary focus of the final words of Jeremiah recorded in chapters 50 – 51. Until recently these additional oracles were considered somewhat superfluous to the organization of the book. However, with the work of Aitken (1983) and Kessler (2003), these oracles are now appreciated as integral to the overall message of MT Jeremiah. To an important extent they provide a summary of the themes which have emerged throughout the collection.

Aitken (1983) identifies in these two chapters five movements organized in chiasm. The first (50:4–20) and last (51:45–53) movements [31] echo images of Israel rushing from Babylon as the Lord prepares to punish the idolatrous city. Graphic pastoral imagery is integral to the prophet's words in chapter 50: [32]

---

[30] 'Flock-masters' is also a suitable translation (Nah. 3:18; Hareuveni 1991: 78), in which case it is in parallel to 'shepherds'.

[31] Aitken's analysis (1983: 30) identifies a framework around the five movements consisting of YHWH's announcements of Babylon's destruction in 50:2–3 and 51:54–58.

[32] The word *ṣō'n* (flock) is the first and last word of this quoted section.

141

> [6] My people have been lost sheep;
> their shepherds have led them astray
> and caused them to roam on the mountains.
> They wandered over mountain and hill
> and forgot their own resting place.
> [7] Whoever found them devoured them; [33]
> their enemies said, 'We are not guilty,
> for they sinned against the LORD, their true pasture,
> the LORD, the hope of their fathers.'
> [8] Flee out of Babylon;
> leave the land of the Babylonians,
> and be like the goats that lead the flock.

(Jer. 50:6–8)

The image of a flock lost/destroyed (*'bd*) may recall the mischief caused by political shepherds in 23:1. However, reference to leading sheep astray (*t'h*, Hiphil) brings to mind false prophets whose deceptive leadership was a grave, though more subtle, threat to the community's destiny (23:13, 32; cf. Mic. 3:5). A similar action is 'causing them to roam' (*qere*: *šwb*, Polel). A favourite verb of Jeremiah's, *šwb* [34] is suitable for emphasizing the literal return from exile as well as the spiritual repentance which would necessarily precede God's favour. Here the form suggests pushing people into apostasy.[35] This defect in their leadership reduced Israel to prey before their enemies, who assumed they could devour God's flock with impunity.

The pastoral imagery in verse 7 includes two unusual expressions for the Lord. The 'hope' (or 'gathering point')[36] of the fathers is unique. YHWH is called their 'true pasture' (*něwēh ṣedeq*) only here and in 31:23, where it refers to Jerusalem. Notice how Jeremiah persists in involving the root *ṣdq* (legitimate/righteous) in pastoral imagery. Consider the subtle shift in the traditional image of the land of promise as Israel's pasture (e.g. Exod. 15:13; Jer. 23:3). The

---

[33] The picture of sheep being devoured (*'kl*) by predators is developed in a gruesome way in v. 17 below: 'Israel is a scattered flock [lit. 'a stray lamb'] that lions have chased away. The first to devour him was the king of Assyria; the last to crush his bones was Nebuchadnezzar king of Babylon.'

[34] This root occurs over 100 times in Jeremiah, more than in any other biblical book.

[35] It is possible to read this line (with the *ketib*) as the 'mountains which led them astray'. See Hareuveni (1991: 98–101) for a geographical explanation of this rendering.

[36] Taking an alternate meaning of the root *qwh* with LXX (cf. Dahood 1967; Hareuveni 1991: 52–54).

conception of the Lord himself as Israel's pasture is a significant theological development, the kind of spiritualizing characteristic of Jesus' teaching.

The final verse has other hints of a new exodus. They are encouraged to flee[37] Babylon,[38] to leave like a flock of sheep and goats whose gate has just swung open. However, the whole community is now encouraged to behave like *'attûdîm*, goat-leaders who determine the pace and direction for the rest of a flock (cf. Isa. 14:9; Zech. 10:3). In this subtle way Jeremiah reinforces the reality anticipated in the new covenant: *every member of the community* will have the ability to respond in faith (Van Hecke 2003: 73), following the law of the true Shepherd written on their hearts.

Second exodus imagery continues in this chapter with God himself gathering his scattered and maimed flock: 'But I will bring Israel back to his own pasture and he will graze on Carmel and Bashan; his appetite will be satisfied on the hills of Ephraim and Gilead' (v. 19). However, the Shepherd will not be content merely to rescue his flock and reverse their fate. They had been abused by the 'lion' Babylon. Israel's redemption, as it was in the first exodus, is tied to God's judgment on their oppressor.

> [44]*Like a lion* coming up from Jordan's thickets
>   to a rich pasture-land,
> I will chase Babylon from its land in an instant.
>   Who is the chosen one I will appoint for this?
>   Who is like me and who can challenge me?
>   And what shepherd can stand against me?
> [45]Therefore, hear what the LORD has planned against Babylon,
>   what he has purposed against the land of the Babylonians:
> The young of the flock will be dragged away;
>   he will completely destroy their pasture because of them.
>
> (Jer. 50:44–45)

As a protective shepherd of his own flock YHWH becomes like a lion who destroys the 'flocks' of the Babylonian 'shepherds'/'lions'. In keeping with biblical justice, Babylon will suffer the fate they determined for themselves by their treatment of others.

---

[37] While this verb (*nwd*) typically means to wander (i.e. aimlessly), in Jeremiah it can be a parallel of *nws* (e.g. 49:30), suggesting flight.

[38] Along with the exodus pattern there is also here an echo of Abraham's call to leave the land of Babylon in Gen. 12 (Kessler 2003: 204–205).

The message of Jeremiah is compatible with the outlook of Kings and Chronicles. Although the history of kingship in the covenant community was more negative than positive, *the prophetic 'solution' is not a return to pure theocracy.* In a sense, this also was a failure. Instead God promises to *reinvigorate* the Davidic covenant with one who truly matches the royal ideal. This promise is matched by a plan to *revive* the Sinai covenant in a way that makes true holiness for everyone in the community possible (31:33–34). Anticipation for the Shepherd of Israel to return is mounting. So also is an expectation for this democratizing of leadership among his flock.

Chapter Eight

Ezekiel: the faithful shepherd

The wilderness covenant

As I judged your fathers in the desert of the land of Egypt, so I will judge you, declares the Sovereign LORD. I will take note of you as you pass under my rod, and I will bring you into the bond of the covenant. (Ezek. 20:36–37)

The prophet Ezekiel, like Jeremiah, ministered in the wake of the destabilizing catastrophe of 586 BC. Both prophets declared the destruction of Jerusalem as inevitable. More specifically, both prophets explained the devastation as God's deliberate *judgment on Judah's shepherd leaders*.[1]

The coming judgment called into question all of Israel's sacred institutions and the 'covenants' or divine promises on which they were founded. Would deportation mark the permanent end of their occupation of the Promised Land? Would the departure of God's Spirit/glory mean the end of his promised presence on Mount Zion? Would the exile of the Davidic kings (with which the book opens) signal the end of the 'eternal' dynasty of God's chosen ruler? These questions reflect a more fundamental concern: was there any hope left for the covenant relationship between YHWH and his people? Ezekiel, like the prophets before him, answers these questions in a positive way. But a hopeful future is described[2] only after a legal justification for the judgment is first detailed.

Ezekiel intentionally employs themes and motifs from the original exodus/wilderness/Sinai traditions to make his case. By recounting Israel's various vices in legal terminology (originating with the Sinai covenant), the prophet effectively justifies God's decision to abandon his people to the natural consequences of their choices and to the curses of the Mosaic covenant. As a Zadokite priest, Ezekiel is acutely aware of the contrast between God's holiness (the intended

---

[1] For the many ways Ezekiel follows Jeremiah see Zimmerli (1979: 43–52).

[2] Hints of the new age (described in full in chs. 34–48) occur in 11:16–21; 14:22–23; 16:60–63; 17:22–24; 20:39–44.

characteristic feature of the covenant community) and the current 'uncleanness' of his land and temple. The root for uncleanness or pollution, *ṭm'*, is primarily used in the Old Testament in Leviticus and Numbers (167 times) and in Ezekiel (35 times). Ezekiel watches the glory cloud (*kĕbôd*) – the manifestation of God's presence first witnessed in the original wilderness – leave the temple as a result of the defilement (9:3ff.; 10:4ff.; 11:22–23). Expressions of religious apostasy were matched by widespread injustice and exploitation of the poor. The prophet's criticism of the rulers for both is scathing (e.g. ch. 11). Like an ungrateful and unfaithful wife (betrothed in the wilderness), they had shamed him before the nations. Therefore he *will* divorce her (ch. 16). The explanatory refrain borrowed from the Sinai covenant is '(for) I am the LORD your God'.[3]

But theodicy[4] is not Ezekiel's final point. God's right to terminate his obligations to Israel becomes the background for underscoring the unmerited and *unexpected* nature of the *restoration* of his people to their favoured status. In their new wilderness, God makes to the purged remnant promises of regathering, resurrection and renewal. The dry bones of Israel would be infused with new life. In place of their hearts of stone would beat new hearts of flesh, freshly empowered to keep the laws of the Torah (36:26–27; cf. 11:16–21). In place of corrupt and sacrilegious leaders, an ideal God-fearing Davidic king would rule (34:23–24; 37:22–25). Like the exiles themselves, the *kĕbôd* of YHWH would return and take up residence in a purified land. There YHWH would inhabit his new temple, purified from its pollution (43:4–5). The question about God's presence would be permanently answered by the name of the ideal city: 'The LORD is there' (48:35).[5]

Ezekiel reveals the prophetic word in unusual ways. His 'living parables' were extreme dramatizations of the fate of Israel (e.g. 24:16ff.). Ezekiel does more than dramatize; like Moses,[6] he is required to join the community in their punishment, to experience personally their corporate destiny. The prophet uses graphic metaphorical language in the communication of his messages (Kohn 2003:

---

[3] For a tradition-historical discussion of this phrase (which occurs 80 times in the Torah and 86 times in Ezekiel), see Zimmerli (1982: 1–28).

[4] See Raitt (1977: 83–105) for a helpful discussion of theodicy (the vindication of God's justice in light of suffering) in Ezekiel.

[5] One can scarcely help but contrast this closing verse of Ezekiel with that of Judges. Anarchy prevailed when there was no (human) king and is only overcome when the divine King reigns in the midst of his people.

[6] For a full survey of the Mosaic elements in Ezekiel's ministry, see McKeating (1994).

19–20). Like the prophets before him (Hosea, Isaiah, Jeremiah), Ezekiel employs traditional images, though often embellishing them into full allegories (e.g. ch. 16) or nuancing them in surprising ways (e.g. chs. 26 – 32).[7] Metaphors are enlisted to engage the affective as well as cognitive faculties of Ezekiel's listeners. One of his extended metaphors involves the scattering of YHWH's sheep at the hands of self-serving shepherds (ch. 34). Though the image is familiar, Ezekiel teases out numerous 'entailments' of the metaphor, first to accuse and then to inspire hope.

Ezekiel and the leaders of Israel[8]

> Her officials within her are like wolves tearing their prey; they shed blood and kill people to make unjust gain. (Ezek. 22:27)

Before we consider Ezekiel's view of leadership more fully, it is helpful to consider the overall structure of the book and to locate the leadership passages within this literary framework. Chapters 1 – 24 describe the judgment of Judah, necessitated especially by their idolatry. The allegory of the unfaithful wife (ch. 16) is a metaphorical replacement for Israel's perspective on their own history. (They questioned why *YHWH* should be unfaithful to *them*!) As in the indictment in the chapters that follow, Ezekiel is explicit about Israel's chronic history of rebellion *since the days of the exodus itself.* We will briefly summarize the prophet's interpretation of the exodus in chapter 20, the basis not only for his criticism but also for his hope for a new exodus.

Following this provocative collection of judgment oracles, the prophet shifts the focus to judgment (also by the hand of Babylon) on surrounding nations who either caused or laughed at Judah's plight (chs. 25 – 32). The prophet's special focus on the hubris of their rulers is noteworthy. The kings of Tyre and Egypt are singled out for the kind of arrogance which presumes divinity (28:2).[9] The humbling of these rulers and their empires is essential to the universal recognition of YHWH as Lord of all.

---

[7] See Newsome's (1984) insightful analysis of these metaphors.

[8] The following section owes much to a book by the same title (Duguid 1994).

[9] Ezekiel maintains the notion from the Torah that setting up anything in place of God (including oneself) is blasphemous, but he also follows the Torah's remarkable teaching that (all) humans (not just kings) are made in the image and likeness of God. Thus his view of human leadership is not totally negative. For an exploration of the subtle dimensions of Ezekiel's anthropology, see Kutsko (2000) and Callender (2000).

The hinge of the book of Ezekiel is chapter 33, a text which serves both as recapitulation [10] of the previous words of judgment and as signal of a new era. The prophet's call as 'watchman' (ṣōpeh) is reissued (3:17; 33:2, 6, 7). As the Babylonian armies invade Jerusalem – confirming Ezekiel's former words of judgment – the prophet's ability to speak returns (33:22). Only now is he free to articulate words of hope.[11] The chapters that follow (34 – 48) are hope-producing descriptions of a new age. We might ask why this new section begins with an extended parable of the shepherds of Israel. This metaphor, like those earlier in the book, graphically supplements and crystallizes Ezekiel's message. It too contains a word of judgment (i.e. against the corrupt shepherds). But the verbal picture ultimately involves the direct involvement of the divine Shepherd who will restore his flock and appoint a worthy (Davidic) shepherd to serve at his side. Thus, the new era of peace, security and blessing *will begin with a change in leadership*. New leadership, as we discuss in more detail below, is not so much a change in form as in substance. All that follows in Ezekiel assumes the proper reign of God as (shepherd) King over his people and the restoration of appropriately loyal regents (undershepherds) who serve him.

Ezekiel not only criticizes Judah's rulers; he *blames* them for the imminent apocalypse. His critique, found throughout the book, takes the shape of both metaphor (chs. 17, 19, 34) and direct address (21:25–27 [H 30–32]; 22:6, 25; 43:7–9; 45:8–9; 46:18). Along with these explicit references are portrayals of ideal future leaders, descriptions that clearly highlight the missing qualities of Israel's final kings. Like the prophetically condemned kings of the surrounding nations, these rulers function as foils for the coming prince.

The parable of chapter 17 is a story of an eagle (Nebuchadnezzar) who is rejected by the cedar sprig (Jehoiachin) and spreading vine (Zedekiah) it planted. Zedekiah is condemned for not keeping faith with the Babylonian king and, by extension, breaking covenant with YHWH himself. The picture in chapter 19 is of a mother lion (Jerusalem?) whose bloodthirsty and reckless cubs (Jehoahaz and Jehoiachin?) learned to 'tear their prey and devour men' (vv. 3, 6).

---

[10] Compare the comments of Zimmerli (1983: 183ff.) with Block (1998: 234–236). Wendland (2001: 91) describes the chapter as both 'transitional and resumptive', but argues for its integral placement at the beginning of chs. 33 – 37.

[11] Ezekiel's loss of speech in 3:26, 24:27 and 33:22 underscores the pivotal nature of these chapters in the structure of the book.

Though their origin was like a vine in a land of fertility (vv. 10–11), their self-imposed destiny became the desert (v. 13). In this indictment is a subtle reference to the loss of the sceptre,[12] once the product of its many branches (cf. 21:10, 13). In righteous anger YHWH demands, 'Take off . . . the crown' (21:26).

Ezekiel finds beastly behaviour characteristic of Israel's leaders in every institution. These provocative but ambiguous images are complemented by decisively direct language punctuated with predatory images:

> [25]There is a conspiracy of her princes within her *like a roaring lion tearing its prey*; they devour people, take treasures and precious things and make many widows within her. [26]Her priests do violence to my law and profane my holy things . . . [27]Her officials within her are *like wolves tearing their prey*; they shed blood and kill people to make unjust gain. [28]Her prophets whitewash these deeds for them by false visions and lying divinations . . . [29]The people of the land[13] practise extortion and commit robbery; they oppress the poor and needy and ill-treat the alien, denying them justice. [30]I looked for a man among them who would build up the wall and stand before me in the gap on behalf of the land so I would not have to destroy it, but I found none. (Ezek. 22:25–30)

The last kings of Judah had, like David (2 Sam. 12:1–12) and Ahab (1 Kgs 21), made a fatal leadership mistake that was built upon a faulty supposition. Abusing others was an expression of the arrogant assumption that power is primarily privilege rather than responsibility. In a succinct summary the prophet says that 'each of the princes of Israel . . . *uses his power to shed blood*' (22:6). By contrast, Ezekiel sees ahead to a day when the community will be led by a prince who is satisfied with his own possessions (45:8–9). He will understand that 'none of my people will be separated from his property' (46:18). The fundamental assumption of the eschatological prince is that *only God can call them 'my people'*.

---

[12] For Gen. 49:10 (the promise of a sceptre to Judah) as background to Ezek. 21:32, see Moran (1958).

[13] The designation *'am hā'āreṣ* ('people of the land') is sometimes used to refer to a group of influential people in Judah (cf. Oppenheimer 1977). In Ezekiel's eyes, they shared the same responsibility for mischief as the official rulers (cf. 7:27; 22:29).

The exodus as paradigm

> I will bring you from the nations and gather you from the countries where you have been scattered – with a mighty hand and an outstretched arm and with outpoured wrath. (Ezek. 20:34)

The first twenty-four chapters of Ezekiel are words of judgment that both implicate Israel and vindicate YHWH. Two chapters in this section identify Israel's rebellion as a characteristic feature since the beginning of her covenant relationship with YHWH. Chapter 16 is the allegory of the unfaithful wife and chapter 20 is the summary of Israel's history. It is important for our purposes to appreciate Ezekiel's view of the exodus, because it will have important implications for his perspective on a *new* exodus.

Ezekiel 20 details Israel's sojourn in Egypt (vv. 5–8), deliverance by YHWH (vv. 9–10), the two wilderness generations (vv. 10–25), the giving of the law in the wilderness (vv. 11–13, 25–26) and entry into the land (v. 28).[14] The prophet emphasizes the idolatrous rebellion of Israel which began even in Egypt (20:7–8; cf. 23:3, 8; Josh. 24:2, 14; Ps. 106:7). The account of rebellion is placed in contrast to the gracious initiative of YHWH, who brought them into the wilderness to give them his laws (vv. 10–12). The summary moves back and forth between the people's rebellion and God's grace. Thankfully, though the people have not changed, neither has YHWH. What brings hope to the current rebellious generation is the continuing commitment of God to honour his own name among the nations (vv. 9, 14, 22; cf. Deut. 9:28; Ezek. 20:9, 14). On this basis Ezekiel holds out hope for another wilderness in which God will cull and reassemble his flock.

> [33] As surely as I live, declares the Sovereign LORD, I will rule over you with a mighty hand and an outstretched arm and with outpoured wrath. [34] I will bring you from the nations and *gather* you from the countries where you have been scattered – with a mighty hand and an outstretched arm and with outpoured wrath. [35] I will bring you into the desert of the nations and there, face to face, I will execute judgment upon you. [36] As I judged your fathers in the desert of the land of Egypt, so I will judge you, declares the Sovereign LORD. [37] I will take note of you as you *pass under my rod*,

[14] For a thorough analysis of this passage in light of Pentateuchal allusions, see Greenberg (1983: 360–388).

and I will bring you into the *bond of the covenant.* [38] I will purge
you of those who revolt and rebel against me. Although I will
bring them out of the land where they are living, yet they will not
enter the land of Israel. Then you will know that I am the LORD.
(Ezek. 20:33–38) [15]

Ezekiel, like Isaiah and Jeremiah before him, understands the exodus
as more than a significant historical event. *It is a paradigm for God's
eschatological work among his people.* Out of their current experience of bondage and 'wilderness', God will again lead his people
like a shepherd (ch. 34). The book ends with this prophet as a *new*
Moses [16] giving *new* law regarding the *new* community and its
new temple.

The shepherd(s) of Israel

I myself will search for my sheep and look after them. (Ezek.
34:11)

Ezekiel's most theologically developed leadership exposé is his *māšāl*
on sheep and shepherds in chapter 34. In this extended metaphor
we find a summary of the themes and perspectives that dominate
the prophetic understanding of leadership. It is quite in keeping with
prophetic tradition that Ezekiel embodies these themes and perspectives in pastoral metaphor. The first half of the chapter begins with an
indictment of the current shepherds of Israel with a vivid depiction of
their incongruous behaviour (vv. 1–10). [17] It is followed by the Lord's
announced intention to judge the shepherds and systematically to
reverse the condition of the flock (vv. 11–16). The second half of the
chapter begins with God's judgment between his sheep and his
appointment of a new shepherd, 'my servant, David' (vv. 17–24).
The final segment paints in the details of the new order, characterized
by peace and prosperity (vv. 25–31). Our discussion will follow
Ezekiel's flow of thought, one section at a time.

The passage begins with a vivid – and tragically ironic – picture of
sheep that are abused by those charged to care for them:

---

[15] On the semantic links between this passage and Exod. 6:6–8, see Fishbane (1979:
131–132).

[16] See Patton (1996: 85–89) and Kohn (2002: 249–250).

[17] While reconstructed divisions in this chapter vary in small details, the following is
satisfactorily defended by Greenberg (1997: 705–709) and Wendland (2001).

[1]The word of the LORD came to me: [2]'Son of man, prophesy against the shepherds of Israel; prophesy and say to them: "This is what the Sovereign LORD says: Woe to the shepherds of Israel who only take care of themselves! Should not shepherds take care of the flock? [3]You eat the curds, clothe yourselves with the wool and slaughter the choice animals, but you do not take care of the flock. [4]You have not strengthened the weak or healed the sick or bound up the injured. You have not brought back the strays or searched for the lost. You have ruled them harshly and brutally. [5]So they were scattered because there was no shepherd, and when they were scattered they became food for all the wild animals. [6]My sheep wandered over all the mountains and on every high hill. They were scattered over the whole earth, and no-one searched or looked for them."' (Ezek. 34:1–6)

Hired shepherds in 'the real world' were expected to be self-sacrificing in their work, increasing a flock's numbers by careful attention to their needs. Those who were faithful were given a modest portion of the produce as pay. In contrast, Ezekiel depicts shepherds who show no regard for the obvious needs of the flock, and – especially to the point – they appear *oblivious to the expectations inherent in their role as undershepherds*. Shepherds were not expected simply to tend a flock; they were serving its owner. The perennial problem with kingship was the tendency to forget *whose* the people were (Deut. 17:20a).

Neglect in shepherding is tantamount to abuse. Without due diligence to the sick and strays – and healthy – a flock is quickly decimated. Consequently Ezekiel can accurately say that the sheep were scattered because there was 'no shepherd'. The details in this account convey how extreme the abuse had become. The 'shepherds of Israel'[18] had been actively consuming the products and the flock,[19] with disregard for the consequences. These shepherds 'ruled them harshly and brutally' (v. 5; cf. Jer. 10:21).[20] The irony of this picture is all the more stark for Ezekiel, who looks back frequently to the Sinai covenant for his perspective. The word translated 'brutally' in

---

[18] The term shepherd is for Ezekiel, like Jeremiah, one that likely encompasses more than the royal office, though. The plural may here reflect his focus on the behaviour of the last kings (since Josiah).

[19] Greenberg (1997: 697) notes the progression from legitimate perquisites to dubious gratuities to gross violation (cf. Lev. 3:17; 7:23; 1 Sam. 2:29).

[20] Contrast the concerns expressed by Jacob for his flocks in Gen. 33:13.

v. 4 (*perek*) is only found in the context of Egyptian slavery (Exod. 1:13–14), a condition Israelites were expressly forbidden to duplicate among themselves (Lev. 25:43, 46, 53).

Israel's rulers had become like the 'wild animals' for which the flock now became food (v. 6). Ezekiel is thus comparing them to the foreign kings under whose harsh rule the people were straining. By their cruel treatment and senseless disregard of God's flock, the kings of Israel had become the accomplices of their enemies, preying on the very people they were called to protect.

The final words of this segment reveal personal pastoral concern behind the forceful indictment: 'My sheep wandered ... they were scattered ... and no-one searched or looked for them' (v. 6). This sentiment prepares the hearers for the unexpected climax in the parable: *God himself will come looking for his lost sheep.*

First, the grounds for the verdict are summarized and a sentence is pronounced:

> [7]Therefore, you shepherds, hear the word of the LORD: [8]As surely as I live, declares the Sovereign LORD, because my flock lacks a shepherd and so has been plundered and has become food for all the wild animals, and because my shepherds did not search for my flock but cared for themselves rather than for my flock, [9]therefore, O shepherds, hear the word of the LORD: [10]This is what the Sovereign LORD says: I am against the shepherds and will hold them accountable for my flock. I will remove them from tending the flock so that the shepherds can no longer feed themselves. I will rescue my flock from their mouths, and it will no longer be food for them. (Ezek. 34:7–10)

As undershepherds Israel's leaders were servants of their heavenly Master, stewards of *God's* flock, not their own. What other choice does the divine Owner have but to give them their just deserts? Rescuing his own sheep from the mouths of these self-serving shepherds (v. 10), YHWH will remove them from office and let them suffer an ignominious death (cf. 12:12–13).

God's gracious intervention is as unexpected as the behaviour of his shepherds. The following verses reveal God's intention personally to reverse their misdeeds.[21]

---

[21] The contents of these first two sections are arranged in chiasm, thus reinforcing the movement of reversal (Greenberg 1997: 706).

[11] For this is what the Sovereign LORD says: *I myself* will search for my sheep and look after them. [12] As a shepherd looks after his scattered flock when he is with them, *so will I* look after my sheep. *I will* rescue them from all the places where they were scattered on a day of clouds and darkness.[22] [13] *I will* bring them out from the nations and gather them from the countries, and *I will* bring them into their own land.[23] *I will* pasture them on the mountains of Israel, in the ravines and in all the settlements in the land. [14] *I will* tend them in a good pasture, and the mountain heights of Israel will be their grazing land. There they will lie down in good grazing land, and there they will feed in a rich pasture on the mountains of Israel.[24] [15] *I myself will* tend my sheep and make them lie down, declares the Sovereign LORD. [16] *I will* search for the lost and bring back the strays. *I will* bind up the injured and strengthen the weak, but the sleek and the strong *I will* destroy. *I will* shepherd the flock with justice. (34:11–16)

Hope for the sheep that are lost or scattered among the nations is anchored in God's determined and direct intervention (cf. 11:17; 20:34, 41; 36:24). He will systematically reverse their fate. Before, no-one 'looked for' them (*drš*; *bqš*; v. 6); now, *the Lord* will 'look for' (*drš*; v. 11) and 'look after' them (*bqr*; vv. 11, 12). Before, they wandered (*šgh*; v. 6) and were scattered (*pwṣ*; vv. 5, 6); now, *the Lord* will deliver (*nṣl*; v. 12) and gather them (*qbṣ*; v. 13). The mountains on which they were once shepherdless (v. 5) will become the mountains on which *the Lord* will shepherd them (v. 13). Instead of brutality (v. 4), they will lie down in green pastures, well fed and without fear (vv. 14–15). The once neglected stray (*ndḥ*), sick (*ḥlh*), weak (*ḥlh*) and abandoned (*'bd*) (v. 4) will have their caring Shepherd search for (*bqš*), recover (*šwb*), bandage (*ḥbš*) and strengthen (*ḥzq*) them (v. 16).

The terms Ezekiel uses are familiar to us from the shorter passage in Jeremiah 23, which perhaps inspired this message. The most

---

[22] This natural image, threatening for both shepherd and flock, is likely a metaphor for God's day of judgment (30:3). Graciously, it is also a day after which God will rescue his flock (Allen 1990: 162).

[23] There may be in these words also an element of confrontation with the kings of Babylon, who used shepherd language in their propaganda. Merodach-baladan II, for example, called himself 'the shepherd who gathers those who have strayed' (Duguid 1994: 39). The emphasis, then, would be on the first person pronoun: '*I* will rescue ... *I* will gather ... *I* will bring them back ...' (i.e. *not* the kings of this world).

[24] Parallels to this verse in Akkadian literature project the association between external peace (achieved by a militant shepherd ruler) and the resultant peaceful grazing and rest of a nation (Tomback 1982: 93–96).

obvious terms come from *r'h* (cf. Jer. 23:1, 2, 4), a root used thirty-two times in Ezekiel 34. Jeremiah also used the conventional image of scattered (*ndḥ*; *pwṣ*) sheep (Jer. 23:2). Similarly, God's response was to gather (*qbṣ*) and recover (*šwb*) his flock (Jer. 23:3).[25] Both passages emphasize the flock (*ṣō'n*) of God. Of its twenty occurrences in Ezekiel 34, the divine owner is in view thirteen times. The compassion of God is stirred for '*my* sheep' (*ṣō'nî*). The metaphor of God the Shepherd, associated with the wilderness traditions, became the touchstone for conceptualizing for the exilic community a new exodus with a renewed covenant in the Promised Land.

The first half of the message closes with the highly charged word 'judgment' (*mišpāṭ*).[26] *Mišpāṭ* can mean justice (the supreme characteristic of good government) or judgment (judicial decree). The word here brings with it a sober realization that harmony will not come simply from the dramatic rescue envisioned. The judgment of the 'sleek and the strong' is a prerequisite for the era of peace. So also is a continuous *reign* of justice.

The second half of the chapter (vv. 17–31) describes a just (*špṭ*; vv. 16, 17, 20) new order which brings with it peace and prosperity. The repetition of key terms from the first half reveals that a comprehensive reversal of bad leadership is planned: fat (*bārî*; vv. 3, 28), weak (*ḥlh*; vv. 4, 21), scattered (*pwṣ*; vv. 5, 6, et al., 21), plunder (*baz*; vv. 8, 22, 28), food for beasts (*'oklâ*; vv. 5, 7, 28) and deliver (*nṣl*; vv. 12, 27).[27]

The first eight verses (vv. 17–24) detail the indictment of bullying animals followed by the appointment of David as a new shepherd. The upbeat vision of regathering is necessarily followed by a depiction of systematic justice on overbearing sheep. Once God's complete purging takes place, then he will place his Davidic deputy on the throne. Notice that judgment among the sheep is predicated on the Lord's ownership of the flock:

[17]As for you, *my flock*, this is what the Sovereign LORD says: I will judge between one sheep and another, and between rams and

[25] Other shared terms from the section below include *qwm* for the appointment of David, *špṭ* for the essential quality of justice in his reign, and *bṭḥ* for the security which that reign provides.
[26] The final comment about justice among the sheep may be an (added) editorial bridge into the next section.
[27] This section shares several elements with Jer. 30:8–11: breaking the yoke, slavery, the appointment of David, quiet, God's presence to deliver, scattering among the nations, and justice.

goats. [18] Is it not enough for you to feed on the good pasture? Must you also trample the rest of your pasture with your feet? Is it not enough for you to drink clear water? Must you also muddy the rest with your feet? [19] Must *my flock* feed on what you have trampled and drink what you have muddied with your feet? [20] Therefore this is what the Sovereign LORD says to them: See, I myself will judge between the fat sheep and the lean sheep. [21] Because you shove with flank and shoulder, butting all the weak sheep with your horns until you have driven them away, [22] I will save *my flock*, and they will no longer be plundered. I will judge between one sheep and another. [23] I will place over them one shepherd, my servant David, and he will tend them; he will tend them and be their shepherd. [24] I the LORD will be their God, and my servant David will be prince among them.[28] I the LORD have spoken. (Ezek. 34:17–24)

There is an animal hierarchy in a mixed flock; males (rams and bucks) typically dominate females, and goats naturally dominate sheep. A shepherd's control over a flock is based on the collaboration of the males and goats with his leadership. The words for ram (*'ayil*) and goat (*'attûd*) consequently became metaphorical terms for community leaders (Ezek. 17:13; Jer. 50:8). Like the abusive shepherds, these sub-leaders are censured for self-serving and destructive behaviour. They feed themselves first and then ruin the pasture for others. They drink first and then befoul the water for others. This intracommunity dysfunction reinforced unacceptable disparities between the 'fat' and the 'lean'.

The metaphor is plumbed further: the indictment includes shoving and butting with the horns. The owner sees the plight of his weak sheep, scattered (*pwṣ*) by the unrestrained force of the ornery and self-absorbed stronger animals (v. 21). Poor leadership by the shepherds was mirrored by the behaviour of the animals with power. With great irony, God must now rescue his own flock *from themselves* (v. 22). Once again, this act of deliverance (for some) rides on the back of judgment (for others): 'I will judge between one sheep and another' (v. 22).

Only after all of this work, attributed to the divine Shepherd, is David introduced as the appointed human shepherd. 'His role begins

---

[28] Though the place of the prince 'among' (*bĕtôk*) the people might suggest an egalitarian view of government, Duguid (1994: 48–49) is right in balancing the collegial aspect with the authority implied by the appointment of a shepherd 'over' (*'al*) them (v. 23).

after the restoration has been achieved by God, at his initiative, and in his time' (Block 1995: 177). Only at this point in the message is the question of the vitality of God's covenant with David answered decisively. The Lord [29] will place over them, or appoint (*qwm*, Hiphil), 'one [30] shepherd, my servant David'.

The role of David is overshadowed by the direct involvement of God and conditioned on the king's subordination. His service to the community is a function of being selected by God to be the servant of God among God's people. Like Isaiah and Jeremiah before him, Ezekiel sees hope for Israel directly located in YHWH's personal role as protecting, providing and judging Shepherd. Only in the wake of God's intervention – *and in deference to God's ultimate rule* – can a human shepherd maintain the divinely established order. In that ideal situation, human leadership understands itself in terms of *service*. The prophetic perspective on human leadership is reinforced in verse 24: 'I the LORD will be their God, and *my servant* David [31] will be prince among them.' [32]

The final segment of this section of Ezekiel 34 guarantees a prosperous and peaceful future, though without any further mention of specifically Davidic rule. Here the language becomes briefly more literal as the scourge of exile is replaced by the bounteous physical blessings of a new covenant.[33] As in the first exodus, God's people will be freed from their bondage, rescued by the Shepherd who calls them, once again, 'my people' and 'the sheep of my pasture':

[25] I will make a covenant of peace with them and rid the land of wild beasts so that they may live in the desert and sleep in the forests in safety. [26] I will bless them and the places surrounding my hill. I will send down showers in season; there will be showers of

[29] YHWH's personal appointment is a prerequisite for Israelite kingship in Deut. 17:14–20 and is here, perhaps, set in contrast to the appointment of kings over Judah by Babylon (Zedekiah) and Egypt (Jehoiakim).

[30] Ezekiel's reference to the singularity (*'eḥād*) of the ruler may be a way of emphasizing his uniqueness, i.e. in the eschatological era, especially in contrast to Israel's previous rulers. The notion of a single ruler may also reinforce the vision of a unified people (cf. 37:22).

[31] The phrase 'my servant David' is used twice in ch. 34 (vv. 23, 24) and twice in ch. 37 (vv. 24, 25).

[32] Ezekiel's preference for the term 'prince' (*nāśî'*) rather than king (*melek*) is important, as will be explained below.

[33] In the background are the original covenant blessings of Lev. 26:4–13 and words of hope for their renewal in Hos. 2:20–23.

blessing. [27]The trees of the field will yield their fruit and the ground will yield its crops; the people will be secure in their land. They will know that I am the LORD, when I break the bars of their yoke and rescue them from the hands of those who enslaved them. [28]They will no longer be plundered by the nations, nor will wild animals devour them. They will live in safety, and no-one will make them afraid. [29]I will provide for them a land renowned for its crops, and they will no longer be victims of famine in the land or bear the scorn of the nations. [30]Then they will know that I, the LORD their God, am with them and that they, the house of Israel, are my people, declares the Sovereign LORD. [31]*You my sheep, the sheep of my pasture, are people, and I am your God, declares the Sovereign LORD.* (34:25–31)

The 'covenant of peace' (v. 25) is an unusual way of referring to guaranteed eschatological blessing (found only in Num. 25:12, Isa. 54:10, Ezek. 37:26 and here). In this passage it echoes the Sinai promise from Leviticus 26:6: 'I will grant peace in the land, and you will lie down and no-one will make you afraid. I will remove savage beasts from the land, and the sword will not pass through your country.'[34]

Ezekiel's references in verses 26–27 to 'showers in season' (*haggešem bĕ'ittô*), the trees providing their fruit (*piryô*) and the land its produce (*yĕbûlâ*), and secure dwelling (*beṭaḥ*) provide conclusive evidence of the prophet's indebtedness to the fuller passage in Leviticus:[35] 'I will send you rain in its season [*gišmêkem bĕ'ittām*], and the ground will yield its crops [*yĕbûlâ*] and the trees of the field their fruit [*piryô*] ... and you will eat all the food you want and live in safety [*beṭaḥ*] in your land' (Lev. 26:4–5).

As the blessings of the Sinai covenant are in the background, so also is the exodus event itself, described in Leviticus 26:13: 'I am the LORD your God, who brought you out of Egypt so that you would no longer be slaves ['*ăbādîm*; cf. Ezek. 34:27] to the Egyptians; I broke the bars of your yoke [*môṭōt 'ullĕkem*; cf. Ezek. 34:27] and enabled you to walk with heads held high.' In the wake of this new deliverance they will enjoy living securely, without fear (Ezek.

---

[34] Isaiah similarly saw such an era of peace and justice associated with a fresh outpouring of the Holy Spirit (Isa. 32:15–18; cf. Ezek. 36:26–27).
[35] For a fuller treatment of the relationship between Lev. 26 and Ezek. 34, see Zimmerli (1979: 51). For a current critical perspective on intertextuality between Ezekiel and the Torah, see Kohn (2002).

34:28b; cf. Lev. 26:5–6; Jer. 30:10), and their shame will be removed (Ezek. 34:29c).[36]

The implementation of a new (or renewed) covenant is highly important for Ezekiel, as it was for Jeremiah. The formulaic language with which this passage comes to a close (v. 31) recalls the original language of Sinai. *The grand visions of the new order constitute a return to the foundations of the old order.* As he was once known in the wilderness of Sinai, YHWH will again be the Shepherd of his people.

The Davidic 'prince'

My servant David will be king over them, and they will all have one shepherd ... and David my servant will be their prince for ever. (Ezek. 37:24–25)

The hope-filled visions of Ezekiel in the rest of the book return to many of the concerns raised in chapter 34. For example, the dry bones prophecy in chapter 37 recapitulates YHWH's regathering of the lost from exile (v. 21) and their resettlement in the Promised Land (vv. 12–14, 25) as a reunified people (vv. 15–19, 22)[37] under the reinstituted rule of David (vv. 22, 24). The specific terminology of chapter 34 is evident especially in the last verses:

My servant David will be *king* over them, and they will all have *one shepherd*. They will follow my laws and be careful to keep my decrees. They will live in the *land* I gave to my servant Jacob, the *land* where your fathers lived. They and their children and their children's children will live there for ever, and *David my servant will be their prince for ever.* I will make a *covenant of peace* with them; it will be an everlasting *covenant.* I will establish them and increase their numbers, and I will put my sanctuary among them for ever. My dwelling-place will be with them; *I will be their God, and they will be my people.* Then the nations will know that I the Lord make Israel holy, when my sanctuary is among them for ever. (Ezek. 37:24–28)

---

[36] 'Heads held high' is taken as the reversal of heads bowed in shame. For a fuller discussion on shame in the literature of the exile and diaspora, see Laniak (1998).

[37] The union of two sticks as images for a newly unified people is comparable to the two symbolic shepherd staffs in Zech. 11:4–17. The unity of 'Israel' as the reconstituted people of God is an important concept in exilic and post-exilic literature.

While this passage uses the term *melek* (king) for David,[38] it also employs *nāśî'* (prince), Ezekiel's preferred designation for leaders.[39] Here again we find the prophet drawing from the well of wilderness traditions to nuance his images of the future. The term *nāśî'* is used extensively in the book of Numbers (over fifty times) for pre-monarchical rulers in the wilderness period. Its occurrence elsewhere in the Bible is minimal, except in Ezekiel where the term is used thirty-three times. While Ezekiel's usage of the term varies, sometimes serving simply as a synonym for *melek*, its prevalence in the wilderness stories contributes to the prophet's larger programme of understanding the future in terms of the past.[40]

The term *nāśî'* is not only a way of recalling the wilderness for Ezekiel, however. It is also a rhetorical mechanism for controlling the typical associations (i.e. abuses) of royalty. As with *rō'eh* (shepherd), servant and *nāgîd*, the choice of this general term emphasizes delegated (and therefore accountable) authority. For Ezekiel, as with his prophetic predecessors, royal prerogatives are regularly placed within the context of divine suzerainty. Ezekiel prefers a term that effectively reveals lines of continuity with Israel's most ancient regime, and one that simultaneously reinforces the boundaries on such leadership as prophetically understood.[41]

With his own unique grammar, Ezekiel summarizes the theology of leadership encountered in earlier traditions. Human leaders are expected – and encouraged – in YHWH's economy. Following episodic direct interventions, divine leadership is willingly entrusted again to human deputies (as it was at the creation). The divine preference for human agency is amazingly resilient. Ezekiel's vision

---

[38] Block (1995: 179 n. 38) explains that *melek* is chosen in this context because *gôy* (nation) rather than *'am* (people) is used (v. 22). The unification of a nation is a specifically royal function.

[39] This passage also refers to David as 'my servant' and 'shepherd'.

[40] The secondary discussion on the term *nāśî'* is extensive and still without consensus. Speiser (1963) understood its use as deliberate archaizing on the part of the prophet, noting its peculiar absence in the literature of the monarchical period (ibid. p. 111). Levenson (1976: 57–107) has made perhaps the strongest case for its exclusive meaning within the Sinai tradition, seeing the *nāśî'* as an apolitical messiah of the coming restoration. But Speiser (1963) also noted the tendency for *nāśî'* to be used for leaders with smaller kingdoms than those described by *melek*. Thus Joyce (1998: 331) can speak of a 'downgrading of royal language' in Ezekiel (cf. 1 Kgs 11:34). Duguid (1994) defends the reasonable view we have adopted that the term is preferred as a way of emphasizing the ruler's contingent or vassal status (i.e. before God).

[41] The LXX solves the ambiguity surrounding Ezekiel's usage of *nāśî'* by employing two different Greek words: *archontes*, for wicked kings in chs. 1 – 39, and *ēgoumenoi*, for idealized kings in chs. 40 – 48 (Raurell 1986: 85–89).

ends with many references to the *nāśî'* as governor in the new city. But the ultimate issue in Ezekiel's programme, as for the other prophets, is the kingdom *of God*. The true *melek* of Israel in Ezekiel is YHWH (Joyce 1998: 332–337). His is the *throne* in 1:26 (cf. 10:1) and his is the *glory* in 1:28. It is the glory of *this* King which returns in 40:1–5 to re-establish *his* throne in 40:7. Since the days of rebellion in the wilderness YHWH was determined to rule his people: '*I will be king over you!*' (*'emlôk 'ălêkem*; Ezek. 20:33). Ezekiel's radically theocentric [42] portrayal of human leadership is overwhelmed (and understood) by a vision of YHWH seated on his throne.

---

[42] For more on this concept, see Joyce (1989: 89–105).

Chapter Nine

Zechariah: the militant, suffering shepherd

The exilic visions of Jeremiah and Ezekiel promoted confidence in the future reign of God in the wake of a (seventy-year) judgment on his people and their leaders. Return from exile began but was intermittent, and the newly rebuilt temple was, like the returned population itself, disappointingly modest in size. During these days (520 BC ff.) the priestly prophets Haggai and Zechariah offered hope on the condition that the people return to YHWH with all their hearts. Like Jeremiah and Ezekiel, Zechariah focused his attention on the question of leadership. Zechariah 1 – 8 contains a series of night visions that climax with the symbolic crowning of Joshua, the high priest. Joshua and Zerubbabel, the Davidic governor, are the two promising leaders in these chapters.

Shepherd imagery is pronounced in the markedly eschatological[1] second portion of Zechariah (chs. 9 – 14). Many scholars assume that this section, made up of two oracles (9 – 11; 12 – 14), comes from a later hand. While this is possible, it is important to appreciate the ways that this later half is linked to the earlier half. Both exhibit a universalistic vision centred in Zion; both emphasize new leadership (and the replacement of old leadership) as the sign of the new age. Some scholars have noticed in both sections a chiastic structure that supports the emphasis on these themes (Lamarche 1961; Baldwin 1972).

Zechariah exhibits a tendency to reuse older prophetic traditions. Allusions to Isaiah, Jeremiah, Ezekiel and Micah predominate (Mason 1976; Meyers 1993: 40–43), many involving pastoral and second exodus imagery. Here, in the period of the restoration, the images are deployed again in critiques of ineffective leaders at all levels of society. Zechariah's theology is quite complementary to his forebears: God is intent on freeing his oppressed flock from their

---

[1] There are apocalyptic features to this section, especially in ch. 14 (P. D. Hanson 1979: 369–380).

oppressors in a second exodus and settling them again in the land of promise. Like previous promises, Zechariah's predictions necessarily involve replacing the false and foolish shepherds who caused the calamity. But in Zechariah there are hints that the end involves a prolonged process with some retraction. The truly novel twist in this book is that God himself will 'strike' his appointed shepherd. Zechariah 9 – 14 is the most quoted section of the Prophets in the Gospels' passion narratives (Lamarche 1961: 9) especially because of this awareness of the Messiah's passion preceding the full restoration of God's people. The book of Revelation depends heavily on Zechariah's symbolic world to depict the ironic victory of the slain Lamb who is also the militant Shepherd.

Oracle 1: Coming judgment and redemption

> The people wander like sheep,
> > they are afflicted, because there is no shepherd...
> I will whistle for them
> > to gather them together.
>
> (Zech. 10:2, 8 NASB)

Zechariah 9:1 marks the beginning of a new oracle (chs. 9 – 11) characterized by judgment on Israel's enemies and hope for the military-pastoral intervention of God for his people. Hope for a royal designate, anticipated in chapter 6, is provided in the call for Zion to welcome her king in 9:9.

Israel's new ruler comes as one 'righteous' (*ṣaddîq*) and 'having salvation' (*nôšā'*).[2] These are familiar terms in royal contexts. While *ṣaddîq* can emphasize character or legitimacy (i.e. Davidic),[3] the Davidic line is not explicit here.[4] In the larger context of chapters 9 – 12, the issue is worthless leadership. In response, God personally rescues his flock from the calamity caused by Israel's shepherds (cf. 10:2–3). This king will execute a reign of peace and justice following holy war initiated by YHWH in verses 1–8 and 14–17. *YHWH* is the

---

[2] The Niphal of *yš'* would typically carry the passive meaning 'to be saved'. Ancient translators preferred a causative meaning, but Meyers & Meyers (1993: 126–127) defend the MT appropriately by insisting that in this context the king is himself dependent on YHWH for salvation (cf. Deut. 33:29; Ps. 33:16). *God* is the 'Saviour' (*yš'*, Hiphil) in this chapter (cf. v. 16).

[3] Or both, as in Isa. 9:7 [H 6]; 11:4–5; Jer. 23:5; 33:15.

[4] There may be an implicit link to David by way of the donkey in the patriarchal blessing for Judah in Gen. 49:11.

one who will defend his house (9:8); *YHWH* will free the prisoners (v. 11); *he* will restore their fortunes (v. 12); and *he* will save 'the flock of his people' (v. 16). The king appears in Zechariah's vision 'gentle and riding on a donkey' (9:9). This is a common Near Eastern image that illustrates solidarity with the people. He is 'humble' (low in status; *'ānî*) or 'afflicted', like the distressed in the community (11:7, 11).[5] It is significant that this term is used for the whole desert community in Isaiah 41:17 (cf. Neh. 9:9) and for Isaiah's Servant in Isaiah 51:21; 54:11; 53:4.

But the donkey could also serve as a traditional signal that the days of warfare (i.e. horses) were over (9:10).[6] Peace would replace war as society's norm (v. 10; cf. Isa. 2:4). Like the shepherd ruler of Micah 5:4, this king's reign would extend to the boundaries of the patri-archal promises (v. 10; cf. Ps. 72:7–8). All this is motivated by the 'blood of my covenant with you', God says (9:11). This phrase, found in the Old Testament only in Exodus 24:8, ties the new order explicitly to the ancient Sinai covenant. The expectation that God will again free his prisoners (9:11; cf. Exod. 5:1–2) was heard in the mission of the Servant in Isaiah 61:1: 'He has sent me . . . to proclaim freedom for the captives and release . . . for the prisoners' (cf. Luke 4:18).

Zechariah 9 concludes with God saving 'the flock of his people', an image of the community that pervades these chapters (10:2; 11:4, 7, 11, 17; 13:7). The background, again, is the ancient exodus by which God 'saved' Israel (Exod. 14:30) and the expectation that he will do so again by means of a new exodus (Ezek. 34:22).

Zechariah 10 expands upon the militant shepherd imagery sug-gested in chapter 9. The anger of the Lord burns against 'the shepherds' (10:3). Without trustworthy shepherd leaders, the people 'wander like sheep' (10:2). Zechariah accuses false prophets of deceptive speech, lying visions, false dreams and vain comfort (v. 2). Because of their self-interested leadership, the people are really leaderless. Abandoned in a wilderness that resembles their ancient predicament,[7] they are 'afflicted' (*'nh*; cf. Exod. 1:11, 12),[8] ironically,

---

[5] The psalmist (David?) is in this state in Pss. 25:16; 86:1. Moses is described as the most 'humble' man in Num. 12:3, a passage that uses the synonym *'ānāw*.

[6] For sources and discussion, see Elliger (1975: 149); Sasson (1976); In der Smitten (1980: 466, 469).

[7] Instead of the typical verb for wandering (*t'h*), the author uses *ns'*, the common term for 'setting out' in Numbers (used there 85 of its 146 MT occurrences).

[8] This term was used in 9:9 to refer to the coming king.

at the hands of their own shepherds. Here Zechariah sounds much like Jeremiah and Ezekiel.

While the false prophets are implied in this immediate context, Zechariah includes all of Israel's leaders in his indictment. In verse 3 'shepherds' is in parallel with 'male goats' (*'attûdîm*), a term for second-tier leaders in the community (cf. Isa. 14:9; Meyers 1993: 196–197). Previously we found the designation 'shepherd' used for prophets, kings and priests. Like Ezekiel (34:17), Zechariah extends his criticism below royalty to the power brokers within the flock who shared responsibility for the demise of Israel. Using a verbal play featured in Jeremiah 23:2, he says that God will 'punish' (*pqd*) these goats and then turn to 'care for' (*pqd*) his flock (10:3; cf. 11:16).[9] The mixing of military and pastoral dimensions is apparent when the 'Lord of Hosts' cares for his flock and then makes them 'like a proud horse in battle' (10:3).

The oracle continues with a promise that Judah will be the source of all leadership to come (10:4).[10] The word for ruler here is the Qal participle of *ngś*, a form often used for oppressive rule (Exod. 3:7; 5:6 et al.). The Lord promises to strengthen his people now to become rulers over others (10:5; cf. Isa. 14:2).

Second exodus imagery intensifies as YHWH declares his intention to 'save' the house of Joseph and 'restore' them out of 'compassion', for 'I am the LORD their God' (10:6). Rescue (*yš'*) from slavery is vital to the exodus account (Exod. 3:8) and to exilic longings (Ezek. 34:10, 12). Returning (*šwb*, Hiphil) is a key notion, especially in Jeremiah.[11] Compassion (*rḥm*) drives God to restore them (10:4; cf. Isa. 49:10, 13, 15; 54:8, 10) and to 'answer' them (*'ānâ*; cf. Isa. 41:17). To this outpouring the afflicted respond with boundless joy (10:7; cf. Isa. 29:19).

When the divine Shepherd whistles[12] for his flock in 10:8, it is clear that he has personally replaced the foolish shepherds of verses 2–3 and has begun the second exodus. The emphasis on the first person is felt throughout: '*I* will whistle . . . *I* will gather . . . *I* will redeem . . . *I* will bring back . . . *I* will gather . . . *I* will strengthen' (vv. 8–12).

---

[9] In the background is also Jeremiah's call for the *'attûdîm* of Israel to lead God's flock out of exile (Jer. 50:8).

[10] Rule is suggested by references to a cornerstone, tent peg and battle-bow in v. 4.

[11] Ps. 23:6 uses a similar mixed form meaning 'return to resettle'. The correct form of the Hiphil is below in Zech. 10:10.

[12] Though whistling (*šrq*) is typically used in a derisive way (i.e. to mock), it is one of the standard means by which a shepherd signals to his own sheep that it is time to move (Judg. 5:16; cf. John 10:3–4).

These are all familiar verbs in our study. For example, gathering (*qbṣ*, Piel) is featured in Isaiah 40:11; 54:7 (with *rḥm*); Micah 2:12; Jeremiah 31:10; Ezekiel 34:13. Redemption (*pdh*) defines the original exodus (Deut. 7:8; Ps. 78:42; Mic. 6:4) and second exodus promises (Isa. 35:10 = 51:11). Returning is accompanied by multiplication (*rbh*) in verse 8, an echo of the patriarchal promise (Gen. 35:11)[13] and the exilic visions of Jeremiah (23:3) and Ezekiel (36:11).

The most obvious link with the exodus is in 10:11: 'They will pass through the sea of trouble; the surging sea will be subdued, and all the depths of the Nile will dry up . . . and Egypt's sceptre will pass away.' Deliverance through the sea was an important memory on which to build exilic hope (Isa. 43:16–19). The depths (*mĕṣûlôt*) of verse 11 (cf. Exod. 15:5; Neh. 9:11) will dry up, another important image from Exodus 14:16ff.; 15:19. In Isaiah 11:15 God had similarly promised to strike (*nkh*) the sea to create a (dry) highway for his people. In the wake of this new deliverance, the people will walk in YHWH's name (cf. Exod. 9:16; Mal. 1:11).

The first oracle continues with pastoral imagery in chapter 11.[14] The opening scene is a cataclysmic devastation of woodlands and pastures that causes shepherds to wail. Though Meyers & Meyers (1993: 240ff.) argue that this literal devastation is the positive result of increased population, it is more likely that the *metaphor* of shepherd leaders is in place. These leaders (pictured as trees, shepherds and lions) mourn the loss of their glory (*'adderet*; v. 3).[15] This passage shares much in common with Jeremiah's woe to shepherd leaders in Jeremiah 25:34–38.

Chapter 11 continues with an extended prophetic narrative explaining the arduous calling of Zechariah to shepherd 'the flock marked for slaughter' (11:4, 7). The prophet replaces those who have ironically exchanged their role as responsible shepherds for callous sellers. Like the shepherds who only (ab)use the flock for products in Ezekiel 34:2–3, these shepherds slaughter the animals in their care and then have the audacity to praise God for their excess income (11:5). Because such leaders (i.e. predators) lack pity (*ḥml*) for the people (11:5), God will deny them pity (11:6). He will hand each one over to

---

[13] This promise is itself an echo of the creation mandate in Gen. 1:22. Recall here that the exodus was a kind of new creation, and second exodus passages often employ creation language.

[14] It is possible that 11:1–3 caps off the section begun in 10:1–3, both referring to the judgment of God's shepherds.

[15] One must concede that this 'glory' is in parallel to lush thicket, and therefore may connote pasture.

his shepherd [16] and king. Though these rulers will oppress (lit. 'beat') the land, the Lord will not deliver (*nṣl*) his people. Into this hopeless scenario the prophet is injected to shepherd the 'flock marked for slaughter' (11:7).

Zechariah takes his job seriously, looking out especially for the afflicted (*'ānî*; [17] 11:7). He begins to use two shepherd staffs, Favour and Union, which symbolize the covenant with YHWH and the unity of the two nations. He purges the community of three unfit shepherds all in one month (11:8). Like Moses and the other prophets who followed him, Zechariah has been called not just to speak God's word but to understand first hand the burden of God for his flock. But this prophet breaks under the pressure: 'The flock detested me, and I grew weary of them' (v. 8). He gives up and decides that the members of the community can determine their own fate (11:9).

The prophet breaks the first staff, symbolizing the end of the covenant.[18] He is watched by the afflicted (*'ānî*) of the flock who understand the ominous significance of the act (11:11). He then collects his pay,[19] trying to end his thankless role as shepherd. He breaks the second staff to illustrate the break-up of the brotherhood of Israel and Judah (11:14).

But God calls him again to take the foolish shepherd's gear (*kĕlî*; 11:15; cf. Meyers 1993: 282). The prophetic parable is not over yet. Zechariah is to play the part of this foolish shepherd, one who is everything a good shepherd is not. He will *not* 'care for the lost, or seek the young, or heal the injured, or feed the healthy, but will eat the meat of the choice sheep, tearing off their hoofs . . .' (11:16). There is a distinct echo of Ezekiel 34:3–4 here. The terminology is even closer to Ezekiel 34:16, where each of the six clauses parallel the indictment in Zechariah 11 in wording, tone and style (Meyers 1993: 285–286). The difference is that Ezekiel is describing what a good shepherd does. Thus, Zechariah follows in the footsteps of previous

[16] The word usually translated 'his neighbour' (*rē'ēhô*) should probably be revocalized to read 'his shepherd' (*rō'ehô*), in which case there is a direct parallel with king. God is giving people up to the leadership they want (cf. v. 8b).

[17] Compare Meyers (1993: 261–262) for the reading 'traders'.

[18] These staffs reflect the two themes of Davidic rule pictured as two sticks in Ezek. 37:15–28. Ezekiel (like Jeremiah) predicts a breaking of the covenant, but only in the context of its promised renewal.

[19] The thirty pieces of silver may represent an insultingly low amount (the cost of a slave in Exod. 22:16), in which case the 'handsome price' in v. 13 is a sarcastic reference. It may also be a substantial wage, almost as much as the governor's salary in Neh. 5:15. Asking for compensation at all may be an ironic gesture for one who criticizes false prophets (who are motivated only by the money).

prophets who use pastoral imagery not only to imbue the afflicted with hope for renewal, but also as the basis for comprehensive critique of failed leadership. Chapter 11 comes to a close with a woe upon this worthless shepherd who abandons (*'zb*) his flock (v. 17). Desertion is the one thing a good shepherd would never do, and what God had repeatedly promised he would never do (cf. Deut. 31:6, 8). A sword is called to strike [20] the shepherd's arm and right eye, permanently incapacitating him as a shepherd. The first oracle is thus complete; the community has been delivered by God not only from their exile under foreign rule but also from the scourge of self-interested leaders in their own community. These are the very issues and images Jesus will later pick up when he chastises the rulers of his day for abusing the flock left in their care.

Oracle 2: Struck shepherd, scattered sheep, and YHWH's reign on Mount Zion

> Strike the shepherd,
>   and the sheep will be scattered,
> and I will turn my hand against the little ones.
>
> (Zech. 13:7)

The final portion of Zechariah predicts the ultimate salvation of Judah and Jerusalem on 'that day',[21] but only after the community and the royal family are purged. Shepherd language is employed again to describe a (royal) figure that the Lord himself will strike. The fatal blow causes the scattering of the sheep and the mourning of the community. But after the people are refined, they will once again enjoy the benefits of a covenant relationship with YHWH.

This new oracle begins as it ends (in ch. 14), with a cataclysmic war between God's people and their enemies in Jerusalem. The centre of God's re-creative work in this post-exilic community is the Davidic family. In the final battle they will be like God's guiding presence in the wilderness: 'On that day ... the feeblest among them will be like David, and the house of David will be like God, like the Angel of the LORD going before them' (12:8; cf. Exod. 32:34). David's line is linked with the Holy Spirit explicitly in 12:10: 'I will pour out on the house

---

[20] 'Strike' is implied by the immediate context (and cf. 13:7).
[21] The phrase 'that day' is used seventeen times in chapters 12 – 14.

of David and the inhabitants of Jerusalem a spirit of grace and supplication.' The pierced figure in verse 10 is mourned by the whole community, beginning with David's house. Purging continues when a cleansing fountain is opened for David and Jerusalem (13:1).

Cleansing is necessitated especially because of the idolatry and impurity introduced by false prophets (13:2–6). In the wake of YHWH's comprehensive purge no-one will even admit to being a prophet (v. 5). It is in the context of this repulsion for deceptive, self-serving prophets that Zechariah's final shepherd image is employed:

> [7]'Awake, O sword, against my shepherd,
>   against the man who is close to me!'
>   declares the Lord Almighty.
> 'Strike the shepherd,
>   and the sheep will be scattered,
>   and I will turn my hand against the little ones.
> [8] In the whole land,' declares the Lord,
>   'two-thirds will be struck down and perish;
>   yet one-third will be left in it.
> [9] This third I will bring into the fire;
>   I will refine them like silver
>   and test them like gold.
> They will call on my name
>   and I will answer them;
> I will say, "They are my people,"
>   and they will say, "The Lord is our God." '
>   (13:7–9)

Commentators wonder whether this shepherd is a royal or priestly figure. Zechariah tends to view these institutions as complicit and inseparable in their leadership (cf. 3:8). Certainly leadership in both civil and cultic spheres – and at all levels – is criticized by this prophet, as we have seen. However, Zechariah's personal replacement of the foolish shepherd who is maimed in chapter 11, the focus on false prophets in 13:2–6 and the striking of 'my shepherd', my assistant,[22] here in 13:7 suggest that a prophet is foremost in mind.

The scattering of the sheep in verse 7 is the inevitable result of becoming shepherdless (Ezek. 34:5). But why does God strike the shepherd and then 'turn [his] hand against the little ones'? Apparently

---

[22] The NIV translates 'āmîtî as 'the man who is close to me'.

this is required judgment for the leadership and the community. From the leader to the least, judgment will come (cf. Jer. 49:20; 50:45). Yet even in judgment there is mercy. A third will remain from the refining fire. This is the remnant motif we saw in the wilderness traditions, resurfacing again in the second exodus passages of the prophets. God promises to re-establish his covenant with this renewed remnant: 'I will say, "They are my people," and they will say, "The LORD is our God"' (13:9; cf. Exod. 6:7; Jer. 31:33; Ezek. 37:27).

The image of a struck shepherd and the scattered sheep is essential background for the Gospel writers as they explain the necessity of Christ's passion. It is arguable that this passage influenced Jesus' own thinking more than any other shepherd passage in the Old Testament (France 1971: 103ff.). Though his death dispersed his flock – and the 'little ones' (cf. Luke 22:28) – they were regathered as his refined community, becoming thereby God's renewed Israel.

IV
The Shepherd Messiah,
his followers and
the second exodus

Prophetic expectations of a better future were cast in terms of Israel's ancient institutions and traditions. An anticipated shepherd ruler (Mosaic and/or Davidic) would lead his renewed community in a second exodus, provide for God's flock in their exilic wilderness, and renew his covenant with them there. This pastoral perspective on redemptive history continued into the New Testament period.

The Ethiopic Apocalypse of Enoch (1 Enoch), written sometime near the turn of the era, summarizes all of Israel's history with pastoral imagery (chs. 89 – 90). The phrase 'Lord of the sheep' appears twenty-three times in these two chapters. During the exodus God saved his sheep from the 'wolves' (Egyptians) that were later drowned in the sea. Moses was one of the sheep that led the others for the Lord, though many went astray following other sheep. The period of the judges – likened to a time when the flock was ravaged by dogs, foxes and wild boars (89:43) – ends when a chosen ram (David) brings security to the flock. The allegory continues with the history of the two kingdoms. The flock ignores (prophet-)sheep and suffers at the hands of lions, leopards, wolves and hyenas (89:55), and destructive shepherds (89:59ff.). The Maccabean rulers are described as a new group of horned lambs that become deliverers. Finally the messianic kingdom comes with judgment for both irresponsible shepherds and blinded sheep (90:26).

Other amplifications of Old Testament wilderness traditions form the backdrop for New Testament writers. The covenanters at Qumran considered themselves 'penitents in the wilderness' (4QpPs^a 3:1) and 'exiles of the wilderness' (1QM 1:2–3), awaiting the coming of God in a second exodus and a new holy war. The theological significance of the wilderness is profound in Jewish literature prior to the teaching of Jesus.[1] Many Jews were expecting the Lord to make the new way in the wilderness promised in Isaiah 40:3. Messianic expectations were of pivotal concern with each effort to establish independence. The Maccabees were never able to claim Davidic blood and so ruled until 'the Prophet should come'. Hope for a coming son of David is alive in the first century BC Psalms of Solomon (17:40–42): 'Faithfully and righteously shepherding the Lord's flock, he will not let any of them stumble in their pasture. He will lead them all in holiness and there will be no arrogance among them, that any should be oppressed. This is the beauty of the king of Israel.' Other kinds of messiahs were expected at the turn of the era. J. J. Collins (1995: 11) outlines hopes in Qumran for royal, priestly, prophetic and heavenly messiah types (cf. VanderKam 1994). The Gospel writers introduce Jesus of Nazareth as a messianic figure in a variety of ways, but consistently in terms of ancient pastoral proto-types and in dialogue with the interpretive traditions that evolved from them.

---

[1] Cf. 1 Macc. 2:29–38; 5:24–28; 9:33, 62.

Chapter Ten

Mark: the shepherd king and the second exodus

Mark is typically understood to be the first Gospel. Its composition probably took place in the late 60s AD, just prior to the destruction of Jerusalem and the temple (cf. Guelich 1989). This setting inevitably contributed to the resonances between Mark and pre-586 BC Old Testament prophecies discussed above.

Mark's Gospel is a brief but powerful story of the life and death of Jesus. The narrative progressively reveals him as the royal son of God (1:1).[1] The answer to Pilate's question in 15:2, 'Are you the king of the Jews?', is answered definitively at the foot of the cross by the centurion: 'Surely this man was the Son of God!' (15:39) Mark presents the true king of the Jews as the serving and suffering shepherd of messianic traditions. He also focuses on the development of the disciples' understanding of this identity as they 'follow' him to the cross, are there 'scattered' and finally 'led' again in Galilee. The long-expected king had come to guide his purged community out of their wilderness and into his eschatological kingdom.[2]

A shepherd in the wilderness

> When Jesus landed and saw a large crowd, he had compassion on them, because they were like sheep without a shepherd. (Mark 6:34)

Mark begins his Gospel with a descriptive statement ('The beginning of the gospel about Jesus Christ, the Son of God'; v. 1) and a highly

---

[1] For this as Mark's primary Christology, see Kingsbury (1983) and Rowe (2002). While Jesus is more frequently called 'son of David' in the Gospel of Matthew, Mark consistently demonstrates his royal identity. C. A. Evans (2001: lxxx–xciii) provides a helpful list of the ways in which Mark appears to be contrasting Jesus with the Roman emperor.

[2] See Rowe (2002: 87ff.) for a thorough summary of contemporary Jewish (and Marcan) views on the kingdom of God and the relation of the Messiah to that kingdom.

significant medley of quotes from the Old Testament (taken from Exod. 23:20; Mal. 3:1; Isa. 40:3).[3] The prologue that follows features the ministry of John, the baptism and temptation of Jesus, his preaching of the kingdom of God, and the calling of his disciples. The first movement[4] of the story is a collection of incidents and teachings that bring the disciples to a critical, though preliminary, understanding of Jesus' nature. Peter's confession in 8:29 marks a major turning point in the story; from this point forward the Lord faces Jerusalem with sombre resolution, repeatedly predicting his coming death at the hands of Israel's leaders. Our particular interest is Mark's use of pastoral and second exodus language just prior to this major break in the narrative.

While commentators disagree over the precise boundaries, it is generally acknowledged that 6:30 – 8:26 forms a discrete unit[5] that brings to a climax the first section of Mark. It is possible that this subdivision extends further on both ends, from 6:7 (the commissioning of the disciples) on one extreme to 8:39 (the call to follow the Son of Man to the cross) on the other (Witherington 2001; Moloney 2002). These three chapters (6 – 8) provide a relatively tight collection of paired stories that take place in Galilee and beyond. Moloney (ibid.) suggests a symmetrical progression from first feeding, first sea journey, first conflict and first healing to second feeding, second sea journey, second conflict and second healing.

Certain motifs are disproportionately evident in these chapters, most notably 'wilderness' and 'bread'. What prompts our deeper investigation is the presence of another familiar image, the shepherd: 'When Jesus landed and saw a large crowd, he had compassion on them, because *they were like sheep without a shepherd*' (6:34). It will soon be clear that Mark intentionally paints his portrait of Jesus using elements of Old Testament wilderness (and second exodus) traditions.

The wilderness/desert (*erēmos*) is an important designation in Mark, clearly carrying symbolic freight from the Old Testament

---

[3] See R. E. Watts (1997) for the significance of this introductory citation in the scheme of Mark's Gospel (cf. Snodgrass 1980).

[4] I generally follow France (2002), who sees three dramatic 'acts' in the book: Galilee (1:14 – 8:21), On the Way to Jerusalem (8:22 – 10:52), and The Passion in Jerusalem (11:1 – 16:8).

[5] While it is defensible to consider 8:22–26 (the two-stage healing) as the beginning of the next section – thus beginning and ending with a blind healing miracle (cf. 10:46–52) and including two confessions, Peter's (8:29) and Bartimaeus's (10:47–48) – it seems equally likely that this story illustrates the disciples' slowly emerging spiritual sight, evident in Peter's correct confession but subsequent 'rebuke' of Jesus (8:32). I therefore see it as a hinge that is both retrospective and prospective.

(Mauser 1963). *Erēmos* is the preferred Septuagint term for Hebrew *midbār* and for similar geographical regions, especially in the Prophetic books. Mark uses the term six times (including the related *erēmos topos*) in the prologue to underscore the desert(ed) setting of the ministry of John and the calling of Jesus and his disciples. As the 'voice of one crying in the *desert*' (Isa. 40:3; Mark 1:3), John [6] preaches and baptizes in the *desert* (v. 4). After his baptism, Jesus was thrust into the *desert* by the Spirit (v. 12), and he was in the *desert* for forty days (v. 13). Prior to choosing his disciples, Jesus retired to a *deserted place* to pray (v. 35) and, as a result of his rapid popularity, attracted great crowds to himself in *deserted places* (v. 45).

While this motif may link Jesus with the prophets Moses and Elijah – both of whom spent forty days in the wilderness (Exod. 34:28; 1 Kgs 19:8; cf. Mark 9:4) – there is a more obvious connection between Jesus and *Israel*. God had called Israel, his 'son', out of Egypt (Exod. 4:22–23; Hos. 11:1) and into the desert where he could initiate his covenant of love (Deut. 7:7ff.; Jer. 2:2). Taking them through the waters of the Reed Sea, he led them by his Spirit (and angel) into the wilderness of Sinai, where they spent forty years. Mark's brief prologue carefully notes that Jesus similarly came through the waters, heard God's word of affirmation as his Son, and was led by his Spirit and angels in the *erēmos*, where he spent forty days.

In the sixth chapter *erēmos* is used in its final appearances with rapid succession. Welcoming the disciples back from their first mission, Jesus calls them to a *deserted place* to rest for a while (6:31). They respond by taking a boat to a *deserted place* (v. 32). But, in keeping with a Marcan pattern, a crowd follows Jesus. The disciples are concerned that, because the place is *deserted* (v. 35), the people will go hungry. Jesus understands that the wilderness, though replete with hostile forces, is the environment in which he, as YHWH in the past, must reveal himself. The 'way in the wilderness' (1:3; Isa. 40:3) is *the way of the Lord*,[7] an important element of second exodus theology.[8] The miracle that the disciples were about to witness was a replication of the miraculous feeding in the

---

[6] Among the Synoptics only Mark mentions John's ministry (and the wild animals) in the *erēmos*.

[7] See R. E. Watts (1997: 221–294) for the relationship between Isaiah's 'way' language and the next section in Mark (8:21/26 – 10:45/11:1). Consider also the designation of the early Christian movement as 'the Way' in Acts 9:2; 19:9, 23; 22:4; 24:14, 22.

[8] Mark was not the only writer who expected YHWH's eschatological reappearance in glory in this same environment (cf. 1:1–3). The desert was important as both physical and theological space in Qumran (Betz 1967; Brooke 1994).

wilderness of the exodus account. By that original miracle (and many others), YHWH had made himself known as compassionate[9] provider to his people.

Upon further investigation, it becomes clear that the term *artos* (bread) is another prominent motif precisely in this section of Mark. Of its twenty-one uses in the Gospel, eighteen of them are in chapters 6 – 8. The first reference, not incidentally, is in the instructions to the disciples who were sent out on their mission with no *bread*, bag or money (6:8). The word is repeated a number of times in the first feeding story (6:37, 38, 44[10]) and in the second (8:4, 5, 6, 14, 16, 17, 19). In between these miracles *artos* is featured in a dispute with the Pharisees and scribes (why do the disciples eat bread with unwashed hands? cf. 7:2, 5) and in the story of the Syro-Phoenician woman (shouldn't the dogs at least get the crumbs? cf. 7:27–28).

Mark's comments after the miracle of walking on the sea (6:47ff.) are intriguing: '[The disciples] were completely amazed, for they had not understood about the loaves [*artois*]; their hearts were hardened' (vv. 51–52). This seems a harsh judgment, but, for Mark, the feeding miracle had failed in its educational and revelatory purpose. Hardening (*pepōrōmenēn*) is only used in Mark here and in 8:17, where Jesus explains the meaning of the feeding miracles. When Jesus warns the disciples to 'Beware of the leaven of the Pharisees and the leaven of Herod' (8:15 NASB), they immediately think it is because they have forgotten to take bread (v. 16). Jesus replies, 'Do you still not see or understand?[11] Are your hearts *hardened*?' (v. 17) He then reminds them of how he provided the bread for the multitudes twice and

---

[9] Perhaps the idea of compassion recalls the words of Isa. 49:10: 'They will neither hunger nor thirst, nor will the desert heat or the sun beat upon them. He who has *compassion* on them will guide them and lead them beside springs of water.' Mark uses the verb *splanchnizomai* (not found in the LXX), a term reserved for Jesus (or God) in the Gospels. The evangelist notes that both feeding miracles were preceded by Jesus being moved with *compassion* (6:34; 8:2; cf. 1:41; 9:22). Interestingly, in all four cases where the verb is used, the disciples are impotent to help. Many of the OT quotes in Mark are employed to emphasize that compassion and mercy are superior to legalism and sterile ritual (cf. Mark 7:1–23; 10:1–12, 17–22). Thus, Jesus is simultaneously encouraging his disciples' growth in efficacious concern while criticizing the careless leaders (i.e. shepherds) of the community (cf. Ezek. 34:4).

[10] There is mixed versional support for the word in v. 44.

[11] The disciples' lack of perception, noted earlier in 4:10–13; 7:15–18, shows that they are still among those who, in the words of Isa. 6:9, are 'ever hearing but never understanding' and 'ever seeing but never perceiving'. The statements in ch. 8 are placed strategically between the healing of the *deaf* (7:31–37) and *blind* (8:22–26; cf. Isa. 6:10; 35:1–7; 42:10–16).

wonders again how they could still not understand (vv. 18–21). The importance of the feeding miracles for revealing the identity of Jesus [12] stands behind the two-phased healing of the blind man that follows immediately, and the subsequent questions to the disciples, 'Who do people say I am?' (v. 27) and 'Who do *you* say I am?' (v. 29)

The wilderness, from the perspective of Deuteronomy, was the place where YHWH *taught* his people that he could provide for them. Miraculously provided bread was daily evidence of God's pastoral concern. But the provision pointed to something more than physical sustenance: 'He humbled you, causing you to hunger and then feeding you with manna, which neither you nor your fathers had known, *to teach you* that man does not live on bread alone but *on every word that comes from the mouth of the LORD*' (Deut. 8:3).

Similarly, Jesus brings a new Israel out into the wilderness to *teach* them to trust his authoritative *word*. *Artos* is, thus, a cipher for God's word. This puts into perspective Christ's response when he looked at the crowd: 'he had compassion on them, because they were like sheep without a shepherd. *So he began teaching them many things*' (6:34). It was the teaching [13] of this shepherd – in contrast to the teaching (i.e. 'leaven') of the scribes and Pharisees – that would bring them life.

There is little doubt that Mark's apology for the identity of Jesus includes an affirmation of his pivotal role in bringing about the second exodus. The Spirit and wilderness are featured provocatively together in the prologue (Wright 1987). The typology of the (forty-year) wilderness as a place of testing, provision (bread) and teaching has already been noted. Mark's interest in the sea [14] is present in the prologue (1:16) and in the miracles of 4:35–41 (the rebuke of the winds), 5:13 (the swine sent into the sea) and 6:47–51 (walking on the water). References to 'gathering', 'rest', 'green' grass and the organization into companies are other likely allusions to (second)

---

[12] These miracles (like all miracles in the Gospels) serve a revelatory function, especially by identifying Jesus in terms of OT traditions (cf. Donahue 1978; Van Oyen 1999).

[13] Given that Mark is three-fifths the size of Matthew or Luke, occurrences of terms for (and therefore his emphasis on) teaching are significant: *didaskalos* (Mark, twelve; Matt., twelve; Luke, seventeen), *didachē* (Mark, five; Matt., three; Luke, once), and *didaskō* (Mark, seventeen; Matt., fourteen; Luke, seventeen). Donahue (1978) appropriately refers to Jesus in Mark's Gospel as 'the parable of God'.

[14] Mark uses the term *thalassa* (sea) nineteen times compared to Matthew (sixteen) and Luke (three). This is the common LXX term for the sea in the exodus account and in predictions of a second exodus (Isa. 43:16; 50:2; 51:10, 15; 63:11; Jer. 51:42).

exodus traditions.[15] Finally, as the last section of Mark begins, Jesus is represented as a new Moses, radiant with the glory of God on a high mountain (9:2ff.).[16]

Of special interest is the phrase 'sheep without a shepherd' in 6:34. This was the representation of Israel that Moses used to express his fear of a future with no successor (Num. 27:17).[17] But the phrase is also a common designation for leaderless people (1 Kgs 22:17). Perhaps in the background is the image in Ezekiel 34 of people whose leaders are so harmful that they are like no shepherds at all (cf. Zech. 10:2). In this case, we are led to understand that Jesus *is* YHWH, coming personally to rescue his sheep. Notice the motifs of feeding, good pasture and rest in LXX Ezekiel 34:

> I will bring them into their own land. I will pasture [LXX *boskō*] [18] them on the mountains of Israel, in the ravines and in all the settlements in the land. I will tend [LXX *boskō*] them in a *good pasture*, and the mountain heights of Israel will be their grazing land. There they will *lie down* in *good grazing land*, and there they will feed [LXX *boskō*] in a *rich pasture* on the mountains of Israel. I myself will tend [LXX *boskō*] my sheep and make them *lie down*, declares the Sovereign LORD. (Ezek. 34:13–15)

In the immediate context of Ezekiel 34 we should not miss references to the divine Shepherd's ministry to the weak and sick (cf. Mark

---

[15] The disciples 'gathered' (*synagō*) around Jesus in 6:30 (cf. Isa. 40:11; 56:8; Jer. 23:8; Ezek. 34:13; 37:21). Mark, alone among the Gospel writers, refers to 'rest' (*anapauō*) for the disciples (6:31). This term is used of flocks lying down generally (Gen. 29:2; 49:14) and in images of the second exodus (Isa. 32:18; 34:14; cf. 28:12; Ezek. 34:14–15). The 'green' grass on which the people are led to sit (6:39) is also a unique Marcan emphasis, suggestive of lush pastures, especially in light of the comparison of the people to sheep in 6:34. This picture may recall the many prophetic images of a blossoming desert in the second exodus (cf. Isa. 35). The most likely allusion to the original wilderness is the seating of the people in groups of hundreds and fifties (6:40). This recalls the organization of the Israelites in the wilderness (Exod. 18:25), a pattern the Qumran sect intentionally followed as they prepared for a second exodus (CD 13:1; 1QS 2:21–22; 1QM 4:1–5; cf. Rule Annexe 1:14–16, 28; 2:1).

[16] Another provocative link with the ancient Sinai account is the reference to the *six days* leading up to the transfiguration (cf. Exod. 24:16; Matt. 17:1). Luke 9:28 simply states, 'about eight days after . . .'

[17] Here stands Jesus, whose namesake was the original answer to Moses' request (Gundry 1993: 323).

[18] Although the general verb for shepherding in Hebrew (*r'h*) has a suitable Greek counterpart (*poimainō*), the translators chose a term that is more focused on feeding (*boskō*), used eleven times in Ezek. 34 (cf. Isa. 49:9). Notice that *esthiō* (to eat) is used six times in Mark 6:31–37.

6:55–56), and his stated intention to judge the abusive members of the flock (cf. Mark 7:1–23; 8:11–21): 'I will search for the lost and bring back the strays. I will bind up the injured and strengthen the weak, but the sleek and the strong I will destroy. I will shepherd the flock with justice. As for you, my flock, this is what the Sovereign LORD says: I will judge between one sheep and another, and between rams and goats' (Ezek. 34:16–17). Situated close to most of Scripture's pastoral words of hope is a critique of current 'shepherds'.[19]

Prophetic judgment of poor leaders typically leads to their replacement, most significantly by a Davidic figure. In Mark's Gospel, Jesus is that David, but the disciples are being prepared – encounter by encounter, teaching by teaching – to understand their role as extensions of the Davidic shepherd's current (and future) ministry. They begin as spectators and learners (*mathētai*). Then Jesus sends them out with the authority to teach, heal and exorcise demons (6:7–13). Twice they are given the job of serving miraculously multiplying bread to the crowds. But now, just as they are becoming aware of their powerful place in the new kingdom, Jesus will insist that the essence of their role as leaders is to *follow the Lamb of God to his death* (8:34–38). Self-sacrificing service is the hallmark of the Lord's deputy shepherds (10:45).

The passion of the shepherd king

For it is written:

> 'I will strike the shepherd,
> and the sheep will be scattered.'
> (Mark 14:27)

The final chapters (11 – 16) of this brief Gospel are given to the details of the passion of Jesus, consistently self-described as the Son of Man who must suffer and die before rising again (8:31; 9:12, 31; 10:33, 45; cf. 14:21, 41). These chapters employ images and allusions taken from three important Old Testament sources: Isaianic Servant songs (esp. ch. 53), the psalms of lament and Zechariah 9 – 14.[20]

[19] The characteristically Marcan interpolation of 6:14–29 adds Herod to the roster of bad leaders in the background (cf. Guelich 1989: 419, 423–424; Fowler 1981: 116–124).

[20] See Bruce (1960–61) and Marcus (1992: 153–198), both of whom give appropriate attention to other interpretive traditions that grew out of Zechariah's prophecies (i.e. in the DSS and Targums).

The Zechariah passages are of most interest because of their sustained use of shepherd/sheep language in discussing the coming judgment[21] and the future Davidic ruler (Bruce 1960–61). The general context of these chapters in Zechariah is the purging of Israel (and the 'house of David') and the establishment of the Messianic Age (i.e. the reign of YHWH; cf. Zech. 14:4, 9).[22] A key image for Mark and the other Gospel writers[23] is the predicted royal shepherd who will be 'struck' and his sheep 'scattered' (Zech. 13:7; Mark 14:27). This quotation from Zechariah 13 accomplishes multiple purposes in Mark. First, like the passages from Psalms and Isaiah, this one emphasizes the *suffering* of God's chosen ruler. As is clear from his baptism onwards, Jesus purposes to take on the full identity and judgment of Israel. Second, it taps the pastoral imagery generously used by Zechariah (Zech. 9:16; 10:3; 11:4–7; 13:7). 'Striking' the shepherd is an obvious reference to his coming crucifixion.[24] But the image of the scattering[25] and regathering of the sheep is clearly central in Jesus' words at this point, as Peter's response confirms. The image of scattered sheep in various Old Testament passages was considered the result of bad (or no) leaders (cf. Jer. 23:2; Ezek. 34:4–6). In Zechariah the Lord promises to save 'the flock of his people' (9:16), people who 'wander like sheep oppressed for lack of a shepherd' (10:2). YHWH's 'anger burns against the *shepherds* ... I will punish the *leaders*' (10:3). The disciples are thus, typologically, among those who are considered victims of abusive leadership. They will become the purified remnant of 13:8–9 (cf. Zech. 9:11–12; 10:6–9).

Just as YHWH promised in his compassion (Zech. 10:6) to regather his flock (10:9–10), so Jesus offers words of hope to the disciples who will soon disperse. The Lord promises that after his

---

[21] R. E. Watts (1997: 183–220) sees the judicial element in Mark's Gospel programmatically introduced in the opening citation from Mal. 3:1.

[22] Note references to 'that day' and the 'kingdom of God' in Mark 14:25 (cf. Marcus 1992: 156–167).

[23] Similarly, the Qumran community shows evidence of viewing this prediction in terms of the Teacher of Righteousness and the members of their community (CD 19:7–13).

[24] Making these statements on the Mount of Olives (Mark 14:26), Jesus recalls the image in Zech. 14:4 of YHWH standing on this same spot as he begins his rescue of the holy city. For eschatological expectations associating the Messiah with this Mount (and other Zecharian motifs), see Marcus (1992: 155–159).

[25] MT Zech. 13:8 also refers to the scattering of the 'little ones', an important concern of Jesus expressed in Mark 9:42 (and, more so, in Matt. 10:42; 18:6–24; cf. Matt. 25:40ff.).

resurrection 'I will go ahead [*proaxsō*] of you into Galilee' (14:28).[26] *Proagō* is a verb of *leading* that Jeremias (1963: 121 n. 26) identifies as a technical term for shepherding. Having earlier *led* the disciples to Jerusalem (10:32), Jesus is promising to *lead* them once again *into* Galilee (C. F. Evans 1954; C. A. Evans 2001: 402, 537). The same verb is used at the end of the Gospel when a young man (angel) tells Mary Magdalene and the mother of James to 'tell his disciples and Peter, "He is *going ahead of you* into Galilee"' (16:7). Thus, the passion account in Mark is framed by the promise of Jesus to lead his scattered sheep once again.

---

[26] On the relationship between vv. 27–28 and the military nuance of the language see Marcus (1992: 161–164; cf. C. F. Evans 1954: 9). Marcus explains the way in which Mark balances both the militancy and the suffering of the messianic traditions: Mark's king is initiating holy war by giving up his life.

Chapter Eleven

Matthew: the compassionate Davidic shepherd

Probably written soon after Mark, Matthew introduces his readers to 'Jesus the Messiah, the son of David, the son of Abraham' (1:1 NASB). These titles are significant indicators of the contours and emphases of this Gospel's portrait.[1] As with the other Gospel writers, Matthew does not limit himself to a singular Christological lens. Jesus is the expected King and Isaianic Servant; new Moses and new David; Son of God and Son of Man; and the new Israel. More than the other Synoptic writers, Matthew employs shepherd language to describe the ministry of Jesus, both in his ministry and in his death.

Understanding Matthew's rendering of the Messiah requires an appreciation for his use of the Old Testament. A good deal of scholarship has been devoted to formulaic citations which far outnumber those in the other Gospels.[2] These are among sixty-one quotations from the Old Testament, twenty-eight of which are unique to Matthew (Senior 1997: 89). But Matthew is also a treasure of almost three hundred allusions to the first Testament.[3] This intertextuality is especially apparent in the opening sections of the Gospel, and in the passion where the shepherd themes of Zechariah 9 – 14 repeatedly surface.

The Davidic shepherd king from Bethlehem

> ... for out of you [Bethlehem] will come a ruler
> who will be the shepherd of my people Israel.
> (Matt. 2:6)

Matthew's prologue (chs. 1 – 2) provides a highly textured introduction to the themes and motifs that will dominate the following

---

[1] Matthew uses 'Messiah' (*christos*) sixteen times (Mark, seven; Luke, twelve), 'son of David' ten times (Mark, three; Luke, twice). Allusions to Jesus as the true Israel(ite) (i.e. son of Abraham; cf. Hos. 11:1 in Matt. 2:15) are numerous.

[2] According to R. E. Brown (1994: 648) there are fourteen in Matthew, three in Luke, one in Mark and nine in John.

[3] See NA[26], pp. 739–769.

narrative. He highlights the contrast between the messianic child and the self-serving Jewish rulers, especially Herod. This tyrannical ruler (and 'all Jerusalem'; 2:3) [4] is threatened by the news of another king in Bethlehem. With the rashness of ancient Pharaoh, [5] he determines to exterminate all newborns who might be considered the next 'king of the Jews'. [6] By contrast, the Magi figure as prototypical Gentiles, eager to worship the Jewish king.

When Herod asks the Jewish religious leaders for information about the birthplace of the predicted Messiah, he is given a quotation that explains his home town and his mission:

> But you, Bethlehem, in the land of Judah,
>   are by no means [7] least among the rulers [8] of Judah;
> for out of you will come a ruler
>   who will be the shepherd of my people Israel.
>
> (Matt. 2:6)

The citation begins with words from Micah 5, a passage that describes a military scene in which Israel will be rescued:

> But you, Bethlehem Ephrathah,
>   though you are small among the clans of Judah,
> out of you will come for me
>   one who will be ruler over Israel,
> whose origins are from of old,
>   from ancient times.
>
> (Mic. 5:2)

Matthew's choice of the verb 'shepherd' may be a reflection of this verse in LXX Micah, [9] but it is more likely a recollection of 2 Samuel 5:2 (1 Chr. 11:2): 'And the LORD said to you, "You shall shepherd my people Israel, and you shall become their ruler." ' The word to the

---

[4] For the way in which Matthew is already contrasting the present and future leaders of Israel in 2:1–6, see Patte (1987: 35).

[5] The many links between Exodus 1 – 2 and Matthew 1 – 2 (e.g. unusual birth, flight, return) are explored by Crossan (1986) and Harrington (1991: 46–50).

[6] This title does not reappear again until the passion account (27:11; 29:37).

[7] Matthew understands the statement of Bethlehem's small status in Mic. 5:2 as an ironic declaration of its *significance* in God's plan. The theme of the 'least' (*elachistos*) is important in Matthew (cf. 25:40, 45).

[8] Matthew interprets the *'alpê* of Mic. 5:2 as chiefs rather than clans, thus emphasizing the issue of leadership.

[9] Or Mic. 5:4: 'He will stand and *shepherd his flock* in the strength of the LORD . . .'

ancestrally illegitimate and ethically irresponsible king Herod is that Israel's true deliverer will be a *shepherd ruler* in *David's* line from *David's* home town. It is likely that the background includes Ezekiel 34, where the future Davidic leader is God's unique shepherd (v. 23) who will shepherd 'my people Israel' (v. 30).[10]

The compassionate shepherd and the lost sheep of Israel

When he saw the crowds, he had compassion on them, because they were harassed and helpless, like sheep without a shepherd. (Matt. 9:36)

The introductory section of Matthew continues through chapter 4, which notes the beginning of Jesus' preaching of the kingdom (v. 17) and his calling of the disciples (vv. 18–22). This is followed by a typical Matthean summary statement:

Jesus went throughout Galilee, teaching in their synagogues, preaching the good news of the kingdom, and healing every disease and sickness among the people. News about him spread all over Syria, and people brought to him all who were ill with various diseases, those suffering severe pain, the demon-possessed, those having seizures, and the paralysed, and he healed them. (4:23–24)

As anticipated in the Servant songs, the ministry of Jesus involves authoritative declarations of God's kingdom and merciful works of healing and liberation.

Such summary statements provide at least one kind of structuring device in Matthew. The next one, located in chapter 9, follows the first major body of new teaching (*tôrâ*) in chapters 5 – 7 and an account of ten miracles in chapters 8 – 9.[11] These miracles are linked[12] to an implicit statement about Jesus' role as Shepherd of Israel: 'Jesus went through all the towns and villages, teaching in their synagogues,

---

[10] Heil (1993: 699–700) makes this observation and notes that the theme of 'God with us' is found in Ezek. 34:30 (cf. Matt. 1:23). The exact phraseology 'my people Israel' (*ho laos mou ho Israēl*) is only found in the Greek Bible with reference to David's leadership (LXX 2 Sam. 5:2; 1 Kgs 8:16; 16:2; 1 Chr. 11:2; Matt. 2:6).

[11] On the possible allusions to the ten plagues in Matt. 8 – 9, see Swartley (1994: 63–67).

[12] See Bauer (1988: 89–90) for the relationship between vv. 34 and 35.

preaching the good news of the kingdom and healing every disease and sickness. When he saw the crowds, he had compassion on them, because they were harassed and helpless, *like sheep without a shepherd'* (Matt. 9:35–36). Compassion (*splanchnizomai*) is a common response of Jesus to specific human need in Matthew (14:14; 15:32; 20:34; cf. 18:27), but here it is a general reaction to the state of the crowds.

What prompts his pastoral compassion specifically is the leaderless fate of the people. The phrase 'sheep without a shepherd' suggests a people without a king, or an army without a commander (Num. 27:17; 1 Kgs 22:17; 2 Chr. 18:16; cf. Isa. 13:14). It is not simply human need that moves Jesus, but *their predicament as a flock not properly led*. Without (good) leadership, this crowd is 'troubled' and 'downcast'.[13] Although these specific verbs (*skyllō; riptō*) are not taken from the Septuagint passages discussed above, the picture is familiar. In Ezekiel 34 God is grieved over shepherds whose harsh and brutal rule (v. 4) was the cause of their flock becoming scattered on the hills and left as food for wild beasts (v. 5).

When Jesus saw the crowd as 'sheep without a shepherd' in Mark, it prompted teaching and a feeding miracle (6:34). In Matthew this vision becomes the basis for a call to more complete discipleship, now with hints of succession (cf. Num. 27:17): 'Then he said to his disciples, "The harvest is plentiful but the workers are few. Ask the Lord of the harvest, therefore, to send out workers into his harvest field" ' (9:37–38).

That prayer, as it turns out in the next verse, will be answered in the sending of the disciples themselves. Jesus first invites them to see people the way he sees them; then he asks them to go where he goes. As his labourers, they are to become extensions of his own ministry, full participants in his mission. Their initial calling as 'followers' (4:19), noted above, took place after Matthew's first summary statement. Now, as the author is signalling the close of the first phase of the Messiah's ministry, the summary of *Jesus'* work becomes a summary of the *disciples'* work: 'He called his twelve [14] disciples to him and gave them authority to drive out evil spirits and to heal every disease and sickness' (10:1; cf. 10:7–8; 4:23–24). They were given the

---

[13] This is a play on the normal translation of *riptō*, to cast.

[14] Matthew's interest in the *twelve* disciples in this section (10:1, 2, 5; 11:1) suits his larger representation of the disciples as the renewed Israel. Grassi (1977) suggests that Gen. 49:1–33 (Jacob's blessing of his twelve sons) may also be informing the content of Matt. 9:35 – 11:1.

responsibility to join their king in the compassionate and powerful work that characterized the messianic kingdom (cf. 11:5).[15]

The focus of this messianic ministry was restricted to 'the lost sheep of the house of Israel' (10:5–6). This is a way of keeping the disciples in tune with his own mission, which chronologically prioritized Jews over Gentiles and Samaritans (15:24).[16] It is also continuous with the concerns of the divine Shepherd expressed in the Old Testament. YHWH was passionate about the 'lost' (*apollymi*) of his flock (LXX Ezek. 34:4, 16, 29; cf. Jer. 23:1). These sheep, continually called 'mine' in Ezekiel 34 (vv. 6, 8, 10, 11, 12, 15, 17, 19, 22), are 'the house of Israel' (34:30–31). The instructions of Jesus empower his under-shepherds to join him in gathering the lost and healing the injured. This mission, as we have seen, is impelled by irresponsible shepherding. The need to 'gather' is necessitated by the mischief of those who 'scatter' (cf. 12:30).[17]

While the involvement of the disciples in the ministry of healing and teaching was no doubt exhilarating (Luke 10:17), Matthew's account shows the commissioning to be a serious occasion.[18] Jesus gives a lengthy description of the opposition they would experience as they join him in his mission to the lost sheep of Israel. Mixing his metaphors, Jesus warns them that they were going not only as shepherds but as 'sheep among wolves' (10:16a). This juxtaposition of images presupposes solidarity both with their Lord and with his flock (Patte 1987: 145). It implies union with the Messiah who will express his greatest act of shepherding by becoming, ironically, the sacrificial Lamb of God.[19]

Here again illegitimate leaders are indicted when pastoral language is used of God's chosen servant(s). We might recall at this point Jeremiah's words, 'My people have become lost sheep; their shepherds have led them astray. They have made them turn aside on the

---

[15] We noted above the prediction in Jer. 23:4 of shepherds (plural) who would tend Israel with the result that none of God's flock would be missing.

[16] Jesus' command to 'go' (*poreuomai*) to the lost sheep of Israel (10:6) anticipates their 'going' (*poreuomai*) to all the nations with the gospel in 28:19. The great message of the name 'Immanuel' (God with us) becomes a promise for those who carry on his mission (28:20; cf. Heil 1993: 707).

[17] Jeremias (1968: 492 n. 72) considers both of these verbs (*synagein*, *skorpizein*) to be shepherding terms.

[18] In Matthew there is no report of the disciples returning from a particular single missionary journey, thus implying that the commission was open ended (though, in a sense, renewed in 28:19–20).

[19] However, like their leader, the disciples were to be 'as shrewd as snakes and as innocent as doves' (10:16b). Self-sacrificing service was not to be understood as handing over authority to one's enemies.

mountains; they have gone along from mountain to hill and have forgotten their resting place' (Jer. 50:6 NASB).

False prophets, the great cause of grief for Jeremiah, were the enemies of Jesus as well. In Matthew 7:15 they are characterized as ravenous wolves in sheep's clothing.[20] In chapter 10 Jesus warns of opposition from religious (v. 17) and civil (v. 18) leaders. His disciples will be the objects of betrayal (v. 21), hatred (v. 22) and persecution (v. 23) at the hands of those who 'kill the body' (v. 28). And this is what they should expect for being followers of the rejected king: 'A student is not above his teacher' (v. 24). Following Jesus involves literally taking up one's 'cross' (v. 38). To serve this shepherd requires laying down one's life in the service of his flock.

The healing ministry of the Son of David

> When Jesus landed and saw a large crowd, he had compassion on them and healed their sick. (Matt. 14:14)

The larger section that begins with 4:23–24 continues until the important summary break at 9:35, and then on until 11:1 (cf. Combrink 1977; Bauer 1988: 84–95). What follows then is an account of increasingly disparate reactions to Jesus' ministry (11:2 – 16:20).[21] Although his ministry is focused on the 'lost sheep of Israel' (15:24), he finds greater receptivity among the Gentiles. These nations (*ethnē*) are certainly part of his plan (24:14; 28:19),[22] but, ideally, as a result of Israel's faith rather than her rebellion (21:43). In a variety of encounters Matthew contrasts the remarkable faith of pagans with the ironic rejection by God's own people. In these encounters one appreciates the importance of healing in the revelation of Jesus as the son of David. Apart from Matthew's introductory verse, the title 'Son of David' is always used in a healing context.

The first encounter is recorded in chapter 12 in the context of a dispute over the Sabbath. Jesus has just finished reminding the religious leaders of a central emphasis of his teaching: God desires

---

[20] Only Matthew among the Synoptics uses this image (cf. 24:11, 24), anticipating the extended metaphor in John 10:12. One recalls political shepherds who devour the flock in Ezek. 22:27 (cf. Zeph. 3:3).

[21] On the structure of 4:12/17 – 16:12/20, see Kingsbury (1975: 7–37). Notice the significance of sending out the disciples at this critical turning point in Matthew's Gospel. As the antagonism to Jesus begins to swell (and his death grows more inevitable), the disciples' role as his future replacements becomes more apparent.

[22] See also 2:1–12; 8:5–13; 12:18–21; 15:21–28; 21:43; 25:32; 27:54.

mercy more than sacrifice (12:7; cf. Hos. 6:6; Matt. 9:13). They follow him into the synagogue, where a man with a withered hand presents an opportunity to test him. 'Is it lawful to heal on the Sabbath?' they ask (12:10). His answer only galvanizes the opposition.

He said to them, 'If any of you has a sheep and it falls into a pit on the Sabbath, will you not take hold of it and lift it out? How much more valuable is a man than a sheep! Therefore it is lawful to do good on the Sabbath.'
Then he said to the man, 'Stretch out your hand.' So he stretched it out and it was completely restored, just as sound as the other. But the Pharisees went out and plotted how they might kill Jesus. (Matt. 12:11–14)

The parabolic saying (unique to Matthew) and healing both under-score the mercy/compassion Jesus has for his lost sheep, each of which has inestimable 'value' (*diapherō*; cf. Matt. 6:26; 10:31).[23] It exposes the discrepancy between the laws and behaviour of his accusers.[24] While it is true that many of the Sabbath healings in the Gospels were long-standing illnesses (cf. Luke 13:10–17; John 5:1–18) – which seemingly could have waited until another day – the greater issue is that Jesus represents *the Day* that they were all (supposedly) waiting for. Sabbath (and jubilee) institutions, prototypes for the Messianic Age, promoted the principles of release and rest.[25] One of the consistent themes in Jesus' teaching is that mercy[26] is not only prioritized over legalism; it is the heart of the law itself. Mercy and compassion, central features of pastoral leadership, involved setting people free from their burdens.

Disputes with the religious leaders continue. In chapter 15 Jesus is asked why his disciples do not wash their hands (ritually) before they

[23] This saying anticipates the longer parable of the lost sheep in ch. 18 and may recall Nathan's provocative story to David in 2 Sam. 12:1–6.
[24] The rabbis would say that a person could rescue an animal or human on the Sabbath but healing could wait (cf. b. Shabbat 128b; b. Mezi'a 32b; m. Yoma 8:6; cf. Mekilta Exod. 22:2; 23:13). More extreme, the Essenes forbid saving humans or animals on the Sabbath (CD 11:13–14).
[25] Matthew reports Jesus' offer of a lighter 'yoke' (the traditional symbol of the law; cf. Acts 15:10) and true 'rest' just prior to the controversy of ch. 12 (Matt. 11:28–30; cf. Jer. 6:16). Rest (*anapauō*) is an important pastoral motif in LXX Ezek. 34:14, 15 (cf. Isa. 14:4, 7, 30; 32:18).
[26] *Eleeō* (to show mercy) is used eight times in Matthew, four times in Luke and three times in Mark. The noun *eleos* (mercy) appears three times in Matthew as well.

eat. He responds with a direct attack on their hypocrisy. Then Jesus moves to the region of Tyre and Sidon, where he has a revealing conversation with a 'Canaanite' woman (v. 22).[27] Seeking healing for her daughter, she cries out, '*Lord*, Son of *David*, have *mercy* on me!' (15:22) Jesus' response, after saying nothing, is to insist on his primary calling: 'I was sent[28] only to the lost sheep of Israel' (15:24). When she persists, his refusal seems to turn to rudeness: 'It is not right to take the children's bread and toss it to their dogs' (v. 26). The woman accepts the canine designation and asks only for the 'crumbs that fall from their masters' table' (v. 27). To this shamelessly persistent faith (which recognizes him as 'Lord' three times) Jesus can only respond with mercy. Her daughter was healed instantly (v. 28). Such exceptions to the primary mission are really *anticipations* of the call to the Gentile nations stated clearly in 28:19–20.

The Canaanite woman makes an important association between healing and the identity of Jesus *as the Son of David*. The 'healing' of a demon-possessed man in 12:22 had raised the question, 'Could this be the *Son of David*?' (12:23) Such an equation is apparent in the stories of the two blind men in 9:27 and 20:30–31. In the last of these accounts Matthew mentions explicitly that Jesus was moved with compassion (*splanchnizomai*).[29] Similarly, in Matthew 14:14, 'When Jesus ... saw a large crowd, he had *compassion* on them and *healed* their sick.'

Matthew is unique in this unprecedented equation between (compassionate) healing and the Davidic Messiah.[30] With little evidence in intertestamental literature for such an association,[31] the most probable source is the Old Testament. But where is David ever considered a healer? Duling (1978) asserts that the 'therapeutic son of David' echoes the Isaianic Servant traditions. Matthew's predilection

---

[27] While the language of 'other sheep' awaits John's Gospel, there are hints here in Matthew.

[28] Jesus was the appointed Davidic shepherd of Israel (Ezek. 34:23). As he was 'sent', so he 'sent' out his disciples to care for the lost sheep (Matt. 10:5, 16). This specific verb (*apostellō*) recalls the commissioning of the Servant in Isa. 61:1.

[29] The healing in 9:27 immediately precedes the summary of Jesus' ministry (19:35) and the comment about his compassion (9:36).

[30] 'Four of the five instances of the verb "to have compassion" (*splanchnizomai*) and five of the eight instances of the verb "to have mercy" (*eleeō*) occur in connection with healing and in almost every case the poly-significant titles Lord and/or Son of David appear as part of the semantic field' (Duling 1992: 112).

[31] Some have tried to find a basis for this in the Psalms of Solomon (17:40; cf. Duling 1992).

for healing verbs [32] may recall key passages like Isaiah 61:1.[33] One might contend that the impulse to reach out to the nations is especially evident in the Servant songs,[34] though in these passages there is no direct link with David. The only passage where compassionate healing and David are mentioned together is Ezekiel 34.[35] While David is not the healer, the divine Shepherd expresses mercy through healing and by the appointment of David as shepherd over the flock of Israel. David is an extension of God's responsive shepherding.[36]

Ezekiel provides background for the story of the lost sheep in Matthew 18.[37] This story, common also to Luke, helps answer a dispute about greatness in Matthew. Jesus points to a child as the ideal representative of his kingdom. The parable illustrates his intention that not one of the 'little ones' (*mikrōn*; 18:6, 10, 14) should be 'lost' (*apollymi*). It is the *lost* sheep of Israel that had been the explicit focus of his (and his disciples') ministry to this point. To the merciful shepherd in Matthew, *each one is valued* (cf. 6:25–30; 10:31, 42; 18:1–19; 19:13–15). Only Matthew's account emphasizes that it is the shepherd's *will* that none should be lost (v. 14).

In the background, again, is the suggestion that the lost are lost because they have been *led astray*. This is the import of *planaō* in verses 12 and 13,[38] a verb used commonly with reference to the effect of false prophets in the Septuagint (e.g. Jer. 23:13, 32).[39] For example,

[32] Matthew often refers to exorcisms (in Mark) as healing (compare Mark 7:31–37 with Matt. 15:30; and Mark 9:14–29 with Matt. 17:14–21). Even some teaching episodes in Mark are summarized as healing in Matthew (compare Mark 10:1 with Matt. 19:2; cf. Paffenroth 1999: 548–551).

[33] *Therapeuō* is used sixteen times in Matthew. *Iaomai*, perhaps echoing the Servant's commission in Isa. 61:1, appears four times. Compare the citations of Isa. 42:1–4 in the context of Matt. 12:18–21, and Isa. 53:4–6 in Matt. 8:17. The association may also be present in LXX Zech. 10:2, a passage which attributes a flock's wandering and injury to the lack of a 'healer' (*iasis*), rather than MT 'shepherd' (cf. Hos. 5:13). A shepherd leader is considered a healer in CD 13:9–10.

[34] See Isa. 42:6; 49:6; 45:22–23; 51:4–5; 56:7; 60:2.

[35] Another possibly relevant messianic passage is Mic. 4:6–7. God promises there to gather the lame and the outcasts as the remnant from which he will build a new nation.

[36] Stanton (1992) demonstrates that the Son of David title in Matthew is linked not only to healing but also to conflict with Jewish leaders. His healing confirmed (to some) a royal identity that was a threat especially to Herod.

[37] Heil (1993) argues that Ezekiel 34 provides the 'narrative strategy' for all of Matthew's references to sheep and shepherds. This overstates the case, but several allusions are certainly clear.

[38] Luke does not use this verb in his retelling of the parable.

[39] This verb, used thirty-one times in Isaiah, is found eight times in Matthew, four times in Mark, once in Luke, and twice in John. Matthew uses it three times in this parable, where Luke maintains the use of *apollymi*.

it is used of the neglected strays in Ezekiel 34:4, 16.[40] In Matthew *planaō* refers to the same kind of *mis*leading (24:4, 5, 11, 24; cf. 22:29). This predicament necessitates the Servant's self-sacrificing ministry in Isaiah 53:6: 'We all, like sheep, have *gone astray*, each of us has *turned* to his own way; and [*as a result*] the LORD has laid on him the iniquity of us all.'

The royal shepherd judge

> When the Son of Man comes in his glory ... he will separate the people one from another as a shepherd separates the sheep from the goats. (Matt. 25:31–32)

The final shepherd passage in the pre-passion section of Matthew is his unique description of the last judgment in chapter 25. There the Son of Man as royal judge (vv. 34, 40; cf. 13:41–43; 16:27) is depicted as a shepherd separating (righteous) sheep from (wicked) goats at the end of the day (cf. 1 Enoch 62 – 63). This image trades on common associations of goats' independence and reckless habits in contrast to the docility and responsiveness of sheep.[41] It also quite likely recalls Ezekiel's metaphor which describes a day of judgment between sheep, and between rams and goats (34:17–22). Concern for the 'little ones' and the 'least' in Matthew (e.g. 25:40, 45) may echo protection of the 'lean' and 'weak' in Ezekiel 34:20–21. Certainly the criterion for judgment is the same: the (mis)treatment of the weak by the powerful. This concern follows closely the priority of mercy in Jesus' ministry. It is a restatement of the pivotal royal ethic in the Old Testament explored above. Only after such justice is in place can God's flock enjoy his eschatological era of peace and security (Ezek. 34:25–29).

Matthew's judgment scene has prompted considerable discussion (S. W. Gray 1989), especially concerning the identity of the 'least' of these, referred to as the 'brothers' of the king in 25:40. Are they (the)

---

[40] It may be important that Matthew's account of the parable has the sheep left on the mountains, not the wilderness as in Luke (Donaldson 1985). The mountains are the setting for the lost sheep in Ezek. 34:6, and they also provide the setting for the ministry of the good shepherd in vv. 13, 14.

[41] Many commentators follow Jeremias (1963: 206, citing the work of G. Dalman), who says that sheep and goats are separated at night because goats need shelter for warmth while sheep prefer the outdoors. It may be more likely that this separation is the daily protocol at feeding time which protects sheep (especially ewes) from overbearing goats. These cultural realities suit the theme of judgment quite naturally.

disciples? The poor? And who are the sheep and goats? Verse 32 pictures 'all the nations'. Are these Gentiles only or both Jews and Gentiles? It is outside the scope of our present discussion to attempt definitive answers to these questions. What is germane is the obvious, though implicit, association between the shepherd and his role as king and judge. This was a standard equation in the ancient world and it is a significant feature in Ezekiel 34.

Another more startling emphasis in this final teaching of the Gospel is the equation between the shepherd king and the 'least'. This may resemble the solidarity assumed between the disciples and the lost sheep to which they were going to minister (10:16). In a much more dramatic way this solidarity between Christ and the least will be expressed at the cross. If, however, the hungry, thirsty, stranger, naked, sick and imprisoned are the *disciples* (cf. 10:17ff.; Hagner 1995: 744–745), then Jesus is stressing his solidarity with those who carry on his mission. In this case, as with the Abrahamic promise,[42] judgment of the nations is determined by their treatment of God's chosen ones.

The 'struck' shepherd and his scattered followers

... for it is written:

'I will strike the shepherd,
and the sheep of the flock will be scattered.'

(Matt. 26:31)

Like the other Gospels, Matthew describes the Messiah's passion by resorting to the Old Testament traditions of the Servant, the psalms of lament and Zechariah 9 – 14 (Moo 1983).[43] We are especially interested in the references and allusions to the final section of Zechariah, because pastoral motifs not only recur in these chapters, they bring coherence to them (Bruce 1960–61). The evangelists depend on Zechariah for their portrait of a humble, God-appointed shepherd ruler who is rejected by his people (Moo 1983: 173–174). We will take each quote or allusion in order.

[42] In support of this comparison note the unique Gospel use of *eulogēmenoi* ('blessed'; v. 34; Gen. 12:2–3) and *katēramenoi* ('cursed'; v. 41; Gen. 12:3).
[43] Matthew also exhibits a particular interest in the Passover as the (divinely determined) timing of his death (26:2). He mentions Passover (without the feast of Unleavened Bread) three times in 26:17–19.

Though all the Gospel writers describe Jesus' entry into Jerusalem on a colt, only Matthew of the Synoptics explicitly references Zechariah:

This took place to fulfil what was spoken through the prophet:

> 'Say to the Daughter of Zion,
> "See, your king comes to you,
> gentle and riding on a donkey,
> on a colt, the foal of a donkey." '
>
> (21:3–4; Zech. 9:9)

Matthew emphasizes the gentleness of the coming ruler who, in LXX Zechariah 9:9, comes with righteousness (*dikaios*) and salvation (*sōzōn*), to put an end to war and oversee an era of global peace (Zech. 9:10).

The next citation comes during the Last Supper:

Then Jesus told them, 'This very night you will all fall away on account of me, for it is written:

> "I will [44] strike the shepherd,
> and the sheep of the flock will be scattered."

But after I have risen, I will go ahead of you into Galilee.' (26:31–32; Zech. 13:7; cf. Mark 14:27)

This is the key quotation discussed above at some length. 'Flock' (*probaton*) is a favourite Matthean term that describes both the lost (9:36; 10:6; 15:24; 18:12) and the disciples (10:16; 26:32). Here the Zecharian image of a struck shepherd and a scattered flock is followed by a further extension of the metaphor: Jesus will *lead them once again* in Galilee.

The virtual quotation (Bruce 1960–61: 340) of Zechariah 11:12b is clearly evident in Matthew's exclusive reference to Judas's pay: 'they counted out for him thirty silver coins' (26:15). The intertextual linkage continues with Matthew's (unique) account of Judas's repentance (returning the money) and suicide, and the chief priests' choice

---

[44] The change from a command to the sword (in Zech.) to a statement that [God] will strike (in Matt.) is a way of emphasizing the implicit *divine* control over the fate of the shepherd.

to buy a potter's field.[45] Matthew writes, 'Then what was spoken by Jeremiah the prophet was fulfilled: "They took the thirty silver coins, the price set on him by the people of Israel, and they used them to buy the potter's field, as the Lord commanded me" ' (27:9–10). Here Matthew's last formal quotation draws both from Zechariah (11:13) and Jeremiah (19),[46] the prophet who is named for the citation. From Zechariah comes the thirty silver pieces (*argyrion*, mentioned four times in Matthew) and their being thrown to the potter/foundry (Heb. *yôṣēr*; Gk *chōneutērion*). Jeremiah's judgment language at the potter's house provides the broader, though more subtle, socio-theological context.

What is especially interesting is the significance of the thirty pieces in Zechariah's account. The work of the shepherd of the worthless flock may be valued here at an insultingly low amount (Schroeder 1975).[47] Matthew is also keen on emphasizing 'innocent blood' (*haima athōon*) in his account (27:4; cf. vv. 6, 8).[48] This echoes the concerns of Jeremiah (7:6; 19:4; 22:3, 17; cf. 1 Sam. 19:5) that rulers would be judged for shedding innocent blood (including the prophet's; Matt. 26:15; LXX Jer. 33:15). The Gospel writer thus understands Jesus to be the rejected righteous shepherd ruler, the one who alone has shown the royal ethic of compassion, and the one whose value is grossly undervalued. This portrait of Jesus, rooted in Zechariah 9 – 14 and in the prophetic tradition generally, is attached to a sustained critique of the false shepherds of Israel.

[45] The irony of the concern to keep the law (27:6) while breaking it (cf. Deut. 27:25) suits Matthew's portrait of Israel's false shepherds.

[46] Jeremiah 19, not 18 or 32 (Gundry 1967: 122–127). See Gundry further for Matthew's mixing of sources.

[47] See the discussion above on Zech. 11:13.

[48] Pilate's wife testifies that Jesus is indeed a righteous (*dikaios*) man (27:19). By washing his hands Pilate attempts to absolve himself formally of this *innocent blood* (27:24).

Chapter Twelve

Luke: the seeking and saving shepherd

Like Matthew, Luke was probably written after Mark, and the shorter Gospel became a primary source for constructing the physician's account. Whether written just before or soon after the destruction of Jerusalem (AD 70), the Synoptics are situated in a similar setting to that of Jeremiah and Ezekiel, who wrote in the context of 586 BC.[1]

Luke is the Gentile companion of Paul whose Gospel provides a detailed biography of Jesus for a Gentile audience. While this Gospel has long been appreciated for its Hellenistic literary forms, there has been a growing respect for the way Luke uses Jewish traditions (especially the LXX) to construct his story. The book of Luke reads like one of the historical books of the Old Testament. He presents the ministry and death of the Lord as a continuation of this canonical 'history of salvation'. Jesus is the long-awaited 'Saviour' (*sōtēr*) who brings 'salvation' (*sōtērios*) to his people.[2] While Matthew presents more explicit quotes from the first Testament, Luke's account breathes with biblical allusions, inferences and analogies. He makes his 'proclamation from prophecy and pattern' (Bock 1987). Allusions to Isaiah are especially important in Luke (Seccombe 1981), particularly for describing Jesus' mission as the suffering Servant-Messiah who leads his people in a new exodus.

References to shepherds in Luke, as in Mark, are few but significant. Their presence is noteworthy in the nativity account and in the parable of the lost sheep. In the former case, they represent the category of person Jesus came to seek and the kind of king they would find. In the parable (and throughout Luke) Jesus presents himself as the seeking and saving Shepherd, in contrast to the religious leaders. This mission of Jesus is clearly exemplified in the story of Zacchaeus that follows in chapter 19. That mission is continued by the disciples in the sequel to the Gospel, the Acts of the Apostles.

[1] Compare Luke 13:33; 19:41–48; 21:20–24 with Jer. 6:6; 32:2; Ezek. 4:4ff.; 26:8ff.
[2] This terminology is unique among the Synoptics.

Shepherds and the birth of the Messiah

And there were shepherds living out in the fields near by, keeping watch over their flocks at night ... the angel said to them ... 'Today in the town of David a Saviour has been born to you; he is Christ the Lord.' (Luke 2:8–11)

Luke 1 – 2 provides a prologue to the Gospel and, to a certain extent, to the combined work of Luke-Acts. Many of the significant themes and motifs of this two-volume work are featured in the seven episodes that comprise the opening scenes (Oliver 1963–64; Talbert 1974: 15–18).

Luke is particularly interested in noting the larger historical and political setting of Christ's birth. The events take place 'in the time of Herod king of Judea' (1:5), in Bethlehem (2:4), as a result of a census ordered by Caesar Augustus (2:1), while Quirinius was governor of Syria (2:2). Though Luke is certainly interested in these details for the accuracy of his 'orderly account' (1:3), such notes also suggest to the reader tensions surrounding Roman rule especially in the years leading up to AD 70. The census was a means to organize the vast empire under Caesar's control (i.e. 'the world') for the purpose of taxation. The widely known designation of then reigning Emperor Octavian was 'divine saviour who brought peace to the world' (Green 1997: 58; cf. Fitzmyer 1981: 394).

In contrast to these notorious rulers (and *their* claims and proclamations), a baby is to be born of whom the angelic herald Gabriel[3] predicts: 'He will be *great* and will be called the *Son of the Most High*. The Lord God will give him the *throne* of his father *David*, and he will *reign* over the house of Jacob for ever; his *kingdom will never end*' (1:32–33).

Mary anticipates the upending of the powerful in her prayer of response (1:52). More audacious still, Zechariah anticipates that the 'horn of *salvation* for us in the house of his servant *David*' will bring '*salvation* from our enemies and from the hand of all who hate us' (1:69, 71). David is mentioned throughout the prologue in references to Joseph's lineage (1:27; 2:4 [twice]; cf. 3:31) and in the announcement to shepherds that a saviour had been born in Bethlehem, the 'city of David'[4] (2:11).

---

[3] Gabriel was recognized in early Judaism as one of the chief angels (cf. Dan. 8:16; 9:21; 1 Enoch 9, 20, 40) and as a militant figure in Qumran (cf. Green 1997: 58–59).

[4] The usual (OT) referent for 'city of David' is Jerusalem (e.g. 2 Sam. 5:7). Luke creates a subtle shift of interest to the city of David's birth (R. E. Brown 1977: 420–424).

Representing Jesus as a descendant of David simultaneously associates him both with his ancestor's humble, pastoral origins and with his later status as conquering, ruling king. Both dimensions are important in Luke's presentation. Mary and Joseph were staying in the multipurpose space under a typical house, used for guests, storage and as a pen for animals at night.[5] Mary's newborn son was wrapped in strips of cloth and laid in a feeding trough (*phatnē*), a datum Luke mentions three times (2:7, 12, 16). The birth announcement went out first not to family members but to shepherds who lived [6] in the nearby fields. To them was given the sign [7] that the baby in the shepherd's trough in the city of David was the Anointed One,[8] *their Saviour* (2:11–12). If these shepherds were keepers of the temple flocks, they become important symbolic witnesses to the birth of the quintessential Lamb of God.[9]

There has been much dispute over what the shepherds represent in Luke's nativity story. This is due in part to the disparate views about the reputation of shepherds in first-century Palestine. Under the influence of Jeremias (1968: 488–489; 1969: 303–312) in particular, many point to the 'despised' nature of shepherds evident in later rabbinic literature.[10] This would suggest that the shepherds were (like the virgin mother, her barren cousin and the widow Anna) among the unlikely classes of people to whom Jesus comes in this Gospel.[11] It is significant that such were chosen to be the first witnesses to the birth of the Messiah

---

[5] *Katalyma* (2:7; cf. 22:11) is a guest room, not an 'inn' (*pandocheion*; cf. 10:34). This could have been a cave dug out of the limestone hillside.

[6] Shepherds who 'lived' (*agrauleō*) in the fields were probably hired shepherds, rather than owners.

[7] The notion of a sign (*sēmeion*) was important in the LXX Exodus account (nineteen times), and also among the prophets. Isaiah uses the term fifteen times.

[8] *Christos* (anointed) is important to Luke's purposes (2:11, 26; 3:15; 4:41 et al.), both for recalling the emphasis on this notion in the books of Samuel and for contrasting 'Christ' with Caesar. The unusual phrase *Christos kyrios* is found in Ps. Sol. 18:7, a source that is rich in Davidic messianism (cf. esp. Ps. Sol. 17).

[9] Shepherds in the Bethlehem area were hired to raise flocks especially in anticipation of the Passover slaughter (cf. Mishnah Sheqalim 7:4; b. Baba Kamma 7:7; Bock 1994: 213).

[10] SB 2:113–114; b. Sanhedrin 25b; Midrash Ps. 23:2 (99b).

[11] More than the other Gospel writers, Luke emphasizes Jesus' interest in and followers from among women (1:42; 8:2; 23:27ff.; 24:5ff.); Samaritans (9:52–55; 10:29–37; 17:11–19); tax collectors (3:12–13; 18:9–14; 19:1–10); 'sinners' (7:36–50; ch. 15; 23:40–43); and the poor (1:48, 51–53; 4:18; 6:20). Luke is interested in the imminent, dramatic reversal of power and privilege (cf. 6:20–26; Green 1997: 58–62). For a social scientific orientation to Luke, see Neyrey (1991).

(2:17–20).[12] Other readers see continuity with the positive image of shepherds in Jewish literature,[13] especially shepherd rulers like Moses and David.[14] It seems probable that Luke would emphasize both the rustic and the royal, because both elements are present in the Davidic/messianic traditions themselves. From the margins of society God was once again selecting a new ruler to shepherd his people (cf. Mic. 5:2, 4).

There are other Old Testament passages that may be informing Luke's presentation of the newborn shepherd ruler. Micah 5:1–5 predicts that the coming ruler will come from Bethlehem (v. 2), and he will '*shepherd* his [God's] flock' (v. 4, LXX). Luke's use of relatively rare terms in the Septuagint provides other clues. In Exodus 15:13 God promises to lead Israel to his holy dwelling (Heb. *nāweh*), translated *katalyma* (guest room) in the Greek text. In 2 Samuel 7:6 God assures David that he was content living among them in a *katalyma*. In LXX Jeremiah 14:8 the 'Hope of Israel, its *Saviour* in times of distress'[15] is asked why he is like a stranger who, literally, turns aside to a *katalyma*. In Isaiah 1:3 YHWH contrasts Israel to a donkey who knows his own *phatnē* (manger). Both of these terms are uncommon, and their use in Luke may suggest that he deliberately equates Israel's hope for God's presence with the manger and the guest room.[16] Another term comes from the Wisdom of Solomon where Solomon states, 'I was nursed with care in *swaddling cloths* [*sparganois*]. For no king has had a different beginning of existence' (7:4–5 NRSV). *Sparganon* is only found in the Septuagint in Ezekiel

---

[12] Derrett (1973a) demonstrates several important links between the manger and grave stories, thereby underscoring the important role of the shepherds (like the two Marys) as key witnesses. His assertion that the baby was born in a cave is plausible, given first-century hillside architecture, but it cannot be verified.

[13] Philo, a Jewish philosopher from Alexandria at the turn of the era, describes the importance of first-hand experience with herding for leaders: 'For the chase of wild animals is a drilling-ground for the general in fighting the enemy, and the care and supervision of tame animals is a schooling for the king in dealing with his subjects, and therefore kings are called "shepherds of their people", not as a term of reproach but as the highest honour ... only the perfect king is one who is skilled in the knowledge of shepherding, one who has been trained by management of the inferior creatures to manage the superior' (*Moses*, LCL 6: 309).

[14] Still others have noted the presence of shepherds at the births of great figures in Greek literature (cf. R. E. Brown 1977: 420–421).

[15] The setting in this chapter is the 'wilderness' of God's judgment.

[16] If R. E. Brown (1977: 421–423) is right about other links between Micah 4 – 5 and Luke 1 – 2, then the mention of birth and birth pains (*ōdinō*) in LXX Mic. 4:10 and Mic. 5:2 may be significant. *Ōdinō* is a common (LXX) Isaianic motif for the turmoil that precedes new beginnings (51:2; 54:1; 66:8; cf. 26:17–18).

16:4 (the parable of Israel's birth), and the rare verb in this verse, *sparganoō*, is used in the New Testament only in Luke 2:7, 12.

There are other allusions to messianic expectations from the wilderness and second exodus traditions in Luke's prologue.[17] Like Elijah, John will turn the hearts of the people in preparation for the Lord (1:17). Similarities between Mary's prayer (Luke 1:46–55) and Hannah's prayer (1 Sam. 2:1–10) are strongly suggestive that a new king(dom) is coming and freedom from foreign rule is imminent.[18] Luke's unique (among Gospel writers) use of *euangelizō* ('bear good news'; 1:19; 2:10) recalls the prominent use of this verb in Isaiah's words of comfort (40:9; 52:7; 60:6; 61:1–2). The 'consolation' (*paraklēsis*) of Israel (LXX Isa. 57:18; Jer. 31:9) was precisely what Simeon believed he had seen in the young Jesus (2:25). This child was already acclaimed as 'Lord' by Elizabeth and the angels (1:43; 2:11).[19] The role of the Holy Spirit surrounding the births (and ministries) of the two boys (1:15, 17, 35, 41, 67, 80; 2:25, 26, 27) recalls the leadership of the Spirit in the wilderness and in the second exodus of Isaiah.[20] The Spirit is, in those contexts, often associated with the glory of God (e.g. Isa. 63:14). And it is the glory of God which overwhelms the shepherds in 2:9 (cf. 2:32).

Luke presents the shepherds as 'watching (in) the night watches',[21] perhaps waiting symbolically for the 'dawn'[22] of God's promised redemption (cf. 1:68; 2:38; Isa. 63:4). The 'today' (*sēmeron*) of the angels' message is the eschatological day of deliverance (2:11; cf. 4:21; Bock 1994: 216).[23] The rejoicing that characterizes Isaiah's second exodus is already apparent as each person and group hears the news (1:14, 44, 47, 58; 2:10; cf. Isa. 49:13; 55:12). Anticipated in the wake of God's deliverance is a new era of peace (1:79; 2:14, 29). The new

---

[17] There are several clear quotations from OT passages in Luke 1 – 2: Mal. 4:6 in 1:17; Ps. 103:17 in 1:50; Ps. 107:9 in 1:53; Ps. 106:10 in 1:71; Mal. 3:1 in 1:76; Isa. 9:2 in 1:79; Isa. 9:2, 42:6, 49:6, 51:4, 60:1–3 in 2:32.

[18] Compare also 1 Sam. 2:26 with Luke 2:52.

[19] *Kyrios* is used with reference to YHWH throughout Luke's prologue (twenty-five times), but it will become a common title for Jesus in the rest of the Gospel.

[20] *Pneuma* is used in the OT especially in LXX Isaiah (thirty-nine) and Ezekiel (thirty-six), and in the NT by Luke (thirty-six in Luke; seventy in Acts; cf. Shelton 1991).

[21] This is an attempt to render into English the cognate accusative, *phylassontes phylakas tes nyktos*, in 2:8. See Derrett (1973a: 89) on the importance of (eschatological) 'watching' in Qumran (cf. 1QS 6:7–8).

[22] The emphasis on shining light in 2:9 is also found in Zechariah's words of praise (1:78–79). Simeon refers to Jesus as Isaiah's 'light to the Gentiles' in 2:32.

[23] This word is especially common in Moses' speeches to the generation leaving the desert in Deuteronomy, a book important to Luke's composition (cf. C. A. Evans 1993a).

age is brought about for God's 'servant' Israel (1:54), by one from the house of God's 'servant' David (1:69), namely, the 'servant' Jesus (2:43).[24]

The Nazareth sermon and the second exodus

> The Spirit of the Lord is on me,
> because he has anointed me
> to preach good news to the poor.
> He has sent me to proclaim freedom for the prisoners
> and recovery of sight for the blind,
> to release the oppressed,
> to proclaim the year of the Lord's favour.
>
> (Luke 4:18–19)

The ministry of Jesus begins in his home town with this quote, summarizing his role as the Isaianic Servant/Messiah. By applying the language of Isaiah 61:1–2 and 58:6 to himself,[25] it is clear that he understands the eschaton to be underway *today*. The Spirit, frequently associated with the ministry of the Servant, empowers Jesus to heal, preach the good news of salvation and free the captives.[26] Like shepherd rulers of the ancient world, Jesus was announcing the beginning of his reign by proclaiming freedom from a variety of forms of bondage. For many Jews, this would be understood in terms of the expected year of jubilee (cf. 11QMelch. Lev. 25).

The prologue provides plenty of hints that the new age had begun. Now Luke details specific associations between the works of Jesus and the programme of the second exodus. Christ's mission to the poor, the lame and the marginalized is central to Luke's Gospel (Green 1995: 76–101). These concerns are not only elements of the Servant's mission anticipated in Isaiah (cf. Mic. 4:6–7); they are central to the work of the divine Shepherd predicted in Ezekiel 34. The Servant is the extension of YHWH's own ministry to the lost, scattered, sick and weak. This understanding of the divine mission *in*

---

[24] Although English versions miss this intertextual allusion, Luke seems conscious of the LXX choice of *pais* (child, servant), rather than *therapōn* or *doulos*, for Isaiah's Servant.

[25] Sanders (1993) explains the relationship between these two LXX passages (on the basis of the noun for 'release', *aphesis*) and the importance of this sermon as a rubric for Jesus' ministry (cf. Seccombe 1981).

[26] Jesus' commission as the Servant begins at his baptism when the Holy Spirit comes upon him and the heavenly voice recites Ps. 2:7 and Isa. 42:1 (Luke 3:22).

the context of the irresponsible behaviour of Israel's current shepherds is important to the theology of all the Gospels.

Luke's account provides other hints of exodus. In a confrontation with a sign-seeking generation (11:14–32), Jesus was accused of casting out unclean spirits by the power of Beelzebub. After exposing the logical weakness of the accusation, he continues: 'But if I drive out demons by the finger of God, then the kingdom of God has come to you' (11:20). The particular phrase 'finger of God' recalls Moses' confrontation with Pharaoh (Exod. 8:19; 31:18).[27] The particular wording may also emphasize the dramatic, and perhaps unsettling, arrival of the new age: 'the kingdom of God has come *upon* [*epi*] *you*'.[28] It is noteworthy that in this context (11:23) Jesus defines his followers as those who 'gather' (*synagō*) with him, and his enemies as those who 'scatter' (*skorpizō*). *Synagō* and *(dia)skorpizō* are key shepherding terms in second exodus passages in the prophets (e.g. LXX Isa. 40:11; Jer. 23:1–2, 8; Ezek. 34: 5–6, 12–13, 21; 37:21).

In the new kingdom that Jesus describes, the twelve apostles will be judges over an equal number of Israelite tribes (22:30). This is an important image in Luke's theology, because these twelve are firstfruits and representatives among the remnant of Israel to be restored (C. A. Evans 1993b). The choice of twelve apostles cannot but be understood against the backdrop of the twelve tribes who constituted the community in the wilderness of Sinai.

In that wilderness context another significant number emerges. Seventy members of Jacob's family left Egypt (Exod. 1:5). This was the beginning of the community that would one day experience the promises made to Abraham. Further, to relieve Moses of the excessive burden of leadership, YHWH had shared his spirit among seventy elders (Num. 11:16ff.; 24:1).[29] Only in Luke, Jesus authorizes seventy of his disciples to share his work of bringing peace and healing, and preaching that 'the kingdom of God has come near to you' (Luke 10:9 NASB; cf. v. 11).

This appointment, though executed with remarkable authority (10:17), was qualified in terms of the Servant's own calling: 'I am sending you out *like lambs among wolves*' (10:3). The disciples are invited to follow the suffering Servant in his mission to bring peace

---

[27] The phrase is only found in the LXX in these two passages and in reference to God's writing on the two tablets of stone in Deut. 9:10. Only Luke has this phrase in the NT.

[28] As in the teaching of the prophets, the Day of the Lord turns out first to be judgment on his own people.

[29] Other 'new Moses' motifs in Luke's Gospel are explored in Tiede (1980: 46–47, 53, 124–125) and Moessner (1982, 1983). Cf. Acts 3:22–23; 7:17–44.

into the world by giving up their own lives (cf. 9:22–23).[30] But this was the only way into the new age: 'Do not be afraid, little flock,[31] for your Father has been pleased[32] to give you the kingdom' (12:32). Luke later describes how the care of Christ's flock was entrusted to others who should be mindful of the cost: 'Keep watch over yourselves and all the flock of which the Holy Spirit has made you overseers. Be shepherds of the church of God, which he bought with his own blood' (Acts 20:28). The self-sacrificing mission of Jesus was already apparent during his transfiguration in 9:28–36. This passage is situated just prior to the large central section of the book which recounts Jesus' movement towards Jerusalem. The language and symbolism of this extraordinary encounter points back to his baptism and ahead to his passion. It is in his conversation with Elijah and Moses that he discusses 'his departure, which he was about to bring to fulfilment at Jerusalem' (9:31). Only Luke uses the word *exodos*[33] for departure, another subtle indication that this writer is particularly aware of the links between the suffering of Christ and the deliverance of his people (cf. Exod. 19:1; Num. 33:38; Heb. 11:22).[34] Only in Luke are the two brightly appearing 'men' (Moses and Elijah?) present when the work of redemption is complete (Luke 24:4; cf. Acts 1:10; Mánek 1957: 8–12).

In all of the Synoptic Gospels Jesus explains the meaning of his death with the phrase 'covenant in my blood' (Luke 22:20). These words recall Moses sprinkling the community in Exodus 24:8 and declaring, 'This is the *blood of the covenant* that the LORD has made with you.' They also anticipate the inauguration of the new covenant described in Jeremiah 31:31 and Ezekiel 34:25; 37:26. The final meal was the Passover (22:1, 7, 8, 11, 13, 15), and the Passover lamb was

[30] Luke's understanding of Jesus as the suffering Servant extends into Acts (cf. 3:18–26; 26:23). Suffering is a typical experience for his followers (5:41; 9:16).

[31] This phrase may echo 'the poor of the flock' in Zech. 11:11 and/or 'the little ones' of Zech. 13:7 (cf. Bruce 1960–61: 346).

[32] *Eudokeō* (to be pleased) is otherwise reserved in the Gospels for God's sentiments about his Son, expressed at his baptism and transfiguration. This may be one more subtle way of hinting that the disciples are inheriting the mission of the suffering Servant/Lamb (cf. Isa. 42:1).

[33] Possibly another exodus term is *exagō* (to lead out), important in the last scene of the Gospel (Luke 24:50). This verb is used three of eight times in the book of Acts with reference to the exodus (7:36, 40; 13:17).

[34] It is possible that Peter's interest in setting up booths (*skēnas*; v. 33) as a response to seeing the glory (*doxa*; 9:31, 32) is reminiscent of Num. 9:17ff. Moessner (1982) explores the exodus typology in this passage, noting the symbolic importance of children (Luke 9:47–48) as the next generation that will inherit the land (in Numbers).

the suffering Servant who submitted willingly to the slaughterer's knife to bear the sins of many (Isa. 53:7, 11).

The seeking and saving shepherd

The Son of Man came to seek out and to save the lost. (Luke 19:10 NRSV)

The central section of Luke begins ominously: 'As the time approached for him to be taken up to heaven, Jesus resolutely set out for Jerusalem' (9:51). From this verse through most of chapter 19 Luke retells Jesus' encounters, miracles and teaching on the way to his death. We find in this section one of the more memorable parables of his teaching ministry, the seeking shepherd (ch. 15).

Before taking up a brief discussion of this familiar story, it is important to consider the nature of parables as extended metaphors.[35] The long history of the secondary discussion of Jesus' parables has come full circle (Snodgrass 2000). Despising the uncontrolled (and uncontrollable) allegorical interpretations of the early church, many modern critics found safer methods, typically restricting each parable to a single meaning (e.g. Jülicher 1888, 1899). In contrast, current trends in literary and biblical criticism attempt to justify polyvalent readings. While some of these 'postmodern' approaches locate meaning(s) in a reader-centred relativism, this is not a necessary conclusion. In a sense, polyvalence is a feature of parables Jesus himself described. He said only few of his listeners could 'hear' and 'see'[36] the deeper meaning that was *intentionally* embedded in his figures of speech (Luke 8:10; cf. Isa. 6:10).

In our introductory chapter we described good metaphors as those that capture and transmit judgments about reality. Like fuller

---

[35] In our analysis of parables, we will follow Dodd's (1935) focus on both the culturally natural and unexpected elements of parables, and the way in which hearers are teased into personal application of their meaning. Funk (1966: 133ff.) has amply defended the view that parables are extended metaphors whose meaning(s) cannot simply be distilled from their supposedly disposable stories. Sider (1995), a literary critic, makes a good case for parables as 'proportional analogies' which communicate correspondences between literal and figurative meaning in varying ways. Snodgrass (2000) has a balanced summary with judicious regard for letting authorial intention control the meaning modern readers derive from Jesus' stories.

[36] The first time Luke uses the ideas of 'seeing' and 'hearing' is in the nativity story. There the shepherds testified concerning what they had 'seen' and 'heard' (2:20). It was a 'sign' (*sēmeion*) that they saw (2:12), a physical reality with a deeper meaning which they successfully perceived. These terms are also used in a rebuke to John, whose faith was weakening (7:22; cf. 10:24).

narratives they contain and promote world views. Effective metaphors can trigger a *gestalt* of imagination, feeling, thought and action. Jesus' parables were effective extended metaphors in just these ways. The parable of the shepherd is found with different elements and emphases in Luke, Matthew and John. The story in Luke and Matthew concerns a shepherd who leaves his flock of ninety-nine in search of one lost sheep.[37] While Matthew's interest is in the restoration of a believer, the parable in Luke is integral to his portrait of Jesus' compassionate, 'evangelistic' ministry as 'the Son of Man [who] came to seek out and to save the lost' (19:10 NRSV).

The contrast between the two Synoptic accounts is revealing. In Luke 15:4 the sheep is 'lost' (*apollymi*); in Matthew 18:12 it 'strays' (*planaō*). In Luke the shepherd leaves (*kataleipō*) the ninety-nine in the wilderness (*erēmos*); in Matthew he leaves (*aphiēmi*) them in the hills (*orē*). In Luke he searches '*until he finds it*'; in Matthew 18:13 he simply searches for the one who went astray to see *if* he might find it. Upon finding the sheep, the shepherd in Luke 15:5 places it on his shoulders (cf. Isa. 40:11; 49:22; 60:4; 66:12). While both stories mention the joy (*chairō*) of recovery, Luke alone mentions community celebration (15:5; cf. 1:58).

Luke emphasizes the passion of the shepherd by his choice of language. One would be over-translating *kataleipō* to say he *abandoned* his ninety-nine for the one; a shepherd in this position would likely have recourse to his donkeys, dogs or fellow shepherds to help him.[38] However, in this moment of loss, a shepherd chooses to give his full personal attention to the recovery of one animal rather than to the safety of the rest of the flock (Nolland 1993: 771, 773).[39] Jesus considers this individualized concern to be a natural expression of anyone's (v. 4) commitment to a flock. Such is the assumption in Ezekiel's metaphor of bad shepherds: 'You have not strengthened the weak or healed the sick [single] or bound up the injured [single]. You have not brought back the strays [single] or searched for the lost [single]' (Ezek. 34:4). Each of these conditions (except the first) is

---

[37] The size of the herd is moderate; it is more than subsistence size but not 'large' (i.e. 300 plus; cf. b. Baba Kamma 6:20).

[38] I have personally witnessed a flock this size stay in one place because of the presence of a shepherd's donkey. It was reported that they would even stay overnight until the shepherd returned. I have also seen shepherds watch another's flock while one of them went in search of a stray.

[39] Cf. the Gospel of Thomas 107, where the explicit point is this disproportionate concern: 'I care for you *more than the ninety nine*' (J. M. Robinson 1988: 137).

described as the state of an individual animal. Individual concern is reflected in the confident words of Psalm 23:1, 'The LORD is *my* shepherd' (cf. Ps. 119: 76). Through these metaphorical statements a compact theology is affirmed that 'God counts by ones' (Barton 2000: 205).

Luke's emphases are made clearer when one looks at the context of the parable. The setting is a dispute that the Pharisees and teachers initiate with Jesus over his indiscriminate choice of eating companions. Their 'grumbling' (*diagongyzō*) recalls the opposition of the leaders to Moses and YHWH in the wilderness.[40] Luke records a string of three parables that include the themes of losing,[41] finding and rejoicing, with explicit correspondence made to the rejoicing in heaven over one sinner who repents (15:7, 10). The lost sheep is contrasted with the rest who 'do not need to repent' (15:7). The longer story of the lost son (which recapitulates the set) creates a more detailed contrast between the older son and those who celebrate with the merciful father.

Clearly Luke's story of the shepherd is part of a critique of Israel's leaders. By beginning with the question, 'Which one of you ...?' (15:4 NRSV), Jesus exposes their ironic hypocrisy in light of natural human sentiment. He begins with stories of lost sheep and coins, valued objects that the average person would naturally expend a significant amount of energy to find. The story of the lost son moves closer to the point by means of a caricature of the religious leaders as the eldest son. The unexpected element in this parable is the *extraordinary* mercy of the father in accepting back his *undeserving* son.

All three stories include the motif of rejoicing (cf. Ezek. 18:23; 33:11), but the third one sets joy in the context of communal eating.[42] Thus, the criticism of Jesus in 15:2 creates a teaching moment about the nature of God[43] and the ministry of his servant(s). Like the Old Testament passages which employ pastoral imagery, Luke 15 subtly combines words of judgment with words of hope.

[40] With one exception this relatively rare word (in the Bible) is only used with reference to the exodus in the LXX (Exod. 15:24; 16:2, 7, 8; Num. 14:2, 36; 16:11; Deut. 1:27; cf. Josh. 9:18). In the NT it is only used in Luke 15:2 and 19:7.

[41] *Apollymi* is used in Luke 15:6, 8, 9, 17, 24, 32.

[42] The image of a great feast carries obvious resonance with expectations for the Messianic Age. Jesus is implying that the 'lavish banquet *for all peoples*' (Isa. 25:6 NASB) has begun.

[43] It was common for Jewish parables of the time to include similar down-to-earth stories to explain the nature of God and his ways (Young 1998). However, in a highly provocative way Jesus was, in this and other parables, also equating *himself* with YHWH.

The unique elements of chapter 15 reinforce Luke's representation of Jesus, whose *persistent compassion* extends especially to the socially and religiously marginalized. The resemblance between the elements in the parable and the story of Zacchaeus (which is only found in Luke) in chapter 19 illustrates the point.[44] The setting is similar: Jesus dines with a 'sinner' (19:7).[45] Jesus' urgent interest in the tax collector (19:5) contrasts with the grumbling (*diagongyzō*) of the Pharisees (19:7). In response to Jesus' inclusive attitude, the tax collector repents (19:8; cf. 15:7). Jesus announces that this 'sinner' is now a recipient of God's 'salvation'; he too is 'a son of Abraham' (19:9). Here is an explicit statement that explains much of the ministry of the Son of God in Luke.[46] The 'lost sheep' include *anyone*, rich or poor, 'righteous' or 'sinner', Jew or Gentile. *To call such people 'lost' is to imply that they belonged in the fold all along.* The resonance between Zacchaeus and the parable is completed by the explanatory statement that follows: 'For the Son of Man came to *seek out* [*zēteō*] and to *save* the *lost*' (19:10 NRSV; cf. Ezek. 34:16; John 6:39).[47] Evangelism is a natural expression of the shepherd's commitment to the whole flock of God, especially those who have not yet found their true home.

---

[44] In a sense, the story of Zacchaeus is the climax to the ministry of Jesus prior to the passion. Marshall (1978: 694) defends an outline of the central section as 9:51 – 19:10.

[45] Ironically, the name Zacchaeus is derived from the Hebrew term for 'pure'.

[46] See Marshall (1970: 77–187) for a full discussion of the importance of 'saving' people in Luke's theology.

[47] Luke's presentation anticipates John's image of the good shepherd seeking 'other sheep' (John 10:16).

Chapter Thirteen

John: the self-sacrificing shepherd and Passover lamb

Among the Gospels, John provides the richest example of pastoral imagery. The famous tenth chapter is a comprehensive *māšāl*[1] on the model shepherd who lays down his life for the flock. This unique emphasis on self-sacrifice is foreshadowed by the witness of John the Baptist regarding the 'Lamb of God, who takes away the sin of the world' in 1:29, the blameless lamb slaughtered on Passover. Pastoral imagery permeates the Gospel's final episode when Jesus commands Peter three times to shepherd/feed 'my sheep' (21:15–17).

The placement of these references within the larger framework of the fourth Gospel is important. Though the structure of John is debated, most agree that between the prologue (1:1–18) and epilogue (ch. 21) there are two main sections, often called the 'Book of Signs' (chs. 2 – 11/12) and the 'Book of Glory' (chs. 13 – 20).[2] The prologue is programmatic (cf. Carson 1991: 111), outlining the primary concerns and themes that follow. Jesus is presented in terms of Old Testament categories, as the divine Word (1:1) and Creator (1:3); life (1:4) and light (1:5ff.); the presence of God (1:14); and one greater than Moses (1:17). The first main section highlights seven 'signs' (*sēmeia*) or revelatory miracles given in the context of increasing opposition.[3] The sign accounts are typically followed by explanatory discourses and disputes which often revolve around one of the seven key 'I am' statements. The author also links several of these episodes to specific biblical feasts (most often the Passover).[4] For example, the discourse of John 10 follows the healing of a blind man (ch. 9), features two 'I am' statements (the door and the good shepherd), and is set during the feast of Hanukkah (10:22).

---

[1] *Māšāl* is the Hebrew term for pithy sayings and stories that often have secondary meanings.

[2] Following Dodd (1953) and R. E. Brown (1966).

[3] The beginning of this section (1:29–34) contains more titles: Lamb of God, Rabbi, Messiah, Son of God, King of Israel and Son of Man.

[4] Passover is mentioned ten times in John, Tabernacles in 7:2, Dedication in 10:22, and 'a feast' in 5:1.

The Book of Glory is about the passion of Christ, set during the Passover festival. More than the other Gospel writers, John emphasizes this liturgical background. The epilogue moves beyond the passion to what some consider a final sign, the miracle of the fish (ch. 21). It is in this setting that Jesus commissions Peter to feed his sheep and intimates that this disciple will follow his master to a similar death.

Second exodus and wilderness imagery

It is not Moses who has given you the bread from heaven, but it is my Father who gives you the true bread from heaven. (John 6:32)

Though John seldom cites the Old Testament directly, his use of typology and allusion is wide-ranging (Carson 1988). The 'I am' sayings undoubtedly recall the divine name revealed to Moses in Exodus 3:14.[5] The original revelation of YHWH's name came both through speaking it and through demonstrations of his character. The 'signs' (*sēmeia*; Exod. 3:12; 4:8 et al.) and 'wonders' (*terata*; Exod. 4:21; 7:3 et al.) in the exodus account were means by which the Egyptians and the Israelites would 'know YHWH'.[6] Similarly in John, the signs are miraculous manifestations of God's glory and revelations of his identity. They trigger two characteristic responses: faith (Exod. 14:31; John 2:11; 20:8) and hardness of heart (Exod. 4:21; 7:3, 13 et al.; John 12:40).

The primary miracles in the wilderness account apparently provided a schema for John. He introduces the key wilderness theme of God's presence in John 1:14: 'The Word became flesh and made his dwelling [*eskēnōsen*][7] among us. We have seen his glory, the glory of the One and Only, who came from the Father, full of grace and truth.' Two of his core symbols[8] are water (e.g. 2:7–9; 4:5ff.; 7:38) and bread (e.g. ch. 6), obvious reminiscences of the

[5] The divine name in LXX Exod. 3:14, *egō eimi ho ōn*, is echoed in John's *egō eimi* sayings, most provocatively when used without a qualifier (4:26; 6:20; 8:24, 28, 58; 18:5, 6, 8).

[6] The verb *ginōskō* (to know) is pivotal in the LXX exodus account. The purpose of the miraculous signs of judgment was that the Egyptians would *know* 'that I (YHWH) am the LORD' (cf. Exod. 5:2; 6:7; 7:5 et al.). This verb is highly significant in John, appearing ninety-five times.

[7] A literal rendering would be 'tabernacled among us'.

[8] A third, light, may recall the pillar of fire for divine guidance in the wilderness. See Koester (1995) for a full discussion of the symbolism in John.

provisions in the wilderness.[9] The offer of 'living water' in 7:38 is made during the festival of Tabernacles, the holiday which commemorates God's provision in the wilderness. After the miraculous feeding story in John 6, the crowd asks for a sign *like the manna in the desert* (v. 31). Jesus replies, 'I tell you the truth, it is not Moses who has given you the bread from heaven, but it is my Father who gives you the *true bread from heaven* ... I am the bread of life. He who comes to me will never go hungry, and he who believes in me will never be thirsty' (vv. 32–35).[10]

The leading figure in the wilderness narratives is, of course, Moses, and the presentation of Jesus as a new Moses is persistent in John (Boismard 1993).[11] Like Moses, Jesus is 'sent' to his own people who reject him (Exod. 2:11, 14; John 1:11). Both perform miraculous signs[12] to reveal God's glory[13] and gather believers (Exod. 4:8–9; John 20:8). While Moses' miracles were primarily acts of judgment on Egypt (which also revealed God's mercy on Israel), Jesus' miracles were primarily acts of mercy for his followers (accompanied by words of judgment on their false leaders). Moses turned water into blood (a symbol of death); Jesus turned water into wine (a symbol of abundant life). Moses brought disease to people and destruction to Egypt's crops; Jesus brought healing to the lame and multiplied their bread. Moses brought darkness to the Egyptians (like blindness; Exod. 10:23); Jesus brought light to the blind. Moses brought death to the firstborn; Jesus raised the dead back to life.

Not surprisingly, John makes use of second exodus language in his Gospel as well. One important precedent for understanding Jesus as a sacrificial lamb comes from Isaiah 53. Here the Servant accomplishes his work of deliverance ironically as he prepares willingly to be 'led like a lamb to the slaughter' (Isa. 53:7). Some of the shepherd motifs (and the interest in 'other sheep') in John 10 likely originate with Isaiah:

[9] Another wilderness symbol is the bronze serpent from Num. 21:9 (John 3:14; cf. 8:28; 12:32, 34).

[10] The phrase 'bread of heaven' (*arton ouranou*), from LXX Ps. 77:24 (E 78:24) and 104:40 (E 105:40), is echoed with variations eight times in John 6 (vv. 31, 32, 33, 41, 50, 51, 58).

[11] Moses is mentioned by name thirteen times in the first nine chapters of this Gospel.

[12] The terms 'signs' (*sēmeia*) and 'wonders' (*terata*) are almost always associated with the works of Moses in the LXX (cf. Deut. 4:34; Ps. 78:43–51).

[13] 'Glory' (most often from *doxa*) is another key OT (wilderness) theme in John (1:14; 2:11; 7:39; 11:4, 40; 12:23, 41; 13:31; 17:5, 22, 24).

And foreigners who bind themselves to the LORD
to serve him . . .
who hold fast to my covenant –
these I will bring to my holy mountain
and give them joy in my house of prayer . . .
The Sovereign LORD declares –
he who gathers the exiles of Israel:
'I will gather still others to them
besides those already gathered' . . .
Israel's watchmen are blind,
they all lack knowledge . . .
They are shepherds who lack understanding;
they all turn to their own way,
each seeks his own gain.

(Isa. 56:6–11)

The most obvious source of inspiration for John 10 is Ezekiel 34, a foundational second exodus passage from the Prophets. This passage (and Jer. 23:1–8) is pertinent because of the contrast it sets up between shepherds who do not care for the flock of YHWH (thereby causing them to be scattered prey for wild animals) and the God of Israel who does care. The divine Shepherd gathers and unifies his scattered flock, which then follows him and his appointed (Davidic) undershepherd. But Ezekiel may have contributed more than just these motifs. Deeley (1997) finds a liberal use of elements from the exilic prophet in John. Ezekiel uses signs to illustrate his message, including his own dumbness. Signs validate a true prophet (Ezek. 33:33; cf. John 4:19; 6:14; 7:40; 9:17). Parables are also more significant in Ezekiel than in any other Old Testament book. Two of his most developed parables are the vine (Ezek. 17; cf. John 15) and the shepherd (Ezek. 34; cf. John 10).

Perhaps Deeley's most important insight is the way Ezekiel's *theology* informs the fourth Gospel. Ezekiel's insistence that, from now on, God's judgment will be on an *individual* basis is a key to the story of the blind man in John 9. This man was blind, not because of generational sin (9:3, 34), but for the *glory of God* – another key theme in Ezekiel. In the dispute prior to the man's healing, a central issue was who the real children of Abraham (and God) are (8:33–58; cf. Ezek. 33:24). Jesus follows Ezekiel's logic: only those who respond to the word of God's messengers are the true heirs of God's promises. The context for Jesus' good shepherd discourse is the ever-increasing tension between him and the religious authorities. Like Ezekiel, he lays hope for God's renewed pastoral leadership on the back of an image of judgment.

John draws broadly from other Old Testament traditions. Like the Synoptic authors, he looks to Zechariah in the framing of his passion narratives. Branch (Zech. 3:8; 6:12) and shepherd (Zech. 9 – 12) symbolism echo in the fourth Gospel.[14] Like Ezekiel and Jeremiah before him, Zechariah emphasized that the coming branch and shepherd would be a *Davidic* ruler. This association was present in the more developed royal traditions of the Psalms.[15] John sees in Jesus both the fulfilment of God's promise to shepherd his people personally *and* the fulfilment of his promise to appoint a Davidic shepherd ruler.[16]

The model shepherd

The good shepherd lays down his life for the sheep. (John 10:11)

Having an awareness of the structure of the fourth Gospel and having noted the importance of second exodus traditions in it, we are now in a position to look in detail at the familiar 'good shepherd' discourse. *Kalos* (10:11, 14) may better be translated 'model' for two reasons. First, 'good' might imply nothing more than a moral quality. While Jesus is certainly contrasting malevolent thieves, bandits and hirelings with a benevolent shepherd, he might have used the more common term *agathos*.[17] *Kalos* implies an attractive quality, something noble or ideal. 'Model' captures these connotations, but also implies a second nuance that is important in this context: Jesus should be emulated. John makes it clear elsewhere that Jesus is ultimately training his followers to be like him in his life and death (4:34–38; 14:12; 17:20; 20:21–23; 21:15–19). They will eventually take care of his flock and risk their lives like their master (21:15–23).

---

[14] Psalm 80, structured around imagery of the shepherd and the vine, may also be in the background.

[15] Daly-Denton (2000) argues that John's allusions to the Psalms contribute significantly to his presentation of Jesus as the royal Son of David.

[16] The language of sonship is heavily used in John: 'Father' (for God) occurs over 100 times and 'Son' (for Jesus) over fifty times. While this certainly had implications for the divinity of Christ (19:7), it was also a traditional way to refer to royalty (Ps. 2:7). See Meeks (1967: 32–99) for the importance of Jesus' kingship in John.

[17] He might also have used the term *dikaios*, which had royal-pastoral connotations (Jer. 23:5).

John 10 is a continuation of the dialogue and dispute[18] surrounding the healing of the blind man in chapter 9 (cf. 10:21). This episode is itself a continuation of previous narrative, beginning with declarations and confrontations during the festival of Tabernacles in chapter 7 (VanderKam 1990). In keeping with festival associations, Jesus had identified himself both as the source of living water (7:38) and as the light of the world (8:12; 9:5). The religious leaders tested him with the case of the adulterous woman in 8:1–11.[19] In response to his audacious self-referential claims (as the true source of light), the religious leaders challenge his authority (8:13ff.) and prepare to stone him (v. 59).[20] In chapter 9 Jesus illustrates his light-giving power by healing a man born blind. This prompts another confrontation with the religious leaders, who expel the man for showing deference to Jesus (9:28). Jesus explains that his signs produce faith for those who can 'see' but judgment for those who are 'blind' (9:35–41).

It is at this point in the Gospel that Jesus launches his extended parable.[21]

> [1] I tell you the truth, the man who does not enter the sheep pen by the gate,[22] but climbs in by some other way, is a thief and a robber. [2] The man who enters by the gate is the shepherd of his sheep. [3] The watchman opens the gate for him, and the sheep listen to his voice. He calls his own sheep by name and leads them out. [4] When he has brought out all his own, he goes on ahead of them, and his sheep follow him because they know his voice. [5] But they will never follow a stranger; in fact, they will run away

---

[18] The plot of John escalates as it moves from one controversy to the next (Culpepper 1983: 89–98).

[19] Although there is considerable text-critical dispute over the authenticity and placement of this passage in John, it certainly fits here as an episode in the progressive escalation of resistance to Jesus' ministry.

[20] The opposition enhances Jesus' solidarity with the woman by dictating for him the same sentence.

[21] John calls this story a *paroimia* in v. 6 (cf. 2 Pet. 2:22). Like *parabolē* (preferred in the Synoptics), this word translates the more general Hebrew term *māšāl* for figurative speech. (The Greek terms are used in parallel in Sirach 47:17.) It is possible that John's preferred term emphasizes the enigmatic nature of the saying. It is noteworthy that Jesus' metaphorical discourses in John (on the shepherd and vine) have allegorical dimensions to them.

[22] Reference to a *thyra* (gate), like that of a watchman, may imply a walled enclosure designed for a flock. This may be suggested similarly by the calling of 'his own' sheep; the flocks of other shepherds may have been sharing the pen.

from him because they do not recognise a stranger's voice. (John 10:1–5)[23]

Introduced with the words *amēn amēn* ('I tell you the truth'), Jesus provides a metaphorical explanation of the current situation (cf. 3:11). The religious leaders are represented by the thief and robber (cf. 9:39–41). They are the strangers whose voice the 'sheep' (i.e. the blind man) do not recognize. A thief (*kleptēs*) was a member of the community, subject to the law (e.g. LXX Exod. 22:1; Derrett 1973b: 45). This term is used of Judas in 12:6. *Lēstēs* is a term for robbers, bandits and outlaws, including revolutionaries like Barabbas (18:40; cf. Luke 23:19). In contrast, Jesus is the *legitimate* shepherd, that is, the one whom both the watchman[24] and the sheep recognize. Because sheep are easily frightened by strangers, their natural responsiveness to their own shepherd indicates whose they are.[25]

Calling them each by name,[26] Jesus leads his flock out (*exagei*; v. 3) as YHWH promised he would in Ezekiel 34:13. There are echoes here also of the prediction of Micah:[27]

> I will surely gather all of you, O Jacob;
>   I will surely bring together the remnant of Israel.
> I will bring them together like sheep in a pen,
>   like a flock in its pasture;
>   the place will throng with people.
> One who breaks open the way will go up before them;
>   they will break through the gate and go out.
> *Their king will pass through before them,*
>   *the LORD at their head.*
>
> (Mic. 2:12–13)

[23] Since J. A. T. Robinson (1955), it has been common to assume the presence of two parables behind these verses (i.e. Jesus as door and as shepherd). Whether or not this is the case in previous oral form, in John's composition this paragraph is closely related (in form and content) to the explanatory expansions that follow: the door in vv. 7–10, the shepherd in vv. 11–18.

[24] We have noted earlier that shepherds were commonly represented as watchmen (cf. Hos. 12:12).

[25] Recall God's emphasis on '*my* sheep' throughout Ezek. 34.

[26] The granting of a special/new name is important not only in traditional animal husbandry but also in one of the OT passages likely influencing these words: 'To [eunuchs] I will give within my temple and its walls a memorial and a name better than sons and daughters; I will give them an everlasting name that will not be cut off' (Isa. 56:5; cf. Isa. 62:2; 6).

[27] A. T. Hanson (1991: 135–136) explores other links between Zech. 3:5–10 and John 10:1–6.

The legitimate shepherd brings [28] *all* of his sheep out (cf. John 18:9), and then they follow (*akoloutheō*) behind him (v. 4). 'Following' is an important emphasis in John, as in all the Gospels. It is the appropriate response of those who recognized Jesus as the Lamb of God (1:36–43). In this chapter it is the familiar voice of the shepherd that inspires 'followership' (10:4, 5, 27). Following takes on an ominous dimension later as Jesus begins to predict his own death (13:36ff.). Following him *to his death* is precisely what he calls Peter to in 21:19–22.

In response to his listeners' lack of understanding (10:6) Jesus draws out the implications of the parable (10:7–18), moving back and forth between literal and figurative speech. He identifies himself as both door and shepherd. As the door he is the exclusive means of entrance into the protected fold. As the shepherd he is the one who leads the flock to pastures (abundant life). By both metaphors Jesus contrasts himself with others – those who do not use the door and those who care for themselves rather than the flock.

The first elaboration explores the door/gate metaphor, which corresponds to 'way' language in John elsewhere (1:23; 14:4–6): [29]

[7]Therefore Jesus said again, 'I tell you the truth, I am the gate [30] for the sheep. [8]All who ever came before me were [31] thieves and robbers, but the sheep did not listen to them. [9]I am the gate; whoever enters through me will be saved. He will come in and go out, and find pasture. [32] [10]The thief comes only to steal and kill and destroy; I have come that they may have life, and have it to the full. (John 10:7–10)

---

[28] Literally, he 'drives' (*ekballō*) them out (cf. 2:15). This detail is puzzling. If the sheep are responsive to the shepherd's voice (v. 3), why does he need to go into the pen and drive them out before they follow him (v. 4)? There may be a hint here that the fold is the Jewish community, out of which only some will follow the Messiah (and then only with prodding). This 'remnant' will then be joined by 'other sheep' (Gentiles) in a reconstituted fold.

[29] The gate of the Lord in Ps. 118:20 may be in the background here.

[30] Because shepherds often sleep in a pen's opening they may, on occasion, consider themselves the 'door' of a pen (cf. Beasley-Murray 1987: 169–170). If this is what Jesus had in mind, it would answer the concern about two competing images. However, the shepherd goes *through* the gate in v. 2. Thus, it is probably best to see this as yet one more case of mixed metaphors.

[31] Jesus may mean messianic pretenders of his day. The Greek verb is present tense: 'All ... *are* thieves and robbers.'

[32] The word for 'pasture' (*nomē*) is used frequently for God's flock in the LXX Psalms (73:1; 78:13; 94:7; 99:3).

Here the contrast in motives and result is made explicit. The religious leaders are serving themselves with the result that the flock is destroyed (*apollymi*). This is precisely the picture at the beginning of Ezekiel 34: shepherds who feed themselves (v. 2), slaughter the sheep (v. 3) and use force to overpower them (v. 4). The result is the scattering (*diaspeirō*) and destruction (*apollymi*) of the flock (vv. 4–5). Jesus' expression 'life to the full' corresponds to Ezekiel's image of sheep lying down in lush pastures (Ezek. 34:13–16).[33] Being saved (*sōzō*; John 10:9) means more than safety in John. Jesus' mission is to bring eternal life, so that none would be lost (*apollymi*; 3:16; cf. 12:12).

The verbs 'come in' (*eiserchomai*) and 'go out' (*exerchomai*) in 10:9, and 'lead out' (*exagō*) in 10:3, are all found in an Old Testament passage to which John may be alluding. When Moses faces his own death, he prays that God will provide a successor.

'May the LORD, the God of the spirits of all mankind, appoint a man over this community *to go out* and *come in* before them, one who will *lead them* out and bring them in, so that the LORD's people will not be like sheep without a shepherd' (Num. 27:16–17). The Lord's response was to appoint Joshua (the namesake of Jesus) as the next spirit-endowed shepherd (Glasson 1963: 82–85).

Jesus now elaborates on his identity as the[34] good shepherd:

[11] I am the good shepherd. The good shepherd lays down his life for the sheep. [12] The hired hand is not the shepherd who owns the sheep. So when he sees the wolf coming, he abandons the sheep and runs away. Then the wolf[35] attacks the flock and scatters[36] it. [13] The man runs away because he is a hired hand and cares nothing[37] for the sheep.

[14] I am the good shepherd; I know my sheep and my sheep know me – [15] just as the Father knows me and I know the Father – and I lay down my life for the sheep. [16] I have other sheep that are not of this sheep pen. I must bring them also. They too will listen to my

[33] Perhaps in the background is the total satisfaction of God's people in the wilderness (Deut. 8:10; 11:15).

[34] Although there is no definite article here, Jesus is certainly emphasizing his singular significance as Israel's shepherd.

[35] It may be significant that 'wolf' is singular. In Jewish law a hired shepherd was liable for any losses due to the threat of a single wolf, but losses to two or more would constitute an 'unavoidable accident' (b. Mezi'a 7:8–9).

[36] Recall that scattering is the result of false teachers/leaders in the OT.

[37] The hired hand is represented as having no concern at all for the sheep, probably a caricature to enhance the criticism of the religious leaders.

voice, and there shall be one flock [38] and one shepherd. [17] The reason my Father loves me is that I lay down my life – only to take it up again. [18] No-one takes it from me, but I lay it down of my own accord. I have authority to lay it down and authority to take it up again. This command I received from my Father. (John 10:11–18)

The threat to the flock is now its vulnerability before a menacing wolf in the absence of the (fleeing) hired shepherd. Wolves are used as symbols in the Bible for destructive leaders such as princes (Ezek. 22:27), judges (Zeph. 3:3) and false teachers (Matt. 7:15; cf. Acts 20:29). This image may recall yet another metaphorical entailment from Ezekiel 34:5.

The emphasis now turns to the truly innovative motif in Gospel shepherd traditions: the shepherd's intention to die for his sheep.[39] *Risking* one's life was occasionally necessary as an expression of protection (cf. LXX Judg. 12:3; 1 Sam. 17:34–37). However, *deliberately dying* for one's flock pushes the metaphor to (beyond?) its limits. The contrast between Jesus and others (thieves, robbers, hirelings and wolves) is drawn sharply: life for the predator entails death for the flock; life for the flock requires death for the shepherd. It is now clear that the shepherd in John's Gospel is also a sacrificial lamb.[40] This paradox is central to John's theology.

'Laying down one's life' (using *tithēmi* and *psychē*) is characteristically Johannine. Among its many occurrences in John all but one are followed by the preposition *hyper*, emphasizing laying down one's life *for*.[41] In 15:13 Jesus explains that laying down one's life *for others* is the model expression of love. The phrase emphasizes Christ's intentional and purposeful decision to submit to death for the sake of those he loves. The irony of this picture of a dying shepherd is diminished by a significant qualification: Jesus has the authority and intention not only to lay his life down but to take it back up (10:18). *He will lead them again.*

A second emphasis in Jesus' explanation is the intimate knowledge [42] between flock and shepherd and between Jesus and his father. This striking language of mutuality and reciprocity anticipates the

---

[38] To preserve the wordplay from the Greek, R. E. Brown (1966: 387) deftly translates *poimnē poimēn*, 'one sheep herd, one shepherd'.

[39] This image is anticipated in Isa. 53:10 and Zech. 13:7 (Moo 1983: 146–147).

[40] The themes of John 10 are inseparably tied to the passion account in John (Meeks 1967: 307–308).

[41] See 10:11, 15, 17, 18; 13:37, 38; 15:13; cf. 1 John 3:16. The exception is 10:17–18.

[42] *Ginōskō* is used four times in vv. 14–15.

vine discourse of chapter 15. There the disciples are considered branches (v. 5) and friends (vv. 13–15).

Another novel entailment of the metaphor is teased out in 10:16. Jesus sees himself taking his own sheep from among the flock of the Jewish fold and adding to them 'other sheep' (v. 16), presumably Gentile believers.[43] Mixing two herds can create conflicts in the natural world (Lancaster 1999: 221) and mixing ethnic groups was certainly a major source of tension in the early church. But this is the messianic mission evident in Matthew's Gospel: to the Jew first, and then to the Gentiles (cf. Rom. 1:16). These Gospel writers stand in the tradition of Isaiah, who anticipated a day when foreigners would bind themselves to the Lord (Isa. 56:6). YHWH promised that after gathering the exiles of Israel, he would *gather still others* (Isa. 56:8). John continues to highlight the importance and benefits of Christ's death for *all*[44] people when he recounts Caiphas's ironic prediction:

'... You do not realise that it is better for you that one man die for the people than that the whole nation perish.'

He did not say this on his own, but as high priest that year he prophesied that Jesus would die for the Jewish nation, and *not only for that nation but also for the scattered children of God, to bring them together and make them one.* (John 11:50–52)

A common responsiveness to the same shepherd holds the diverse flocks together (10:16; cf. vv. 3–5). Jesus has already emphasized this point in his dispute with the opposition (8:47; cf. 18:37). The *legitimate* children of Abraham, the *true* children of God, are those who respond to the word of the one sent by God.

The theme of unity was a feature of metaphorical shepherd passages in the Old Testament (Ezek. 34:23; Zech. 11). The visions of these prophets suggested the reunification of Israel's tribes under a single Davidic king, like the unity David himself had brought to the twelve tribes, and which Hezekiah and Josiah had attempted. But the vision in John has the unity of Jew and Gentile in mind. Unity will be the featured topic in Jesus' priestly prayer for his disciples in John 17.

---

[43] The theme of gathering the scattered sheep *of Israel* is common in the OT as we have seen (e.g. Mic. 2:12; Jer. 23:3; 31:10; Ezek. 34:11–13).

[44] Jesus' emphasis on salvation for the 'world' (*kosmos*) complements this theme (e.g. 3:16). John uses this word seventy-eight times.

John is intent on showing the escalation of opposition to Jesus in this Book of Signs. There is diverse reaction to his words in 10:19–21 (cf. 7:12, 25–27, 31, 40–41; 9:16). He is accused of madness (cf. 7:20; 8:48) and some prepare (again) to stone him (10:31–32; cf. 8:59). The dispute in 10:22–42 is set during Hanukkah, a feast that celebrates the deliverance of the Jews from their foreign enemies.[45] Perhaps, with typical Johannine irony, the author subtly recalls the disappointment the Hasmoneans turned out to be. They were illegitimate heirs to David's throne who became increasingly self-serving and abusive in their rule. There is some evidence that during this time of year Ezekiel 34 was read in the synagogue liturgy (Guilding 1960: 129–132).[46] If this was so, the contrast between good and bad shepherds would have been even more apropos.

Elements of the shepherd parable are recalled throughout the dispute. Jesus tells his accusers that they do not believe because they are not of his flock (v. 26). Twice he insists that no-one can 'snatch' (*harpazō*; vv. 27, 28) any of his sheep from his hand. This is the verb used of the wolf in verse 12.

The final miracle of the Sign section in John is the raising of Lazarus in chapter 11. Here Jesus demonstrates dramatically his power to give life. He *is* the resurrection and the life (11:25). This event hardens the opposition completely (11:53) and the narrative moves towards the inevitable death of the shepherd-lamb. But this will come in Jesus' own time, after he discloses more fully his expectations for those who, 'following' him, will continue his ministry in the wake of his resurrection.

The passion and the Passover lamb

> Behold, the Lamb of God who takes away the sin of the world!
> (John 1:29 NASB)

John's Gospel begins with a singularly important testimony to the identity of Jesus. John the Baptist – twice identified in the prologue as a reliable witness (1:6–7, 15) – twice hails Jesus as the 'the Lamb of God' (1:29, 36). Neither the phrase nor the word *amnos* (lamb) is used by other Gospel writers. The title may allude to the *amnos* led

---

[45] Hanukkah had become a smaller version of the feast of Tabernacles by this period (cf. 2 Macc. 1:9) and had accumulated strong messianic elements (Borchert 1996: 328).

[46] Though see the important critiques of Crockett (1966) and Heinemann (1968).

to slaughter in LXX Isaiah 53:7 (cf. Hos. 4:16; Zech. 10:3).[47] In keeping with the fourth Gospel's interest in the Passover holiday, there is an obvious association between this lamb and the paschal sacrifice.[48] The Baptist's emphasis in 1:29 is the expiatory mission of Christ; he is the 'Lamb of God *who takes away the sin of the world*' (cf. 11:50).

In ways unique to this Gospel, the mission and passion of the Son of God are tied to the Passover. Only in John, Jesus' ministry begins with his cleansing of the temple in Jerusalem on Passover (2:13ff.; cf. v. 23; 4:45).[49] The feeding of the multitude takes place only in John near the time of Passover (6:4).[50] Only John records the great sign of Lazarus's resurrection and notes that it takes place during the feast of Passover (mentioned three times in 11:55 and 12:1).[51] John sets the events of the final week in the context of the feast (13:1), and reminds his readers of this throughout (18:28, 39).[52]

John links the passion events to the Passover in other explicit ways. Only in John is Jesus' death timed[53] to the slaughtering of the paschal lambs prior to the Passover festival (19:14).[54] With characteristic Johannine irony, the Jewish leaders meticulously maintain their own purity so that they can partake in the Passover meal (18:28), all the while rejecting the ultimate paschal Lamb (cf. Culpepper 1983: 169). Also unique to John's account is the reference

---

[47] While some commentators see the phraseology rooted in Ps. 34:20 (God's care for the righteous sufferer), John's overriding interest in Passover (lamb) motifs suggests otherwise.

[48] Though see Carson's (1991: 149–151) summary of the problems with this view and a qualified defence for an apocalyptic (rather than sacrificial) lamb.

[49] Jesus' anger in John's account was provoked not because of excessive exchange rates charged during the Passover season, but because of commerce itself in the sacred area (Carson 1991: 179; cf. Zech. 14:21).

[50] The symbolism of Jesus as the bread of life may also involve his ideal replacement of the unleavened bread in the festival.

[51] Lazarus's death and resurrection is the climax of the Book of Signs and it anticipates the passion of Christ, the climax of the Book of Glory.

[52] John 18:39 identifies the Roman substitution tradition with the Jewish *Passover* (cf. 'Feast' in Matt. 27:15; Mark 15:6). The meaning of Passover is ironically enacted by the death of a blameless individual in place of a criminal (v. 40).

[53] There is a good deal of debate about the exact chronology of the passion week and which calendar John is following in his account. See R. E. Brown (1994: 1350–1378) for a summary of possible explanations.

[54] The Synoptic writers were also intent on linking Jesus with the Passover, but accomplished this primarily through the association of the Last Supper with the traditional Passover meal (cf. Matt. 26:17ff.; Mark 14:12ff.; Luke 22:7ff.). Jesus is the paschal (lamb) in 1 Cor. 5:7 and the sacrificial (paschal?) lamb in 1 Pet. 1:19.

to the bones of Jesus which go unbroken (19:33, 36; cf. Exod. 12:46; Num. 9:12).[55]

It is accurate to say that the 'story world' of John's Gospel follows a 'Passover plot' (Stibbe 1994: 38; cf. Dodd 1953: 384–386). Brodie (1993) has good reason to outline the structure of the book in terms of the three years of ministry bracketed by this symbolic holiday. The movement of Jesus' ministry towards Jerusalem each year anticipates his passion. Each year the conflict surrounding his identity increases, but his destined 'hour' will only come with the final Passover (13:1; cf. 2:4; 7:30; 8:20).

It is now generally recognized that John's Book of Glory is the culmination of the themes and interests introduced in the Book of Signs (Senior 1991: 144–159). The death of the messianic Lamb is his greatest act of love (15:13). When he is 'lifted up' he will draw all persons to himself (3:14; 12:32–34). By this single death, like a seed fallen to the ground (12:24), many will gain new life (8:34–36).[56] By the unique death of this Shepherd who lays down his life for his sheep, he will gather and unify the 'scattered children of God' (11:52).

The passion is about many other themes in John. It is clearly about the authority Jesus has over the powers of this world (both Jewish and Roman) and over death itself (10:18). Jesus controlled his own destiny; it was only in the 'hour' of *his* choice that death would come (cf. 17:1). John presents the true 'king of the Jews' (19:12, 15, 20–22) whose moment of glory and triumph comes, ironically, with his death on a cross. For John, this triumph is the pivot of salvation history (cf. Carson 1991: 97, 152–153).

'Feed my sheep'

The final chapter of the book of John is an epilogue to the Gospel, recounting the story of the amazing catch of fish and the Lord's final encounters with Peter (and John).[57] Though previous commentators have often treated this chapter as a later and somewhat extraneous addition,[58] Spencer (1999) has good grounds for defending it as

[55] Here John joins the Synoptic writers with a citation from Zechariah that identifies Jesus as the pierced (shepherd) (Zech. 13:1; John 19:37; cf. Rev. 1:7). John's Christology (here as in Revelation) freely juxtaposes shepherd and lamb images.
[56] The *redemptive* nature of Christ's death is an important element in this Gospel, emphasized often in the context of the 'I am' statements (e.g. 6:51; 10:15, 28; 12:24).
[57] Bruce (1983: 405) wryly suggests another title for this passage: 'By Hook and by Crook'.
[58] See Keener (2003: 1219–1222) for a review of positions.

integral and summative with respect to the preceding narrative and the prologue.

As in the Synoptics, the denouement in the fourth Gospel explores the new realities that have begun with Christ's resurrection.[59] Having given the disciples his promised Spirit (20:22) and authority to forgive sins (20:23), he has revived their faith, even that of Thomas (20:25–28). In the epilogue, the disciples are now (re)called from their fishing nets to follow him.[60] They are fed miraculously again by their Lord. This last sign[61] is followed, characteristically, by a challenging encounter. Peter is specifically charged to shepherd the flock of the model Shepherd (21:15–17),[62] and he is called to follow that Shepherd in death (vv. 18–19). Jesus reveals himself again as the controller of nature, the generous host, and the one who calls disciples to follow him.

Much attention has been given to the semantics of the discussion between Jesus and Peter in this passage. The roots of four sets of synonymous Greek terms are provided in brackets.

[15]When they had finished eating, Jesus said to Simon Peter, 'Simon son of John, do you truly love me [*agapaō*] more than these?'

'Yes, Lord,' he said, 'you know [*oida*] that I love [*phileō*] you.'

Jesus said, 'Feed [*boskō*] my lambs [*arnion*].'

[16]Again Jesus said, 'Simon son of John, do you truly love [*agapaō*] me?'

He answered, 'Yes, Lord, you know [*oida*] that I love [*phileō*] you.'

Jesus said, 'Take care of [*poimainō*] my sheep [*probaton*].'

[17]The third time he said to him, 'Simon son of John, do you love [*phileō*] me?'

Peter was hurt because Jesus asked him the third time, 'Do you love [*phileō*] me?' He said, 'Lord, you know [*oida*] all things; you know [*ginōskō*] that I love [*phileō*] you.'

Jesus said, 'Feed [*boskō*] my sheep [*probaton*].' (John 21:15–17)

[59] The timing of the encounter at 'dawn' (20:1) is symbolic of new beginnings.

[60] Peter's decision to go fishing (v. 3) suggests a kind of aimlessness. Only after the following encounter with Jesus is his future course focused.

[61] There is debate over whether or not this last miracle should be seen as one of the 'signs' of the Gospel. Certainly the resurrection of Christ is the climactic eighth sign of the Gospel. However, the way in which the epilogue recalls the terms and themes of the prologue suggests that this scene re-emphasizes the nature of Christ (revealed in the signs) and the call to follow him.

[62] John's call, implied in v. 24, is to be a witness to the words and works of Jesus.

While it is important for the exegete to be sensitive to lexical differentiation, most scholars agree that these synonyms (here and elsewhere in John) are virtually interchangeable (R. E. Brown 1966: 1102–1106). This has been demonstrated especially in terms of the most debated pair (*agapaō* and *phileō*),[63] and the herding terms (*boskō*, *poimainō*) are both translations for Hebrew *rā'āh* in LXX Ezekiel 34.[64] Still, the use of interchangeable terms emphasizes their shared meanings all the more. *True love* must be expressed by the *comprehensive care* of Jesus' flock.[65]

The element that is most germane to our discussion of this passage is the conceptualization of discipleship in terms of shepherd functions. As we have seen in all the Gospels, 'following'[66] Jesus ultimately entails 'shepherding' his sheep. John's epilogue makes this most explicit. While Jesus had placed an enormous emphasis on the disciples' relationship with him, this final scene demonstrates the intended outcome of that intimacy. Verbs convey the emphasis on action;[67] three times Peter is told to 'feed/shepherd my sheep'.

But Peter is also called to follow the model Shepherd in his death. If the three questions about love remind Peter of his three denials, so the call to die for Jesus recalls the disciple's empty promise in 13:37 (cf. 18:25–27). In this ultimate expression of union with Christ and his mission,[68] Peter is commanded, 'Follow me!' (vv. 19, 22). It is not surprising, therefore, that this apostle will encourage other leaders in the church to understand their suffering and service in terms of the self-sacrificing shepherd of John's Gospel (1 Pet. 5:1–4).[69]

---

[63] Cf. Bruce (1983: 405) and Carson (1991: 676–677).

[64] *Boskō* is the common translation, used eleven times in Ezek. 34, though *poimainō* is used in Ezek. 34:10, 23 (cf. Jer. 23:2, 4).

[65] The emphasis on 'my' sheep (three times) prohibits Peter from treating them as his own. It also equates Jesus with YHWH, the owner of the flock in the OT passages surveyed above. This reflects the consistent assumption in John's Gospel that Jesus is YHWH.

[66] 'Following' is a motif in this section. Some form of the verb *akoloutheō* is used in vv. 19, 20 and 22 (cf. its four occurrences in 1:37–43; also 8:12; 10:4–5, 27; 12:26; 13:36–37).

[67] The focus of this passage is not the office, but the work of a shepherd.

[68] Carson (1991: 99) notes that the theme of the people of God in John is tied to the mission and person of the Son of God. Thus, John's revelation of Christ is essentially a call to join those who follow him.

[69] Quoting the words of Ps. 44:22, Paul frames the destiny of Christians similarly: 'For your sake we face death all day long; we are considered as sheep to be slaughtered' (Rom. 8:36).

V
Following and serving the Shepherd-Lamb

Chapter Fourteen

1 Peter: on being aliens and shepherds

The letter known as 1 Peter was written by the apostle Peter (1:1) probably during the mid-60s AD when the churches in Asia Minor were experiencing persecution under Nero. At this time the apostle was awaiting his own death in Rome ('Babylon', 5:13). Peter encourages these churches as 'aliens and sojourners', understanding their identity[1] as God's renewed covenant community, freshly formed in a new wilderness of testing, and anticipating glory in their future home.[2] The letter prescribes holy living in the face of unjust suffering, motivating the churches by the example of Christ, their Shepherd (2:25), whose sufferings they share. In the last chapter elders are called to be humble and willing undershepherds of this Chief Shepherd's flock.

This short epistle is heavily rooted in Old Testament language and imagery. Without suggesting any tension between 'Israel' and 'the church', Peter freely uses the designations 'diaspora' (1:1), 'elect' (1:1), and 'a chosen people, a royal priesthood, a holy nation, a people belonging to God' (2:9).[3] He calls his fellow elders to 'shepherd the flock of God' (5:2).

The letter is clearly aligned with the Gospel traditions, especially those involving Peter. Obvious examples include the metaphors of rock (1 Pet. 2:4–8; Matt. 16:18–19; cf. Acts 4:10–11) and shepherd (1 Pet. 2:25; 5:1–4; John 21:15–17).[4]

---

[1] Identity is the focus of Peter's parenetic composition (Martin 1992: 270). Consequently metaphors of the community (and their leaders) will play an important role in his exhortation.

[2] 1 Peter has a strong eschatological perspective, perhaps even apocalyptic (Michaels 1988: xlvi–xlix; Davids 1990: 15–17).

[3] Although these designations would have obvious meaning to Jews, their use for predominantly Gentile readers is remarkable. Evidence that they are Gentiles is found in 1:14, 18; 2:9–10, 25; 3:6; 4:3–4.

[4] Also consider Satan's interest in devouring believers (1 Pet. 5:8; Luke 22:31). For more on Gospel traditions in 1 Peter, see Selwyn (1949: 28) and Gundry (1966/67).

The church as diaspora: 'aliens and sojourners' and a second exodus

Live in reverent fear during the time of your exile. (1 Pet. 1:17 NRSV)

Peter's epistle begins programmatically[5] with significant theological designations for the community: 'To God's *elect, strangers* in the world, *scattered* throughout Pontus, Galatia, Cappadocia, Asia and Bithynia . . .' (1:1). 'Elect' (or chosen; *eklektos*) may recall Septuagint references to God's people (Pss. 88:4, 20 [E 89:3, 19]; 104:6, 43 [E 105:6, 43]) or, more specifically, the Isaianic Servant (Isa. 42:1; 45:4; cf. 65:9, 15, 23).[6] The term 'stranger' (*parepidēmos*) echoes an important biblical motif associated first with the patriarchs. Abraham was an 'alien' (*paroikos*; Heb. *gēr*) and a 'stranger' (*parepidēmos*; Heb. *tôšāb*) among the Hittites (Gen. 23:4; cf. Ps. 39:12 [E 38:13]).[7] The patriarch of Israel is among the great people of faith mentioned in Hebrews, those who 'admitted that they were aliens and strangers [*parepidēmoi*] on earth' (Heb. 11:13).[8]

Peter characterizes his readers as strangers who are 'dispersed' (*diasporas*) among the nations he lists. This term carries the theological allusion further. They are not only, like the patriarchs, living as strangers on this earth. They are also, like Old Testament Israel, a people in exile, awaiting their promised homeland (i.e. heaven; 1:4).[9] Diaspora becomes a controlling metaphor for the rest of the book (Martin 1992: 144 ff.).

By situating his audience in a theological diaspora[10] Peter sets the

---

[5] Cf. Furnish (1975).

[6] Consider the central role of the Holy Spirit here (1 Pet. 1:2), in the exodus account (Isa. 63:10–14) and in the description of the Servant's work (Isa. 42:1; 61:1).

[7] *Parepidēmos* is only found in the Greek Bible in Gen. 23:4; Ps. 38:13; Heb. 11:13; 1 Pet. 1:1; 2:11.

[8] Michaels (1988: 6–7) summarizes Peter's point: 'Their divine election is a sociological as well as theological fact, for it has sundered them from their social world and made them like strangers or temporary residents in their respective cities and provinces . . . *parepidēmois* is the corollary of *eklektois*.'

[9] Heavenly hope is key to the prologue (1:3–12) which, in turn, is paradigmatic for understanding the body of the letter (Kendall 1986).

[10] Diaspora appears in the LXX twelve times, beginning with predictions of it in Deut. 28:25. In Isa. 49:6 the Servant's mission is to restore the dispersion of Israel. The scattering of God's people in the exile was commonly described with pastoral images, as we have seen (e.g. Ezek. 34).

stage for encouraging holy and hopeful living.[11] The central section of
the epistle begins with these key terms from 1:1: 'Dear friends, I urge
you, as aliens [*paroikous*][12] and strangers [*parepidēmous*][13] in the
world, to abstain from sinful desires, which war against your soul'
(2:11). Here we meet the other term used in Genesis 23:4 and Psalm
39:13 [E 12]. An alien or sojourner (*paroikous*; Heb. *gēr*), in biblical
traditions, is a person who does not have permanent rights within the
community. Though they settle among other nations, their identity is
defined by citizenship in their home country.[14] Peter has already
elicited this image in 1:17 where he encourages believers to 'pass the
time of your sojourning [*paroikias*] here in fear' (KJV). The NRSV
emphasizes the diaspora connotations: 'live in reverent fear *during the
time of your exile*' (cf. 4:2).[15] This book, written from 'Babylon'
(5:13), is an epistle *'from the homeless to the homeless'* (Michaels
1988: 9).[16] Their only secure identity is in the 'household of God'
(2:5; 4:17).[17]

The language of sojourning in 1:17 contributes to a fuller
association between these churches and the ancient Israelites in
1:13–21. Pilgrimage language is preceded by a call to holiness,
repeating the covenantal refrain given to the wilderness community, 'Be holy, because I am holy' (1:16; Lev. 11:45; 19:2

---

[11] The agenda of Peter is similar to that of the writer of Hebrews. Although perhaps
overstated, Käsemann (1984) shows how central the motif of the 'wandering people of
God' is to that epistle.

[12] *Paroikoi* became a common designation for the church in the epistles written by
the early church fathers (Michaels 1988: 8).

[13] Elliott (1981: 232) notes that these terms were conventional socio-religious
designations used in the Roman Empire for foreigners and other marginal groups.

[14] Recall the confession of the Israelites in Deut. 26:5 (NASB): 'My father was
a wandering Aramean, and he went down to Egypt and sojourned [*paroikēsen*]
there.'

[15] Israel's 'time of sojourning' (*paroikia*) in Egypt (Acts 13:17; cf. Wis. 19:10) ended
when God powerfully led them out. Peter similarly holds out hope that the church's
pilgrimage on earth will one day end.

[16] The terms 'diaspora' and 'Babylon' in the first and last verses of the letter confirm
the importance of this metaphorical identity to its message. Elliott (1981) demonstrates how the whole epistle is framed by the concern that those who were literally
strangers and aliens in Roman society would find their true identity in the 'household'
(*oikos*) of God. Like *paroikous* and *parepidēmous*, *oikos* and its variants permeate the
book (ibid., 165–266). For a critique of the extremes in Elliott's sociological analysis,
see Balch (1986).

[17] Elliott (1981: 270) sees the household of God (*oikos tou theou*) metaphor as the
central integrating rubric for the letter, though tied to the notion of homelessness. We
follow Martin (1992), who identifies diaspora as the key and *oikos* language as its
theological counterpart.

et al.).[18] This transcendent, transient community was 'redeemed . . . with the precious blood of Christ, a lamb without blemish or defect' (1:18–19; cf. 2:22–23; 3:18). It is possible that Leviticus 19 is the background for this whole passage (Michaels 1988: 61). Peter sees his readers as having been liberated (*lytroomai*; cf. Exod. 6:6; 15:13; Deut. 7:8) from their spiritual slavery by the blood of the ultimate sacrificial Lamb.[19] The confluence of terms from Israel's exodus and Sinai traditions situates the apostle's readers in a new wilderness, re-engaging afresh the covenant of YHWH.[20]

The perspective that Peter's diaspora is a new wilderness community is evident in the second chapter, where he quotes again from the Sinai tradition. In 2:9 the churches are called 'a chosen people, a royal priesthood, a holy nation, a people belonging to God' (cf. Exod. 19:6; Isa. 43:20–21).[21] Peter sees this reconstituted priestly nation offering 'spiritual sacrifices' acceptable to God (2:5). The idea of metaphorical sacrifices is already present in the Old Testament (e.g. Ps. 51:17) and is found elsewhere in the New Testament (Heb. 13:15–16; Rom. 12:1; Eph. 5:2). But in this context the focus is on the community as a living temple. This priestly community will declare the 'wonderful deeds' (*aretas*) of the one who called them (2:9).[22] As holy 'aliens and strangers in the world' they would abstain from 'sinful desires which war against your soul' (2:11).[23]

---

[18] The community's liminal status in the empire created enormous pressures to conform to majority culture (cf. Elliott 1981: 225). Peter seizes the opportunity to challenge believers to affirm their sectarian identity through their holiness/separation. In historical perspective it was precisely this self-perception as a 'third race' that contributed both to widespread persecution and, ironically, eventual victory over the Roman world (Colwell 1970: 57).

[19] While the unblemished Passover lamb may be in mind, the word in LXX Exod. 12:5 is *teleios* rather than *amōmos* as in 1 Peter. However, both are used to translate the same Hebrew word *tāmîm*.

[20] The significance of Christ's blood is evident in 1:2 where Peter mentions its sprinkling. The specific term he uses (*rantismos*) refers to the heifer ritual described in Num. 19 (19:9, 13, 20, 21; cf. Heb. 12:24). This ritual required the priest to deposit the ashes of the heifer *outside* the camp (19:9).

[21] The term 'priesthood' (*hierateuma*) is found in the NT only here (2:5, 9) and in the LXX only in Exod. 19:6 and 23:22. Exod. 19:6 is also the source for the phrase 'holy nation' (cf. Elliott 1966).

[22] *Aretas* is precisely the term used in LXX Isa. 43:21 and 63:7 to describe God's awe-inspiring deeds in the first exodus.

[23] The enemies of this new wilderness community are spiritual (cf. 5:8).

Other second exodus allusions abound in 1 Peter 2.[24] Deterding (1981: 60–63) cites the images of the people of God (2:9–10; Hos. 1:9; 2:1, 23), the day of visitation (2:12; Exod. 4:31; 13:19), free men who are slaves of God (2:16; Deut. 32:36), and Christ as Shepherd in 2:25 (cf. 5:4). He notes other exodus images in the short letter: loins girded (1:13; Exod. 12:11), the spirit of glory that rests on the community (4:14; Exod. 24:16 et al.), and the mighty hand of God (5:6; Exod. 13:3 et al.). As sojourners in this virtual wilderness, the people of God look ahead in hope to a permanent land of promise, their 'inheritance that can never perish ... in heaven' (1:4).[25]

Suffering like Christ; suffering with Christ

Christ suffered for you, leaving you an example. (1 Pet. 2:21)

The central section of this small epistle (2:11 – 4:11) provides direction for Christian [26] behaviour (as resident aliens) in this world. We have already seen how Peter uses exodus language to describe redemption by the blood of Christ. Beginning in chapter 2, he encourages believers to look to Christ's suffering not only as the basis for their salvation but also as the model for their suffering.[27]

Peter elaborates on both aspects of Christ's suffering:

[21] To this you were called, because Christ suffered for you, leaving you an example, that you should follow in his steps.

[22] 'He committed no sin,
and no deceit was found in his mouth.'

[23] When they hurled their insults at him, he did not retaliate; when he suffered, he made no threats. Instead, he entrusted himself to

---

[24] The view (F. L. Cross 1954) that 1 Peter is a baptismal liturgy framed by Passover rites and themes has been vigorously disputed (Moule 1956; Thornton 1961). However, the motifs from the wilderness literature are clear, and resemblances to the order and content of the Passover Haggadah of this time are very suggestive (Leaney 1963–64: 248). Elements from the feast of Tabernacles may also be present in 1 Peter (Hillyer 1970). In either case Peter may be involving the ancient festival associations for theological purposes rather than as a basis for ritual.

[25] Inheritance (*klēronomia*) in 1:3 is a central concept in the conquest traditions (LXX Josh. 1:15 et al.).

[26] Peter uses the term *christianos* in 4:16.

[27] For a helpful discussion of suffering in 1 Peter in the broader context of NT teaching, see Davids (1990: 30–44).

him who judges justly. [24]He himself bore our sins in his body on the tree, so that we might die to sins and live for righteousness; by his wounds you have been healed. [25]For you were like sheep going astray, but now you have returned to the Shepherd and Overseer of your souls. (1 Pet. 2:21–25)

While 'following' Jesus is a common motif in the Gospels, the term used in v. 21 (*epakoloutheō*) means to devote oneself to someone or something. Significantly, this term is used in Leviticus 19:4, 31; 20:6 (with regard to idols and familiar spirits), a passage that was apparently in mind in chapter 1 as well (vv. 15–16).

Peter moves freely from the exemplary aspect of Christ's suffering to its redemptive dimensions. With Isaiah 53 in the background, the apostle develops a 'Servant Christology' (Kirkpatrick 1982: 78) in which Christ's suffering is the source of healing.[28] As straying sheep they were rescued by the Shepherd and Overseer (*episkopos*)[29] of their souls (2:25). Here is Peter's first reference to the shepherd-sheep relationship between Jesus and his followers. In the background is language from Isaiah[30] and Ezekiel 34, where the shepherd is a healer.[31] Peter may be reflecting the Gospel traditions as well. There, Jesus represented himself as the Shepherd who had come to gather the scattered children of God from every nation.

The influence of Isaiah's Servant characterization on Peter's understanding of Christ is noteworthy. The Servant was unique in his mission but was, in an important sense, the personification of the mission and ministry of the *community*. Peter assumes that the suffering of Jesus in his priestly and sacrificial role was a model for his followers.

Jesus is presented as an example of suffering again: 'It is better, if it is God's will, to suffer for doing good than for doing evil. For Christ died for sins once for all, the righteous for the unrighteous, to bring you to God. He was put to death in the body but made alive by the

[28] There are allusions or quotes from Isa. 53:9 in v. 22, and Isa. 53:4–6, 12 in v. 23 (cf. Heb. 9:28).
[29] This term is used synonymously with shepherds as a designation for elders in Acts 20:28.
[30] Along with the clear allusion to Isa. 53:6, turning and healing are found together in Isa. 6:10.
[31] Zechariah's smitten shepherd of 13:7 may be in the background here as well. In Zech. 13:9 the people are refined by fire (cf. 1 Pet. 1:7). Remember that in Zechariah leaders are called shepherds (10:3; 11:3, 5, 8; cf. 1 Pet. 5:2).

Spirit' (3:17–18). The phrase *hoti kai christos* ('for Christ also') from 2:21 is used again in 3:18 to signal the exemplary significance of his suffering. Here too Peter moves beyond the exemplary aspect to the redemptive. In both passages he identifies believers as the cause of Christ's suffering before they are asked to suffer with him.[32] The beginning of their identity with Christ is signalled by baptism (3:20–21). This is followed naturally by a life characterized by Christ's own gracious humility and holy character: 'Therefore, since Christ suffered in his body, arm yourselves also with the same attitude, because he who has suffered in his body is done with sin. As a result, he does not live the rest of his earthly life for evil human desires, but rather for the will of God' (1 Pet. 4:1–2).

Peter's most profound statement regarding suffering is found at the close of this section:

Dear friends, do not be surprised at the painful trial you are suffering, as though something strange were happening to you. But rejoice that *you participate in the sufferings of Christ*, so that you may be overjoyed when his glory is revealed. If you are insulted because of the name of Christ, you are blessed, for the Spirit of glory and of God rests on you. (1 Pet. 4:12–14)

The apostle asserts that believers not only imitate their suffering Servant, they also participate in his sufferings. This is not to say that the atoning work of Christ continues in their suffering, for the 'once' in 3:18 is categorical and final. However, there is a sense in which the followers of Jesus are extensions of a ministry characterized by suffering (Matt. 10:16, 38; John 21:18–19). Paul shared a similar view in Colossians 1:24: 'Now I rejoice in what was suffered for you, and I fill up in my flesh what is still lacking in regard to Christ's afflictions, for the sake of his body, which is the church.' The same perspective is evident in Revelation, where the suffering of those who follow the slain Lamb is a mark of their identity with him. Finally vindicated, they will join him in his future glory as Shepherd King.

---

[32] Consider, in this regard, the ominous words given regarding Paul following his conversion: 'But the Lord said to Ananias, "Go! This man is my chosen instrument to carry my name before the Gentiles and their kings and before the people of Israel. *I will show him how much he must suffer for my name*"' (Acts 9:15–16).

Serving the Chief Shepherd

Be shepherds of God's flock that is under your care. (1 Pet. 5:2)

Before Peter picks up the topic of suffering again[33] in 5:6–11,[34] he provides a metaphorically rich charge to the leaders in the dispersed communities which make up the flock of God. He prefaces his comments with a statement of his own identity[35] as a fellow elder and sufferer.[36]

> [1]To the elders among you, I appeal as a fellow-elder, a witness of Christ's sufferings and one who also will share in the glory to be revealed: [2]Be shepherds of God's flock that is under your care, serving as overseers – not because you must, but because you are willing, as God wants you to be; not greedy for money, but eager to serve; [3]not lording it over those entrusted to you, but being examples to the flock. [4]And when the Chief Shepherd appears, you will receive the crown of glory that will never fade away. (1 Pet. 5:1–4)

The elders are to shepherd (*poimainō*) God's flock under their care. Only here and in Acts 20:28 is the imperative form of this verb used in this way. There Paul urged the Ephesian elders, 'Keep watch over yourselves and all the flock of which the Holy Spirit has made you overseers. *Be shepherds* of the church of God, which he bought with his own blood.'[37] In both contexts the association between shepherding and careful oversight is clear. In Acts the 'overseers' (*episkopoi*) are expected to guard or pay close attention to (*prosechō*) the needs of the flock (in the context of wolves; v. 29). Similarly, leaders in

---

[33] Peter's address to his fellow elders assumes the context of suffering which constitutes the overall theme of this larger section (Davids 1990: 174).

[34] Although Peter will shift his focus from the elders to the community in 5:6–11, pastoral imagery may resurface with the reference to the devil as a lion in v. 8.

[35] Peter makes his 'appeal' (*parakaleō*) on the basis of the leaders' identity as elders and shepherds. In 2:11 he appealed to the community as aliens and strangers. From chapter 2 also comes the Isaianic image of the shepherd and the sheep (2:22–25). Identity images are foundational to Peter's exhortations.

[36] Though Peter does not explicitly refer to his own sufferings in v. 1, he has already made the case that sharing in the glory of Christ must be preceded by sharing in his suffering. Recall here that Peter is distinguished from John in John 21 as one who would die in the manner that his Lord did. It may be that Peter is writing from Rome where he is awaiting his execution.

[37] The only other place Paul uses the metaphor of shepherds is in Eph. 4:11, where '*pastors* and teachers' are among the gifts given to the church.

Hebrews 13:17 'watch over' (*agrypneō*) your souls as they serve the 'great Shepherd of the sheep' (Heb. 13:20). In 1 Peter 5:2 the elders are to oversee (*episkopeō*) the flock.[38] This is the flock of 'the Shepherd and Overseer [*episkopon*] of your souls' (2:25). Watching, noted frequently in this study, is a comprehensive summary of shepherding tasks. It is the vigilant attention to threats that can disperse or destroy the flock. As in Acts 20:28, the sacrifice of the Shepherd-Lamb is the source of motivation for this vigilance.

Peter's concern is that the hard work of oversight be done 'willingly' (*hekousiōs*; 5:2). Although this particular adverb is used rarely in the Greek Bible,[39] the concept of willing service is common in the Old Testament. There, as in later Essene material, the emphasis exceeds voluntarism to include a joyful embrace of God's will (Michaels 1988: 284).[40] In contrast to this response is the self-seeking interest in financial gain mentioned in verse 2 (cf. Ezek. 34:3; Acts 20:32–35; 2 Cor. 11:7–21; 1 Tim. 3:8). Feeding on the flock is a sign of predators, not shepherds (Ezek. 34:7; 1 Tim. 6:5–6).

Peter reminds the elders that the nature of leadership among Jesus' followers is that of eager (*prothymōs*) service (5:2). Echoing the Lord's disdain for overbearing rulers, the apostle rejects the approach that 'lords it over' (*katakyrieuō*; v. 3)[41] others (Matt. 20:25; Mark 10:42; cf. Luke 22:24–27).[42] This was precisely the concern of Ezekiel: 'You have ruled them harshly and brutally' (34:4). The abuse of power consistently triggers biblical critiques of leadership that feature the shepherd metaphor.

Authority is a feature of the shepherd's role, but one comprehensively qualified by the reminder that elders are caring for the flock *of God*. There is no room for pretence in the service of the divine

---

[38] This verb is not found in all manuscripts.

[39] It is used for voluntary service (Exod. 36:2), personal sacrifice (Ps. 53:8 [H 54:6]) and endurance in suffering (4 Macc. 5:23) in the LXX and once in the NT (Heb. 10:26). Cf. also 1QS 1:7, 11; 5:1–10, 21–22.

[40] In CD 13:7–9 the community overseer (*mebaqqer* = *episkopos*) is to love the congregation as a father would, and carry them in all their distress like a shepherd his sheep. But notice, in contrast to the hierarchical order of the Essene community (1QS 6:8; as in Judaism generally), the church's shepherds are not to insist on rank.

[41] Although this verb can be used in a positive way to refer to dominion (Gen. 1:28; 9:1; Ps. 48:15 [E 49:14]), it can connote a treacherous abuse of power (Ps. 9:31 [E 10:9–10]).

[42] The context in the (Matt./Mark) Gospel accounts is a request by some disciples to have a place of prestige in the imminent kingdom. Jesus' reply was that leadership in his kingdom meant service and even death. In Luke it is part of the passion narrative in which Jesus will emphasize his own role as Servant among them (22:27). 1 Peter shares the themes and language of both Synoptic traditions (Elliott 1970: 374–375).

Shepherd. Elders 'have no proprietary rights' (Davids 1990: 178). The fundamental issue here is accountability, as it is in Acts 20:28 and Hebrews 13:17 and in virtually every passage we have surveyed. Undershepherds are each charged with their discrete 'portion' (*klēros*) of the Chief Shepherd's flock (v. 3; cf. 2:25; Heb. 13:20; 2 Kgs 3:4). The use of *klēros*, found most frequently in Septuagint Numbers–Judges, suggests that the 'real estate' in the new community is the people themselves, clustered under caring guardians.

Ever mindful of their contingent role in caring for *his* flock, shepherds will model [43] the kind of humility [44] and service that the 'sheep' will embrace. Like Jesus, good shepherd elders can say, 'Follow me as I lay my life down for you.' Those who lead the flock of marginalized suffering members are to be exemplars in self-sacrifice. Humility is the distinguishing mark of their service (5:5–6).

The 'crown of glory' reinforces an important theme in 1 Peter and the Gospels: the suffering of the great Shepherd led ultimately to his glory. [45] That glory will be shared by those who suffer with him, like him and for him (4:13; 5:1). A deferred reward will vindicate all those who are identified with the sacrificial Lamb.

Peter and many of his fellow elders did share completely in the fellowship of Christ's sufferings. Martyrdom became commonplace for the early generation of followers. With the intense focus that comes from being close to death, Peter may well be recalling the solemn charges he received from Christ at the shore of Galilee: '*Feed my sheep*' and '*Follow me*'.

---

[43] The idea of shepherds as examples for their sheep stretches the metaphor. Members of the church are not only sheep but also emerging shepherds who will become like their leaders in serving others.

[44] Submissive humility (*tapeinōsis*) is the chief characteristic of the Servant-Lamb in Isa. 53:8 and of the flock that follows their shepherd in 1 Pet. 5:5 (Martin 1992: 261).

[45] Peter twice uses the verb *phaneroō* (reveal), once for the revelation of Christ as the sacrificial Lamb (1:19–20) and here as the one who will appear in glory.

Chapter Fifteen

Revelation: the slain Lamb and ruling Shepherd

The book of Revelation provides a fitting conclusion to the Bible's shepherd and sheep imagery. In this apocalyptic letter, rich with animal symbolism, we find a conquering royal Lion-Shepherd who is, ironically, a slain Lamb. This figure's followers are those who, like him, overcome the personified powers of evil by giving up their lives as martyrs. Dying for the Lamb gives them the right to reign with him as his fellow victors.

Revelation is typically dated to the end of the first century AD. During a period of intense persecution and suffering, churches in Asia Minor were tempted to compromise their loyalty to Christ. The author John[1] describes personal visions which provide hope of ultimate victory for those who stay true to their Lord. As apocalyptic literature,[2] John's Revelation exhibits intense interest in the events that comprise the end of 'history'. Malevolent and benevolent forces bifurcate dramatically in his dualistic universe. Images of paradise are preceded by a cosmic conflict during which God and the Lamb execute judgment on the earth.

The apocalypse is rich in allusions to other biblical traditions. In many ways it is a continuation of the themes of the Gospel of John,

---

[1] The author is identified by name in 1:1, 4, 9; 22:8. Contemporary scholarship continues to debate the specific identity of this John.

[2] The secondary discussion on apocalyptic literature is vast. One helpful summary of current thinking is found in *Semeia*, vol. 14. There J. J. Collins (1979: 9) provides the following definition: ' "Apocalypse" is a genre of revelatory literature with a narrative framework, in which a revelation is mediated by an otherworldly being to a human recipient, disclosing a transcendent reality which is both temporal, insofar as it envisages eschatological salvation, and spatial, insofar as it involves another, supernatural world.' Many have also emphasized the significance of the social environment (i.e. suffering) out of which apocalyptic literature typically emerges (Hellholm 1986). While Revelation shares many of these literary and sociological elements with Jewish apocalyptic literature of this period, it is a distinctly Christian expression of the genre (Hurtado 1985).

traditionally assumed to be written by the same author.[3] Both structure their accounts in sevens; both are rich in enigma and irony; both feature the suffering and glory of the Lamb of God. Many of the motifs in this final book of the Bible recollect the original Passover, the exodus from Egypt and the wilderness period during which God's protective presence was directly experienced. There are hundreds of allusions[4] to other Old Testament passages, especially from the second part of Daniel and from the second exodus sections of Isaiah and Ezekiel (cf. Fekkes 1994; Beale 1998).

Before beginning our selective exegetical journey, we should consider the structure of Revelation.[5] Though commentators have outlined the book in a variety of ways, there is general agreement that the first three chapters are introductory, launching the description of the dramatic visions with an identification of the author and Christ, the Lord of the churches to whom seven messages are given. Chapters 4 – 16 recount the visions of seven seals, trumpets, visions and bowls. These are followed by descriptions of the judgment of Babylon, the Beast and God's other enemies (chs. 17 – 20). The book concludes with a vision of a new world order and a new Jerusalem at its centre (chs. 21 – 22).

Finally, a word is in order regarding the interpretation of Revelation. Most commentaries exhibit one or more of the following interpretive approaches to the referents of the apocalypse: preterist (first or fifth century), historicist (major movements in church history), futurist (end times) and idealist (primarily symbolic). A helpful presentation is made by Beale (1999: 44–49), who summarizes these various approaches and defends a position that appreciates both historical and transhistorical dimensions in the prophetic collection. The visions of Revelation invite readers into a symbolic world that is, on its own terms, descriptive of real historical events. At the same time it provides a theological perspective on forces evident throughout history and beyond.

It is especially important to remember the capacity and purpose of symbols and metaphors to affect readers on multiple levels. They have the power to bear cognitive-imaginative content and to incite

---

[3] Although differences between Revelation and the fourth Gospel are regularly noted (e.g. Whale 1987), there is a remarkable concurrence of certain words and phrases (e.g. water of life, shepherd, overcome, witness, etc.; cf. Kistemaker 2001: 22).

[4] Because of differences in methodology and definition, the number of allusions commentators cite ranges from 250 to 700 (Fekkes 1994: 62).

[5] For an overview of structural indicators, see Bauckham (1993a). On the cycles of seven, see A. Y. Collins (1976: 13–44).

emotional and volitional responses. Furthermore, symbolic language is intentionally multivalent. Using Wheelwright's (1975) distinction, Revelation employs both 'steno' (one-to-one correspondence) and 'tensive' (range of meanings) symbols.[6]

The messianic Lion-Lamb and the eschatological exodus

[5]Then one of the elders said to me, 'Do not weep! See, the Lion of the tribe of Judah, the Root of David, has triumphed. He is able to open the scroll and its seven seals.'

[6]Then I saw a Lamb, looking as if it had been slain, standing in the centre of the throne, encircled by the four living creatures and the elders. He had seven horns and seven eyes, which are the seven spirits of God sent out into all the earth. [7]He came and took the scroll from the right hand of him who sat on the throne ... [9]And they sang a new song:

> 'You are worthy to take the scroll
>   and to open its seals,
> because you were slain,
>   and with your blood you purchased men
>   for God
>   from every tribe and language and people
>   and nation.
> [10]You have made them to be a kingdom
>   and priests to serve our God,
>   and they will reign on the earth.'
> (Rev. 5:5–10)

Messianic King

The Lion of the tribe of Judah ... has triumphed. (Rev. 5:5)

Revelation 5 continues a description of the first of seven heavenly throne room scenes begun in chapter 4. The events of the end of the world can commence with the opening of the sealed scroll. The only one worthy is introduced first, significantly, as the 'Lion of the tribe of Judah, the Root of David' (v. 5; cf. 22:16). These titles

---

[6] Asserting multiple meanings is not implying that meaning is indeterminate. See the comments of Heyman (1976: 352).

have long-standing messianic/royal associations we have noted in prophetic and Gospel passages above.[7] The scene in Revelation 5 is clearly reminiscent of the account of the Son of Man in Daniel 7 (Beale 1999: 315–316). In Daniel's vision there is a rare biblical glimpse of a distinct heavenly (divine?) figure approaching the Ancient of Days (Dan. 7:13; cf. Rev. 1:13–16). In words that are echoed in Revelation 5, this figure is given supreme and eternal authority[8] over humankind: 'He was given authority, glory and sovereign power; all peoples, nations and men of every language worshipped him. His dominion is an everlasting dominion that will not pass away, and his kingdom is one that will never be destroyed' (Dan. 7:14). In both passages this giving of authority takes place in a royal enthronement or investiture ceremony.[9]

The Lion of Judah is capable of opening the scrolls because he has 'triumphed' (5:5). The verb *nikaō*, variously translated 'conquer', 'overcome' or 'triumph', is used seventeen times in Revelation, far more than any other New Testament (or LXX) book. Emphasis on the sovereign conqueror is central to the theology of the apocalypse (Bauckham 1993b: 54–65). He is a militant victor who subdues his enemies with deadly force. John elsewhere uses the royal language of Psalm 2 to describe this apocalyptic king as one who 'rules' ('shepherds'; *poimainō*) the nations *with a rod of iron*.[10]

Sacrificial horned Lamb?

> Worthy is the Lamb, who was slain,
> to receive power...
>
> (Rev. 5:12)

---

[7] Biblical sources include Gen. 49:9; Isa. 11:10 (cf. Rev. 22:16). Extrabiblical continuation of these traditional images can be found in 4 Ezra 11:36–46; 12:31–34; 4Qpatr3.

[8] 'Authority' (*exousia*) is a central term in both accounts and in both books. Leading all other biblical books, LXX Daniel has twenty-two occurrences of the term and Revelation has twenty-one.

[9] While most commentators see this scene as one in which the Lamb is granted kingship, Aune (1997: 336–338) explains why it should be viewed as a ceremony of investiture.

[10] John follows the LXX rendering of Ps. 2:9 (*poimainō* for r'h rather than MT r'') in 2:27; 12:5; 19:15. John is certainly aware of the 'pastoral' associations of *poimainō* (cf. 7:17).

Though John *hears* of a capable one introduced as the Davidic Lion, what he *sees* is 'a Lamb [*arnion*],[11] looking as if it had been slain' (v. 6; cf. v. 12; 13:8). This Lamb is not only an *able* conqueror (v. 5); he is *worthy* (*axios*)[12] to open the scroll *because of his redemptive death* (v. 9). The power of this messianic figure is matched by his self-sacrifice. The title 'Lamb' becomes the most common designation for the Lord, featured twenty-eight times in the apocalypse.[13]

This image is obviously related to the crucifixion of Christ, who is identified in John's Gospel as the 'Lamb of God who takes away the sin of the world' (John 1:29). The death of the Messiah became the climax of the whole sacrificial system.[14] Like the *amnos* (lamb) of LXX Isaiah 53:7, Jesus was 'slaughtered' (*esphagēs*; 5:6, 9, 12), thereby bearing the sins of many (Isa. 53:11–12). More particularly, as the fourth Gospel emphasizes, this death was the ultimate Passover sacrifice (Hillyer 1967). Like the blood of the spotless lambs that had redeemed the ancient Israelites from their bondage in Egypt, the blood of Jesus 'purchased men for God' (Rev. 5:9).[15] This was the mission of the messianic Lamb who was 'slain from the creation of the world' (13:8). As in John, the theological crux in Revelation is that the cross is the means of glory (cf. 19:13; cf. 1 Cor. 1:23–24). The blood of the Lamb certifies his kingship.

While the image of the Lamb draws on sacrificial associations, it could also have depicted a warrior much like the conquering Lion.[16] There is some evidence of an apocalyptic *military* Lamb who would wage war on behalf of God's elect (Test. Jos. 9:3; cf.

[11] While the term *arnion* is technically a diminutive of *arēn*, meaning '*small sheep*' (lamb), there is some dispute about whether or not this meaning was in place during the first century. Whale (1987) provides an important reminder not to overemphasize the choice of vocabulary here (i.e. in contrast to *amnos* in the fourth Gospel and LXX).

[12] Worthiness is a capacity *demonstrated*, i.e. through a test (cf. Wis. 3:5). In Aramaic, perhaps John's first language, *zeka'* means both worthy and able (van Unnik 1970).

[13] Casey (1982: 149) summarizes: the Lamb receives worship (5:8, 12ff.; 7:9, 10), is ruler of the eschaton (14:1) and the sustaining essence of the heavenly city (21:22, 23; 22:1). He is judge and warrior (6:1, 16; 14:10; 17:14) and pastoral provider for the church (7:17; 14:4; 19:7, 9; 21:9, 14). Cf. Hillyer (1967: 232–236).

[14] The book of Hebrews explores the rich imagery of Jesus as ultimate high priest offering himself as the ultimate sacrifice.

[15] See Str-B I, 85 and IV, 40 for rabbinic reflections on the *eschatological* redemption effected by the blood of the Passover lamb.

[16] Michaels (1992: 131) observes that though 'the Lion turns out to be a sacrificial Lamb, the Lamb through the rest of the book behaves very much like a Lion'!

1 Enoch 90:9, 37; cf. Sandy 1991: 451–455). Within the context of Revelation, the Lamb is often described in this military role (17:14; cf. 13:8; 21:27; Aune 1997: 369). It is the wrath of the Lamb that is dreaded in 6:12–17. It is his wrath that explains the seven plagues of 6:1 – 8:1.[17]

The militant dimension of the Lamb is also visualized by horns (5:6), which are suggestive of royal power.[18] These horns may be characteristically symbolic features of the vision (e.g. 17:12), or they may suggest that a *ram* is in mind, rather than a lamb (cf. 13:11; Aune 1997: 368). If what John saw was a ram, this would reinforce the association with royal power clearly evident in Daniel's vision (Dan. 8:3).

While some commentators have chosen to understand John's Lamb as *either* royal conqueror *or* willing sacrifice (Aune 1997: 367–373), it seems wiser to appreciate the mixing of metaphors (and Old Testament traditions) [19] so characteristic of Johannine literature (cf. Moyise 1995: 123–138). Self-sacrifice and authoritative rule *both* describe the Lamb, and both, as we will see, are foundational to John's understanding of discipleship.

The ransomed

> ...with your blood you purchased men for God...
> ...to be a kingdom and priests.
>
> (Rev. 5:9–10)

The Lamb is worthy not simply because of his willingness to die, but also because his shed blood was the acceptable means by which a universal community was *purchased* (5:9). The language of ransom and redemption is commonly used in the New Testament to describe the effect of the cross (e.g. 1 Cor. 6:20; 7:23; 2 Pet. 2:1). The obvious Old Testament prototype is the redemption/ransom of Israel from Egypt (e.g. Deut. 7:8; 13:5). This was secured by the blood of a spotless lamb, the centre of the original Passover rite.

---

[17] The wrath of the Lamb brings justice to his enemies and vindicates his followers who have suffered with him (A. T. Hanson 1957: 200).

[18] Cf. Süring (1982). Horns are symbols of powerful nations (Zech. 1:18–21 [MT 2:1–4]), and of power exercised by nations (Jer. 48:25) and kings (Ezek. 29:21; Ps. 132:17 [H 131:17]; Dan. 7:7–12, 20–21; 8:3–4, 8). Cf. 1 Enoch 90:37.

[19] Barker (2000: 133–135) explores the interpretation of Isaiah's Servant as both royal and sacrificial figure in a variety of Second Temple texts. She notes that the Aramaic word *tly'* can mean either 'lamb' or 'servant'.

The possibility that John has a Passover precedent[20] in mind is reinforced by the description of the renewed community as a 'kingdom of priests' (*basileian kai hiereis*; 5:10; cf. 1:5–6). This phrase recalls the original designation of Israel on Mount Sinai as a *basileion hierateuma* (Exod. 19:6; cf. 1 Pet. 2:9). John's new Passover/exodus vision is of a newly reconstituted people of God, purchased by the blood of the Lamb, and reigning with him as priests[21] in his kingdom. This new people is comprised of members of every nation and language, as anticipated by the 'mixed multitude' of Exodus 12:38 (KJV), the second exodus language of Isaiah 66:18 and Zechariah 8:22, and Jesus' intention to gather 'other sheep' in John 10:16 (cf. Rev. 7:9; 10:11; 11:9; 13:7; 14:6; 17:15).

The faithful followers of the Shepherd-Lamb and the eschatological feast of Tabernacles

> After this I looked and there before me was a great multitude that no-one could count, from every nation, tribe, people and language, standing before the throne and in front of the Lamb. They were wearing white robes and were holding palm branches in their hands ... These are they who have come out of the great tribulation; they have washed their robes and made them white in the blood of the Lamb. (Rev. 7:9, 14)

Followers of the Lamb

> They follow the Lamb wherever he goes. (Rev. 14:4)

While the visions of John are cosmic in scope, they exhibit a sustained focus on Christ's followers – on their loyalty, sacrifice and final destiny. The letters in chapters 2 – 3 are intended to encourage the

---

[20] Jewish expectations of a great eschatological Passover/exodus are evident in 1 Enoch 1:4; 1QM 1 – 2; Ap. Abr. 30:2 – 31:1; Josephus, *Antiquities* 20:97–98; *Lives of the Prophets* 2:11–19; 12:12–13. Cf. Betz (1967); Bauckham (1993b: 70–71). Exodus allusions in Revelation include references to Balaam and Balak (2:14; Num. 22 – 23); seven plagues (6:1 – 8:1; Ps. 78:44–51 followed in vv. 52–54 by a description of God's shepherd guidance; cf. Rev. 7:15–17); 'affliction' (*thlipsis*) (7:14 et al.; Exod. 4:31); being carried on eagles' wings into the wilderness (12:14; Exod. 19:4); the mark/seal that saves (7:3; Exod. 12:23); tribal counting beginning with Judah (7:5; Num. 2:3; 7:12; 10:14); 'washing' (*plynō*) garments (7:14; Exod. 19:10, 14); the song of Moses (15:2–4; Exod. 15).

[21] The priestly dimension of the whole community is important in the original covenant and in Rev. 1:5–6; 5:10; 21:7; 22:3.

followers of Jesus to persevere through suffering and remain true in doctrine so that they would 'overcome' (*nikaō*; 2:7, 11, 17, 26; 3:5, 12, 21). When the fifth seal is broken in chapter 6 John sees 'under the altar the souls of those who had been slain [*sphazō*] because of the word of God and the testimony they had maintained' (6:9). Overcoming is the ironic outcome of suffering unto death. The wrath of the Lamb (v. 16) is unleashed on the ungodly partly to avenge the blood of these martyrs. But first, *more* would die: 'Then each of them was given a white robe, and they were told to wait a little longer, until the number of their fellow-servants and brothers who were to be killed as they had been was completed' (6:11; cf. 13:7, 10; 20:4).

Death is the ultimate cost to pay for maintaining one's 'testimony' (v. 9). *Martyria* (translated 'testimony' or 'witness') for these disciples entails *martyrdom*. The equation between their deaths and that of their Lord is reinforced by the perfect passive participle of *sphazō* ('to have been slain'), the same verb and form used of the Lamb in 5:6, 12 (cf. 13:8).[22] Similarly, the countless multitudes of faithful in 7:9ff. wear robes which are washed white 'in the *blood of the Lamb*' (7:14). While it is true that the sealed 144,000[23] mentioned earlier in that chapter were *spared* death, the paradox of Christ's victory (*nikaō*) *through* death is the norm for his followers throughout the book (cf. 2:10; 12:11; Michaels 1992: 134–137). This is in keeping with Christ's challenges to his disciples in the fourth Gospel to give up their lives willingly (12:25; 15:13; 21:18–19; cf. Rev. 2:11, 16; 3:1–5, 16).

Revelation 14:4 describes those who have been 'purchased from among men' (i.e. by the blood of the Lamb) as those who keep themselves 'pure' and 'blameless',[24] who are 'offered as firstfruits[25] to God and the Lamb'. In other words, to follow the Lamb means to be, *like him*, a pure and blameless sacrifice (cf. Isa. 53:7–9). They are made followers by Christ's death and they qualify as his followers *by their deaths*. Perhaps the best summary of discipleship in Revelation is given in 14:4: '*They follow the Lamb wherever he goes*' (Aune 1996).

---

[22] Compare the slaughter (*sphazō*) of the prophets and saints in 18:24 and the deaths of the two witnesses killed in the 'great city ... *where also their Lord was crucified*' (11:8).

[23] The identity of the 144,000 here and in ch. 14 is among the most disputed issues in Revelation scholarship. I understand them to be a separate group from the international multitude (cf. Aune 1998: 439–448).

[24] These terms have both moral and ritual dimensions to them (cf. Aune 1998: 810–818).

[25] The priestly role continues with this reference to firstfruits (Num. 3:11–13; 8:14–18).

Following the Lamb ultimately leads beyond death to an eternity serving the Lamb. While the book of Revelation emphasizes the suffering and death of the Lamb's followers, they are also comrades of Christ who accompany him in holy war (17:14; cf. 14:1 [26]).[27] In 2:26–28 they are promised a share in the Lamb's authority; they will rule over/shepherd (*poimainō*) the nations with an iron rod. At the climax of John's visions those who have died for the Lamb will reign with him for ever and ever (22:5; cf. 5:10; 20:6), even inheriting with him the Davidic promise (21:7). These promises are in keeping with New Testament teaching elsewhere that the followers of Christ will one day rule with him (e.g. Luke 19:12–19; 1 Cor. 6:2–3). However, as we have so often seen, their authority will be eternally qualified by their role as *his servants* (22:3).

The Shepherd-Lamb and the eternal feast of Tabernacles

> ... he who sits on the throne will spread his tent over them ...
> For the Lamb at the centre of the throne will be their
> shepherd.
>
> (Rev. 7:15, 17)

'Following' (*akoloutheō*) the 'Lamb' reflects a mixed metaphor. As was apparent in the Gospels, following Jesus meant following him as their Shepherd. At the end of John's Gospel, Peter was commanded to follow Jesus to his death (John 21:18–19). Implicitly Jesus was asking him both to follow him as Shepherd (feeding his sheep) and to follow him as sacrificial Lamb. In Revelation John uses shepherd language also for the Lamb. Of those who have washed their robes in his blood it is said:

> Therefore, they are before the throne of God
> and serve him day and night in his temple;
> and he who sits on the throne will spread his tent over them.
> Never again will they hunger;
> never again will they thirst.

---

[26] The background of a common Near Eastern 'combat myth' in Rev. 14 recalls its presence in stories of the exodus (A. Y. Collins 1976: 101–155; Day 1985: 88–101).

[27] It is quite likely that the supposed virginity of the 144,000 (14:4) is really a reference to their sexual purity in the context of holy war (Deut. 23:9–14; 1 Sam. 21:5; 2 Sam. 11:9–13; 1QM 7:3–6). Like Christ, their purification for war is equated with purity for sacrifice; Christ and his followers declare holy war through martyrdom (cf. Bauckham 1993b: 76–80).

The sun will not beat upon them,
nor any scorching heat.
For the Lamb at the centre of the throne will be their shepherd;
he will lead them to springs of living water.
And God will wipe away every tear from their eyes.
(Rev. 7:15–17; cf. Isa. 49:10; Ezek. 34:23)

The presence of imagery from Israel's ancient wilderness journey in this passage is unmistakable. Protection (from natural threats), provision (of food and water) and guidance are given by the Lamb who shepherds (*poimainei*) and guides (*hodēgēsei*)[28] them. 'Living water' recalls Jesus' use of the phrase in John 7:38 during the feast of Tabernacles (cf. John 4:10–11). Similarly, there is bread that keeps one from hungering again (John 6:27ff.).[29] But, as was clear in John, these statements of Jesus recalled lessons that were offered originally in Israel's wilderness experience (John 6:31–35). There God comprehensively demonstrated his intent and capacity to satisfy each of their basic human needs (Deut. 8:3).

It was in the wilderness that God first camped ('spread his tent'; *skēnōsei*; Rev. 7:15) among his people.[30] This endearing image of God's presence (cf. 2 Sam. 7:6) is highlighted in the climax of the apocalypse: 'And I heard a loud voice from the throne saying, "Now the dwelling of God is with men, and *he will live with* [*skēnōsei*] *them. They will be his people, and God himself will be with them and be their God*" ' (Rev. 21:3; cf. Exod. 6:6–7). This restatement of God's eternal covenant relationship with his people echoes the language of the original sojourn in the desert of Sinai.

God's pastoral presence among his people is the object of celebration during the feast of Tabernacles, the festival background of the imagery in Revelation 7 (and much of the book; Ulfgard 1989). Tabernacles celebrations began with the waving of palm branches (Lev. 23:40; Rev. 7:9; cf. 2 Macc. 10:7) and involved seven days of living in booths. By the first century this probably had become the most popular feast among the Jews.[31] As an autumnal rite, it incorporated prayers for the early rains (Keener 2003: 722–725; cf. John 7:37ff.).

---

[28] *Hodēgeō* is a key LXX verb used for God's leadership in the wilderness (Exod. 13:17; 15:13; Num. 24:8; Deut. 1:33; Neh. 9:12, 19; Pss. 76:21 [MT 77:20]; 77:14, 53 [MT 78:14, 53]; 105:9 [MT 106:9]; 106:30 [MT 107:30]; Isa. 63:14).
[29] Cf. the 'hidden manna' of Rev. 2:17.
[30] *Skēnoō* is used of Jesus' mission in John 1:14.
[31] Josephus, *Antiquities* 8:4, 1.

Tabernacles was a holiday whose meaning was informed in part by Zechariah 14, a passage read during the feast in the Second Temple period (b Meg. 31a). In Zechariah's vision the Day of the Lord would involve 'living water' (*hydōr zōn*; Zech. 14:8)[32] flowing out of Jerusalem, where YHWH would reign as king (Zech. 14:9; cf. Rev. 7:10, 17). The survivors (i.e. 'remnant') of the Jewish population would be joined by Gentiles who had survived the plagues (Zech. 14:12–15; cf. Rev. 7:9). The rulers of the world will join the annual worship of Israel's King *at the feast of Tabernacles* (Zech. 14:16). The visions of Zechariah 14 and Revelation 7 reveal the *eschatological* dimension of a holiday ordained to remember God's historic presence in the wilderness. Like Passover, this feast was ordained to teach God's people as much about the future as about the past.

As the Passover and exodus represent paradigmatic moments in the history of salvation, so the wilderness sojourn and the feast of Tabernacles became symbolic of an age of comprehensive divine provision. The great climax to Tabernacles imagery occurs at the end of the apocalypse. The wedding (19:7; 21:2ff.) consummates the betrothal initiated in the wilderness of Sinai (Hos. 2:2; Ezek. 16) and offered by the Bridegroom in the Gospels. The holiday's symbols of water and light are provided by the reigning Lamb (21:6; 22:1, 17; 21:23–24; 22:5[33]). God's tabernacling presence, no longer located within a temple, is directly available for all of his servants. God and the Lamb *are* the temple (21:22). Here is one of the richest ironies in the history of salvation: the heavenly Jerusalem, it turns out, was all along as much anticipated by the deserts and dispersions of the community's journey as by the earthly city bearing its name. In both experiences the Shepherd-Lamb was teaching them to follow him to their real home.

---

[32] Cf. the *zōēs pēgas hydatōn* of Rev. 7:17.
[33] The all-night burning of 'candlesticks' described in b. Sukkah 5:2–4 is reminiscent of God's pillar of fire.

VI
Concluding observations and reflections

After such a sweeping survey of texts and topics it will serve us well to summarize the themes that have resurfaced throughout. These observations will, in turn, help us consider implications for 'pastoral' ministry.

The first observation is that shepherd leadership is *comprehensive* in scope. It represents a diverse and changing 'role set'. For the sake of convenience we have in places summarized the inter-related pastoral roles as protector, provider and guide. Fundamentally, however, the task of shepherds is determined daily by the changing needs of the flock under their care. 'Pastors' are generalists. This 'underlying paradigm of ministry . . . contains within it references to the authority, tender care, specific tasks, courage and sacrifice required of the pastor' (Tidball 1997: 54). To be a *good* shepherd – and this is consistently the biblical concern – means to be accountable for the lives and well-being of the sheep. For this reason the designation is used for prophets, priests and kings in the Old Testament, and for ruling elders in the New Testament church.[1]

Good shepherding is expressed by decisions and behaviours that benefit the 'flock', often at great personal cost. It calls for *the benevolent use of authority*, what Tidball (1997: 46) describes as a 'subtle blend of authority and care'. Some situations require militant protection and discipline, others beckon for gentle nurture. The shepherd ruler of Psalm 2 rules with an iron rod. The shepherd ruler of Isaiah 40 tenderly carries the nursing ewes. The shepherd image is especially useful for *holding in tension* these essential features of leadership. Authority without compassion leads to harsh authoritarianism. Compassion without authority leads to social chaos. Shepherds must be able to express their leadership in a variety of

---

[1] While one might conclude from the preceding study that pastoral identity is anchored in OT royal traditions, it is perhaps more accurate to say that various leadership roles (including OT kings and NT elders) are understood in terms of the shepherd metaphor.

ways. 'The work of the shepherd', notes Tidball (1997: 48), 'involved as much toughness as tenderness, as much courage as comfort.' The apostle Paul lets the Corinthians choose which posture he will take when he comes: 'What do you desire? Shall I come to you with a rod,[2] or with love and a spirit of gentleness?' (1 Cor. 4:21 NASB)

The second point is closely related. Bad or 'false' shepherds are those who use their position to serve their own needs. *They forget whose flock they serve.* Contrast Jacob, who wearied himself day and night in the care of Laban's sheep (Gen. 31:40), with the hired hand in Jesus' parable who cares only about himself (John 10:13). The principle here is reiterated throughout the Bible: *God* is the ultimate Shepherd of *his* people. He calls human deputies to work for him, though at the risk that they presume prerogatives reserved for the Owner. To be a shepherd is to be both *responsible for* (the flock) and *responsible to* (the Owner). Nathan resorted to a shepherd story to remind King David how he had forgotten this fundamental principle. Those who are called to leadership in the covenant community are called to take care of those whom God calls '*my* sheep' (John 21:15–17).

A third observation involves what we have called the 'divine preference for human agency', a trend which appears already in the creation account. The God of Scripture passionately seeks humans to enlist in his mission, risking it regularly in their hands. This predilection is rooted in an ideal whereby human rule is a derivative extension of divine rule. Our theology of leadership is informed by this breathtaking choice of God to grant royal prerogatives to his creatures. To be made in his image is to rule with him and for him. Reigning with him is the destiny of all those who follow the Lamb in the book of Revelation.

Already the temptation to hubris is present throughout the accounts of biblical leaders, beginning with the first couple. In order to qualify this tendency, leaders are constantly reminded of their contingent status. Every shepherd leader is first and always a sheep who relates to God as 'my Shepherd'. A discernible preference for ambiguous terms keeps this dependent relationship primary. Leaders are called shepherd, steward, servant, son, *nāśî'* (prince) and *nāgîd* (leader). As such they are explicitly *appointed* by God and only effective as they are *empowered* by God's Spirit. They are depicted regularly as vassals, vice-regents and deputy rulers, as Psalm 2 so provocatively portrays.

---

[2] Paul elicits pastoral imagery with the word *rabdos*, the shepherd's club.

To place the emphasis on accountability to God is to safeguard the image of shepherd from becoming simply a means to prompt obedience by a human 'flock' to its (often self-appointed) 'shepherd'. When human rule turns despotic, the biblical writers prefer this image as the basis for their critique. Shepherd leadership requires humility before God and responsiveness to God's people. It resists pretence, posturing and privilege.

When conventional Near Eastern shepherd language appears in the Bible, it is most often used with reference to YHWH as the King of Israel. No human king of Israel was ever given the title 'Shepherd'. When Jesus came as the divine-human Shepherd of Israel, he once again delegated authority to his human ambassadors. Only when endowed with his Spirit and provided with his continued presence were they able to fulfil their tasks as his undershepherds. In this way they became God's co-workers (cf. 1 Cor. 3:9), always in a supporting role.

The biblical understanding of human rule as an extension of divine rule helps explain why a biblical theology of leadership necessarily involves a journey into theological terrain classically categorized as Christology and theology (proper). Our exploration of leadership has carried us into ecclesiology, soteriology and anthropology as well. While these dimensions of the discussion may have been unexpected, they reflect an important fourth observation. Biblically, leadership can only be understood in terms of a fully integrated theological vision of God and his work on earth. A comprehensive pastoral theology engages leaders in this rich vision.

The integrally related notions of leadership and community have been present throughout this study. Though we have focused our attention on the metaphor of shepherd leader, this is essentially connected to the ecclesial image of the flock of God. The root metaphor of shepherd and flock throws certain concerns into bold relief. Most notable is the vulnerability and dependence of God's people in the face of bad leadership. They easily 'wander' (*t'h*; *planaō*), 'scatter' (*pws*; *diaspeirō*) and get 'lost' (*'bd*; *apollymi*). Consequently shepherd leaders are all the more accountable for neglect and abuse. The Bible will use other corporate metaphors to convey different themes, but this particular one suits critiques of poor leadership.

A fifth observation is that pastoral imagery is part of a larger redemptive-historical *narrative* that depicts God's leadership in wilderness settings. Beginning with the original Passover, re-emerging in the exile and crescendoing at the inauguration of the new age in the

Gospels, God revealed himself as the Shepherd of his people, leading them by undershepherds through the desert to their promised home. By the diligent oversight and guidance of God's gifted shepherds, every member of the flock makes it home.

Thus, shepherd language is not only linked to the fuller metaphor of the community as God's flock. This matrix of images is integrally connected to the *metanarrative* of Scripture. The vision of Revelation brings this great story to a climax as God spreads his tent over his chosen ones and provides for their every need:

> Never again will they hunger;
> > never again will they thirst.
> The sun will not beat upon them,
> > nor any scorching heat.
> For the Lamb at the centre of the throne will be
> > their shepherd;
> he will lead them to springs of living water.
> And God will wipe away every tear from their eyes.
> > > (Rev. 7:16–17)

The festival of Tabernacles, which recalled the ancient sojourn, had all along anticipated the age to come when God would shepherd his people for ever.

A sixth observation concerns the 'mixing' of metaphors. For the sake of this study we have limited our interest to passages that clearly engage pastoral motifs. However, many of these texts also pictured God as divine Warrior, King, Father or Lamb. While this metaphorical collage at times creates an exegetical challenge, the mixing and merging is important for theological reasons. We stated in the Introduction that metaphors are not only uniquely creative in meaning-making, they are also constrictive and limiting. The divine Shepherd is an important metaphor in Scripture. But it is one of many biblical 'portraits' of God (Coppedge 2001). We should not expect it to provide an exclusive or exhaustive presentation of divine attributes and behaviours. Rather we ought to appreciate the inclination of most biblical authors to engage a variety of images to express the dynamic and ultimately inexpressible nature of God.

Finally, let us consider the Bible's predilection for ordinary metaphors. There is a deliberate divine choice to use the common elements in our world as revelatory vehicles. Nature itself is a form of revelation (Ps. 19:1–6) and, judging from the evidence, cultural occupations and institutions are too. The resilience of the pastoral image for a variety of leadership roles in different contexts (prophet, priest, king, church leader) – and at times when cultural associations were less favourable – is evidence of its enduring usefulness. Any person in 'pastoral' ministry is heir to a remarkable heritage that stretches back four thousand years. With the ancient Israelites we confess, 'My father was a wandering Aramean.' With a later generation we affirm that the Great Shepherd 'pitched his tent' among us (John 1:14; cf. 2 Sam. 7:6) and showed us how to live and die for those sheep who recognize his name.

Epilogue

We are left, finally, with an important question: knowing the primary emphases and themes associated with shepherd imagery, are there common, *contemporary* metaphors that might convey these inter-related truths about God and leadership? Some have resorted to CEO, coach or 'wounded healer'.[1] Should these contemporary images seem somehow less sacred or profound, perhaps it is because we have been mesmerized by occasional safaris among legendary biblical landscapes and forgotten that those original images were chosen because of their ordinariness. These common images were drafted for serious and often subversive purposes that could only be accomplished if the images were *commonly* experienced. Through *ordinary* word-pictures biblical writers prompted the imaginations of their audiences to consider perspectives that were often quite extra-ordinary. The inspired authors invite us to join them in visualizing timeless truths in contextually meaningful ways.

Although the challenge to find what translators call a 'dynamic equivalent' is justified, we will need to resort to a mix of metaphors to convey the same set of inter-related notions the biblical writers communicated with pastoral imagery. This is, apparently, what the apostle Paul chose to do. Resorting at times to servant, slave, friend, midwife, father or overseer, the apostle made sure that his readers understood the nature of leadership (Bennett 1993). The search for revelatory vehicles among the 'associated commonplaces' of modern life is the task now before us.

---

[1] See Messer (1989) for others. These metaphors, just like the shepherd, can have negative as well as positive associations. Scripture's preference for the shepherd is qualified by its emphasis on the quality of leadership.

Appendix A

Mesopotamian deities with shepherd titles

Sumerian terms[1]

Ab-ba, Shepherd of the lands

An(u) (sky god), Shepherd of the whole earth

Asimbabbar acts as your shepherd

Dumuzi, Shepherd of the heavens; Shepherd of the underworld; Abundant Shepherd

Enbilulu, Faithful shepherd

Enlil (Father of Utu/Shamash; Husband of Ninlil), Faithful shepherd; Shepherd of the teeming multitudes; the herdsman; the 'shepherd-crook' of the gods is under your care; the shepherd upon whom you gaze; Shepherd of the dark-headed; True shepherd

Etana, a shepherd who ascended to heaven

Ishum/Hendursag (protective watchman), Holder of the lofty sceptre, Guardian of the dark-headed, Shepherd to human beings

Ishtar/Inana, Shepherdess of the darkness of men(?), Shepherdess of the weary people, 'Shepherdess Ishtar who walks in front of the herd'

Marduk, Shepherd of the whole entirety, Shepherd of humankind

Mullil, Shepherd, Shepherd of the black-headed

Nabu (divine scribe of the destinies; wisdom, agriculture), Shepherd of all heaven and earth

Nanna-Sin, Shepherd of the heavens, Shepherd of the homeland

(Nin-)amash-ku-ga, Shepherd of the goats of Enlil

Ningal, 'I, Ningal – like an unworthy shepherd . . . '

Nin-gun-a, Shepherd of the Herds

Nin-ma-dib-dib, Shepherd of the (yellow?) goats of Enlil

Ninurta, Shepherd of the weak, who is merciful to the destitute

---

[1] Translated from Seux 1967: 441–450.

255

Nusku, God of fire and light, sorcery, Shepherd Shamash, Faithful
    shepherd of humankind, Shepherd of the black-headed,
    Shepherd of humankind, Shepherd of the lower world,
    Guardian of the upper

Appendix B

Mesopotamian kings with shepherd titles and epithets

Sumerian terms[1]

Shepherd: Gudea, Ur-nammu, Shulgi, Lipit-Ishtar, Enlil-bani, Rim-Sin, Samsu-ilanu

Righteous shepherd: Rim-Sin and Nebuchadnezzar I

Obedient shepherd: Lipit-Ishtar, Abisare

Son (of An), obedient shepherd: Ur-Ninurta

Obedient shepherd to the Great Mountain: Rim Sin

Shepherd of the assembly of the country and the territory of Nippur: Rim Sin

Shepherd of the first class of (god's name): Lipit-Ishtar, Ur-Nammu, Gudea

Shepherd of the country: Shulgi

Shepherd of the whole country: Lipit-Ishtar

Shepherd of his country: Guidea

Shepherd of equity/justice: Nur-Adad, Sin-iddinam, Sin-iqisham

Shepherd who brings stability to Nippur: Sin-iddinam

Shepherd of justice: Warad-Sin

Shepherd who loves justice: Ishme-Dagan

Zealous shepherd: Rim-Sin, Ammi-ditana

Shepherd who reveres Nippur: Zambia

Shepherd of the black-headed: Shulgi, Shu-Sin, Rim-Sin

Powerful shepherd: Lugalzagesi

Humble shepherd: Sin-iddinam, Kudurmabuk, Ammisaduqa, Burnaburiash II

Humble shepherd of Nippur: Lipit-Ishtar

Shepherd according to his (Enlil's) heart: Iddin-Dagan

Favoured shepherd of An: Damiq-ilishu

Favoured shepherd of Enlil, of Utu and of Marutu: Shamash-shum-ukin

---

[1] Translated from Seux 1967: 441–450.

His (god's) favourite shepherd: Hammurabi, Karaindash,
   Adad-shum-usur, Assurbanipal, Assur-etel-ilani
Faithful shepherd: Enannatum I, Gudea, Ur-Nammu, Shulgi,
   Iddin-Dagan, Ishme-Dagan, Lipit-Ishtar, Ur-Ninurta,
   Nur-Adad, Rim-Sin, Samsu-iluna, Ammi-saduqa,
   Burnaburiash II, Kadashman-Enlil
Faithful shepherd according to the irrevocable word of Ningirsu:
   Gudea
Faithful shepherd of the country: Sin-iddinam
Faithful shepherd of (city name): Shulgi, Sin-iddinam, Anam

Akkadian terms[2]

Shepherd (Neo-Assyrian):
   Shalmanasar I, Tukuti-Ninurta I, Assur-nadin-apli,
   Tiglath-Pileser I, Tukulti-Ninurta II, Shalmaneser III,
   Sargon II, Esarhaddon, Assurbanipal, Sin-shar-ishkun
Shepherd (Neo-Babylon):
   Kurigalzu II, Nazimaruttash, Shagarakti-Shuriash,
   Nebuchadnezzar I, Marduk-apla-iddina II,
   Shamash-shum-ukin, Nebuchadnezzar II, Nabonidus
Shepherd sage: Tukulti-Ninurta I
Shepherd superlatively strong: Gandash (early Kassite)
Experienced shepherd: Sennacherib, Assurbanipal, Nabonidus
Submissive shepherd: Nabonidus
Faithful shepherd: (used widely)
Faithful shepherd and zealous towards Enlil and Marduk:
   Sargon II
Your (Marduk's) faithful shepherd: Nebuchadnezzar II
Shepherd who safeguards: Hammurapi
Reflective shepherd: Nabonidus
Pious shepherd: Sennacherib
Zealous shepherd: Tukulti-Ninurta I, Tiglath-Pileser I
Shepherd full of awe: Simbarshipak, Nabonidus
Shepherd of confidence: Asarhaddon
Shepherd provider: Nabonidus
Shepherd, provider for Marduk: Assurbanipal
Shepherd of the holy places: Shamshi-Adad V
Shepherd of the subjects: Sennacherib

[2] Translated from Seux 1967: 244–250.

Shepherd of the four regions: Assurnasirpall II
Shepherd of Assyria: Sargon II
Shepherd of populations: Hammurapi
Shepherd of great populations: Nebuchadnezzar II
Shepherd of large populations: Agumkakrime, Nebuchadnezzar II,
    Nabonidus
Shepherd of the assembly of the inhabited places: Shalmaneser I
Shepherd of the people of Susa: Attapakshu, Tetep-Mada
Shepherd of the black-headed: Ipiq-Adad II, Asarhaddon,
    Assurbanipal
Shepherd of Shushinak: Attapakshu
Marvellous shepherd: Assurnasirpal II, Sardur I, Adad-nerari III

Other formulaic titles from Neo-Assyrian and Neo-Babylonian kings

Shepherd of the work of their hands
Shepherd who assures the stability of the throne of his father
Shepherd who maintains the populations in good order
Shepherd who gathers the dispersed
Shepherd who satisfies his (or their) heart
Shepherd who fears (his divinity)
Shepherd who is on guard

In association with divine names

Shepherd, favoured of Enlil, of Shamash, and of Marduk
Shepherd, loved of Ninurta
Shepherd, named for Marduk (or Enlil)
Shepherd who reveres Nippur
Shepherd, protector of the regions
Shepherd who provides for/attends to the needs of the sanctuaries of
    the great gods

Bibliography

Aitken, K. T. (1983), 'The Oracles Against Babylon in Jeremiah 50 – 51: Structures and Perspectives', *Tyndale Bulletin* 35: 25–63.

Alexander, T. D. (1995), 'Messianic Ideology in the Book of Genesis', in P. E. Satterthwaite, R. S. Hess & G. J. Wenham (eds.), *The Lord's Anointed: Interpretation of Old Testament Messianic Texts*, Carlisle, UK: Paternoster: 19–39.

Allen, L. C. (1990), *Ezekiel 20 – 48*, WBC; 29, Waco, TX: Word.

Alt, A. (1989), *Essays in Old Testament History and Religion*, trans. R. A. Wilson, Sheffield: Sheffield Academic.

Anderson, B. W. (1962), 'Exodus Typology in Second Isaiah', in B. W. Anderson & W. Harrelson (eds.), *Israel's Prophetic Heritage: Essays in Honor of J. Muilenburg*, New York: Harper: 177–195.

———(1976), 'Exodus and Covenant in Second Isaiah and Prophetic Tradition', in F. M. Cross, W. E. Lemke & P. D. Miller (eds.), *Magnalia Dei: The Mighty Acts of God: Essays on the Bible and Archaeology in Memory of G. Ernest Wright*, Garden City, NY: Doubleday: 339–360.

———(1983), *Out of the Depths: The Psalms Speak for Us Today*, Philadelphia: Westminster.

Aune, D. E. (1996), 'Following the Lamb: Discipleship in the Apocalypse', in R. N. Longenecker (ed.), *Patterns of Discipleship in the New Testament*, Grand Rapids: Eerdmans: 269–284.

———(1997), *Revelation 1 – 5*, WBC; 52, Dallas: Word.

———(1998), *Revelation 6 – 16*, WBC; 52B, Nashville: Thomas Nelson.

Baines, J. (1995), 'Kingship, Definition of Culture, and Legitimation', in D. O'Connor & D. P. Silverman (eds.), *Ancient Egyptian Kingship*, Leiden: Brill: 3–47.

Balch, D. L. (1986), 'Hellenization/Acculturation in 1 Peter', in C. H. Talbert (ed.), *Perspectives on First Peter*, Macon, GA: Mercer University: 79–101.

Baldwin, J. G. (1972), *Haggai, Zechariah, Malachi*, TOTC, London: Inter-Varsity.

Barker, M. (2000), *The Revelation of Jesus Christ*, Edinburgh: T. & T. Clark.

Barré, M. L. & J. S. Kselman (1983), 'New Exodus, Covenant, and Restoration in Psalm 23', in C. L. Meyers & M. O'Connor (eds.), *The Word of the Lord Shall Go Forth*, Winona Lake, IN: Eisenbrauns: 97–127.

Barstad, H. M. (1989), *A Way in the Wilderness: The 'Second Exodus' in the Message of Second Isaiah*, JSS 12, Manchester: University of Manchester.

Barton, S. C. (2000), 'Parables of God's Love and Forgiveness', in R. N. Longenecker (ed.), *The Challenge of Jesus' Parables*, Grand Rapids: Eerdmans: 199–216.

Bauckham, R. (1993a), 'Structure and Composition', in R. Bauckham, *The Climax of Prophecy: Studies in the Book of Revelation*, Edinburgh: T. & T. Clark: 1–37.

———— (1993b), *The Theology of the Book of Revelation*, Cambridge: Cambridge University.

Bauer, D. R. (1988), *The Structure of Matthew's Gospel: A Study in Literary Design*, JSNTS 15, Sheffield: Almond.

Beale, G. K. (1998), *John's Use of the Old Testament in Revelation*, JSNTS 166, Sheffield: Sheffield Academic.

———— (1999), *The Book of Revelation: A Commentary on the Greek Text*, NIGTC, Grand Rapids: Eerdmans.

Beasley-Murray, G. R. (1987), *John*, WBC; 36, Waco, TX: Word.

Beckman, G. M. (1988), 'Herding and Herdsmen in Hittite Culture', in O. Heinrich (ed.), *Documentum Asiae Minoris Antiquae*, Wiesbaden: Harrassowitz: 33–44.

Beegle, D. M. (1972), *Moses, the Servant of Yahweh*, Grand Rapids: Eerdmans.

Bennett, D. W. (1993), *Metaphors of Ministry: Biblical Images for Leaders and Followers*, Grand Rapids: Baker.

Bentzen, A. (1948), *Messias, Moses Redivivus, Menschensohn: Skizzen zum Thema Weissangung und Erfüllung*, ATANT 17, Zurich: Zwingli Verlag.

Berges, U. (1989), *Die Verwerfung Sauls: Eine thematische Unter-suchung*, Forschung zur Bibel 61, Würzburg: Echter Verlag.

———— (2000), 'Who Were the Servants? A Comparative Inquiry in the Book of Isaiah and the Psalms', in J. C. De Moor & H. F. Van

Rooy (eds.), *Past, Present, Future: The Deuteronomistic History and the Prophets*, Leiden: Brill: 1–18.

Betz, O. (1967), 'The Eschatological Interpretation of the Sinai-Tradition in Qumran and in the New Testament', *Revue de Qumran* 6: 89–107.

Beuken, W. A. M. (1990), 'The Main Theme of Trito-Isaiah: "The Servants of YHWH" ', *JSOT* 47: 67–87.

——— (2003), 'The Unity of the Book of Isaiah', in J. C. Exum & H. G. M. Williamson (eds.), *Reading from Right to Left: Essays on the Hebrew Bible in Honour of David J. A. Clines*, JSOTS 373, Sheffield: Sheffield Academic: 50–62.

Beyerlin, W. (ed.) (1978), *Near Eastern Religious Texts Relating to the Old Testament*, trans. J. Bowden, Philadelphia: Westminster.

Bimson, J. J. & J. P. Kane (eds.) (1985), *New Bible Atlas*, London: Inter-Varsity.

Black, J. & A. Green (1992), *Gods, Demons and Symbols of Ancient Mesopotamia*, Austin: University of Texas.

Black, M. (1962), *Models and Metaphors: Studies in Language and Philosophy*, Ithaca, NY: Cornell University.

——— (1979), 'More About Metaphor', in A. Ortony (ed.), *Metaphor and Thought*, Cambridge: Cambridge University Press: 19–43.

Blenkinsopp, J. (1992), *The Pentateuch: An Introduction to the First Five Books of the Bible*, New York: Doubleday.

Block, D. I. (1988), *The Gods of the Nations*, Grand Rapids: Baker Academic.

——— (1995), 'Bringing Back David: Ezekiel's Messianic Hope', in P. E. Satterthwaite, R. S. Hess & G. J. Wenham (eds.), *The Lord's Anointed: Interpretation of Old Testament Messianic Texts*, Carlisle, UK: Paternoster: 167–188.

Bock, D. L. (1987), *Proclamation from Prophecy and Pattern: Lucan Old Testament Christology*, JSNTS 12, Sheffield: JSOT.

——— (1994), *Luke Volume 1: 1:1 – 9:50*, BECNT, Grand Rapids: Baker.

Boismard, M. E. (1993), *Moses or Jesus: An Essay in Johannine Christology*, trans. B. T. Viviano, Minneapolis: Fortress.

Bolman, L. G. & T. E. Deal (1997), *Reframing Organizations: Artistry, Choice, and Leadership*, 2nd edn, San Francisco: Jossey-Bass.

Borchert, G. L. (1996), *John 1 – 11*, NAC 25A, Nashville: Broadman & Holman.

Borowski, O. (1998), *Every Living Thing: Daily Use of Animals in Ancient Israel*, Walnut Creek, CA: AltaMira.

Breasted, J. H. (1906–7), *Ancient Records of Egypt* 1–5, Chicago: University of Chicago.

Brettler, M. Z. (1989), *God is King: Understanding an Israelite Metaphor*, *JSOTS* 76, Sheffield: Sheffield Academic.

―――― (1998), 'Incompatible Metaphors for YHWH in Isaiah 40 – 66', *JSOT* 78: 97–120.

Brewer, D. (2002), 'Hunting, Husbandry and Diet in Ancient Egypt', in B. J. Collins (ed.), *A History of the Animal World in the Ancient Near East*, Leiden: Brill.

Brief, A. P. & H. K. Downey (1983), 'Cognitive and Organizational Structure: A Conceptual Analysis of Implicit Organizing Theories', *Human Relations* 36 (12): 1065–1090.

Brodie, T. L. (1993), *The Gospel According to John: A Literary and Theological Commentary*, New York: Oxford University.

Brooke, G. J. (1994), 'Isaiah 40:3 and the Wilderness Community', in G. J. Brooke (ed.), *New Qumran Texts and Studies*, Leiden: Brill: 117–132.

Brown, R. E. (1966), *The Gospel According to John (1 – 12)*, AB, New York: Doubleday.

―――― (1977), *The Birth of the Messiah: A Commentary on the Infancy Narratives in Matthew and Luke*, London: Geoffrey Chapman.

―――― (1994), *The Death of the Messiah: From Gethsemane to the Grave*, 2 vols., New York: Doubleday.

Brown, R. H. (1977), *A Poetic for Sociology*, Cambridge: Cambridge University.

Bruce, F. F. (1960–61), 'The Book of Zechariah and the Passion Narrative', *Bulletin of the John Rylands Library* 43: 336–353.

―――― (1968), *New Testament Development of Old Testament Themes*, Grand Rapids: Eerdmans.

―――― (1983), *The Gospel of John: Introduction, Exposition and Notes*, Grand Rapids: Eerdmans.

Brueggemann, W. (1968), 'David and His Theologian', *CBQ* 30: 156–181.

―――― (1990), *First and Second Samuel*, Interpretation, Louisville: John Knox.

Bruins, H. J. (1986), *Desert Environment and Agriculture in the Central Negev and Kadesh-Barnea During Historical Times*, Nijkerk, Netherlands: Midbar Foundation.

Budde, K. (1895), 'The Nomadic Ideal in the Old Testament', *New World* 4: 726–745.

Bullinger, E. W. (1968), *Figures of Speech Used in the Bible*, Grand Rapids: Baker.

Burden, T. L. (1994), *The Kerygma of the Wilderness Traditions in the Hebrew Bible*, American University Studies Series VII, vol. 163, New York: Peter Lang.

Caird, G. B. (1980), *The Language and Imagery of the Bible*, Philadelphia: Westminster.

Callender, D. E. (2000), *Adam in Myth and History: Ancient Israelite Perspectives on the Primal Human*, HSS 48, Winona Lake, IN: Eisenbrauns.

Camp, C. V. & D. R. Fontaine (eds.) (1993), *Women, War, and Metaphor: Language and Society in the Study of the Hebrew Bible*, *Semeia* 61, Atlanta: Scholars.

Carlson, R. A. (1964), *David the Chosen King: A Traditio-Historical Approach to the Second Book of Samuel*, Stockholm: Almqvist & Wiksell.

Carr, D. M. (1995), 'Isaiah 40:1–11 in the Context of the Macrostructure of Second Isaiah', in W. R. Bodine (ed.), *Discourse Analysis of Biblical Literature: What it is and What it Offers*, Atlanta: Scholars: 51–74.

———— (2001), 'Genesis in Relation to the Moses Story: Diachronic and Synchronic Perspectives', in A. Wénin (ed.), *Studies in the Book of Genesis*, Leuvin: Leuvin University: 273–295.

Carson, D. A. (1988), 'John and the Johannine Epistles', in D. A. Carson & H. G. M. Williamson (eds.), *It is Written: Scripture Citing Scripture*, New York: Cambridge University: 245–264.

———— (1991), *The Gospel According to John*, Grand Rapids: Eerdmans.

Casey, J. S. (1982), 'Exodus Typology in the Book of Revelation', PhD dissertation, Southern Baptist Theological Seminary.

Caws, P. (1974), 'Operational, Representational, and Explanatory Models', *American Anthropologist* 76 (1): 1–11.

Charpin, D. (1986), *Le clergé d'Ur au siècle d'Hammurabi*, Geneva: Librairie Droz.

Childs, B. (1974), *The Book of Exodus*, OTL, Louisville: Westminster.

———— (1979), *An Introduction to the Old Testament as Scripture*, Philadelphia: Fortress.

Clements, R. E. (1967), *Abraham and David: Genesis 15 and its Meaning for Israelite Tradition*, SBT, 2nd series 5, Naperville, IL: A. R. Allenson.

Clifford, R. (1989), 'Narrative and Lament in Isaiah 63:7 – 64:11', in M. P. Horgan & P. J. Kobelski (eds.), *To Touch the Text: Biblical and Related Studies in Honor of Joseph A. Fitzmyer, SJ*, New York: Crossroad: 93–102.

Clines, D. (1978), *The Theme of the Pentateuch*, Sheffield: University of Sheffield.

Coats, G. W. (1968), *Rebellion in the Wilderness: The Murmuring Motif in the Wilderness Traditions of the Old Testament*, Nashville: Abingdon.

——— (1972), 'An Exposition for the Wilderness Traditions', *VT* 22: 288–295.

——— (1988), *Moses: Heroic Man, Man of God, JSOTS* 57, Sheffield: Sheffield Academic.

——— (1993), *The Moses Tradition, JSOTS* 161, Sheffield: Sheffield Academic.

Cohn, R. L. (1981), *The Shape of Sacred Space: Four Biblical Studies*, Studies in Religion 23, Chico, CA: Scholars.

Collins, A. Y. (1976), *The Combat Myth in the Book of Revelation*, Montana: Scholars.

Collins, B. J. (ed.) (2002), *A History of the Animal World in the Ancient Near East*, Leiden: Brill.

Collins, J. J. (1979), 'Introduction: Toward the Morphology of a Genre', *Semeia* 14: 1–20.

——— (1995), *The Sceptre and the Star: The Messiahs of the Dead Sea Scrolls and other Ancient Literature*, New York: Doubleday.

Colwell, E. C. (1970), 'Popular Reactions Against Christianity in the Roman Empire', in J. T. McNeill et al. (eds.), *Environmental Factors in Christian History*, New York: Kennikat: 53–71.

Combrink, H. J. B. (1977), 'Structural Analysis of Mt. 9:35 – 11:1', *Neotestamentica* 11: 98–114.

Coppedge, A. (2001), *Portraits of God: A Biblical Theology of Holiness*, Downers Grove, IL: InterVarsity.

Craigie, P. (1983), *Psalms 1 (1 – 50)*, WBC; 19, Waco, TX: Word.

Craigie, P. C., P. H. Kelley & J. F. Drinkard, (1991), *Jeremiah 1 – 25*, WBC; 26, Dallas: Word.

Creach, J. (1998), 'The Shape of Book Four of the Psalter and the Shape of Second Isaiah', *JSOT* 80: 63–76.

Cribb, R. (1991), *Nomads in Archaeology*, Cambridge: Cambridge University Press.

Crockett, L. (1966), 'Luke iv. 16–30 and the Jewish Lectionary Cycle: A Word of Caution', *JJS* 17: 13–46.

Cross, F. L. (1954), *1 Peter – A Paschal Liturgy*, London: A. R. Mowbray.

Cross, F. M. (1973), *Canaanite Myth and Hebrew Epic*, Cambridge, MA: Harvard University.

Crossan, J. D. (1986), 'From Moses to Jesus: Parallel Themes', *Bible Review* 2: 18–27.

Culpepper, R. A. (1983), *Anatomy of the Fourth Gospel*, Philadelphia: Fortress.

Dahood, M. (1967), 'The Metaphor in Jeremiah 17, 13', *Biblica* 48: 109–110.

Daly-Denton, M. (2000), *David in the Fourth Gospel: The Johannine Reception of the Psalms*, Leiden: Brill.

Davids, P. H. (1990), *The First Epistle of Peter*, NICNT, Grand Rapids: Eerdmans.

Davies, G. I. (1974), 'The Wilderness Itineraries: A Comparative Study', *Tyndale Bulletin* 25: 46–81.

Davies, W. D. (1997), 'Paul and the New Exodus', in C. A. Evans & S. Talmon (eds.), *The Quest for Context and Meaning: Studies in Biblical Intertextuality in Honor of James A. Sanders*, Leiden: Brill: 443–463.

Davis, S. J. M. (1987), *The Archaeology of Animals*, New Haven: Yale University.

Day, J. (1985), *God's Conflict with the Dragon and the Sea*, Cambridge: Cambridge University.

——— (1998), 'The Canaanite Inheritance of the Israelite Monarchy', in J. Day (ed.), *King and Messiah in Israel and the Ancient Near East*, JSOTS 270, Sheffield: Sheffield Academic: 72–90.

Deeley, M. K. (1997), 'Ezekiel's Shepherd and John's Jesus: A Case Study in the Appropriation of Biblical Texts', in C. A. Evans & J. A. Sanders (eds.), *Early Christian Interpretation of the Scriptures of Israel: Investigations and Proposals*, JSNTS 148, Sheffield: Sheffield Academic: 252–264.

del Olmo Lete, G. (1993), 'Sheep and Goats at Ugarit: Alphabetic Texts', *Bulletin on Sumerian Agriculture* 7: 183–197.

Derrett, J. D. M. (1973a), 'The Manger at Bethlehem: Light on St Luke's Technique from Contemporary Jewish Religious Law', *Studia Evangelica* 6: 86–94.

——— (1973b), 'The Good Shepherd: St John's Use of Jewish Halakah and Haggadah', *Studia Theologica* 27: 25–50.

Deterding, P. E. (1981), 'Exodus Motifs in 1 Peter', *Concordia Journal* 7: 58–65.

Dijkstra, M. (1999), 'YHWH as Israel's *go'el*: Second Isaiah's Perspective on Reconciliation and Restitution', *ZAR* 5: 236–257.

Dittmer, L. (1977), 'Political Culture and Political Symbolism: Toward a Theoretical Synthesis', *World Politics* 29: 552–583.

Dodd, C. H. (1935), *The Parables of the Kingdom*, London: Nisbet & Co.

——— (1953), *The Interpretation of the Fourth Gospel*, Cambridge: Cambridge University.

Donahue, J. R. (1978), 'Jesus as the Parable of God in the Gospel of Mark', Interpretation 32: 369–386.

Donaldson, T. (1985), *Jesus on the Mountain: A Study in Matthean Theology*, *JSNTS* 8, Sheffield: Sheffield Academic.

Driver, G. R. (1956), *Canaanite Myths and Legends*, Edinburgh: T. & T. Clark.

Dubbink, J. (2001), 'Cedars Decay, A Sprout will Blossom: Jeremiah 23:5–6: Conclusion of the Prophecies on Kingship', in J. W. Dyk et al. (eds.), *Unless Someone Guides Me . . . Festchrift for Karel A. Deurloo*, Maastricht: Uitgeverij Shaker: 157–165.

Duguid, I. M. (1994), *Ezekiel and the Leaders of Israel*, Leiden: E. J. Brill.

Duling, D. C. (1978), 'The Therapeutic Son of David: An Element in Matthew's Christological Apologetic', *NTS* 24: 392–410.

——— (1992), 'Matthew's Plurisignificant "Son of David" in Social Science Perspective: Kinship, Kingship, Magic, and Miracle', *BTB* 22: 99–116.

Du Mesnil du Buisson, R. (1973), *Nouvelles Études sur les Dieux et les Mythes de Canaan*, Leiden: Brill.

Durham, J. I. (1987), *Exodus*, WBC; 3, Waco: Word.

Earle, T. (ed.) (1991), *Chiefdoms: Power, Economy, and Ideology*, Cambridge: Cambridge University.

Edelman, M. J. (1971), *Politics as Symbolic Interaction*, Orlando: Academic.

Eissfeldt, O. (1962), 'The Promises of Grace to David in Isaiah 55:1–5', in B. W. Anderson & W. Harrelson (eds.), *Israel's Prophetic Heritage: Essays in Honor of James Muilenburg*, New York: Harper: 196–207.

Elliger, K. (1975), *Das Buch der zwölf kleinen Propheten II*, Göttingen: Vandenhoeck & Ruprecht.

Elliott, J. H. (1966), *The Elect and the Holy: An Exegetical Examination of 1 Peter 2:4–10 and the phrase 'Basileion ierateuma'*, Leiden: Brill.

———(1970), 'Ministry and Church Order in the NT: A Traditio-Historical Analysis (1 Pt 5, 1–5 & plls)', *CBQ* 32: 367–391.

———(1981), *A Home for the Homeless: A Sociological Exegesis of 1 Peter*, Philadelphia: Fortress.

Engnell, I. (1967), *Studies in Divine Kingship in the Ancient Near East*, 2nd edn, Oxford: Blackwell.

Eph'al, I. (1984), *The Ancient Arabs: Nomads on the Borders of the Fertile Crescent 9th – 5th Centuries* BC, Jerusalem: Magnes Press.

Eslinger, L. M. (1985), *Kingship of God in Crisis: A Close Reading of 1 Samuel 1 – 12*, Sheffield: Almond.

———(1994), *House of God or House of David: The Rhetoric of 2 Samuel 7*, Sheffield: JSOT.

Evans, C. A. (1993a), 'Luke 16:1–18 and the Deuteronomy Hypothesis', in C. A. Evans & J. A. Sanders (eds.), *Luke and Scripture: The Function of Sacred Tradition in Luke-Acts*, Minneapolis: Fortress: 121–139.

———(1993b), 'The Twelve Thrones of Israel: Scripture and Politics in Luke 22:24–30', in C. A. Evans & J. A. Sanders (eds.), *Luke and Scripture: The Function of Sacred Tradition in Luke-Acts*, Minneapolis: Fortress: 154–170.

———(2001), *Mark 8:27 – 16:20*, WBC; 34B, Nashville: Thomas Nelson.

Evans, C. F. (1954), 'I Will Go Before You into Galilee', *JTS* 5: 3–18.

Evenari, M., L. Shanan & N. Tadmor (1971), *The Negev: The Challenge of a Desert*, Harvard: Harvard University.

Fekkes, J. (1994), *Isaiah and the Prophetic Traditions in the Book of Revelation: Visionary Antecedents and their Development*, JSNTS 93, Sheffield: JSOT.

Ferré, F. (1987), 'In Praise of Anthropomorphism', in R. P. Scharlemann & G. E. M. Ogutu (eds.), *God in Language*, New York: Paragon House: 182–193.

Fiedler, K. (1982), 'Casual Schemata: Review and Criticism of Research on a Popular Construct', *Journal of Personality and Social Pscyhology* 42: 1001–1013.

Fishbane, M. (1979), *Text and Texture: Close Readings of Selected Biblical Texts*, New York: Schocken.

———(1985), *Biblical Interpretation in Ancient Israel*, Oxford: Clarendon.

Fitzmyer, J. A. (1981), *The Gospel According to Luke (1 – 9)*, AB, Garden City, NY: Doubleday.

Flanagan, J. W. (1988), *David's Social Drama: A Hologram of Israel's Early Iron Age*, *JSOTS* 73, Sheffield: Almond.

Flight, J. W. (1923), 'The Nomadic Idea and Ideal', *JBL* 42: 158–226.

Fokkelman, J. P. (1990), *Narrative Art and Poetry in the Books of Samuel* 3, Assen/Maastricht, Netherlands: Van Gorcum.

Fowler, R. M. (1981), *Loaves and Fishes: The Function of the Feeding Stories in the Gospel of Mark*, SBLDS 54, Chico, CA: Scholars.

Fox, M. (1973), 'Jeremiah 2:2 and the "Desert Ideal"', *CBQ* 35: 441–450.

France, R. T. (1971), *Jesus and the Old Testament: His Application of Old Testament Passages to Himself and His Mission*, London: Tyndale.

———(2002), *The Gospel of Mark: A Commentary on the Greek Text*, NIGTC, Grand Rapids: Eerdmans.

Frankfort, H. (1939), *Cylinder Seals: A Documentary Essay on the Art and Religion of the Ancient Near East*, London: Macmillan.

Frayne, D. (1990), *Old Babylonian Period (2003–2595 BC)*, The Royal Inscriptions of Mesopotamia: Early Periods 4, Toronto: University of Toronto.

Freedman, D. N. (1980), *Pottery, Poetry, and Prophecy*, Winona Lake, IN: Eisenbrauns.

———(1987), 'The Structure of Isaiah 40:1–11', in E. W. Conrad & E. G. Newing (eds.), *Perspectives on Language and Text*, Winona Lake, IN: Eisenbrauns: 167–193.

Fretheim, T. E. (1991), *Exodus*, Interpretation, Louisville: John Knox.

Funk, R. W. (1966), *Language, Hermeneutic, and Word of God: The Problem of Language in the New Testament and Contemporary Theology*, New York: Harper & Row.

Furnish, V. P. (1975), 'Elect Sojourners in Christ: An Approach to the Theology of 1 Peter', *Perkins School of Theology Journal* 28: 1–11.

Gadd, C. J. (1948), *Ideas of Divine Rule in the Ancient East*, London: Oxford Press.

Galaty, J. G. (1990), 'Pastoral Systems in Global Perspective', in J. G. Galaty & D. L. Johnson (eds.), *The World of Pastoralism: Herding Systems in Comparative Perspective*, New York: Guilford Press: 1–31.

Gardiner, A. H. (1931), *The Library of A. Chester Beatty*, Oxford: Oxford University.

Geertz, C. (1966), 'Religion as a Cultural System', in M. Banton (ed.), *Anthropological Approaches to the Study of Religion*, London: Tavistock: 1–46.

Geertz, C. (ed.), (1971), *Myth, Symbol and Culture*, New York: Merton.

Gerbrandt, G. E. (1986), *Kingship According to the Deuteronomistic History*, SBLDS 87, Atlanta: Scholars.

Glasson, T. F. (1963), *Moses in the Fourth Gospel*, SBT 40, London: SCM.

Glück, J. J. (1963), 'Nagid-Shepherd', *VT* 13: 144–150.

Glueck, N. (1967), *Hesed in the Bible*, trans. A. Gottschalk, Cincinnati: Hebrew Union College.

Goffman, E. (1974), *Frame Analysis*, New York: Harper & Row.

Good, R. M. (1983), *The Sheep of His Pasture: A Study of the Hebrew Noun 'Am(m) and Its Semitic Cognates*, Harvard Semitic Monographs 29, Chico, CA: Scholars.

Goodenough, E. R. (1928), 'The Political Philosophy of Hellenistic Kingship', *Yale Classical Studies* I: 51–103.

————(1929), 'Kingship in Early Israel', *JBL* 48: 169–208.

Gottlieb, H. (1967), 'Die Tradition von David als Hirten', *VT* 17: 190–200.

Grant, D. & C. Oswick (eds.) (1996), *Metaphor and Organizations*, London: Sage.

Grassi, J. A. (1977), 'The Last Testament-Succession Literary Background of Matthew 9:35 – 11:1 and Its Significance', *BTB* 7/4: 172–176.

Gray J. (1952), 'Canaanite Kingship in Theory and Practice', *VT* 2: 192–220.

Gray, S. W. (1989), *The Least of My Brothers: Matthew 25:31–46: A History of Interpretation*, SBLDS 114, Atlanta: Scholars.

Grayson, A. K. (1987), *Assyrian Rulers of the Third and Second Millennia* BC, Toronto: University of Toronto.

————(1991), *Assyrian Rulers of the Early First Millenium* BC, vol. 1, Toronto: University of Toronto.

————(1996), *Assyrian Rulers of the Early First Millennium* BC, vol. 2, Toronto: University of Toronto.

Green, J. B. (1995), *The Theology of the Gospel of Luke*, Cambridge: Cambridge University.

————(1997), *The Gospel of Luke*, NICNT, Grand Rapids: Eerdmans.

Greenberg, M. (1969), *Understanding Exodus*, New York: Behrman House.

————(1983), *Ezekiel 1 – 20*, AB, Garden City, NY: Doubleday.

————(1997), *Ezekiel 21 – 37*, AB, Garden City, NY: Doubleday.

Gregory, K. L. (1983), 'Native View Paradigms: Multiple Cultures and Cultural Conflict in Organizations', *Administrative Science Quarterly* 28: 359–376.

Guelich, R. A. (1989), *Mark 1 – 8:26*, WBC; 34A, Dallas: Word.

Guilding, A. (1960), *The Fourth Gospel and Jewish Worship: A Study of the Relation of St John's Gospel to the Ancient Jewish Lectionary System*, Oxford: Clarendon.

Gundry, R. H. (1966/67), ' "Verba Christi" in 1 Peter: Their Implications Concerning the Authorship of 1 Peter and the Authenticity of the Gospel Tradition', *NTS* 13: 336–350.

———(1967), *The Use of the Old Testament in the Gospel of Matthew*, *NTS* 18, Leiden: Brill.

———(1993), *Mark: A Commentary on His Apology for the Cross*, Grand Rapids: Eerdmans.

Hagner, D. A. (1995), *Matthew 14 – 28*, WBC; 33B, Dallas: Word.

Hallo, W. W. (1957), *Early Mesopotamian Royal Titles*, New Haven: American Oriental Society.

Hallo, W. W. (ed.) (1997), *The Context of Scripture* 1, Leiden: Brill.

———(2000), *The Context of Scripture* 2, Leiden: Brill.

Halpern, B. (1981), *The Constitution of the Monarchy in Israel*, HSM 25, Chico, CA: Scholars.

———(2001), *David's Secret Demons: Messiah, Murderer, Traitor, King*, Grand Rapids: Eerdmans.

Hanson, A. T. (1957), *The Wrath of the Lamb*, London: SPCK.

———(1991), *The Prophetic Gospel: A Study of John and the Old Testament*, Edinburgh: T. & T. Clark.

Hanson, P. D. (1979), *The Dawn of Apocalyptic*, rev. edn, Philadelphia: Fortress.

Hareuveni, N. (1980), *Nature in Our Biblical Heritage*, Neot Kedumim, Israel.

———(1991), *Desert and Shepherd in Our Biblical Heritage*, Neot Kedumim, Israel.

Harrington, D. J. (1991), *The Gospel of Matthew*, Sacra Pagina Series 1, Collegeville, MN: Liturgical.

Hayes, W. C. (1953), *The Scepter of Egypt* 1, Cambridge: Harvard University.

Heil, J. P. (1993), 'Ezekiel 34 and the Narrative Strategy of the Shepherd and Sheep Metaphor in Matthew', *CBQ* 55: 698–708.

Heinemann, J. (1968), 'The Triennial Lectionary Cycle', *JJS* 19: 41–48.

Hellholm, D. (1986), 'The Problem of Apocalyptic Genre and the Apocalypse of John', *Semeia* 36: 13–64.

Herrmann, S. (1985), '2 Samuel 7 in the Light of the Egyptian Königsnovelle Reconsidered', in S. Israelit-Groll (ed.), *Pharaonic Egypt: The Bible and Christianity*, Jerusalem: Magnes: 119–128.

Hesse, B. & P. Wapnish (2002), 'An Archaezoological Perspective on the Cultural Use of Mammals in the Levant', in B. J. Collins (ed.), *A History of the Animal World in the Ancient Near East*, Leiden: Brill: 457–491.

Heyman, L. W. (1976), 'Indeterminacy in Literary Criticism', *Soundings* 59: 345–356.

Hillyer, N. (1967), ' "The Lamb" in the Apocalypse', *Evangelical Quarterly* 39: 228–236.

——— (1970), 'First Peter and the Feast of Tabernacles', *Tyndale Bulletin* 21: 39–70.

Hoffmeier, J. K. (1997), *Israel in Egypt: The Evidence for the Authenticity of the Exodus Tradition*, New York: Oxford University.

Holladay, W. L. (1986), *Jeremiah 1: A Commentary on the Book for the Prophet Jeremiah, Chapters 1 – 25*, Hermeneia, Philadelphia: Fortress.

——— (1989), *Jeremiah 2*, Hermeneia, Minneapolis: Fortress.

Holmgren, F. (1973), *With Wings as Eagles: Isaiah 40 – 55, An Interpretation*, Chappaqua, NY: Biblical Scholars.

Hopkins, D. (1993), 'Pastoralists in Late Bronze Age Palestine: Which Way Did They Go?', *BA* 56: 200–211.

Hornung, E. (1982), *Conceptions of God in Ancient Egypt*, trans. J. Baines, London: Routledge & Kegan Paul (originally Ithaca: Cornell, 1982).

Hugenberger, G. P. (1995), 'The Servant of the Lord in the "Servant Songs" of Isaiah', in P. E. Satterthwaite, R. S. Hess & G. J. Wenham (eds.), *The Lord's Anointed: Interpretation of Old Testament Messianic Texts*, Carlisle, UK: Paternoster: 105–140.

Hurtado, L. W. (1985), 'Revelation 4 – 5 in the Light of Jewish Apocalyptic Analogies', *JSNT* 25: 105–124.

Iggers, G. G. (1975), *New Directions in European Historiography*, Middleton, CN: Wesleyan University.

In der Smitten, W. T. (1980), 'hămôr', *TDOT* 4: 465–470.

Isaac, B. (1990), *The Limits of Empire*, Oxford: Clarendon Press.

Ishida, T. (1977), *The Royal Dynasties in Ancient Israel: A Study on the Formation and Development of Royal-Dynastic Ideology*, Berlin: Walter de Gruyter.

Jacobsen, T. (1987), *The Harps that Once*, New Haven: Yale University.

Japhet, S. (1989), *The Ideology of the Book of Chronicles and its Place in Biblical Thought*, New York: P. Lang.

Jeremias, J. (1963), *The Parables of Jesus*, New York: C. Scribner's Sons.

——— (1968), '*poimēn*', in *Theological Dictionary of the New Testament* 6, trans. G. W. Bromiley, Grand Rapids: Eerdmans: 485–502.

——— (1969), *Jerusalem in the Time of Jesus: An Investigation into Economic and Social Conditions during the New Testament Period*, London: SCM.

Jobling, D. (1998), *1 Samuel*, Berit Olam Studies in Hebrew Narrative and Poetry, Collegeville, MN: Liturgical.

Johnson, D. (1969), *The Nature of Nomadism*, Chicago: University of Chicago.

Joyce, P. M. (1989), *Divine Initiative and Human Response in Ezekiel*, *JSOTS* 51, Sheffield: Sheffield Academic.

——— (1998), 'King and Messiah in Ezekiel', in J. Day (ed.), *King and Messiah in Israel and the Ancient Near East*, *JSOTS* 270, Sheffield: Sheffield Academic: 323–337.

Jülicher, A. (1888, 1899), *Die Gleichnisreden Jesu*, 2 vols., Freiburg: Akademische Verlagsbuchhandlung von J. C. B. Mohr.

Kaiser Jr, W. C. (1978), *Toward an Old Testament Theology*, Grand Rapids: Zondervan.

——— (1995), *The Messiah in the Old Testament*, Grand Rapids: Zondervan.

Käsemann, E. (1984), *The Wandering People of God*, Minneapolis: Augsburg.

Keener, C. S. (2003), *The Gospel of John: A Commentary*, 2 vols., Peabody, MA: Hendrickson.

Keller, W. P. (1970), *A Shepherd Looks at Psalm 23*, Minneapolis: World Wide Publications.

Kelley, P. H. (1970), 'Israel's Tabernacling God', *Review and Expositor* 67: 488–489.

Kemp, B. J. (1989), *Ancient Egypt: Anatomy of a Civilization*, London: Routledge.

Kendall, D. W. (1986), 'The Literary and Theological Function of 1 Peter 1:3–12', in C. H. Talbert (ed.), *Perspectives on First Peter*, Macon, GA: Mercer University: 103–120.

Kessler, M. (1999), 'The Function of the Chapters 25 and 50 – 51 in the Book of Jeremiah', in A. R. P. Diamond et al. (eds.), *Troubling Jeremiah*, *JSOTS* 260, Sheffield: JSOT: 64–72.

—— (2003), *Battle of the Gods: The God of Israel Versus Marduk of Babylon*, Assen, Netherlands: Royal Van Gorcum.

Keys, G. (1996), *The Wages of Sin: A Reappraisal of the 'Succession Narrative'*, *JSOTS* 221, Sheffield: Sheffield Academic.

Kingsbury, J. D. (1975), *Matthew: Structure, Christology, Kingdom*, Philadelphia: Fortress.

—— (1976), 'The Title "Son of David" in Matthew's Gospel', *JBL* 95: 591–602.

—— (1983), *The Christology of Mark's Gospel*, Philadelphia: Fortress.

Kirkpatrick, W. D. (1982), 'The Theology of 1 Peter', *SWJT* 25: 58–81.

Kistemaker, S. J. (2001), *New Testament Commentary: Exposition of the Book of Revelation*, Grand Rapids: Baker.

Kitchen, K. A. (1993), *Ramesside Inscriptions: Translated and Annotated Translations* 1, Oxford: Blackwell.

—— (2003), *Ramesside Inscriptions: Translated and Annotated Translations* 4, Oxford: Blackwell.

Klein, R. W. (1980), 'Jeremiah 23:1–8', Interpretation 34: 167–172.

—— (1983), *1 Samuel*, WBC, Waco, TX: Word.

Knapp, A. B. (1988), *The History and Culture of Ancient Western Asia and Egypt*, Belmont, CA: Wadsworth.

Knierim, R. (1985), 'The Composition of the Pentateuch', in K. Richards, *Society of Biblical Literature 1985 Seminar Papers*, Atlanta: 393–405.

Knoppers, G. (1995), 'Images of David', *Biblica* 76: 449–470.

—— (1997), 'The Vanishing Solomon: The Disappearance of the United Monarchy from Recent Histories of Ancient Israel', *JBL* 116: 19–44.

Koehler, L. (1956), 'Psalm 23', *ZAW* 68: 227–234.

Koester, C. R. (1995), *Symbolism in the Fourth Gospel: Meaning, Mystery, Community*, Minneapolis: Fortress.

Kohn, R. L. (2002), 'A Prophet Like Moses? Rethinking Ezekiel's Relationship to the Torah', *ZAW* 114: 236–254.

—— (2003), 'Ezekiel at the Turn of the Century', *Currents in Biblical Research* 2.1: 9–31.

Korpel, M. C. A. (1990), *A Rift in the Clouds: Ugaritic and Hebrew Descriptions of the Divine*, Münster: Ugarit-Verlag.

Kramer, S. N. (1940), *Lamentation over the Destruction of Ur*, The

Oriental Institute of the University of Chicago Assyriological Studies 12, Chicago: University of Chicago.

—— (1972), *Sumerian Mythology: A Study of Spiritual and Literary Achievement in the Third Millennium* BC, rev. edn, Philadelphia: American Philosophical Society.

—— (1974), 'Kingship in Sumer and Akkad: The Ideal King', in P. Garelli (ed.), *Le palais et le royaute XIX Rencontre Assyriologique Internationale*, Paris: Paul Geuthner: 163–176.

Kuhn, T. (1970), *The Structure of Scientific Revolutions*, 2nd edn, Chicago: University of Chicago.

Kutsko, J. F. (2000), 'Ezekiel's Anthropology and Its Ethical Implications', in M. S. Odell & J. T. Strong (eds.), *The Book of Ezekiel: Theological and Anthropological Perspectives*, SBLSS 9, Atlanta: Society of Biblical Literature: 119–141.

Kuyvenhoven, R. (2003), 'Jeremiah 23:1–8: Shepherds in Diachronic Perspective', in A. D. Hollander et al. (eds.), *Paratext and Megatext as Channels of Jewish and Christian Traditions*, Leiden: Brill.

Laansma, J. (1997), ' "I will give you rest": the "rest" motif in the New Testament', Tübingen: Mohr Siebeck.

Laato, A. (1997), 'Second Samuel 7 and the Ancient Near Eastern Royal Ideology', *CBQ* 59: 244–269.

Lakoff, G. & M. Johnson (1980), *Metaphors We Live By*, Chicago: University of Chicago.

Lamarche, P. (1961), *Zacharie IX – XIV: Structure Littéraire et Messianisme*, Paris: Gabalda.

Lambert, W. G. (1960), *Babylonian Wisdom Literature*, Oxford: Clarendon.

Lancaster, W. & F. (1999), *People, Land, and Water in the Arab Middle East*, Amsterdam: Harwood Academic Publishers.

Langdon, S. (1905), *Building Inscriptions of the Neo-Babylonian Empire: Part I, Nabopolassar and Nebuchadnezzar*, Paris: Ernest Leroux.

Laniak, T. S. (1998), *Shame and Honor in the Book of Esther*, SBLDS 165, Atlanta: Scholars.

—— (2003), 'Esther's *Volkcentrism* and the Reframing of Post-Exilic Judaism', in S. W. Crawford & L. J. Greenspoon (eds.), *The Book of Esther in Modern Research*, JSOTS 380, London: Continuum: 77–90.

Larsen, M. T. (ed.) (1979), *Power and Propaganda: A Symposium on Ancient Empires*, Copenhagen: Akademisk Forlag.

Lasswell, H. D. et al. (eds.) (1979–80), *Propaganda and Communications in World History*, Honolulu: University Press of Hawaii.

Leaney, A. R. C. (1963–64), '1 Peter and Passover: An Interpretation', *NTS* 10: 238–251.

Lee, W. W. (2003), *Punishment and Forgiveness in Israel's Migratory Campaign*, Grand Rapids: Eerdmans.

Lemche, N. P. (1976), 'The Manumission of Slaves, the Fallow Years, the Sabbatical Year, the Yobel Year', *VT* 26: 38–59.

——— (1985), *Early Israel: Anthropological and Historical Studies on the Israelite Society before the Monarchy*, Leiden: Brill.

Levenson, J. D. (1976), *Theology of the Program of the Restoration*, HSM 10, Missoula, MT: Scholars.

——— (1985), *Sinai and Zion: An Entry into the Jewish Bible*, Minneapolis: Winston.

——— (1988), *Creation and the Persistence of Evil: The Jewish Drama of Divine Omnipotence*, San Francisco: Harper & Row.

Lichtheim, M. (1973), *Ancient Egyptian Literature* 1, Berkeley: University of California.

Locke, J. (1894), *An Essay Concerning Human Understanding*, Oxford: Oxford University.

Long, G. A. (1994), 'Dead or Alive?: Literality and God-Metaphors in the Hebrew Bible', *JAAR* 62: 509–537.

Long, V. P. (1989), *Reign and Rejection of King Saul: A Case for Literary and Theological Coherence*, SBLDS 118, Atlanta: Scholars.

Luckenbill, D. (1926), *Ancient Records of Assyria and Babylon* 1, Chicago: University of Chicago.

Lundbom, J. R. (1986), 'Psalm 23 – Song of Passage', Interpretation 40: 6–16.

——— (1997), *Jeremiah: A Study in Ancient Hebrew Rhetoric*, Winona Lake, IN: Eisenbrauns.

Lundquist, J. M. (1984), 'The Common Temple Ideology of the Ancient Near East', in T. G. Madsen (ed.), *The Temple in Antiquity*, Provo, UT: Brigham Young University: 53–76.

Lutz, H. F. (1919), *Selected Sumerian and Babylonian Texts*, Philadelphia: University Museum.

Ma, W. (1999), *Until the Spirit Comes: The Spirit of God in the Book of Isaiah*, JSOTS 271, Sheffield: Sheffield Academic.

Macky, P. W. (1990), *The Centrality of Metaphors to Biblical Thought: A Method for Interpreting the Bible*, Lewiston, NY: Edwin Mellen.

Malamat, A. (1980), 'A Mari Prophecy and Nathan's Dynastic

Oracle', in J. A. Emerton (ed.), *Prophecy: Essays Presented to Georg Fohrer on His Sixty-Fifth Birthday, 6 September, 1980*, Berlin: Walter de Gruyter: 68–82.

Mánek, J. (1957), 'The New Exodus in the Books of Luke', *NovT* 2/1: 8–23.

Mann, T. W. (1977), *Divine Presence and Guidance in Israelite Traditions: The Typology of Exaltation*, Baltimore: Johns Hopkins University.

——— (1979), 'Theological Reflections on the Denial of Moses', *JBL* 98: 481–494.

——— (2000), 'Stars, Sprouts, and Streams: The Creative Redeemer of Second Isaiah', in W. P. Brown & S. D. McBride Jr (eds.), *God Who Creates: Essays in Honor of W. Sibley Towner*, Grand Rapids: Eerdmans: 135–151.

Marcus, J. (1992), *The Way of the Lord: Christological Exegesis of the Old Testament in the Gospel of Mark*, Louisville: Westminster John Knox.

Marshall, I. H. (1970), *Luke: Historian and Theologian*, Exeter: Paternoster.

——— (1978), *The Gospel of Luke: A Commentary on the Greek Text*, NIGTC, Grand Rapids: Eerdmans.

Martin, T. W. (1992), *Metaphor and Composition in 1 Peter*, SBLDS 131, Atlanta: Scholars.

Mason, R. (1976), 'The Relation of Zech 9 – 14 to Proto-Zechariah', *ZAW* 88: 227–238.

Matthews, V. H. (1978), *Pastoral Nomadism in the Mari Kingdom (c. 1830–1760 BC)*, Cambridge: American Schools of Oriental Research.

Mays, J. L. (1994), *The Lord Reigns: A Theological Handbook to the Psalms*, Louisville: Westminster John Knox.

Mauser, U. W. (1963), *Christ in the Wilderness: The Wilderness Theme in the Second Gospel and Its Basis in Biblical Tradition*, SBT 39, Naperville, IL: A. R. Allenson.

Mazar, A. (1990), *Archaeology of the Land of the Bible: 10,000–586 BCE*, New York: Doubleday.

McCann, J. C. (1993), *A Theological Introduction to the Book of Psalms*, Nashville: Abingdon.

McCarter, P. K. (1984), *II Samuel*, AB 9, Garden City, NY: Doubleday.

McCarthy, D. J. (1965), 'II Samuel 7 and the Structure of the Deuteronomic History', *JBL* 84: 131–138.

———— (1982), 'Compact and Kingship: Stimuli for Hebrew Covenant Thinking', in T. Ishida (ed.), *Studies in the Period of David and Solomon and Other Essays*, Tokyo: Yamakawa-Shuppansha: 75–92.

McFague, S. (1982), *Metaphorical Theology*, Philadelphia: Fortress.

McKane, W. (1983), *Prophets and Wise Men*, London: SCM.

———— (1986), *Jeremiah* 1 (Jeremiah 1 – 25), ICC, Edinburgh: T. & T. Clark.

McKeating, H. (1994), 'Ezekiel the "Prophet Like Moses"', *JSOT* 61: 97–109.

Meeks, W. A. (1967), *The Prophet-King: Moses Traditions and Johannine Christology*, NT Supp. 14, Leiden: Brill.

Mercer, S. A. B. (1952), *The Pyramid Texts in Translation and Commentary*, vols. 1–4, New York: Longmans, Green & Co.

Merrill, E. H. (1987), *Kingdom of Priests: A History of Old Testament Israel*, Grand Rapids: Baker.

———— (1988), 'Pilgrimage and Procession: Motifs of Israel's Return', in A. Gileadi (ed.), *Israel's Apostasy and Restoration: Essays in Honor of Ronald K. Harrison*, Grand Rapids: Baker: 261–272.

Messer, D. E. (1989), *Contemporary Images of Christian Ministry*, Nashville: Abingdon.

Mettinger, T. (1976), *King and Messiah: The Civil and Sacral Legitimation of the Israelite Kings*, Lund: G. W. K. Gleerup.

Meyers, E. & C. (1993), *Zechariah 9 – 14*, AB, New York: Doubleday.

Michaels, J. R. (1988), *1 Peter*, WBC; 49, Waco, TX: Word.

———— (1992), *Interpreting the Book of Revelation*, Grand Rapids: Baker.

Miller, P. D. (1993), '"Moses My Servant": The Deuteronomic Portrait of Moses', in D. L. Christensen (ed.), *A Song of Power and the Power of Song: Essays on the Book of Deuteronomy*, Winona Lake, IN: Eisenbrauns: 301–312.

Moberly, R. W. L. (1983), *At the Mountain of God: Story and Theology in Exodus 32 – 34*, Sheffield: JSOT.

Moessner, D. P. (1982), 'Jesus and the "Wilderness Generation": The Death of the Prophet Like Moses According to Luke', *SBL 1982 Seminar Papers*: 319–340.

———— (1983), 'Luke 9:1–50: Luke's Preview of the Journey of the Prophet Like Moses of Deuteronomy', *JBL* 102/4: 575–605.

Moloney, F. J. (2002), *The Gospel of Mark: A Commentary*, Peabody, MA: Hendrickson.

Moo, D. J. (1983), *The Old Testament in the Gospel Passion Narratives*, Sheffield: Almond.

Moran, W. L. (1958), 'Gen 49,10 and its use in Ez 21,32', *Biblica* 39: 405–425.

Morgan, G. (1986), *Images of Organization*, Beverly Hills, CA: Sage.

Motyer, A. (1993), *The Prophecy of Isaiah: An Introduction and Commentary*, Downers Grove, IL: InterVarsity.

Moule, C. F. D. (1956), 'The Nature and Purpose of 1 Peter', *NTS* 3/1: 1–11.

Mowinckel, S. (1962), *The Psalms in Israel's Worship*, trans. D. R. Ap-Thomas, Nashville: Abingdon.

Moyise, S. (1995), *The Old Testament in the Book of Revelation*, *JSNTS* 115, Sheffield: Sheffield Academic.

Muller, V. (1944), 'The Prehistory of the "Good Shepherd"', *JNES* 3: 87–90.

Mulzac, K. D. (2000), ' "Creation" in the Book of Jeremiah', in J. Moskala (ed.), *Creation, Life, and Hope: Essays in Honor of Jacques B. Doukham*, Berrien Springs, MI: Andrews University.

Murray, D. F. (1998), *Divine Prerogative and Royal Pretension: Pragmatics, Poetics and Polemics in a Narrative Sequence about David (2 Samuel 5.17 – 7.29)*, *JSOTS* 264, Sheffield: Sheffield Academic.

Na'aman, N. (1986), 'Habiru and Hebrews: The Transfer of a Social Term to the Literary Sphere', *JNES* 45: 271–288.

Netzer, E. (1992), 'Domestic Architecture in the Iron Age', in A. Kempinsky & R. Reich (eds.), *The Architecture of Ancient Israel: From the Prehistoric to the Persian Periods*, Jerusalem: Israel Exploration Society: 193–201.

Newsome, C. A. (1984), 'A Maker of Metaphors: Ezekiel's Oracles Against Tyre', Interpretation 38: 151–164.

Neyrey, J. H. (ed.) (1991), *The Social World of Luke-Acts: Models for Interpretation*, Peabody, MA: Hendrickson.

Nielsen, K. (1989), *Hope for a Tree: The Tree as a Metaphor in Isaiah*, *JSOTS* 65, Sheffield: Sheffield Academic.

Nohrnberg, J. (1995), *Like Unto Moses: The Constituting of an Interruption*, Bloomington: Indiana University.

Nolland, J. (1993), *Luke 9:21 – 18:34*, WBC; 35B, Dallas: Word.

Noth, M. (1972), *A History of Pentateuchal Traditions*, trans. B. W. Anderson, Englewood Cliffs, NJ: Prentice-Hall.

——— (1981), *The Deuteronomistic History*, *JSOTS* 15, Sheffield: Redwood Burn, Trowbridge and Esher.

O'Connor, D. & D. P. Silverman (eds.) (1995), *Ancient Egyptian Kingship*, Leiden: Brill.

Oden, T. C. (1983), *Pastoral Theology: Essentials of Ministry*, San Francisco: Harper & Row.

O'Kane, M. (1996), 'Isaiah: A Prophet in the Footsteps of Moses', *JSOT* 69: 29–51.

Oliver, H. H. (1963–64), 'The Lucan Birth Stories and the Purpose of Luke-Acts', *NTS* 10: 202–226.

Oppenheimer, A. (1977), *The 'Am Ha-aretz: A Study in the Social History of the Jewish People in the Hellenistic-Roman Period*, trans. I. H. Levine, Leiden: Brill.

Ortony, A. (1975), 'Why Metaphors are Necessary and Not Just Nice', *Educational Theory* 25: 45–52.

Oswalt, J. (1986), *The Book of Isaiah: Chapters 1 – 39*, Grand Rapids: Eerdmans.

Oswick, C., T. Keenoy & D. Grant (2002), 'Metaphor and Analogical Reasoning in Organizational Theory: Beyond Orthodoxy', *Academy of Management Review* 27/2: 294–303.

Paffenroth, K. (1999), 'Jesus as Anointed and Healing Son of David in the Gospel of Matthew', *Biblica* 80: 547–554.

Patrick, D. A. (1985), 'Epiphanic Imagery in Second Isaiah's Portrayal of a New Exodus', in R. Ahroni (ed.), *Hebrew Annual Review 8, 1984: Biblical and Other Studies in Honor of Sheldon H. Blank*, Columbus: Ohio State University: 125–141.

Patte, D. (1987), *The Gospel According to Matthew: A Structural Commentary on Matthew's Faith*, Philadelphia: Fortress.

Patton, C. (1996), ' "I Myself Gave Them Laws that were not Good" ': Ezekiel 20 and the Exodus Traditions', *JSOT* 69: 73–90.

Paul, S. M. (1968), 'Deutero-Isaiah and Cuneiform Royal Inscriptions', in W. W. Hallo (ed.), *Essays in Memory of E. A. Speiser*, AOS 53, New Haven, CT: American Oriental Society: 180–186.

Pepper, S. (1942), *World Hypotheses*, Berkeley: University of California.

Petersen, D. L. (1986), 'Portraits of David Canonical and Otherwise', Interpretation 40: 130–142.

Plastaras, J. (1966), *The God of the Exodus: The Theology of the Exodus Narratives*, Milwaukee: Bruce.

Polanyi, M. (1964), *Personal Knowledge: Towards a Post-Critical Philosophy*, New York: Harper and Row.

Polzin, R. (1993), *Samuel and the Deuteronomist: A Literary Study of the Deuteronomic History*, 2nd edn, Bloomington, IN: Indiana University.

Porter, J. R. (1963), *Moses and the Monarchy: A Study in the Biblical Tradition of Moses*, Oxford: Blackwell.

Posener, G. (1960), *De la divinité du pharaon*, Cahiers de la Société Asiatique 15, Paris: Imprimerie Nationale.

Postgate, J. N. & S. Payne (1975), 'Some Old Babylonian Shepherds and Their Flocks', *Journal of Semitic Studies* 20/1–2: 1–21.

Postgate, J. N. (1986), 'The Equids of Sumer, Again', in R. H. Meadow & H. P. Uerpmann (eds.), *Equids in the Ancient World*, Wiesbaden: Dr Ludwig Reichert Verlag: 194–213.

Power, E. (1928), 'The Shepherd's Two Rods in Modern Palestine and in some Passages of the Old Testament', *Biblica* 9: 434–442.

Pritchard, J. B. (ed.) (1969), *Ancient Near Eastern Texts Relating to the Old Testament*, 3rd edn, Princeton: Princeton University.

Provan, I. W. (1995), 'The Messiah in the Book of Kings', in P. E. Satterthwaite, R. S. Hess & G. J. Wenham (eds.), *The Lord's Anointed: Interpretation of Old Testament Messianic Texts*, Carlisle, UK: Paternoster: 67–85.

Quinn, N. (1987), 'Culture and Cognition', in D. Holland & N. Quinn (eds.), *Cultural Models in Language and Thought*, Cambridge: Cambridge University: 3–40.

——— (1991), 'The Cultural Basis of Metaphor', in J. W. Fernandez (ed.), *Beyond Metaphor: The Theory of Tropes in Anthropology*, Stanford: Stanford University: 56–93.

Raitt, T. M. (1977), *A Theology of Exile: Judgment/Deliverance in Jeremiah and Ezekiel*, Philadelphia: Fortress.

Raurell, F. (1986), 'The Polemical Role of the *arxontes* and *afygoymenoi* in Ez LXX', in J. Lust (ed.), *Ezekiel and His Book: Textual and Literary Criticism and their Interrelation*, Leuven: Leuven University: 85–89.

Redford, D. B. (1992), *Egpyt, Canaan, and Israel in Ancient Times*, Princeton: Princeton University.

Rendtorff, R. (1997), 'Some Reflections on the Canonical Moses: Moses and Abraham', in E. E. Carpenter (ed.), *A Biblical Itinerary: In Search of Method, Form and Content*, JSOTS 240, Sheffield: Sheffield Academic: 11–19.

Reviv, H. (1989), *The Elders in Ancient Israel: A Study of a Biblical Institution*, trans. L. Plitmann, Jerusalem: Magnes Press.

Richards, I. A. (1936), *The Philosophy of Rhetoric*, London: Oxford University.

Ricoeur, P. (1974), 'Creativity in Language: Word, Polysemy,

Metaphor', in E. Straus (ed.), *Language and Language Disturbances*, Pittsburgh: Duzuesne University: 49–72.

——— (1979), 'The Metaphorical Process as Cognition, Imagination, and Feeling', in S. Sacks (ed.), *On Metaphor*, Chicago: University of Chicago: 141–157.

Roberts, J. J. M. (1983), 'The Divine King and the Human Community in Isaiah's Vision of the Future', in H. B. Huffmon, F. A. Spina & A. R. W. Green (eds.), *The Quest for the Kingdom of God: Studies in Honor of George E. Mendenhall*, Winona Lake, IN: Eisenbrauns: 127–136.

——— (1987), 'In Defense of the Monarchy: The Contribution of Israelite Kingship to Biblical Theology', in P. D. Miller, P. D. Hanson & S. D. McBride (eds.), *Ancient Israelite Religion: Essays in Honor of Frank Moore Cross*, Philadelphia: Fortress: 377–396.

Robinson, J. A. T. (1955), 'The Parable of John 10:1–5', *ZNW* 46: 233–240.

Robinson, J. M. (ed.) (1988), *The Nag Hammadi Library in English*, 3rd edn, San Francisco: Harper & Row.

Rooke, D. W. (1998), 'Kingship as Priesthood: The Relationship between the High Priesthood and the Monarchy', in J. Day (ed.), *King and Messiah in Israel and the Ancient Near East*, JSOTS 270, Sheffield: Sheffield Academic: 187–208.

Rosch, E. (1978), 'Principles of Categorization', in E. Rosch & B. Lloyd (eds.), *Cognition and Categorization*, Hillsdale, NJ: Lawrence Erlbaum: 27–48.

Rost, L. (1926), *Die Überlieferung von der Thronnachfolge Davids*, Stuttgart: W. Kohlhammer.

Rowe, R. D. (2002), *God's Kingdom and God's Son: The Background to Mark's Christology from Concepts of Kingship in the Psalms*, Leiden: Brill.

Rowton, M. B. (1974), 'Enclosed Nomadism', *Journal of Economic and Social History of the Orient* 17: 1–30.

Ryder, M. L. (1993), 'Sheep and Goat Husbandry with Particular Reference to Textile Fibre and Milk Production', *Bulletin on Sumerian Agriculture* 7: 9–32.

Ryken, L., J. C. Wilhoit & T. Longman (eds.) (1998), *Dictionary of Biblical Imagery*, Downers Grove, IL: InterVarsity.

Sade, M. (1988), *Domestic Mammals in the Iron Age Economy of the Northern Negev*, M.A. Thesis, Tel Aviv University (Hebrew).

Safrai, Z. (1994), *The Economy of Roman Palestine*, London: Routledge.

Sailhamer, J. H. (1992), *The Pentateuch as Narrative*, Grand Rapids: Zondervan.

Sakenfeld, K. D. (1978), *The Meaning of Hesed in the Hebrew Bible*, Missoula, MT: Scholars.

Sanders, J. A. (1993), 'From Isaiah 61 to Luke 4', in C. A. Evans & J. A. Sanders (eds.), *Luke and Scripture*, Minneapolis: Fortress: 46–69.

Sandy, D. B. (1991), 'John the Baptist's "Lamb of God" Affirmation in its Canonical and Apocalyptic Milieu', *JETS* 34/4: 447–460.

Sarbin, T. R. (ed.) (1986), *Narrative Psychology: The Storied Nature of Human Conduct*, New York: Praeger.

Sarna, N. M. (1991), *Exodus*, The JPS Commentary, Philadelphia: Jewish Publication Society.

Sasson, J. (1976), 'Ass', *IDB* Supplement: 72–73.

Satterthwaite, P. E. (1995), 'David in the Books of Samuel: A Messianic Expectation?', in P. E. Satterthwaite, R. S. Hess & G. J. Wenham (eds.), *The Lord's Anointed: Interpretation of Old Testament Messianic Texts*, Carlisle, UK: Paternoster: 41–65.

Schroeder, R. P. (1975), 'The "Worthless" Shepherd: A Study of Mark 14:27', *CurTM* 2: 342–344.

Schultz, R. (1995), 'The King in the Book of Isaiah', in P. E. Satterthwaite, R. S. Hess & G. J. Wenham (eds.), *The Lord's Anointed: Interpretation of Old Testament Messianic Texts*, Carlisle, UK: Paternoster: 141–165.

Seccombe, D. (1981), 'Luke and Isaiah', *NTS* 27: 252–259.

Sefati, Y. (1998), *Love Songs in Sumerian Literature*, Ramat Gan, Israel: Bar-Ilan University.

Segert, S. (1987), 'The Ugaritic nqdm After Twenty Years: A Note on the Function of Ugaritic nqdm', *UF* 19: 409–411.

Seitz, C. R. (1989), 'The Prophet Moses and the Canonical Shape of Jeremiah', *ZAW* 101: 3–27.

——— (1990), 'The Divine Council: Temporal Transition and New Prophecy in the Book of Isaiah', *JBL* 109: 229–247.

——— (1991), *Zion's Final Destiny: The Development of the Book of Isaiah: A Reassessment of Isaiah 36 – 39*, Minneapolis: Fortress.

Selwyn, E. G. (1949), *The First Epistle of Peter*, London: Macmillan.

Senge, P. M. (1990), *The Fifth Discipline: The Art and Practice of the Learning Organization*, New York: Doubleday/Currency.

Senior, D. (1991), *The Passion of Jesus in the Gospel of John*, Collegeville, MN: Liturgical.

——— (1997), 'The Lure of the Formula Quotations: Re-assessing Matthew's Use of the Old Testament with the Passion Narrative as Test Case', in C. M. Tuckett, *The Scriptures in the Gospels*, BETL 131, Leuven: Leuven University: 89–115.

Seux, M.-J. (1967), *Epithetes royals akkadiennes et sumeriennes*, Paris: Letouzey et Ane.

Shelton, J. B. (1991), *Mighty in Word and Deed: The Role of the Holy Spirit in Luke-Acts*, Peabody, MA: Hendrickson.

Sider, J. W. (1995), *Interpreting the Parables: A Hermeneutical Guide to Their Meaning*, Grand Rapids: Zondervan.

Smith, G. A. (1966), *A Historical Geography of the Holy Land*, Jerusalem: Ariel.

Smith, M. S. (1997), *The Pilgrimage Pattern in Exodus*, JSOTS 239, Sheffield: Sheffield Academic.

Snell, D. C. (1997), *Life in the Ancient Near East 3100–332 BCE*, New Haven: Yale.

Snodgrass, K. R. (1980), 'Streams of Tradition Emerging from Isaiah 40:1–5 and their Adaptation in the New Testament', *JSNT* 8: 24–45.

——— (2000), 'From Allegorizing to Allegorizing: A History of the Interpretation of the Parables of Jesus', in R. N. Longenecker (ed.), *The Challenge of Jesus' Parables*, Grand Rapids: Eerdmans: 3–29.

Soskice, J. M. (1985), *Metaphor and Religious Language*, Oxford: Clarendon.

Speiser, E. A. (1963), 'Background and Function of the Biblical "Nasi"', *CBQ* 25: 111–117.

Spencer, P. E. (1999), 'Narrative Echoes in John 21: Inter-textual Interpretation and Intratextual Connection', *JSNT* 75: 49–68.

Stanton, G. N. (1992), *A Gospel for a New People*, Edinburgh: T. & T. Clark.

Sternberg, R. J. & P. A. Frensch (eds.) (1991), *Complex Problem Solving*, Hillsdale, NJ: Lawrence Erlbaum.

Stibbe, M. W. G. (1994), *John's Gospel*, New York: Routledge.

Stienstra, N. (1993), *YHWH is the Husband of His People*, Kamen: Kok Pharos.

Stigers, H. G. (1980), '*ṣdq*', in R. L. Harris et al. (eds.), *Theological Wordbook of the Old Testament*, Chicago: Moody: 752–755.

Stuhlmueller, C. (1970), *Creative Redemption in Deutero-Isaiah*, Rome: Biblical Institute.

Süring, M. L. (1982), *The Horn Motif in the Hebrew Bible and Related Ancient Near Eastern Literature and Iconography*, Berrien Springs: Andrews University.

Swartley, W. M. (1994), *Israel's Scripture Traditions and the Synoptic Gospels: Story Shaping Story*, Peabody, MA: Hendrickson.

Tadmor, H. (1982), 'Traditional Institutions and the Monarchy: Social and Political Tensions in the Time of David and Solomon', in T. Ishida (ed.), *Studies in the Period of David and Solomon and Other Essays*, Tokyo: Yamakawa-Shuppansha: 239–257.

Talbert, C. H. (1974), *Literary Patterns, Theological Themes, and the Genre of Luke-Acts*, SBLMS 20, Missoula, MT: SBL & Scholars.

Talmon, S. (1966), 'The "Desert Motif" in the Bible and in Qumran Literature', in A. Altmann (ed.), *Biblical Motifs: Origins and Transformations*, Cambridge: Harvard University: 31–63.

Terrien, S. (1978), *The Elusive Presence: Toward a New Biblical Theology*, New York: Harper & Row.

Thomas, D. W. (1962), '*clmwt* in the Old Testament', *JSS* 7: 191–200.

Thompson, J. A. (1980), *The Book of Jeremiah*, NICOT, Grand Rapids: Eerdmans.

Thompson, S. (1996), 'Politics Without Metaphors is Like a Fish Without Water', in J. S. Mio & A. N. Katz (eds.), *Metaphor: Implications and Applications*, Mahwah, NJ: Lawrence Erlbaum: 185–201.

Thornton, T. C. G. (1961), '1 Peter, A Paschal Liturgy?', *JTS* 12/1: 14–26.

Thureau-Dangin, F. (1907), *Sumerischen und Akkadischen Königsinschriften*, Leipzig: J. C. Hindrichsche Buchhandlung.

Tidball, D. J. (1997), *Skilful Shepherds: Explorations in Pastoral Theology*, Leicester: Apollos.

Tiede, D. L. (1980), *Prophecy and History in Luke-Acts*, Philadelphia: Fortress.

Tomback, R. S. (1982), 'Psalm 23:2 Reconsidered', *JNSL* 10: 93–96.

Tunyogi, A. C. (1962), 'The Rebellions of Israel', *JBL* 81: 385–390.

Ulfgard, H. (1989), *Feast and Future: Revelation 7:9–17 and the Feast of Tabernacles*, Lund: Almqvist & Wiksell.

Unnik, W. C. van (1970), ' "Worthy is the Lamb": The Background of Apoc. 5', in A. Descamps et al. (eds.), *Mélanges Bibliques en homage au R. P. Béda Rigaux*, Gembloux: Duculot: 445–461.

Van Buren, E. D. (1945), *Symbols of the Gods in Mesopotamian Art*, Rome: Pontificium Institutum Biblicum.

SHEPHERDS AFTER MY OWN HEART

Vancil, J. W. (1975), *The Symbolism of the Shepherd in Biblical, Intertestamental, and New Testament Material*, PhD dissertation: Dropsie University.

Van de Mieroop, M. (1993), 'Sheep and Goat Herding according to the Old Babylonian Texts from Ur', *Bulletin on Sumerian Agriculture* 7: 161–182.

VanderKam, J. C. (1990), 'John 10 and the Feast of the Dedication', in H. W. Attridge, J. J. Collins & T. H. Tobin (eds.), *Of Scribes and Scrolls: Studies on the Hebrew Bible, Intertestamental Judaism, and Christian Origins*, Lanham: University Press of America.

——— (1994), 'Messiah in the Scrolls', in E. Ulrich & J. VanderKam (eds.), *The Community of the Renewed Covenant: The Notre Dame Symposium on the Dead Sea Scrolls*, Notre Dame: University of Notre Dame: 211–234.

van der Lingen, A. (1992), 'BW'-YS' ('To Go Out and To Come In') as a Military Term', *VT* 42/1: 59–66.

Van der Toorn, K. (1995), 'Shepherd', *Dictionary of Deities and Demons in the Bible*, Leiden: E. J. Brill: 1457–1459.

Van Driel, G. (1993), 'Neo-Babylonian Sheep and Goats', *Bulletin on Sumerian Agriculture* 7: 219–258.

Van Hecke, P. J. P. (2003), 'Metaphorical Shifts in the Oracle against Babylon (Jeremiah 50 – 51)', *Scandinavian Journal of the Old Testament* 17/1: 68–88.

Van Oyen, G. (1999), *The Interpretation of the Feeding Miracles in the Gospel of Mark*, Brussel: Koninklijke Vlaamse Academie Voor Wetenschappen.

von Rad, G. (1962), *Old Testament Theology* 1, trans. D. M. G. Stalker, New York: Harper & Row.

Walton, J. H. (2003), 'The Imagery of the Substitute King Ritual in Isaiah's Fourth Servant Song', *JBL* 122/4: 734–743.

Watts, J. D. W. (1987), *Isaiah 34 – 66*, WBC; 25, Waco, TX: Word.

Watts, J. W. (1992), *Psalm and Story: Inset Hymns in Hebrew Narrative*, JSOTS 139, Sheffield: JSOT.

Watts, R. E. (1997), *Isaiah's New Exodus and Mark*, WUNT 88, Tübingen: Mohr Siebeck.

Weick, K. E. & M. G. Bougon (1986), 'Organizations as Cognitive Maps', in H. P. Sims Jr, D. A. Gioia & Assoc. (eds.), *The Thinking Organization*, San Francisco: Jossey-Bass.

Weinfield, M. (1995), *Social Justice in Ancient Israel and in the Ancient Near East*, Minneapolis: Fortress.

Wendland, E. R. (2001), ' "Can these Bones Live Again?" ': A Rhetoric of the Gospel in Ezekiel 33 – 37', Part 1, *Andrews University Seminary Studies* 39/1: 85–100.

Westenholz, J. (1997), *Legends of the Kings of Akkade*, Winona Lake, IN: Eisenbrauns.

——— (2000), 'The King, the Emperor, and the Empire: Continuity and Discontinuity of Royal Representation in Text and Image', in S. Aro & R. M. Whiting (eds.), *Melammu Symposia* 1, Helsinki, University of Helsinki: 99–125.

——— (2004), 'The Good Shepherd', in A. Panaino & A. Piras (eds.), *Melammu Symposia* 4, Milano: University of Bologna.

Westermann, C. (1969), *Isaiah 40 – 66: A Commentary*, OTL, London: SCM.

Whale, P. (1987), 'The Lamb of John: Some Myths about the Vocabulary of the Johannine Literature', *JBL* 106/2: 289–295.

Wheelwright, P. (1975), *Metaphor and Reality*, 6th edn, Bloomington: Indiana University.

Whitelam, K. W. (1979), *The Just King: Monarchial Judicial Authority in Ancient Israel*, *JSOTS* 12, Sheffield: JSOT.

Widengren, G. (1984), 'The Gathering of the Dispersed', in W. B. Barrick & J. R. Spencer, *In the Shelter of Elyon: Essays on Ancient Palestinian Life and Literature in Honor of G. W. Ahlström*, *JSOTS* 31, Sheffield: JSOT: 227–245.

Wiggermann, F. A. M. (1985–86), 'The Staff of Ninshubura', *Jaarbericht Ex Oriente Lux* 29: 3–34.

Wildavsky, A. (1984), *The Nursing Father: Moses as a Political Leader,* University, AL: University of Alabama.

Wildberger, H. (1965), 'Das Abbild Gottes, Gen. 1:26–30', *Theologische Zeitschrift* 21: 245–259.

Williams, R. J. (1964), 'Literature as a Medium of Political Propaganda in Ancient Egypt', in W. S. McCullough (ed.), *The Seed of Wisdom*, Toronto: University of Toronto: 14–30.

Williamson, H. G. M (1998), 'The Messianic Texts in Isaiah 1 – 39', in J. Day (ed.), *King and Messiah in Israel and the Ancient Near East*, *JSOTS* 270, Sheffield: Sheffield Academic: 238–270.

Willis, J. T. (1990), ' "Rod" and "Staff" in Isaiah 1 – 39', *Old Testament Essays* 3: 93–106.

Willis, T. M. (1987), 'A Fresh Look at Psalm XXIII 3A', *VT* 37: 104–106.

Wilson, G. H. (1985), *The Editing of the Hebrew Psalter*, SBLDS 76, Chico, CA: Scholars.

────(1986), 'The Use of Royal Psalms at the "Seams" of the Hebrew Psalter', *JSOT* 35: 85–94.

────(1993), 'Shaping the Psalter: A Consideration of Editorial Linkage in the Book of Psalms', in J. C. McCann (ed.), *The Shape and Shaping of the Psalter*, JSOTS 159, Sheffield: Sheffield Academic: 72–82.

Wilson, J. (1951), *The Burden of Egypt*, Chicago: University of Chicago.

Wilson, R. R. (1999), 'Who Was the Deuteronomist? (Who Was Not the Deuteronomist?): Reflections on Pan-Deuteronomism', in L. S. Schearing & S. L. McKenzie (eds.), *Those Elusive Deuteronomists: The Phenomenon of Pan-Deuteronomism*, JSOTS 268, Sheffield: Sheffield Academic: 67–82.

Witherington, B. (2001), *The Gospel of Mark: A Socio-Rhetorical Commentary*, Grand Rapids: Eerdmans.

Wright, J. (1987), 'Spirit and Wilderness: The Interplay of Two Motifs Within the Hebrew Bible as a Background to Mark 1:2–13', in E. W. Conrad & E. G. Newing (eds.), *Perspectives on Language and Text: Essays in Honor of Francis I. Andersen's Sixtieth Birthday*, Winona Lake, IN: Eisenbrauns: 269–298.

Young, B. (1998), *The Parables: Jewish Tradition and Christian Interpretation*, Peabody, MA: Hendrickson.

Zimmerli, W. (1960), 'Le nouvel "exode" dans le message des deux grands prophètes de l'exil', in *La Branche d'Amandier: Hommage à Wilhelm Vischer*, Montpellier, France: La Faculté Libre de Théologie Protestante: 216–227.

────(1979), *Ezekiel 1*, Hermeneia, trans. R. E. Clements, Philadelphia: Fortress.

────(1982), *I Am Yahweh*, trans. D. W. Scott, ed. W. Brueggemann, Atlanta: John Knox.

────(1983), *Ezekiel 2*, Hermeneia, trans. J. D. Martin, Philadelphia: Fortress.

Index of modern authors

Index of Scripture references

Index of ancient sources